Lecture Notes in Artificial Intelligence 2033

Subseries of Lecture Notes in Computer Science
Edited by J. G. Carbonell and J. Siekmann

Lecture Notes in Computer Science
Edited by G. Goos, J. Hartmanis and J. van Leeuwen

Springer
Berlin
Heidelberg
New York
Barcelona
Hong Kong
London
Milan
Paris
Singapore
Tokyo

Jiming Liu   Yiming Ye (Eds.)

E-Commerce Agents

Marketplace Solutions, Security Issues, and Supply and Demand

Series Editors

Jaime G. Carbonell, Carnegie Mellon University, Pittsburgh, PA, USA
Jörg Siekmann, University of Saarland, Saarbrücken, Germany

Volume Editors

Jiming Liu
Hong Kong Baptist University
Department of Computer Science
Kowloon Tong, Hong Kong, China
E-mail: jiming@comp.hkbu.edu.hk

Yiming Ye
IBM T.J. Watson Research Center
30 Saw Mill River Road (Route 9A)
Hawthorne, NY 10532, USA
E-mail: yiming@watson.ibm.com

Cataloging-in-Publication Data applied for

Die Deutsche Bibliothek - CIP-Einheitsaufnahme

E-commerce agents : marketplace solutions, security issues, and supply and demand / Jiming Liu ; Yiming Ye (ed.). - Berlin ; Heidelberg ; New York ; Barcelona ; Hong Kong ; London ; Milan ; Paris ; Singapore ; Tokyo : Springer, 2001
(Lecture notes in computer science ; Vol. 2033 : Lecture notes in artificial intelligence)
ISBN 3-540-41934-9

CR Subject Classification (1998): I.2.11, K.4.4, C.2, K.6.5, H.3.5-7, D.4.6

ISBN 3-540-41934-9 Springer-Verlag Berlin Heidelberg New York

Springer-Verlag Berlin Heidelberg New York
a member of BertelsmannSpringer Science+Business Media GmbH

http://www.springer.de

Printed in Germany

Typesetting: Camera-ready by author, data conversion by PTP Berlin, Stefan Sossna
Printed on acid-free paper SPIN 10782400 06/3142 5 4 3 2 1 0

Table of Contents

Introduction to E-Commerce Agents: Marketplace Solutions, Security Issues, and Supply and Demand

Jiming Liu and Yiming Ye

Introduction

The Internet has swept over the computing world like a hurricane. The scope and rate of change of WWW are stunning and are influencing almost every aspect of human society. Among the many changes brought by the Internet is the emergence of electronic commerce over the Web. Electronic commerce activities, such as on-line exchange of information, services, and products etc., are bringing business to a whole new level of productivity and profitability. In parallel with the emergence of electronic commerce, there have been interesting developments in the area of intelligent software agents, or software entities that are capable of independent action in open, unpredictable environments. The Internet will never reach its full potential as an electronic marketplace unless e-commerce agents, or proactive Web Programs, are used to (semi) autonomously perform tasks such as:

- mediating among various heterogeneous Web sites,
- monitoring contents and notify customers,
- performing precision information filtering and comparison,
- providing tailored services according to the specialized needs of customers,
- assisting customers in making decisions, and
- acting on behalf of customers in matchmaking, server monitoring, negotiation, bidding, auction, transaction, transfer of goods, and follow-up support.

As e-commerce agent technology becomes more mature and standardized, we may envision that the richness and depth of electronic commerce services will increase and at the same time new forms of products and services as well as new business opportunities will emerge.

This book is aimed at providing an explicit account for the current state of the art in intelligent software agent-mediated electronic commerce. The contributed chapters are organized according to the key issues addressed in the following areas: marketplace solutions, security, and supply and demand.

J. Liu and Y. Ye (Eds.): E-Commerce Agents, LNAI 2033, pp. 1-6, 2001.

Marketplace Solutions

Many existing Web sites are at present constructed based on a set of static projections and fixed assumptions. It would be helpful to develop and deploy on-line intermediaries in the electronic marketplace that can provide or pawn auxiliary services, evaluate the quality of products, and provide recommendations on related or similar products. Chapters 1-8 concern agent-based solutions for electronic marketplaces, covering such topics as brokering and negotiation support.

Tewari and Maes present an agent-based intermediary architecture, called MARI (Multi-Attribute Resource Intermediary), for the specification, valuation, and brokering of heterogeneous resources in electronic marketplaces. It enables both buyers and sellers of non-tangible goods and services to provide relative preferences for the transaction partners and for the attributes of products in question. MARI provides the algorithmic supports for gathering user utility functions, valuating potential transaction partners, and optimally matching buyers and sellers. This multi-attribute utility-based approach to brokering is appealing as it supports multiple sellers and buyers within multiple product domains.

Zacharia, Evgeniou, Moukas, Boufounos, and Maes's work presents an interesting approach to the problem of setting prices in a knowledge marketplace, i.e., a marketplace where services are transacted. A framework is presented which incorporates a reputation brokering mechanism and dynamic pricing algorithms. The authors studied the microeconomic effects in a reputation-brokered, agent-mediated knowledge marketplace. This marketplace is enriched by dynamic pricing algorithms for agents that adjust their prices based on the success of the previous bid and/or their owners' dynamically updated reputations.

Barbosa and Silva propose a new electronic marketplace architecture based on intelligent agents, contemplating the search and aggregation roles of an intermediary and provide an example of the proposed marketplace, i.e., medicine purchase and sale. Their architecture has some interesting features compared to the existing ones; for instance, it allows various parameters such as the delivery time of the product to be used in the process of product comparison and uses ontologies to share the knowledge among the entities that exist in the marketplace.

When the number of buyers and sellers increases, according to Gallego and Delgado, the activities in an electronic marketplace will involve various types of business processes and may require more than one intermediary. While focusing on multimedia products and services, the authors provide a comprehensive classification of broker agents according to their characteristics and levels of complexity (namely, products, customized products, services, and multi-broker).

Sim and Chan describe an information brokering protocol for establishing a connection between buyers and sellers by matching advertisements and requests based on predefined multiple criteria. Experiments have been conducted to test the proposed protocol. Results show that given a reasonable amount of time, connections established based on their approach yield a good user satisfaction rating.

Gjerstad and Dickhaut provide a model of belief-based expected surplus maximization strategies for buyers and sellers in a double auction scenario. In the model, beliefs of traders are formed based on observed market data, and actions of traders are selected to maximize their expected surplus. Buyers and sellers are assumed to have preferences over monetary rewards that are monotonically increasing. The authors show that the trading activities resulting from such strategies can quickly and reliably reach competitive equilibrium prices and complete market efficiency.

Lei, Heywood, and Chatwin propose a decentralized/distributed agent architecture to support real-time manufacturing decision-making for on-the-spot orders in a garment industry application. In order to perform robust scheduling task under uncertain demand patterns, the proposed approach consists of a framework for global control and management, local ordering heuristics, and a user interface incorporating a Quality Function Definition (QFD) decision table for capturing user preferences. To reflect the complex nature of the task, resources and orders are viewed as producers and customers in a supply chain, and agents use a market-based model of double auction during the negotiation process.

Rasmusson's work addresses the specification of suitable options to capture the structure of the payoff functions of agents to be designed for a given application. He provides a model of agents as self-interested actors in a market and presents a framework for reasoning about their actions. The agents can be equipped with a set of resources for trading with other agents based on the requests of a user. The proposed resource network-based model can not only be used in traditional agent programming such as travel agents, but also be used in situations such as when agents negotiate market-based bandwidth reservations over a computer network.

Security Issues

The emerging growth of electronic commerce over the Internet is bringing exciting opportunities for companies. However, the risk is also imminent. As more and more Web citizens such as customers, merchants, system integrators, insiders, and especially hackers are spending more and more time on the "wild" Web, the exposure of a company to the Internet is the physical equivalent of placing its front door on every browser in the world. To fully enjoy the benefits of electronic commerce, security issues such as how to reliably identify an authorized user, how to detect a malicious agent, how to establish a secure communication, and how to conduct a secure transaction over the Internet must be considered. Chapters 9-15 address the issues of security in e-commerce agent access, communication, and transaction.

Maes, Navratil, and Chaudhari propose a high security voice-based authentication method for electronic commerce applications. Their method is capable of performing the task of determining the identity of a speaker over a very large population and the task of verifying the identity claim of a speaker based on his or her voice. The former task combines dialogs to reduce the set of ambiguous speakers and text-independent speaker identification to accurately recognize the actual user, whereas the latter task utilizes dialogs with knowledge-based and acoustic-based personal random or predefined questions. They have successfully demonstrated their conversational speech biometrics method in a telephony prototype.

Claessens, Preneel, and Vandewalle's chapter addresses the communication security for e-commerce agents. It presents a lightweight agent framework that provides agent communication and agent autonomy facilities to application developers. The framework is implemented in Java, and the communication security is enabled by using a Java SSL/TLS library. The SSL (Secure Sockets Layer) and TLS (Transport Layer Security) protocols provide entity authentication, data authentication, and data confidentiality at the socket level.

Ding et. al discuss the issues of system security and application security related to software agents. In an electronic marketplace, malicious agents can do harm in many ways, from attacking authorized agents to creating market chaos. In order to prevent such agents from reproducing and propagating, they suggest a protocol for trusted third party-based user identity verification and a protocol for agent migration from one market to another. They also provide reviews of related works.

In order to allow a user to purchase and pay for goods and services on the Internet, Romao and Mira da Silva previously proposed a payment system protocol, called SET/A. In their present chapter, they discuss one of the problems of SET/A, namely, the exposure of private keys when an agent has to digitally sign documents that prove the occurrence of its operations (something that can be done only by verifying the user's private key). Correspondingly, they propose a solution to this problem based on a proxy certificate mechanism in which the owner of an agent can delegate some power to the agent. The work of Yi, Siew, and Miao focuses on applying software agent technology together with cryptographic technology to automate and to secure electronic transaction for a series of on-line interdependent purchases. The proposed agent-mediated secure electronic transaction (SET) protocol incorporates a trusted agent service center into the payment system, and hence the secure payment agent is able to order and pay for a series of interdependent goods and services according to the purchase condition of a customer after it is launched from the customer device.

Lee, Yip, Tsang, and Ng introduce an agent-based transaction model for processing micropayment transactions in a distributed environment and demonstrate this model in a system implemented on an OMG MASIF compliant agent platform. A mobile agent mechanism, based on the integration of the SET protocol and the MilliCent protocol, is used to provide services for micropayment. The idea is to bundle and send the initial request and set-up information together to the server in a form of agent. This technique eases local processing, hence reducing the communication load. The authors develop a prototype system to justify the approach. Their experience shows that the agent-based approach is better in reducing network traffic than the original protocol.

Chari, Kermani, Smith, and Tassiulas explicitly address various security and privacy issues when mobile devices and agents enter into the scene of electronic commerce. They provide a taxonomy that unifies different mobile commerce scenarios into a single framework and analyze the related security challenge. They identify the entities that are involved in mobile commerce: client devices, kiosk devices, and infrastructure servers. They then examine the corresponding security and privacy issues associated with the application scenarios of these entities, such as disconnected interaction, bi-connected interaction, and full connected interaction. Their analysis suggests several checkpoints for security before a mobile commerce system is deployed.

Supply and Demand

Electronic commerce and Internet are changing many factors that can influence the dynamics of supply and demand in the new economy. E-commerce is not just an Internet presence or an electronic storefront, it is a complex enterprise infrastructure consisting of networks, Internet connections, servers, and other support systems such as databases and business intelligence. Chapters 16-19 of this book deal with the emerging applications of e-commerce agents in areas that may influence the forces of supply and demand in the new market.

Loke and Zaslavsky address the issue of e-commerce agents in workflow management. Mobile agent-based workflow offers a distributed means of automating and streamlining business process enactment, such as virtual enterprises and supply-chain management. The authors present an algebra of mobile agent itineraries that specifies the executable workflow. They then illustrate the mechanism by applying the algebra to scenarios such as voting, meeting scheduling, and sales order processing.

Enterprise federation is a self-organizing network of partner enterprises. Tianfield's chapter looks into the life-cycle organization of enterprise federation and provides a blueprint for creating, configuring, and operating such a network. It also offers a multi-agent based dynamic system model for the operations of enterprise federation, which covers both inter-level coordination and intra-level cooperation.

Business intelligence will be one of the forces that influence supply and demand. Software agents as information content mediators can play an important role in dynamically creating pull-and-push advertising. The work of Wu, Ngu, and Pradhan is concerned with how to develop information search agents by applying data mining techniques with incremental learning facilities. Agents that perform different functions are discussed: a Relevance Agent that verifies the relevance of recommended documents from sellers and Web users using a dictionary; a SitHelper that incrementally learns each user's areas of interest from the user's access log; and a Document Agent that checks and reports any updates of Web documents. The significance of this work is that the developed agents can add new capabilities to electronic commerce systems in building and serving their user communities.

A good user interface can serve as a favorable channel connecting supply and demand in the electronic markets. Devlin and Scott study the user interface aspect of electronic commerce agents. They argue that multi-modal interface agents can provide better interactions than single-modal interface. They perform experiments to test and analyze the role of speech agents in tasks involving electronic transactions. The speech agent used in their experiment is a three-dimensional talking face and the storefront is a CD store. User testing is evaluated based on usability and usefulness. Testing results show that users are willing to embrace the speech technology; however, there exist several technical and usability limitations. This chapter is worth reading for multi-modal e-commerce agent developers.

We wish you enjoy reading the book.

Acknowledgements. We would like to take this opportunity to thank Bulent Basaran, Aslihan Celik, Anindya Datta, Kaushik Dutta, Takeshi Furuhashi, Avigdor Gal, Richard Goodwin, Paul Y. Huang, Pinar Keskinocak, Juhnyoung Lee, John Muller, Sun Park, Michael Rothkopf, Timothy K. Shih, Debra VanderMeer, Gulcan N. Yesilkokcen, and Eric Yu for reviewing the chapters. We would also like to thank the special issue authors for their efforts in cross-reviewing process. We would like to express our gratitude to Mr. Alfred Hofmann of Springer-Verlag for his help in editing and publishing this special volume. Jiming Liu would like to acknowledge the support provided by Hong Kong Baptist University during this book project. Yiming Ye would like to thank Dr. Stephen Boies for his support.

A Generalized Platform for the Specification, Valuation, and Brokering of Heterogeneous Resources in Electronic Markets

Gaurav Tewari and Pattie Maes

MIT Media Lab, E15-305, 20 Ames Street
Cambridge, MA 02142 USA
{gtewari, pattie}@media.mit.edu

Abstract. This paper describes MARI (Multi-Attribute Resource Intermediary), a project which proposes to improve online marketplaces, specifically those that involve the buying and selling of non-tangible goods and services. MARI is an intermediary architecture intended as a generalized platform for the specification and brokering of heterogeneous goods and services. MARI makes it possible for both buyers and sellers alike to more holistically and comprehensively specify relative preferences for the transaction partner, as well as for the attributes of the product in question, making price just one of a multitude of possible factors influencing the decision to trade. Ultimately, we expect that the ability to make such specifications will result in a more efficient, richer, and integrative transaction experience.

1 Introduction

1.1 Overview

This paper describes MARI (Multi-Attribute Resource Intermediary) – a research project being conducted in the Software Agents Group at the MIT Media Lab [2]. MARI proposes to radically improve online marketplaces, specifically those that involve the buying and selling of non-tangible goods and services. MARI is an agent-based intermediary architecture intended as a generalized platform for the specification and brokering of heterogeneous goods and services. MARI lies at the intersection of three general areas of research -- multi-agent systems, highly-mediated communications, and electronic commerce. Of these three general areas, MARI is positioned primarily from a "highly-mediated communications" perspective.

J. Liu and Y. Ye (Eds.): E-Commerce Agents, LNAI 2033, pp. 7-24, 2001.

1.2 Research Focus and Objectives

State of the art online marketplaces, such as Chemdex [29], Priceline [30], Elance [31], etc. accentuate the importance of price in determining which seller the buyer transacts with and vice versa. This results in a static, impersonal bidding experience, and in an inability for the buyer and seller to transcend price as the only negotiative dimension. There is simply no means to convey the full "value proposition" of the holistic product offering. Online auction systems have a tendency to foster a spirit of adversarial competitiveness in the buying process. In systems such as Ebay [16] and Amazon Auctions [17], not only must a buyer first undergo the burden of uniquely identifying the exact product she is seeking, but furthermore, she must then enter into a inflexible and antagonistic bidding interplay with the seller. MARI attempts to overcome these limitations. MARI makes it possible for both buyers and sellers to more holistically and comprehensively specify relative preferences for the transaction partner, as well as for the attributes of the product in question, making price just one of a multitude of possible factors influencing the choice of trading partner and the decision to trade. MARI is unique in the sense that it allows both the buyer as well as the seller to exercise control. By allowing each party to choose and implicitly associate weights with relevant features from the underlying ontology, MARI makes it possible to take into account subtle differences in characteristics of each party, so as to facilitate a more accurate match.

2 Related Work

Unlike most online shopping systems which generally operate in only one stage of the online shopping process [4], MARI operates in three core stages -- namely product brokering, merchant brokering, and negotiation -- to provide a unified experience that better facilitates economically efficient and socially desirable transactions. MARI amalgamates features of the 'Market Maker' [11] and 'Tête-à-Tête' [12] projects at the Media Lab, and extends these to create a more comprehensive solution. In particular, MARI builds upon multi-attribute utility theory formulations, as introduced in Tête-à-Tête, to model relative user preferences and quantify tradeoffs.

MARI relates to first generation price-comparison systems such as BargainFinder [7] and Jango [8], but goes much further than the rudimentary functionality afforded by such tools. MARI goes beyond just bid and ask prices to include the attributes of the transaction parties as dimensions for consideration and differentiation.

MARI relates to second generation value comparison shopping systems such as Personalogic [5], MySimon [13], and the Frictionless ValueShopper [6] in that it offers an advanced decision support engine, based upon multi-attribute utility theory, that meaningfully facilitates the exchange of complex and heterogeneous products. It differs from these systems in that it (i). allows both parties (buyers and sellers) to search for an optimal transaction partner, and (ii). it automates the match making between buyers and sellers. Further, MARI supports a non-linear and iterative user-interaction model, that accurately reflects the true nature of real-life transactions.

MARI relates to online negotiation systems and auctions, such as Kasbah [9] and AuctionBot [10], and commercial systems provided by Moai [32], TradingDynamics [33] and others. It differs from them in proposing an integrative negotiation protocol and interaction model. This model, based upon bilateral argumentation, embodies an appropriate blend of formality and efficiency, and provides an alternative to the adversarial competitiveness of online auctions.

Additionally, MARI relates to work in operations research done in the domain of dynamic pricing of inventories [19], [20], [21]. Specifically, we address the issue of how sellers should dynamically shift their valuations when demand is price sensitive and stochastic, and the seller's objective is to maximize expected revenues. Moreover, our algorithms for matching buyers and sellers are fundamentally based on flow algorithms as encountered in combinatorial optimization and network theory [22].

Finally, MARI builds on work done in the area of market-oriented allocation mechanisms [23], [24], [26]. We build upon economic theory in general, and game theory in particular, to formulate our problem in economics terminology [15], [25] with optimization heuristics, such as maximization of aggregate surplus, that derive directly from the literature.

3 Research Domain

3.1 Functional Overview

MARI embodies a trend, expected to be key to the electronic marketplaces of tomorrow. Specifically, we believe that negotiations will be highly complex and participants will engage in integrative negotiation over various aspects of a transaction, price being only one of many considerations.

MARI represents a general purpose architecture that is capable of supporting multiple sellers and buyers within multiple product domains. For the purposes of our project we envision deploying the MARI infrastructure in the context of a "services marketplace" in which language translation services are bought and sold. Hence, MARI is specifically encoded with a "language translation service" ontology and suitable complementary data.

3.2 Services Marketplaces

A substantial motivation for the choice of "services marketplaces" in general, and a language-translation marketplace in particular, as the application domain for this project lies in our belief [27] that in the future, as people become increasingly networked, it will be easier for individuals to mutually help one another. People who share each other's notions of quality and other such intangible attributes are in a much better position to be helpful to one another, at least until agents become truly "intelligent," and can be the ones helping people with complex tasks. For instance, given the extremely rudimentary capabilities of current state of the art automated translation systems [28], a (networked) person would be much better off if she could receive help with a language translation problem from a *human* expert located somewhere else. In this context, it is reasonable to postulate that the importance of technologies that mediate communications amongst end users will emerge as being of critical importance.

3.3 The Language Translation Marketplace

In order to be able to participate in the MARI marketplace, a "seller" creates a "selling agent" that is aware of its owner's level of expertise, availability, compensation expectations, and other special constraints, such as requirements for the buyer. Similarly, a "buyer" creates a "buying agent" that understands the exact needs of its owner such as degree of expertise desired, time-sensitivity or urgency with which information is needed, range and type of compensation that the buyer is willing to offer the seller, and other special constraints, such as minimum requirements on the seller's reputation level. Additionally, the buying (selling) agents also encapsulate information on how different qualified sellers (buyers) can be rank ordered in degree of relative preference. Subsequently, the "market" automatically matches buyers and sellers. Once a match has been made, other media (such as email, cell-phone, as well as richer media) may be employed to implement the "knowledge transfer relationship" in practice.

A benefit of focusing specifically on "services marketplaces" and "information goods" is that it allows us to concentrate more on the attributes relevant to the parties attempting to engage in the transaction without getting overwhelmed by the material details inherent to the product itself. For many information goods, the characteristics of the seller actually serve to define the good itself. For instance, in a language translation marketplace, the fact that the seller of the translation service is considered an expert, and has a high reputation rating associated with her to substantiate this claim, implicitly conveys the nature and quality of the "good," in this case the translation service. Indeed, one can argue that in the context of services marketplaces, in which the service being bought and sold lacks tangible manifestation and is hence not as easily susceptible to objective evaluation, the ability to be able to ontologically segregate and prioritize the various subtle impinging factors gains significance and relevance. Hence, the choice of services marketplaces, in which intangible services and information are bought and sold, is an appropriate and fitting choice as the target application domain for this project.

The electronic services marketplace embodied within MARI allows us to instantaneously match buyers and sellers in real-time. Ultimately, we hope, market forces will push the system towards an equilibrium where the time and efforts of a true expert are optimally used for just those questions that cannot easily be answered by anyone else. Resources will be bid up or down to reflect their true worth based upon a continuously updating balance between supply and demand of the scarce resource, and will thus be optimally allocated.

4 Implementation

4.1 Algorithms and Technologies Used

4.1.1 Overview. All interaction between a given user[1] (buyer or seller) and MARI is mediated by the User Interface Manager (UIM) (see Figure 4). When a user initially logs onto MARI, he or she must specify whether her intent is to put a product or service up for sale or to purchase a product or service. Depending upon the user's choice, the UIM presents the appropriate interface to the user, such that the system is able to adequately capture all relevant parameters. The buyer's and seller's interfaces are, in fact, remarkably similar since, in both cases, our intent is to gauge the user's multi-attribute utility function so as to be able to accurately assess how the user would value products he or she has not explicitly seen or "rated" before. Being able to make such inferences is integral to the successful functioning of MARI's core matching algorithm.

MARI's market structure most closely resembles a "*monopolistic competition*" -- each seller has the ability to differentiate her products or services from those of other sellers[2]. The market structure is monopolistic in the sense that each seller has the ability to set her own price, rather than merely accept the prevalent "market price" as under perfect competition and, thus, can be said to exercise market power. On the other hand, each seller must still compete, in terms of price and the range of products offered, with other sellers since they are all effectively trying to find transaction partners from a common underlying set of buyers. Moreover, there are no barriers to entry, and new sellers are free to enter the market. In this way, the market structure also resembles that of a competitive industry.

4.1.2 Capturing User Preferences. Each distinct buyer or seller is represented within MARI by an agent. The "buyer agent" embodies the buyer's revealed preferences with respect to the desired resource. Similarly, "seller agents" embody the preferences and interests of sellers. Each agent is customized to the needs and desires of its owner, and attempts to advocate on the owner's behalf when finding suitable transaction partners. These agents are then used by the system to coordinate the preferences and interests of each party involved. MARI's interaction with the user, via which the user agent is initialized, can be decomposed into several steps, enumerated below. Each ontology-

---

1 We use the term "user" to refer specifically to a buyer or seller. By contrast, we use the term "market maker" to refer to the system administrator who instantiates MARI within the context of a specific product domain.

2 Since we specifically focus on complex products and services that consists of multiple, often non- tangible, attributes (such as seller reputation, for example), one could argue that the merchant offerings are differentiated a priori. Indeed, one can reasonably argue that in such product domains, it is extremely difficult, if not simply infeasible, for a given seller to perfectly replicate another seller's product offering.

specific attribute has a predefined "default" value associated with it, and the user can accept or override these defaults.

Step 1: Specifying the Ideal Offer (see Figure 1). The user specifies a "referential" or "preferred" configuration, or *offer*, which consists of specific product and transaction partner attribute values, as derived from the underlying domain ontology. The user can modify which attributes are *fixed* and which are *flexible* and must also associate a monetary valuation ("bid" or "ask") with this offer (referred to as the *pbsvalue*).

The attributes of any given product can be classified as being either fixed or flexible. A fixed attribute is one whose value, as specified by the user, is used for transaction party *qualification*. By contrast, flexible attributes have associated ranges, and are used for transaction party valuation. For instance, in the example of language translation services (buyer's perspective), the number of words to be translated could be a fixed attribute, while the reputation of the seller, the degree of expertise of the seller, and the amount of time within which the translation will be completed could be flexible attributes. Each fixed attribute has a predefined set of permissible values, and the user must select acceptable values from this set. For instance, the permissible values for 'number of words to be translated' might be the set of non-negative integers.

Step 2: Gathering Ranges of Flexible Attributes (see Figure 2). Having specified which attributes ought to be considered flexible and which ought to be fixed, a user must also associate a permissible range of values with each flexible attribute. Further, in order to exercise some constraint on automatically generated bids and asks, the user must also specify the range (defined by a pair of highest and lowest endpoints, referred to as *maxvalue* and *minvalue*, respectively) of permissible valuations. This range corresponds to valuating the best and least qualified transaction partner, respectively.

Step 3: Inferring Attribute Weights. Once the User Interface Manager (UIM) has captured the above parameters, it automatically infers relative weights to be associated with each flexible attribute. The existence of weights is indicative of the fact that the user associates different degrees of importance with the various attributes, when evaluating a given offer.

Asking a user to explicitly specify weights for each attribute would no doubt be the most accurate and transparent technique. However, doing so imposes additional burden and tedium on the user. Moreover, it is not at all clear whether users themselves are able to accurately quantify these numerical relative preferences. MARI automatically derives relative "weights" for flexible attributes by using the heuristic that an attribute's weight or relative importance is proportional to how constrained the range of permissible values is, relative to the ranges of other flexible attributes [18]. A tightly constrained range indicates that the user is relatively unwilling to compromise and hence the attribute is relatively more significant to her. With this in mind, we use the following formula to calculate the numerical weight factor to be associated with a given (flexible) attribute, p:

$$Weight(p)=\frac{1-\left(\dfrac{\text{Permissible Range of p}}{\text{Possible Range of p}}\right)}{\sum_{i}\left[1-\left(\dfrac{\text{Permissible Range of i}}{\text{Possible Range of i}}\right)\right]} \quad (i\ \textit{ranges over all flexible attributes}) \tag{1}$$

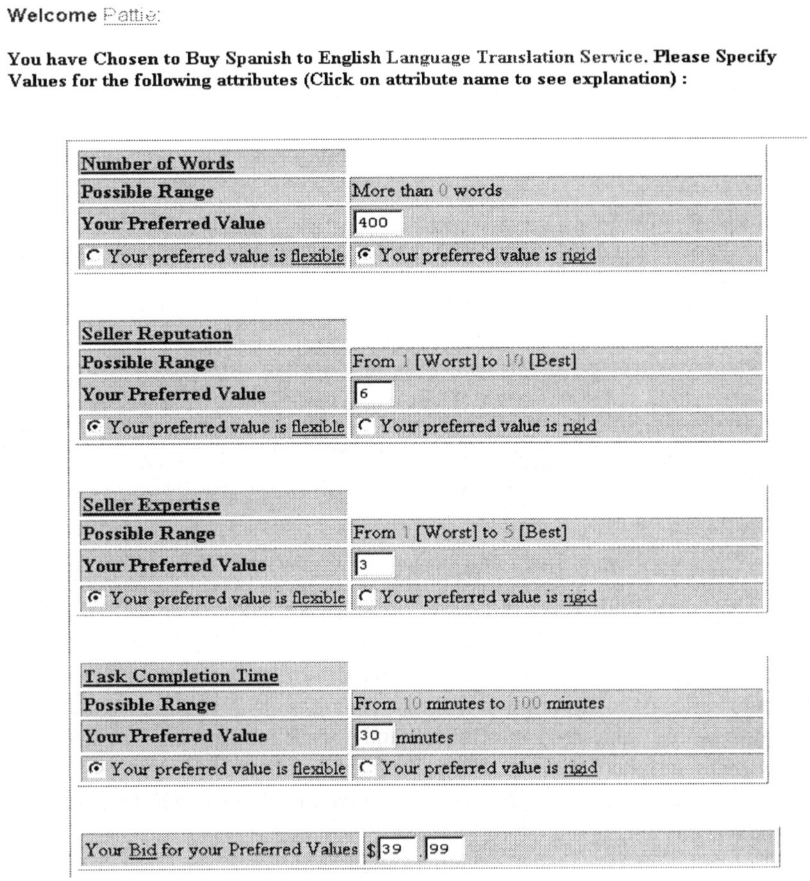

Welcome Pattie:

You have Chosen to Buy Spanish to English Language Translation Service. Please Specify Values for the following attributes (Click on attribute name to see explanation) :

Number of Words	
Possible Range	More than 0 words
Your Preferred Value	400
○ Your preferred value is flexible	● Your preferred value is rigid

Seller Reputation	
Possible Range	From 1 [Worst] to 10 [Best]
Your Preferred Value	6
● Your preferred value is flexible	○ Your preferred value is rigid

Seller Expertise	
Possible Range	From 1 [Worst] to 5 [Best]
Your Preferred Value	3
● Your preferred value is flexible	○ Your preferred value is rigid

Task Completion Time	
Possible Range	From 10 minutes to 100 minutes
Your Preferred Value	30 minutes
● Your preferred value is flexible	○ Your preferred value is rigid

Your Bid for your Preferred Values $39 .99

Fig. 1. Specifying a "Referential" Configuration or "Offer"

4.1.3 Modeling User Utility Functions. Since MARI is fundamentally an infrastructural tool, we expect that each "market maker" will create an instantiation of MARI specific to their product domain. When instantiating MARI, the market maker must specify the product ontology as well as a set of parameters which determine how user utility functions are modeled and what heuristics are optimized in the match making process.

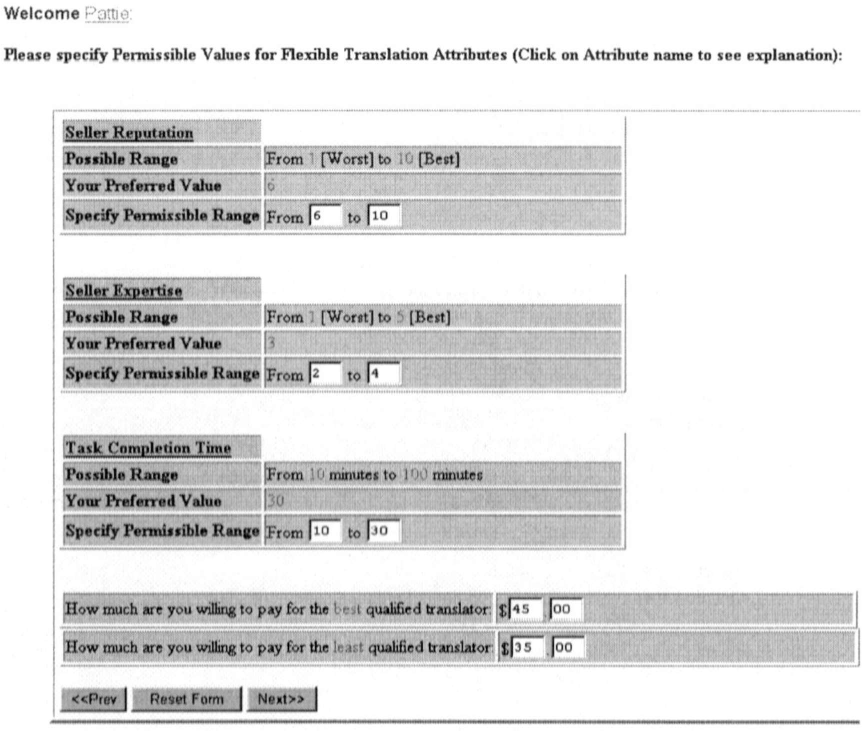

Welcome Pattie:

Please specify Permissible Values for Flexible Translation Attributes (Click on Attribute name to see explanation):

Seller Reputation	
Possible Range	From 1 [Worst] to 10 [Best]
Your Preferred Value	6
Specify Permissible Range	From 6 to 10

Seller Expertise	
Possible Range	From 1 [Worst] to 5 [Best]
Your Preferred Value	3
Specify Permissible Range	From 2 to 4

Task Completion Time	
Possible Range	From 10 minutes to 100 minutes
Your Preferred Value	30
Specify Permissible Range	From 10 to 30

How much are you willing to pay for the best qualified translator:	$45 . 00
How much are you willing to pay for the least qualified translator:	$35 . 00

<<Prev | Reset Form | Next>>

Fig. 2. Specifying Ranges for Flexible Attributes

The market maker initializes the Buyer or Seller Valuation Manager (B/SVM) (see Figure 4), whose purpose is to gather sufficient information from the user so as to be able to accurately infer how her (uni-dimensional) utility might change as each flexible attribute varies over its permissible range. Doing so enables us to accurately assess how the user would value product offerings and transaction partners that have not been explicitly seen or "rated" before. The process of automatically valuating a potential transaction partner then simply becomes a matter of taking a weighted sum of uni-dimensional utility functions.

Based upon the market maker's configuration parameters, the Valuation Managers model the user's utility function as follows:

Step 1: Visually Selecting Utility Functions. When first instantiating MARI, the market maker is required to initialize the Valuation Function Generalizer (VFG). The purpose of the VFG is to model the user's utility for various ontology attributes by allowing the market maker to visually associate a generic (pre-defined) mathematical function with each flexible attribute [12] (see Table 1 and Figure 3). Of course, users have the option of being able to override these "default" values during the offer specification process.

Table 1. MARI's Predefined Generic Utility Functions (x is a place-holder variable for a value of the flexible attribute over its permissible range)

Name	**Functional Generalization** *(a, b, c represent arbitrary, non-negative constants)*	**Graph Shape**
UF_1	$(ax \pm b)$	
UF_2	$(ax^2 \pm bx \pm c)$	
UF_3	$(-ax^2 \pm bx \pm c)$	
UF_4	$(-ax \pm b)$	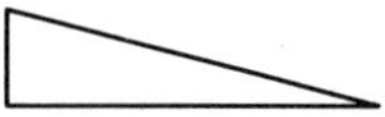
UF_5	$(ax^2 \pm bx \pm c)$	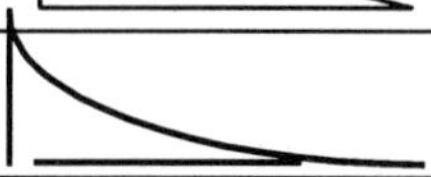
UF_6	$(-ax^2 \pm bx \pm c)$	
UF_7	x < (midpoint of permissible range) ? $(ax \pm b) : (-ax \pm b)$	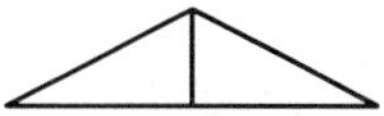
UF_8	x < (midpoint of permissible range) ? $(ax^2 \pm bx \pm c) : (ax^2 \pm bx \pm c)$	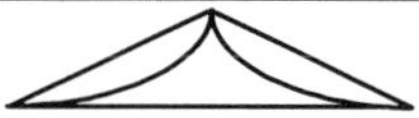
UF_9	x < (midpoint of permissible range) ? $(-ax^2 \pm bx \pm c) : (-ax^2 \pm bx \pm c)$	
UF_{10}	x < (midpoint of permissible range) ? $(-ax \pm b) : (ax \pm b)$	
UF_{11}	x < (midpoint of permissible range) ? $(ax^2 \pm bx \pm c) : (ax^2 \pm bx \pm c)$	
UF_{12}	x < (midpoint of permissible range) ? $(-ax^2 \pm bx \pm c) : (-ax^2 \pm bx \pm c)$	
UF_{13}	x = (high end point of permissible range) ? 1 : 0	
UF_{14}	x = (high end point of permissible range) ? 0 : 1	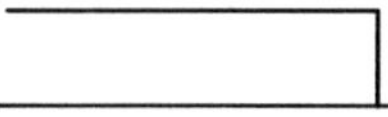
UF_{15}	x = 1	
UF_{16}	x = (low end point of permissible range) ? 1 : 0	
UF_{17}	x = (low end point of permissible range) ? 0 : 1	

Seller Reputation
Possible Range
From 1 [Worst] to 10 [Best]
Function Which Best Describes How User Preference Changes as Reputation Varies over its Permissible Range:
UF2
Seller Expertise
Possible Range
From 1 [Worst] to 5 [Best]
Function Which Best Describes How User Preference Changes as Seller Expertise Varies over its Permissible Range:
UF1
Task Completion Time
Possible Range
From 10 minutes to 100 minutes
Function Which Best Describes How User Preference Changes as Task Completion Time Varies over its Permissible Range:
UF3
<<Prev
Reset Form
Next>>
Name
Graph Shape

Fig. 3. Visually Associating Utility Functions with Flexible Attributes

Step 2: Quantifying Utility Functions. Using the generalized equation form of the utility function selected by the market maker (see Table 1), in conjunction with the *pbsvalue*, *maxvalue*, and *minvalue* parameters specified by a given user (see Figures 1 and 2), the Valuation Function Generalizer (VFG) is able to compute a mathematical approximation to the utility function corresponding to each flexible attribute. The polynomial used to represent the function can be at most of degree two (quadratic). Higher order polynomial approximations can subsequently be created by the Valuation Function Trainer (VFT) using Lagrange interpolation, as described in Step 3 below.

For example, let us assume that a given buyer is willing to accept a "seller reputation" ranging from 6 to 10. Assume that in her "referential offer" the buyer specifies a preferred value of 6. Further, say the market maker has pre-associated UF2 with this flexible attribute as it varies over its range – the choice of this utility function would reflect the fact that the buyer is willing to bid higher as the seller's reputation increases, and that her valuation increases exponentially as reputation approaches the maximum possible. In this case we can derive the equation[3] which captures the change in the buyer's utility as reputation varies, as:

$$UF_2(x)=\left(\frac{maxvalue-pbsvalue}{(x_{hi}-x_{low})^2}\right)x^2+\left(\frac{(-2)(maxvalue-pbsvalue)(x_{low})}{(x_{hi}-x_{low})^2}\right)x+\left(pbsvalue+\frac{(maxvalue-pbsvalue)(x_{low})^2}{(x_{hi}-x_{low})^2}\right). \tag{2}$$

Where:

x_{low} = the value of the attribute specified in the referential offer (i.e. 6);
x_{hi} = high endpoint of the permissible range (i.e. 10).

Step 3: Refining Utility Functions through Revealed Preferences. In this stage, the Valuation Manager attempts to fine-tune the rough utility function captured by the VFG. During system initialization, the VFG invokes the Valuation Function Trainer (VFT), which requires that the market maker iteratively "train" the system. At that time, the market maker is asked to explicitly "valuate" hypothetical product offerings strategically chosen to representatively span the space of all relevant product offerings. Essentially, the preferences expressed by the market maker are taken to be a benchmark set of "reasonable" preferences. Using these revealed preferences in conjunction with offer data that is specific to a particular user, the VFT facilitates the construction of a (iteratively refined) piecewise, linear approximation of the user's utility function.

If there are *n* flexible attributes, then the user's utility function can be visualized as an *n* dimensional hyper plane in *(n+1)* dimensions (where the $(n+1)^{st}$ dimension is the numerical "monetary" valuation associated with each point on the hyper plane). The VFT uses Lagrange Interpolation, in conjunction with an iterative scheme we shall refer to as "*delta scaling,*" in order to determine higher degree polynomial approximations for utility functions.

In general, we can use Lagrange Interpolation to approximate the value of any $(n-1)^{st}$ degree polynomial, f, at any arbitrary point, x, provided that we already know the values of the function ($f_0, f_1, \ldots, f_{n-1}$) at n distinct points ($x_0, x_1, \ldots, x_{n-1}$), by using the following expression:

$$f(x)=\underbrace{f_0\frac{(x-x_1)(x-x_2)\ldots(x-x_{n-1})}{(x_0-x_1)(x_0-x_2)\ldots(x_0-x_{n-1})}+\ldots+f_{n-1}\frac{(x-x_0)(x-x_1)\ldots(x-x_{n-2})}{(x_{n-1}-x_0)(x_{n-1}-x_1)\ldots(x_{n-1}-x_{n-2})}}_{n\ terms}. \tag{3}$$

---

[3] This function is derived using standard algebraic techniques along with special properties of quadratic functions. In particular, we have used the fact that the global minima of a quadratic, of the form $y=ax^2+bx+c$, occurs at –(b/2a), that the quadratic function corresponding to UF_2 is monotonically increasing, and that the user has already revealed two data points, *(x, y)*, on the curve: (x_{low}, *pbsvalue*) and (x_{hi}, *maxvalue*).

The term "delta scaling" refers to the technique by which the VFT picks points in the attribute space to be valuated by the market maker. The algorithm goes through iterations referred to as "delta phases." In each delta phase, the algorithm uni-dimensionally varies the value of a single flexible attribute (by "delta") and asks the market maker to explicitly associate a valuation with the feature set, thus effectively obtaining an additional data point relevant to this attribute. Subsequently, the algorithm performs Lagrange interpolation to computer a higher degree (uni-dimensional) utility function for the attribute. In a given delta phase, the algorithm does this for each attribute, thereby improving the degree of each attribute's associated utility function by at least one. The market maker thus provides MARI with an internal model of reasonable user preferences. This model can be though of as a "template," that is subsequently adapted to user-specific data.

4.1.4 Delineating Transaction Partners. MARI operates by using the notion of "market cycles." At the beginning of every market cycle, MARI goes through two phases. In the first phase, for each buyer, MARI identifies the sellers who are qualified to meet the buyer's request. This corresponds to the subset of sellers who are able to satisfy the buyer's fixed attribute requirements. In the second phase, MARI uses its internal mathematical approximation of the buyer's and sellers' utility functions to calculate "bids" and "asks." For instance, given an arbitrary seller, s, we can compute buyer b's valuation or "bid" for s as:

$$\text{Valuation}_{b,s} = \sum_i f_i\left(x_{i,s}\right) * w_i \quad . \tag{4}$$

Where:

i, ranges over all flexible attributes;

f_i is the buyer's revealed utility function corresponding to attribute i;

$x_{i,s}$ is the seller-specific value of attribute i;

w_i is the weight associated with attribute i by the buyer.

Then, for each buyer, MARI evaluates the "cost" that would be incurred if the buyer were to engage in a transaction with any of the qualified sellers. Currently, we take this "cost" to be equal to the "bid-ask spread," which can be interpreted as the aggregate surplus[4] [14], [15] that the two parties would derive if the transaction were to take place. We use this metric of "cost" since our indicator of the "goodness" of an allocation is welfare, which, in this case, is measured by the surplus that the allocation generates.

Subsequently, we can conveniently formulate the problem of optimally pairing up buyers and sellers as a "matching" problem. Mathematically, we can represent the state of the marketplace as a graph, G, in which sellers and buyers represent nodes. We refer to the set of buyers and seller as B and S, respectively, and to the set of arcs as A. Each

---

[4] Aggregate surplus is the sum of consumer and producer surplus. Consumer surplus is defined as the difference between the amount a consumer is willing to pay for a good and the amount she actually pays. Producer surplus is defined as the difference in the market price the producer receives for a good and the marginal cost incurred in its production [15].

individual buyer node $b \in B$ is connected to a subset of seller nodes $S' \subseteq S$, via some arc (b, s) with associated arc "cost" c_{bs}. Given this formulation, our goal is to find a sub-graph $G' \subseteq G$, such that the sub-graph represents a feasible[5] pairing of buyers and sellers with the largest overall "cost" (surplus), defined as the sum of the costs of its constituent arcs. To accomplish this, our solution strategy mirrors that of a (modified)[6] *minimum* cost flow problem. With this formulation the matching problem can now be expressed as the following linear program [22]:

$$\text{Minimize} \sum_{(i,j)\in A} c_{ij} x_{ij} \; . \tag{5}$$

subject to the constraints:

$$\sum_{\{j:(i,j)\in A\}} x_{ij} = 1 \text{ for all } i \in S \; , \tag{6}$$

$$\sum_{\{j:(i,j)\in A\}} x_{ji} = 1 \text{ for all } i \in B \; , \tag{7}$$

$$x_{ij} \geq 0 \text{ for all } (i,j) \in A \; . \tag{8}$$

We solve this to identify buyer-seller pairings for which the aggregate surplus of transaction parties is globally maximized. The "clearing price" for any given transaction pair is, by default, set at the midpoint between the original bid and ask prices, thereby equally dividing the surplus between the buyer and the seller. The market maker can, however, modify this distribution of surplus, choosing to retain the bid-ask spread as operating profit for instance.

4.2 System Architecture

Overall, the MARI system architecture consists of the following major functional components (see Figure 4):

1). User Interface Manager (UIM): Controls the (HTML) interface that is presented to the user. The UIM allows the user to specify and initiate a buy or sell request, to examine the status of previous requests, and to view market statistics and history. The Valuation Managers, discussed below, are invoked by the UIM during the course of initializing a user request to buy or sell. The UIM ensures that all relevant parameters are collected from a user in the context of any request, and that only valid requests are propagated.

---

[5] In this case the "feasibility" condition maintains that for a given buyer, the seller should be *qualified* to serve the buyer *and* that the buyer should meet the *qualification* criteria, if any, specified by the seller. Moreover, the buyer's bid can be no less than the seller's ask.

[6] Since we are actually trying to *maximize* the sum of our costs (aggregate surplus), we redefine costs in the min cost flow formulation to be the negative of the computed surpluses. Minimizing the sum of the *negatives* of the original quantities is equivalent to maximizing the sum of the original quantities.

2). Buyer Valuation Manager (BVM): Gathers sufficient information from a potential buyer so as to be able to accurately infer the buyer's valuation for previously unseen products.

2.1). Valuation Function Generalizer (VFG): Models a buyer's utility for multiple attributes by allowing the market maker to select from generic, pre-defined mathematical functions.

2.2). Valuation Function Trainer (VFT): Fine-tunes the rough utility function captured by the VFG by giving the market maker the option of iteratively "training" the system. Essentially, the VFT facilitates the construction of an (iteratively refined) piecewise, linear approximation of the buyer's utility function.

3). Seller Valuation Manager (SVM): Gathers information from a potential seller so as to be able to accurately infer the seller's valuation for previously unseen products. Like the BVM, the SVM works by having the market maker initialize the VFG and VFT.

4). Market Cycle Manager (MCM): Manages and enforces market cycles. The frequency of market cycles is a system variable that must be pre-specified, or can be set to be triggered by the simultaneous presence of certain (pre-specified) environmental conditions (such as number of users currently waiting to be matched).

4.1). Optimization Heuristic Manager (OHM): Allows the specification of which optimization heuristic ought to be employed. For instance, in some cases, the market maker's aim might be to maximize the *number* of buyers and sellers matched, while in other cases one may want to maximize the minimum surplus amongst all transaction partners (Rawlsian approach [15]), etc. The OHM enforces the specified optimization heuristic throughout the system by setting key *global* parameters appropriately, in a mutually consistent fashion. These parameters can then be referenced by other modules in the process of optimally pairing transaction partners.

The MCM invokes the Match Maker (MM) at the start of every market cycle. The MCM also ensures that buying and selling requests are time-stamped and queued appropriately so that precedence and priority relationships can be established if needed. At the end of every market cycle, the MCM examines the results output by the MM and notifies the User Status Manager (USM) and User Notification Manager (UNM), so as to update the status of user requests, as appropriate.

5). Match Maker (MM): Invoked by the MCM, the MM optimally pairs up buyers and sellers. The exact optimization heuristic to be used by the MM is specified by the MCM at the time of invocation. The MM gets the IDs of "active" users to be included in the matchmaking process from the User Status Manager (USM).

6). User Status Manager (USM): The USM monitors the status of each user. The USM keeps track of which requests are "active" and ought to be included in the matchmaking process in any given market cycle. For instance, the market maker may require that any given user should remain active for at least *n* market cycles, or, perhaps, that a given user should remain active until she is involved in market cycles with an *aggregate* of at least m other users, at least m_1 of whom are sellers and m_2 are buyers.

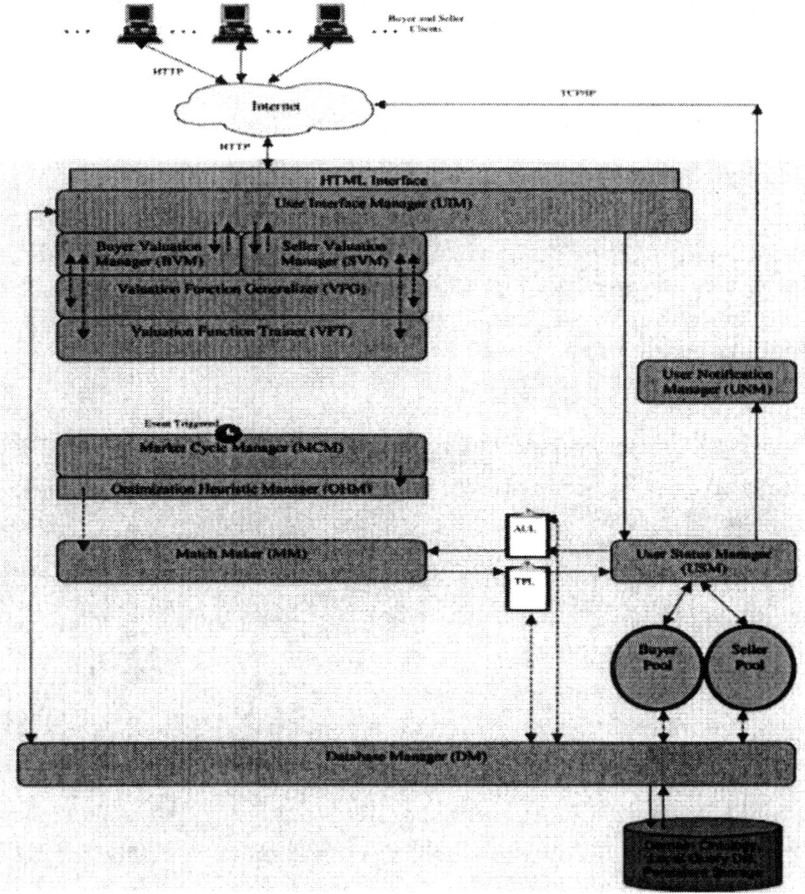

Fig. 4. System Schematic

7). User Notification Manager (UNM): The UNM notifies a given user of the outcome of their buying or selling request once a definitive outcome has been established or the time permitted by the user has expired. "Notification" can be "active" (sending an e-mail to the user) or "passive" (writing the outcome to a local database which is queried when the user logs in to check the status of her request).pairs up buyers and sellers. The exact optimization heuristic to be used.

8). Database Manager (DM): The DM presents each of the above components with an interface to a back-end database, thus abstracting away the specific details by which data is stored and retrieved from the rest of the system.

9). Active User List (AUL): At the beginning of each market cycle, the Match Maker (MM) *reads* the AUL to identify "active" buyers and sellers who need to be matched. The User Status Manager (USM) *updates* the AUL when a new user enters the system and at the end of each market cycle.

10). Transaction Partner List (TPL): The TPL is a list of transaction partners as determined by the Match Maker (MM) at the termination of the most recent market cycle.

The AUL, TPL, and Buyer and Seller Pools effectively comprise a system "*log*" that capture the state of the system at the end of a Market Cycle. In the event of a system failure, we revert back to the last logged state.

As of now, we have completed implementing a prototype of the system using an HTML front end, driven by Java servlets to manage content and user interaction, and integrated with a back-end SQL database for persistent storage. Additionally, we are in the process of writing DTDs for product ontologies and buyer and seller profiles, since these will be created, maintained and stored in XML.

5 Future Work

As of now, we have precisely defined MARI's design framework and functional modules, and have delineated the core algorithms that will be used in gathering user utility functions, "valuating" potential transaction partners, and optimally matching buyers and sellers. In the near future, we expect to actually deploy the MARI infrastructure to build a language translation marketplace within the context of the visionary Nation1 virtual youth community established by the Media Lab [3]. We expect that actually deploying our system in such a setting and using it to broker translation services will allow us to benefit from direct user feedback to address considerations such as privacy preservation, individual rationality, incentive compatibility, market liquidity, and stability of matchings (sensitivity analysis), as well as more mundane concerns such as speed, accuracy, data integrity, ease of use, and scalability.

As we further refine the MARI architecture and implementation, we expect to face a number of key questions. In particular, even though we have identified one set of models by which agents will interact and transaction partners will be determined, several issues remain to be addressed. We are keen to explore what algorithms and technologies our system can leverage in the process of information integration and representation, decision analysis, modeling and reasoning about utilities, heuristical learning and inference from user-interaction, facilitating inter-agent communication and negotiation, and attuning pre-existing knowledge bases in developing and managing shared product ontologies. Further, in the near future, we would like to explore the usage of standardized agent communication languages, we would like to see how machine learning techniques can be used in assisting decision support and negotiation, and will also facilitate dynamic alteration of bids and asks based upon stochastic demand and supply patterns over finite horizons [19], [20], [21].

Having completed a satisfactory implementation of the MARI infrastructure, we would next like to undertake simulations that employ different optimization heuristics, welfare metrics, and matching algorithms. We are curious to study how the quality of the outcome changes as we vary these parameters. Currently we are in the process of evaluating what additional concerns our system needs to address, and what kinds of simulations might be particularly compelling to undertake.

References

1. MARI: http://www.media.mit.edu/gtewari/MARI/
2. Software Agents Group: http://agents.www.media.mit.edu/groups/agents
3. Nation1: http://www.nation1.net
4. Maes, P., Guttman , Robert H., Moukas, Alexandros G.: Agents That Buy and Sell. Communications of the ACM, Vol. 42. 3 (1999)
5. Personalogic: http://www.personalogic.com
6. Frictionless ValueShopper: http://compare.frictionless.com
7. Bargainfinder: http:// bf.cstar.ac.com/bf
8. Jango: http://www.jango.com
9. Kasbah: http://ecommerce.media.mit.edu/Kasbah/
10. Wurman, Peter R., Wellman, Michael P., Walsh, William E.: The Michigan Internet AuctionBot: A Configurable Auction Server for Human and Software Agents. Proceedings of the Second International Conference on Autonomous Agents (Agents-98). Minneapolis, MN, USA (1998)
11. Wang, David Yi: Market Maker: An Agent-Mediated Marketplace Infrastructure. Master of Engineering Thesis, Department of Electrical Engineering and Computer Science, MIT, Cambridge, MA (1999)
12. Guttman, Robert H: Merchant Differentiation through Integrative Negotiation in Agent-mediated Electronic Commerce. Masters Thesis, MIT Media Laboratory, Cambridge, MA (1998)
13. MySimon Buyers Guide: http://www.mysimon.com/consumer_resources/Buyers_Guides/index.anml.
14. Pindyck, Robert S., Rubinfeld, Daniel R.: Microeconomics. Prentice-Hall, New Jersey (1997)
15. Varian, Hal R.: Intermediate Microeconomics. W. W. Norton & Company, New York (1999)
16. Ebay: http://www.ebay.com.
17. Amazon Auctions: http://www.amazon.com/auctions.
18. Morris, J., Maes, P.: Negotiating Beyond the Bid Price. Workshop Proceedings of the Conference on Human Factors in Computing Systems (CHI 2000). The Hague, The Netherlands (2000)
19. Gallego, Guillermo, Ryzin, Garrett: Optimal Dynamic Pricing of Inventories with Stochastic Demand over Finite Horizons. Management Science 40(8) (1994) 999-1020
20. Bitran, Gabriel R., Mondshein S.: Periodic Pricing of Seasonal Products in Retailing. Management Science 45(8) (1997) 64-79

21. Raman, Kalyan, Chatterjee R.: Optimal Monopolistic Pricing under Demand Uncertainty in Dynamic Markets. Management Science 41(1) (1995) 144-162
22. Ahuja, Ravindra K., Magnanti Thomas L., Orlin, James B.: Network Flows: Theory, Applications and Algorithms. Prentice-Hall, New Jersey (1993)
23. Boutilier, C., Shoham, Y., Wellman, M.: Economic Principles of Multi-Agent Systems. Artificial Intelligence 94 (1997) 1-6
24. Sandholm, T., Ygge, F.: On the Gains and Losses of Speculation in Equilibrium Markets. Proceedings of the Sixteenth International Joint Conference on Artificial Intelligence. Nagoya, Japan (1997) 632-638
25. Fudenberg, D., Tirole, J.: Game Theory. MIT Press, Cambridge, MA (1995)
26. Walsh, W., Wellman M., Wurman P., MacKie-Mason, J.: Some Economics of Market-Based Distributed Scheduling. Proceedings of the Eighteenth International Conference on Distributed Computing Systems. (1981) 612-621
27. Pattie Maes' statement: http://pattie.www.media.mit.edu/people/pattie/statement.html
28. Altavista online translation system: http://world.altavista.com/
29. Chemdex: http://www.chemdex.com
30. Priceline: http://www.priceline.com
31. Elance: http://www.elance.com
32. Moai: http://www.moai.com
33. TradingDynamics: http://www.tradingdynamics.com

Economics of Dynamic Pricing in a Reputation Brokered Agent Mediated Marketplace

Giorgos Zacharia[1], Theodoros Evgeniou[2], Alexandros Moukas[1], Petros Boufounos[1], and Pattie Maes[1]

[1]MIT Media Laboratory, Cambridge, MA 02139, USA
{lysi,moux,petrosb,pattie}@media.mit.edu
[2]INSEAD, 77305 Fontainebleau Cedex, France
theodoros.evgeniou@insead.fr

Abstract. We present a framework to study the microeconomic effects in a reputation brokered Agent mediated Knowledge Marketplace, when we introduce dynamic pricing algorithms. We study the market with computer simulations of multiagent interactions. In this marketplace, the seller reputations are updated in a collaborative fashion based on the performance of the user in the delegated tasks. To the best of our knowledge, this is the first agent mediated marketplace where the agents use dynamic pricing based on "dynamically" updated reputations. The framework can be used to investigate the different equilibria reached, based on the level of intelligence of the selling agents, the level of price-importance elasticity of the buying agents, and the level of unemployment in the marketplace. Preliminary experiments addressing these issues are presented.

1 Introduction

Prior work in Agent mediated Electronic Commerce has investigated the use of software agents in marketplaces where agents do much of the bidding and negotiating on their users behalf in marketplaces of tangible goods. This paper presents a framework for an Agent mediated Knowledge Marketplace, where buyers are the users with questions and sellers are the users who can potentially answer those questions. Unlike marketplaces of tangible goods, in a marketplace of services, we have to face additional complexities like measuring seller competency and performance. We use collaborative reputation mechanisms to estimate the sellers' performance based on their past transactions.

In this Agent mediated Knowledge Marketplace we automate the processes of matchmaking, scheduling, and pricing of the posted tasks. The buyers configure their agents with their budget and time constraints and the importance of the specific task. These agents try to maximize their owners' utilities. In order to achieve this, the buyer agents estimate the expected performance of each seller based on the reputation of that seller in the marketplace and the seller's price, and choose the seller that maximizes their expected utility. Selling agents respond to buyers by bidding on behalf of their owners for the available tasks based on their owners' reputations and their time availability. In this marketplace, the seller reputations are updated in a collaborative fashion based on the performance of the user in the delegated tasks.

J. Liu and Y. Ye (Eds.): E-Commerce Agents, LNAI 2033, pp. 25-38, 2001.

Due to the nature of our reputation mechanisms, there is an inherent market inefficiency [3] because initially sellers are undervalued until their reputation values come close to their actual ability. In order to solve, or at least minimize this problem, we suggest dynamic pricing algorithms. Dynamic pricing allows us to price as efficiently as possible by considering the current reputation of each seller. The purpose of this paper is to present a framework within which dynamic pricing algorithms for reputation driven agents can be tested, and to suggest that such algorithms can be used to overcome the inherent market inefficiency.

The paper is organized as follows. First we give a brief overview of other agent mediated marketplaces, and then we describe the knowledge marketplace framework and the reputation mechanism we developed. Within this framework we suggest some simple dynamic pricing algorithms that the agents can use, we discuss some theoretical issues regarding optimal pricing and price limits of the agents, and finally we present some preliminary experimental results for the simple dynamic pricing methods used.

2 Background

Kasbah [1], [6] is an ongoing research project to help realize a fundamental transformation in the way people transact goods. In Kasbah, a user wanting to buy or sell a good creates an agent, gives it some strategic direction, and sends it off into the agent marketplace. Kasbah agents pro-actively seek out potential buyers or sellers and negotiate with them on their creator's behalf [1], [6]. In Kasbah, the reputation values of the individuals trying to buy/sell books/CDs are major parameters of the behavior of the buying, selling or finding agents of the system. The latest version of Kasbah, which is implemented using the MarketMaker [9] infrastructure, allows users to trade intangible goods like translation services. The interface and the backend of our Knowledge Marketplace will also be implemented using MarketMaker but its major difference from Kasbah is the negotiation strategies of the buyers and sellers.

In Kasbah the price negotiation is based on a limited number of predefined negotiation strategies provided by the system. Agents created with these strategies cannot adjust their negotiation behavior according to the market conditions and the user has to make sure that his/her price ranges are close to the market prices. In the Knowledge Marketplace we wanted to have software agents automate the task of monitoring the market conditions for their users. This means that, instead of using predefined time-varying price functions we need to incorporate adaptive pricing for the sellers and utility evaluation functions for the buyers.

So far, there has been quite extensive research in adaptive pricing agents [2], [8] and it was shown that with minimally intelligent agents (Zero Intelligent Plus) we can achieve economically efficient equilibria without the agents knowing each other's strategy or the market conditions from a macroscopic level [2]. It was also shown that in a marketplace with quality differentiation and quality sensitive users, we can have stable price equilibria, as predicted by game theory [2].

Since our Knowledge Marketplace will be targeting low budget markets, like amateur translation services, we believe that it is important for the success of our marketplace to preserve both the user anonymity and the free identity switching features. Since the reputation mechanisms of our Knowledge Marketplace allow user anonymity and free identity switching, our marketplace incurs the inherent inefficiency of mistreatment of new users until they manage to establish themselves in the marketplace. [3]. The goal of this paper is to suggest that adaptive pricing can be used to decrease the inefficiencies incurred due to anonymity and identity switching: we propose to enrich this marketplace with adaptive pricing algorithms that allow pricing based on temporal reputation changes. To the best of our knowledge, this is the first agent-mediated marketplace where the agents use dynamic pricing based on "dynamically" updated reputations. In this paper we only discuss simple dynamic pricing algorithms and show preliminary experimental results. Future work will focus on designing better algorithms and testing them more thoroughly within the framework of this paper.

3 Knowledge Marketplace

For the purposes of our model, we assume that the marketplace consists of the same number of buyers and sellers. The equilibria of this marketplace are evaluated for two different scenarios: unemployment (less demand than supply), and overemployment (more demand than supply). Since we keep the number of buyers and sellers fixed, we created the scenarios by changing the rate of creation of tasks for each buyer. In particular, the market operates in periods. In every period, each buyer has a probability ***P*** to generate a problem. Once a problem is generated, the buying agent dispatches a request for bids to all sellers. Upon receipt of this query, all available seller agents respond with a price bid and wait for the buyer's decision. A selling agent already engaged in another task, cannot undertake a second one, so it does not respond. However, the buyers may have multiple tasks served at the same time.

After the sellers respond to the buyer, the buyer evaluates the expected utility function for each bid and picks the available seller that offers the highest expected utility. Note that the buyer is allowed to reject all bids. Once it makes its selection, the buyer delegates the task to the chosen seller. The chosen seller then becomes engaged for some market periods, in order to perform its task. In the current model, all tasks are assumed to take the same amount of time. The cycle repeats for all the buyers in the market. We repeat the simulation for a number of periods, and record all the contracts established, as well as the total utilities of the buyers and the total profits (sum of prices at which they managed to sell) of the sellers.

At every period each buyer can generate a problem of importance ***I*** with probability P. The importance ***I*** of the problem is a uniformly distributed random variable from 0 to 1. If a problem is generated, the buyer will request bids from the sellers without providing information about the importance of the task, so that it does not lose its bargaining power. The sellers, on the other hand, have uniformly distributed abilities ***A*** ranging from 0 to 1. The sellers reputation is updated over time based on the seller's ability. We discuss the reputation update mechanism below.

4 Reputation Mechanisms

Consumer to Consumer marketplaces like Kasbah [1], [6], MarketMaker [9], eBay, Yahoo Auctions and Amazon Auctions introduce some major issues of trust [5]: Potential buyers have no physical access to the product of interest while they are bidding or negotiating. Therefore sellers can easily misrepresent the condition or the quality of their products. Additionally, sellers or buyers may decide not to abide by the agreement reached at the electronic marketplace, asking later to renegotiate the price, or even refuse to commit the transaction. Even worse, they may receive the product and refuse to send the money for it, or the other way around. Almost all of these concerns are also true for marketplaces of intangible goods, except that instead of the uncertainty about the condition of the products we have the uncertainty about the competency or actual performance of the seller.

One way of solving the above mentioned problems would be to incorporate in the marketplace a reputation brokering mechanism, so that each user can customize his/her pricing strategies according to the risk implied by the reputation values of his/her potential counterparts. In our previous work [10], we have developed elaborate reputation mechanisms for open online marketplaces or communities that are robust against common abuses of online rating systems. A simple version of these reputation mechanisms is incorporated in our Knowledge Marketplace. For the full reputation mechanism, we refer the reader to [10]. After a seller completes a task, his/her reputation will be updated, using the rating received from the buyer as an indication about his/her ability. Suppose that at time t=i, a user with reputation R_{i-1} is rated with a score W_i, which is a random value normally distributed around the user's ability **A,** truncated between 0 and 1. Let $E_i = R_{i-1}/D$, where D is the reputation range. At equilibrium, E_i can be interpreted as the expected value of W_i, which is the ability of the user A, though early in a user's activity it will be an underestimate. Let θ>1 be the effective number of ratings considered in our reputation evaluation [10]. We then propose the simplified Sporas formula [Equation 1], which is a recursive estimate of the reputation value of a user at time t=i, given the user's most recent reputation, R_{i-1}, and the rating W_i:

$$R_i = R_{i-1} + \frac{1}{\theta} \bullet \Phi(R_{i-1})(W_i - E_i) \ , \ \Phi(R_{i-1}) = 1 - \frac{1}{1 + e^{\frac{-(R_{i-1} - D)}{\sigma}}} \ , \ E_i = R_{i-1}/D \qquad \textbf{(1)}$$

The parameter σ controls the dumping function Φ so that the reputation of highly reputable users is less sensitive to rating fluctuations. In order for the agents to have no incentive to switch identities, we choose the initial reputation of the agents to be minimal. For the experiments we set the initial reputation to be 0.01.

5 Buying Agents

In picking the most suitable seller for its task, the buyer tries to maximize the following Cobb-Douglas utility function:

$$U = (1 - P)^{1-I} O^{I} \tag{2}$$

Where P is the price the buyer will pay, normalized by his budget cap (P_{actual}/P_{cap}) so that it is between 0 and 1, I is the importance of the problem to the buyer, and O is the outcome of the problem in the range [0,1], where 1 is perfect and 0 is terrible. We chose this function for our simulation because it has the following properties:

1. For an important problem, the buyer is willing to spend more.
2. For an unimportant problem, the buyer will sacrifice quality for price.

Furthermore, we assume that a buyer always has the option to turn to some external market (for example, the traditional consulting market) with reputation 1, and price P_m to solve his problem. If none of the sellers' offers provides a greater utility to the buyer than the traditional market, then the buyer will employ the traditional market in solving his problem. The Theoretical Analysis section describes formulas and conditions for this case.

In order to evaluate the expected utility, our buyers use the certainty equivalent principle. In other words, they treat the performance of the seller as a deterministic variable, represented by the value of his reputation. Thus they evaluate their utility function using Outcome = Reputation of the seller, which, as noted above, changes over time.

6 Selling Agents

There are several kinds of selling agents (sellers). In this work we experimented with very simple pricing strategies: we used Derivative Followers, Reputation Followers, and Random Sellers. Designing more intelligent sellers is the subject of ongoing research.

6.1 Derivative Followers

Derivative Followers (DF) are sellers who decide their next bid according to the success of the previous one. So, these sellers focus on increasing their prices from one contract to another as long as they can get the contracts. Likewise, they decrease their bid when they do not get contracts. We assume that Derivative Followers increase their price bids by a fixed step S_{up} multiplied by a random number picked from a uniform distribution with range [0,1] for the next (inertia+1) periods. The random number is different every time it offers a bid. Our preliminary experiments showed that the value of inertia does not have much effect on the results because there are no local maximums or minimums in the profit landscapes of the derivative follower sellers. Therefore, for this paper the inertia is set to 0. If a derivative follower fails to receive a contract, it will start decreasing its price bids by S_{dn} `*random`. In other words, if `idle` is the number of periods after the inertia time passes, the derivative follower's price offer will be:

$$P = LastContractPrice + S_{up} * random_1 - S_{dn} * random_2 * idle\ . \tag{3}$$

The random numbers are different for the two monomials, and they are both recomputed every time an offer is made. Such agents have also been used in other work (see for example [2] and [8]).

6.2 Reputation Followers

Reputation followers maintain a shadow price P_s on which they apply the derivative follower algorithm, assuming that they would offer that price if they had a perfect reputation. However, the price they actually announce is the product of the shadow price and the current reputation value, i.e. $P_s * R$. We decided to implement this scheme, in order to make agents who will actually respond fast to their reputation changes. Indeed, our experiments showed that reputation followers set bids that followed their reputation patterns very effectively and very closely. In a sense our reputation followers are derivative followers but with a step that depends on their reputation and therefore is dynamically changing. Low reputation agents change their prices slowly; therefore we expect that in the case of unemployment they would initially perform better than low reputation derivative followers since they would undercut them. After many trades, when they all reach a "steady state" (their reputation is the same as their ability - does not change any more therefore neither does the reputation followers' price step - and the prices they bid converged to some steady state prices) we expect both reputation followers and derivative followers to behave similarly. These observations were in fact verified by the experiments, as shown below.

6.3 Random Sellers

Random sellers have no pricing or bidding strategies. They just bid random prices. Naturally, these agents are not expected to perform adequately, but they provide a measure to compare against. Other benchmarks can also be used. For example, one can use the optimal pricing (given complete information) described in the theoretical analysis section (a sort of "socially optimal pricing").

7 Theoretical Analysis

7.1 Sellers' Price Range Computation

Given reputation R, external market price P_m, and importance I, the maximum price that the seller can charge is the following:

$$P \leq 1 - \frac{(1 - P_m)}{R^{1/1-I}} \tag{4}$$

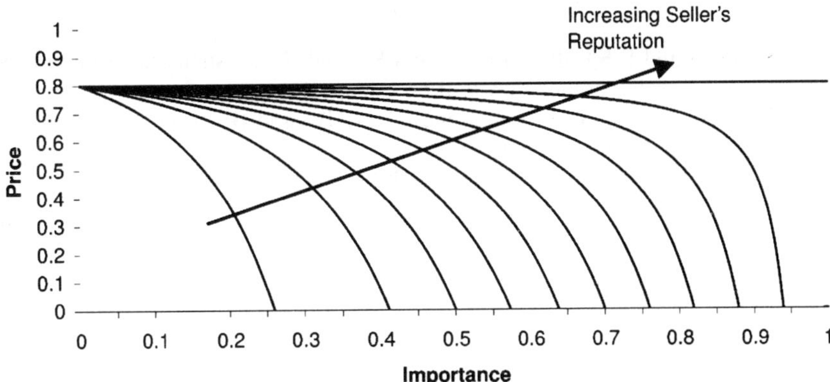

Fig. 1. The range of bids allowed for a seller, as his reputation increases, starting from 0.01, going to 1. Sellers have a chance of receiving the contract only if they bid below the curve given their reputation and the importance of the buyer's problem (which they do not know when placing the bid).

Furthermore, initially the sellers have a very low reputation (=0.01 in our case), therefore they can only receive low importance jobs. Even if they bid for zero price, they can only get a contract if:

$$R^I \geq (1-P_m)^{1-I} \leftrightarrow I \leq \log(1-P_m) \Big/ \log(R(1-P_m)) \quad (5)$$

where $\boldsymbol{I}$ is the importance of the job, and $\boldsymbol{R}$ is the initial reputation of the selling agent. This is expected, since agents will opt to build reputation, in order to be able to actively bid for a larger share of the contracts.

7.2 Optimal Pricing under Complete Information

Suppose we have n sellers and m buyers, and let us represent the set of our sellers as $\{S_1,S_2,S_3,\ldots,S_n\}$, sorted by reputation such that:

$R(S_1)>R(S_2)>R(S_3)>\ldots>R(S_n)$

and our buyers $\{B_1,B_2,B_3,\ldots,B_m\}$, sorted by quality sensitivity such that

$I(B_1)>I(B_2)>I(B_3)>\ldots>I(B_n)$

We have unemployment conditions when n>m, full employment when n=m, and overemployment when n<m.

Under any conditions the maximum number of trades that can take place in each round is: `t=min(n,m)` .

We will now prove that *if there is perfect information in the marketplace, such that the sellers know each other's reputation, the buyers' utility functions, then there exists a Nash equilibrium. In the Nash equilibrium, the prices are such that the sellers and the buyers will pair according to their respective ability and quality sensitivity. Therefore, we will observe trades among the following pairs:*

$(S_1, B_1), (S_2, B_2)\ldots(S_t, B_t)$

Proof: We have a Nash equilibrium if for every consecutive pairs of sellers and buyers (S_i, B_i), (S_j, B_j) such that

$1\leq i<j\leq t$ then:

The prices $P(S_i)$ and $P(S_j)$ offered by sellers S_i and S_j are such that if any of the sellers prices higher or lower then they will be worse off,.

Given the prices $P(S_i)$ and $P(S_j)$, then the buyers B_i and B_j are both better off by selecting sellers S_i and S_j respectively.

Therefore seller S_i will price its services such that:

$$U_i(P(S_i),R(S_i),I(B_i)) > U_i(P(S_j),R(S_j),I(B_i)) \quad \textbf{(6)}$$

otherwise B_i could have selected S_j (if B_i was choosing first), and

$$U_j(P(S_i),R(S_i),I(B_j)) < U_j(P(S_j), R(S_j), I(B_j)) \quad \textbf{(7)}$$

otherwise B_j could have selected S_i (if B_j was choosing first).

Since,

$R(S_i)>R(S_j)$, $I(B_i)>I(B_j)$, (2), (6), and (7)

$\Rightarrow P(S_i)>P(S_j)$

Since this is true for any i, j such that $1\leq i<j\leq t$ it means for any seller S_k, where $1\leq k<t$, its closest competitor is S_{k+1}. Therefore, given $P(S_{k+1})$, the optimal price for S_k is the maximum (in order to maximize profit) price $P(S_k)$ for which if i=k and j=k+1, then (*) still holds. Indeed, if S_k offers slightly higher price $P(S_k)^+$, then S_{k+1} would undercut S_k by offering $P(S_{k+1})$, since we would have

$$U_k(P(S_{k+1}),R(S_{k+1}),I(B_k)) > U_k(P(S_k)+,R(S_k),I(B_k)). \quad \textbf{(8)}$$

In the case of unemployment , the seller S_{t+1} will have to shout a price of 0 to maximize the probability of undercutting seller S_t. Therefore, the seller S_t will have to shout an $P(S_t)$ according to the assumption that $P(S_{t+1})=0$, and all the sellers will have to optimize the shouted prices according to the same assumption. In the case of full employment or overemployment, nobody can undercut seller S_t, therefore S_t will give the maximum price that meets the threshold of the minimum utility of the respective buyer B_t, so if there is no minimum utility requirement on the buyers' side, all sellers should be able ask for the maximum price. As it was discussed above, the minimum utility is the one enjoyed when the buyer transacts outside the online marketplace with a perfectly reputable sellers for the market price P_m.

This equilibrium state does not depend on the dynamics of the reputation algorithm itself. If the reputations of the sellers are stationary then the optimal pricing strategy would be the one that would price as close as possible to the optimal prices derived above at every trading period. However, since our system involves dynamically changing reputations, the dynamic pricing algorithms need to also adapt to these changes. Furthermore, we assume that sellers do not have complete information. In the following sections, we evaluate the effectiveness of the commonly used Derivative Follower seller, and enhanced Reputation Followers in various market conditions.

8 Results of Simulations

We ran several simulations to evaluate the behavior of our system and test the three pricing algorithms in the two market conditions. Without loss of generality, each seller also started with a minimal price, 0.01 (so that none of the sellers started with any advantage). The performance of the algorithms is evaluated based on the profits of each seller as a function of his/her ability. The three algorithms are also evaluated in competition settings where each third of the agents price with one of the algorithms. In this section we present some preliminary results.

8.1 Unemployment

Figure 2 shows the profits of the sellers in the case that they are all either random, or derivative followers, or reputation followers (no competition among different pricing strategies). As shown, in the case of unemployment both followers perform better than random sellers, since random sellers often charge high prices even when they have low reputations, and therefore miss more contracts than the followers do. Regarding the two followers, we observe that when they do not compete both kinds of followers perform about the same: figure 2 shows that for the particular simulation run reputation followers performed slightly better than derivative followers did (especially at the low ability range), but the difference is small.

On the other hand, when the three types of agents compete with each other, then all the agents with more than random intelligence were observed to drive their prices down in order to attract the agents of the buyers. Therefore random sellers were not able to get contracts so, as the experiments showed, almost all random sellers had zero profit. Furthermore, we observed that some followers also could not escape from their initial low reputation by offering low enough prices (that can be attributed to the randomization in following the derivative). Even some agents with very high abilities were not able to engage in trade and could not raise their reputations. Other agents that initially offered lower prices raised their initial reputation, and, thus, attracted even more buyers. This scenario is a good example of how initial history might affect such a marketplace with positive reputation mechanisms. Furthermore, as shown in figure 3, reputation followers tend to escape from their initial low reputation more often than other agents do. This is because at the initial states they increase their prices slowly (since they have low reputation) therefore undercutting the derivative followers and the random sellers, and therefore accumulating more profit. In figure 4 we show the average difference between the profits of the reputation followers and the derivative followers over time. As shown in the figure, at the beginning (when all agents have low reputations) the difference between the profits of the reputation followers and the derivative followers increases (reputation followers undercut the derivative followers most of the time), while over time this difference decreases (as suggested above, over time the reputation of the agents is the same as their actual ability so both reputation followers and derivative followers behave similarly). The figure shows the difference of profits for two kinds of agents: low ability ones (in this case we chose the agents with ability less than 0.3 and measured their average profit) and high ability ones (agents with ability larger than 0.7). The phenomenon appears for both types of agents, and it is stronger for the high ability ones.

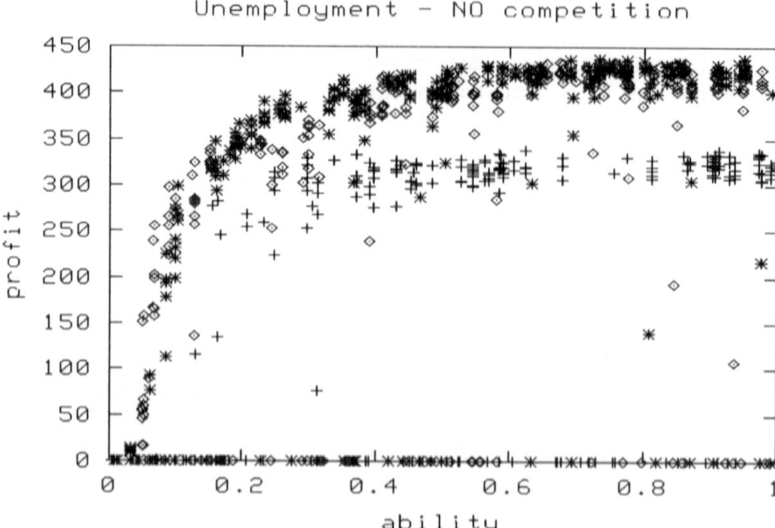

Fig. 2. Unemployment simulations: plus signs (+) are random sellers, stars signs (*) are derivative followers, and circle signs (•) are reputation followers. We run three experiments where for each one all sellers had the same strategy. The figure compares their final profits.

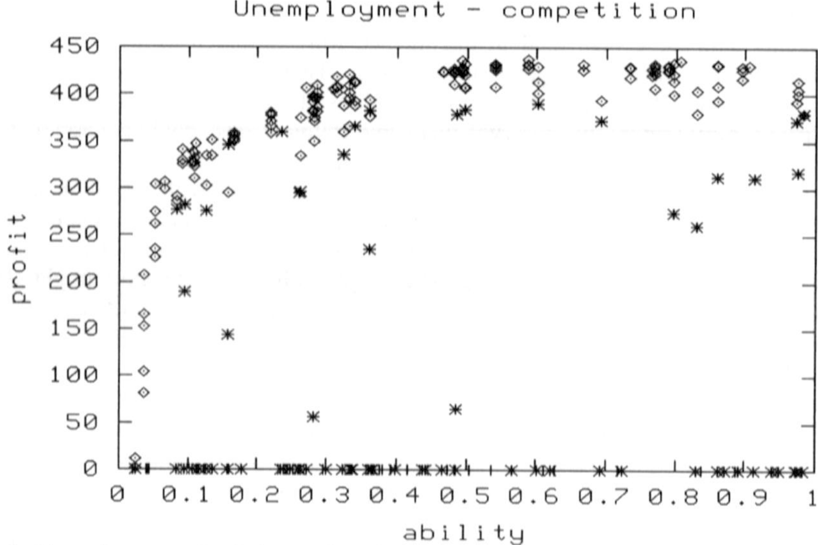

Fig. 3. Unemployment simulations: plus signs (+) are random sellers, stars signs (*) are derivative followers, and circles signs (•) are reputation followers. We run one experiment where a third of the sellers where random, the other third derivative followers, and the remaining reputation followers.

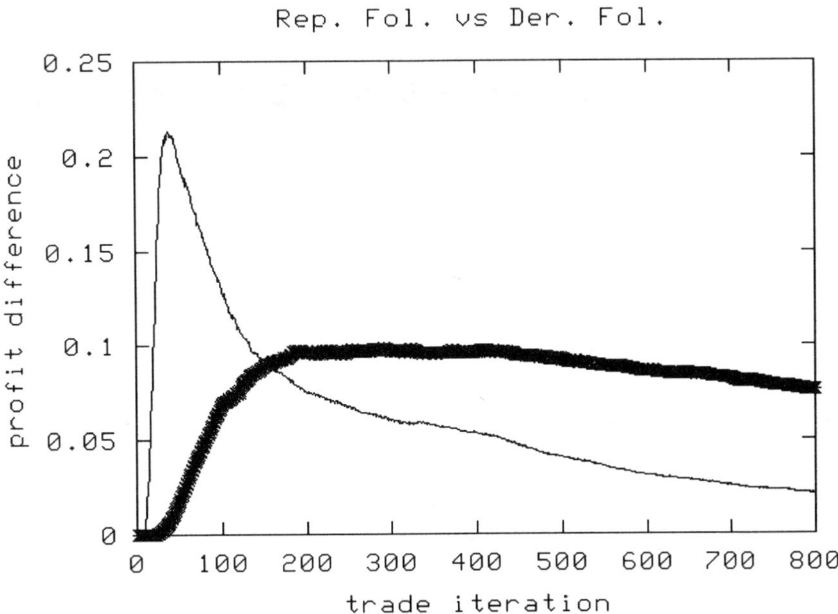

Fig. 4. Unemployment simulations: Average profit difference between reputation and derivative followers over time (y-axis: (avg. profit of rep. fol. – avg. profit of der. fol.) / (# of trade iterations), x-axis: # of trade iterations). Bold line for low ability sellers, thin line for high ability sellers.

8.2 Overemployment

We have overemployment when we expect that a seller will be "guaranteed" to get a job. This occurs when p*B*d>S, where S is the number of sellers, B is the number of buyers, p is the probability of a job being created by the buyer at a market period, and d is the duration of jobs. Satisfaction of this condition guarantees that the seller will make a deal in the next d periods (assuming that B is large enough, so that the standard deviation of the number of job created/period is very small). In fact, if the p*B>S, then the seller can be employed continuously (without having a single period of unemployment), as long as his price offers fall within the acceptable range of the buyers.

In the case of overemployment, all the sellers have the potential of enormous profit. However, the random sellers do not behave that well (since they do now take advantage of the overemployment), as expected, while the reputation followers perform according to their abilities. In the case of overemployment the derivative followers perform overall the best, as shown in figures 5, 6, and 7 (which show the same results as figures 2, 3, and 4 for the case of overemployment).

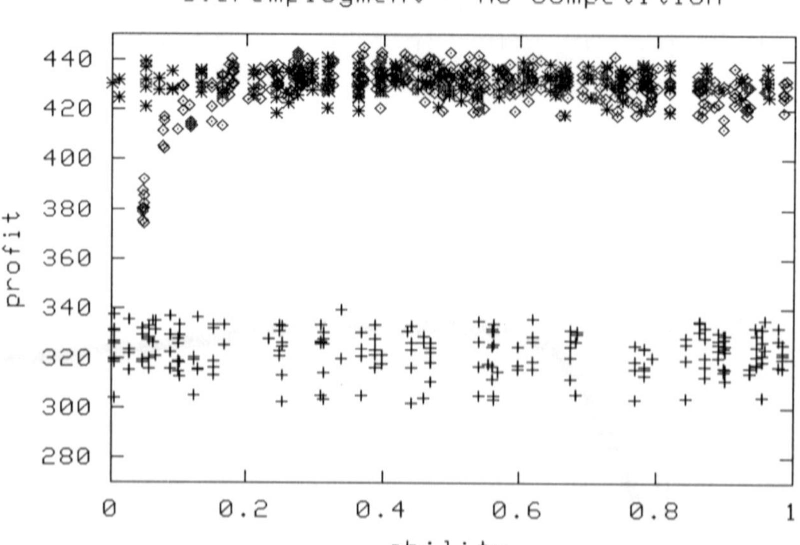

Fig. 5. Overemployment simulations: convention as in Figure 2.

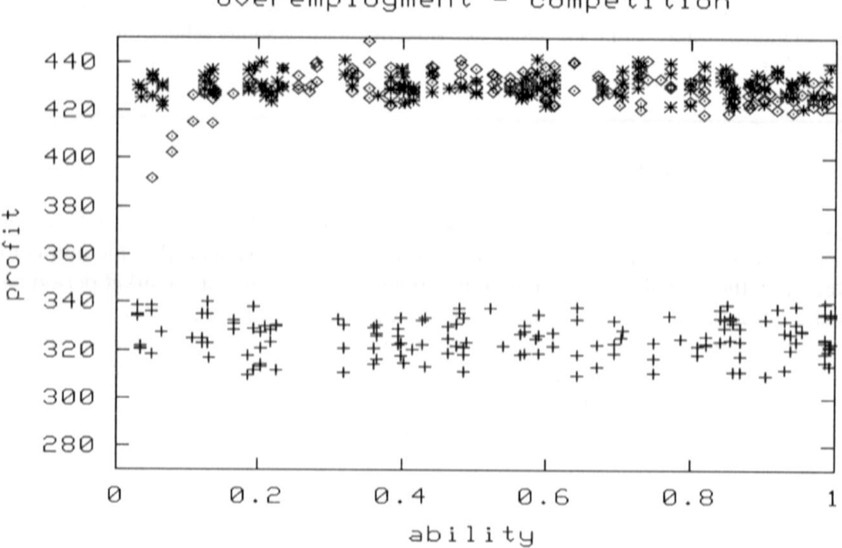

Fig. 6. Overemployment simulations: convention as in Figure 4.

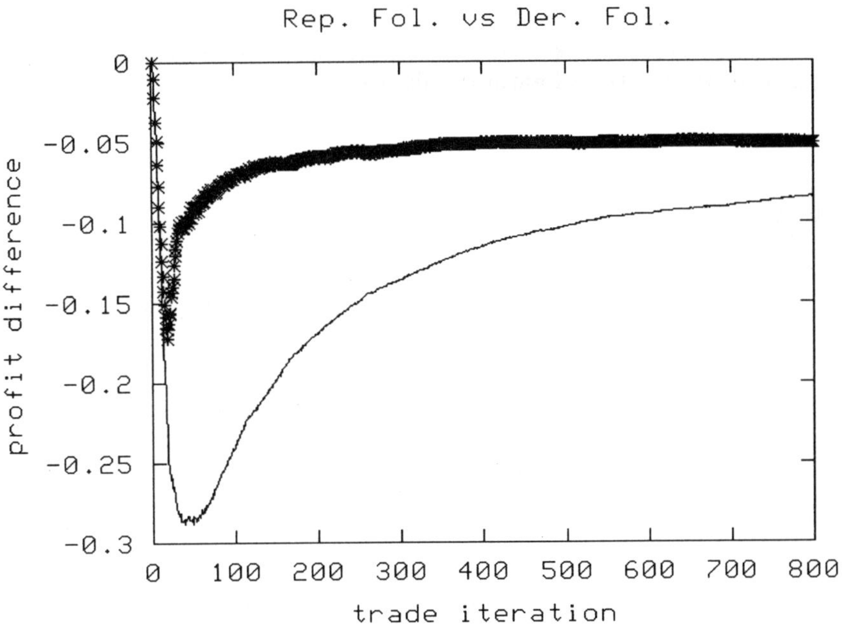

Fig. 7. Overemployment simulations: convention as in Figure 5.

9 Conclusion

We have presented a framework for an Agent mediated Knowledge Marketplace in which users' reputations are established through collaborative mechanisms. We enriched our marketplace with dynamic pricing algorithms in order to get better price during the bootstrapping process, when all users start with minimal reputations. The proposed implementations were simple derivative follower agents, which adjust their prices based on the success of the previous bid, and reputation follower agents who adjust their prices based on both their owners' reputations and the success of their previous bid. Both mechanisms are successful in getting the marketplace bootstrapped and reaching stable market equilibrium conditions, while reputation followers achieve this more effectively. The overall performance of the agents depends also on the market conditions: in the case of unemployment, reputation followers do perform better than derivative followers since the first manage to undercut the second. However, in the case of overemployment where undercutting is not as important (since all agents get a contract as long as they price in a way that they are not "undercut" by the external market price P_m), derivative followers perform better than reputation followers. It is therefore important for the agents to be able to identify the market conditions, according to the requests for bids they receive, and adapt their pricing strategies accordingly. Therefore the optimal strategy may be a combination of the two strategies we have presented here, with which the sellers decide which algorithm they want to use based on their perceived ability and market conditions.

Future work will address the issue of designing more intelligent agents within the proposed framework. The theoretical work presented in this paper, namely the computation of a "socially optimal" dynamic pricing mechanism, can be also used in the future to evaluate the performance of the agents.

References

1. Chavez A, Maes P.: Kasbah: an agent marketplace for buying and selling goods. PAAM 96. Proceedings of the First International Conference on the Practical Application of Intelligent Agents and Multi-Agent Technology. Practical Application Company. 1996, pp.75-90. Blackpool, UK.
2. Cliff, D. and Bruten, J.: "More Than Zero Intelligence Needed for Continuous Double-Auction Trading", HP Technical Report HPL-97-157, CEFES'98, 1998 U. of Cambridge, England.
3. Friedman, E. and Resnick, P.: The Social Cost of Cheap Pseudonyms: Fostering Cooperation on the Internet. In Proceedings of the 1998 Telecommunications Policy Research Conference (1998). Alexandria, VA. Lawrence Erlbaum Associates, Inc., Mahwah, NJ.
4. Glickman, M. "Parameter estimation in large dynamic paired comparison experiments" Journal of the Royal Statistical Society: Series C (Applied Statistics) vol. 48, no. 3, (1999) pp 377-394, Publisher: Blackwell Publishers, Oxford, UK.
5. Kollock, P. The Production of Trust in Online Markets, Advances in Group Processes, vol. 16, (1999), E. J. Lawler, M. Macy, S. Thyne, and H. A. Walker (eds), JAI Press, Greenwich, CT.
6. Moukas, A., Zacharia, G., Guttman, R., Maes, P. Agent-mediated electronic commerce: an MIT Media Laboratory perspective. International Journal of Electronic Commerce, vol.4, no.3, (Spring 2000), pp.5-21. M.E. Sharpe, Armonk, NY, USA; ISSN: 1086-4415
7. Oliver, J. Artificial agents learn policies for multi-issue negotiation. International Journal of Electronic Commerce, vol. 1 (4) , (1997) pp. 49-88, M.E. Sharpe, Armonk, NY.
8. Sairamesh J., and Kephart, J., O. 1998. Price Dynamics of Vertically Differentiated Information Markets. In Proceedings of International Conference on Information and Computation Economies, Charleston, SC.
9. Wang, D., Market Maker: an Agent-Mediated Marketplace Infrastructure, MEng Thesis, (1999), Massachusetts Institute of Technology, Cambridge, MA.
10. Zacharia, G., Maes P. Trust management through reputation mechanisms, Applied Artificial Intelligence Journal, Vol. 14 (9) , (October 2000), pp. 881-908, Taylor and Francis Ltd, London, UK; ISSN: 0883-9514

An Electronic Marketplace Architecture Based on Technology of Intelligent Agents and Knowledge

Georgia Pinto Barbosa[1] and Fabio Q. B. Silva[2]

[1] Cesar – Recife Center for Advanced Studies and Systems, PO Box 7115, 50780-350
Informatics Center, Federal University of Pernambuco, PO Box 7851, 50740-540
Recife - Pernambuco – BRAZIL
gpb@cin.ufpe.br

[2] State Technological Institute of Pernambuco, Av. Prof. Luiz Freire, 700, 50740-540
Informatics Center, Federal University of Pernambuco, PO Box 7851, 50740-540
Recife Pernambuco – BRAZIL
fabio@cin.ufpe.br

Abstract. The Internet, with its speed, agility, scalability and wide reach characteristics, can be used to create a wide and open business market, able to offer efficiency to the process of buying and selling products, reducing transaction costs. However, most e-commerce applications do not exploit the synergy of the Internet because they only involve a single enterprise with its own suppliers and customers. It is necessary to take the communication and cooperation idea to an environment that integrates virtual enterprises and buyers, allowing the creation of an agile and efficient electronic marketplace. With the goal of constructing an efficient and extensible marketplace, this article proposes an electronic marketplace architecture based on intelligent agents and knowledge, contemplating the search and aggregation roles of an intermediary. The process of medicine purchase and sale is used to exemplify the use of this architecture.

1 Introduction

Through the use of information technology of global networks, such as Internet, with their speed, agility, scalability and wide reach characteristics, one can imagine the creation of a wide and open business market, able to offer efficiency to the process of buying and selling products and to reduce transaction costs.

Nowadays, there are many categories of virtual enterprise applications found in Web, which are classified by several researchers, depending on the application context ([1], [2]).

In a general way, these applications can be classified according to the entities which are involved in the commercial transaction: buyers and sellers. Table 1 presents these categories and exemplify them with existent application in Internet.

Consumer-to-Consumer category is related to applications that support commercial transactions among consumers. In this category, there is not the figure of an enterprise, legal entity, but a consumer who offers some product or service for another consumer. Virtual auctions, like E-bay and Lokau, are examples of this category.

J. Liu and Y. Ye (Eds.): E-Commerce Agents, LNAI 2033, pp. 39-60, 2001.

Table 1. Categories of Electronic Commerce

	Consumer	**Business**
Consumer	Consumer-to-Consumer Ex: Lokau[1], E-bay[2]	Consumer-to-Business Ex: PriceLine[3]
Business	Business-to-Consumer Ex: Amazon[4], Dell[5]	Business-to-Business Ex: IBM[6]

In Business-to-Business category, the entities involved in the commercial transaction are enterprises, not final consumers. This way, the enterprise buys products which are used as raw material to products that are sold to consumers. This category groups applications that facilitate, among other activities, the management of suppliers, inventories and distribution.

Business-to-Consumer category is related to applications that support commercial transactions among final consumers and enterprises. This category is well exemplified through the several enterprise Web sites that offer their products using electronic catalogs in Internet. Through these Web sites, the final consumer can place electronic orders and pay for them. Web sites as Amazon and Dell are examples of this category.

Consumer-to-Business category is also related to the electronic commerce among final consumers and enterprises. The difference between this category and the Business-to-Consumer one is related to how the product or services are traded. In this category, the final consumers indicate to the enterprise what they want to buy and how much they would like to pay for the product. In Business-to-Consumer category, the process is the opposite: the enterprise gives the exact price of their products. There is a tendency in Internet where the applications classified in the Business-to-Consumer category become more flexible to consumers and, as a result, they would be classified as Consumer-to-Business applications.

Each one of these categories has particular characteristics that should be analyzed and treated differently, because they involve different entities and ways of relationship. For this reason, it is necessary that strategies of marketing and application development be suitable to imposed situations by the commerce environment, so that electronic commerce application can assist well the involved entities.

The rest of this article is focused in Consumer-to-Business applications, but the result reached by this article can be adjusted to assist the needs of the other categories. Some directions for these adjustment are presented in Section 5.

A common aspect among the virtual enterprises that exist nowadays is that their applications do not exploit the synergy of the Internet because they only involve a single enterprise with its own suppliers and customers [10]. So, they get linked to a virtual environment, which does not take advantage of one of the main Internet/Web's potential: the ability of providing a global and open marketplace.

---

[1] http://www.lokau.com.br

[2] http://www.ebay.com

[3] http://www.priceline.com

[4] http://www.amazon.com

[5] http://www.dell.com

[6] http://www.ibm.com

It is necessary to take the communication and cooperation idea to an environment that integrates virtual enterprises and buyers, allowing the creation of an agile and efficient electronic marketplace.

To accomplish this, the need of electronic intermediaries arises in this environment, with the role of coordinating the relevant information to the process of buying and selling products, reducing the transaction costs.

For a complete commercial transaction, many steps of the process of buying and selling need to be contemplated. This process is not related only to place an order and its payment: it includes many other activities.

Walid Mougayar, in [1], divides the process of buying and selling into three steps: pre-sale, sale and post-sale. Besides, for each one of these steps, he specifies their activities, producing a model of buying and selling, called Buyer/Seller Model (Table 2).

Table 2. Buyer / Seller Model

	Buyers	*Sellers*
Pre-sale	Search/Inquire for product Discover product Compare products Negotiate terms	Distribution Promotion Display Pricing policy
Sale	Place order Receive acknowledgement Initiate payment Receive product	Receive order Authorize payment Schedule order Build/Retrieve from inventory
Post-sale	Request support Give feedback	Ship product Receive payment Support products Market research

This model presents different perspectives of the process of buying and selling: the seller and buyer perspectives. The activities that are presented in these perspectives can be mapped to the electronic commerce environment of Internet. Appendix presents examples of how each one of these activities affect the electronic environment provided by Internet.

It is important to highlight that the usage of intermediaries in this process of buying and selling should be accomplished considering the systems that already exist in the enterprises, which already give support to some of the activities presented in Table 2. The intermediaries should be integrated with all legacy systems, allowing that the process be as automatic as possible. For example, an enterprise which sells through credit cards, possibly has already used systems that have a direct communication with the credit card management company. This way, the intermediaries in this scenery should not accomplish this activity. They should integrate themselves to the existent systems giving the necessary information so that the process of buying and selling can follow the rest of its natural flow. In spite of this article does not exploit the activities that are accomplished by legacy systems, it refers to some of their elements, joining them with the information flows used to support the buying and selling decisions.

This way, Joseph Bailey groups the intermediary functions into those following roles [3]:

- *Aggregation* – Intermediaries can aggregate products among suppliers to reduce transaction costs. They can aggregate the demand of many buyers or the products of many sellers, while still maintaining the interaction between buyers and sellers.
- *Pricing* – The intermediary determines the price of products based on their demand and offer, gotten in the marketplace.
- *Search* – As the intermediaries are repositories of marketplace information, they can turn more accessible the information of sales product to buyers, reducing the search costs.
- *Trust* – With this role, intermediaries will have the objective to protect buyers and sellers from opportunistic behavior of the marketplace participants. The behavior of this participants will be monitored and when there is some kind of irregular situation, the intermediary will associate it to the participant and this one will have his reputation shaken.

As these intermediaries need to interact in a distributed and adaptable manner with the other present actors in this environment (buyers and sellers) and this interaction is based on the rich and dynamic knowledge inherent to this environment, the technology of intelligent agents, ontologies[7] and knowledge bases get appropriated to the development of this electronic marketplace.

This article proposes an electronic marketplace architecture based on intelligent agents and knowledge, contemplating the search and aggregation roles of an intermediary. The process of medicine purchase and sale is used to exemplify the use of this architecture.

This article is organised as follows. Section 2 presents the proposed electronic marketplace architecture based on intelligent agents. In this section, the agents that take part of this marketplace are defined, as well their transaction and information models. How the marketplace will make commercial transactions possible is presented in Section 3. Section 4 presents some related works in this area and Section 5 presents some conclusions.

2 Marketplace Architecture

In the aggregation and search roles that the proposed marketplace contemplates, these activities are emphasized:

- *Help the buyer* in the process of the product choice based on its functionality, even when he/she does not know exactly what he/she wants to buy;
- *Matching* demand and offer of products;
- *Suggestions of purchase* based on complement and similar products;
- *Notification of buyers* about the existence of the offer of products, based on their profiles (including the purchase history);
- *Identify the level of consumer satisfaction*;

This last activity is about the identification of the buyer feedback as to the product functionality bought by him. This information is taken into consideration in the activity of *helping the buyer in the process of a product choice*, although it can be used as the basis for a trust mechanism.

---

[7] Ontology is an explicit specification of a conceptualization [4].

One of these activities requirements is that the system marketplace must foresee that existing processes are accomplished in a distributed manner and the behavior of buyers and sellers has a dynamic nature. Besides, the system is based on the rich knowledge that already exists about the application domain and the knowledge acquired from buyers, sellers and transactions that involve them. According to these characteristics, the use of intelligent agents technology is suitable. Besides, an information model based on ontologies and knowledge bases is used to represent the sharing of information in this environment.

Based on the proposed compositional design of multi-agents systems in [5], the marketplace architecture definition presented in this section is divided into three modules. The first identifies which agents are involved in this system. These agents will be specialized from the generic model for the weak agent notion [6] and their general objectives will be introduced. The second presents the transactional models of the marketplace, in the view of each agent defined in the previous module. The last module corresponds to the information model, based on ontologies and knowledge bases definition, that is used by the agents of marketplace. Those modules are presented in the following sections.

2.1 Definition of the Agents That Exist in the Marketplace

There are three kinds of agents in the proposed marketplace: buyer agent, seller agent and intermediary agent.

The buyer agent has as objective the representation of the buyer needs. To accomplish this, it owns information related to the profile of the buyer and his needs. The seller agent will be the seller interface in this marketplace. It is responsible for informing which products are for sale and the ways of negotiation that are allowed in a commercial transaction of products with the buyer. The intermediary agent exists with the objective to coordinate the information related to the marketplace. This includes information about buyers and sellers and what is being offered and demanded. In the proposed marketplace, it is responsible for allowing the activities about the aggregation and search of products presented in the beginning of this section. The architecture of this marketplace is shown in Figure 1.

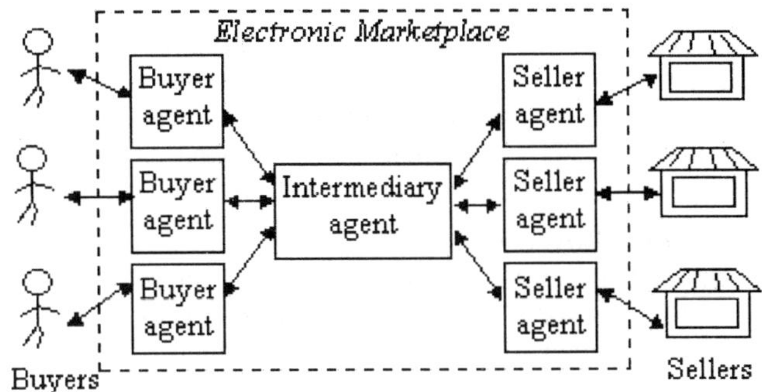

Fig. 1. The electronic marketplace architecture

As can be seen in Figure 1, the communication between buyers and sellers agents is accomplished by an intermediary agent. Only after the successful negotiation of the buying and sales terms, the buyer himself will interact with the seller application to finish the commercial transaction, using the parameters already traded by the marketplace agents.

The marketplace agents were specialized from a generic model of a broker which describes agents who are able to reason, act and communicate, not only based on coming information from the outside world, as well as the coming information from other agents [6]. Figure 2 presents the generic model for the weak agent notion. This model consists of six components: own process control (OPC), maintenance of world information (MWI), world interaction management (WIM), maintenance of agent information (MAI), agent interaction management (AIM), and agent specific tasks (AST).

Table 3 summarizes these components according to the view of participant agents of this marketplace. The AST component will be presented through the transactional models of each agent in Section 2.2.

Table 3. Components of generic module *versus* participant agents of the marketplace

	Buyer agent	**seller agent**	**intermediary agent**
OPC	defines different characteristics of the agent (e.g., negotiation rules)		
MWI	stores the world information (e.g. information on attributes of products)		
WIM	models interaction with the world		
	(e.g., with databases and buyers)	(e.g., with databases and sellers)	(e.g., databases and other intermediary agents)
MAI	keeps information about intermediary agent (e.g., products that are offered in the marketplace)	keeps information about intermediary agent (e.g., which products are demanded in the marketplace and there is no offer for them).	keeps information about buyer and seller agents (e.g., which buyers and sellers take part of the marketplace and what they want to buy and sell)
AIM	manages communication with the intermediary agent	manages communication with the intermediary agent	manages communication with buyer and seller agents

2.2 Transactional Models

About the activities of the marketplace presented previously, transactional models which are based on the perception of the involved agents were developed. These models describe the interactions among the marketplace agents that are necessaries to accomplish these activities, showing which alternative ways can be followed.

2.2.1 Perception of the Buyer Agent

The main interactions between the buyer agent and the intermediary agent occurs in two ways: actively or passively. In the active interaction, the buyer agent needs to shop for something, although it cannot even know which product fits better to its needs. In the passive interaction, the buyer agent waits for a contact of the intermediary agent that will notify it about the products that are been offered and eventually can be of its interest. Figure 3 presents the active transactional model through the buyer agent's perception and Figure 4 presents the passive transactional one.

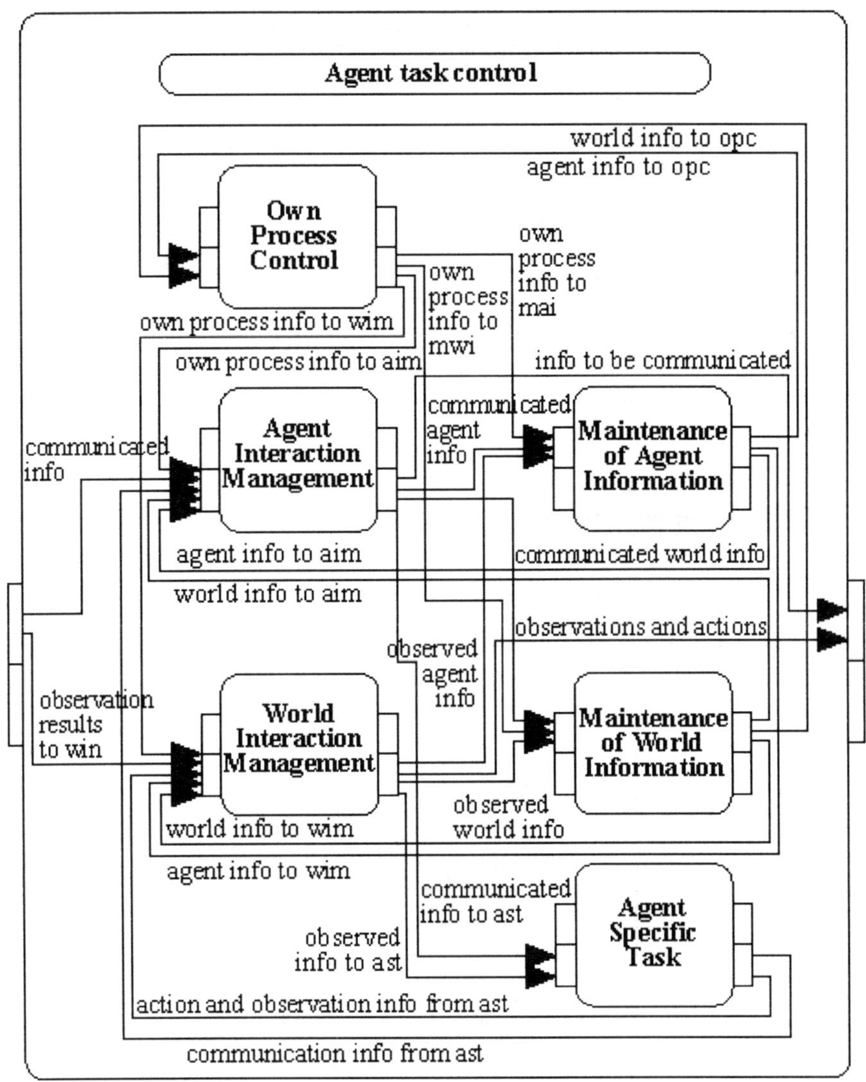

Fig. 2. Generic model for the weak agent notion

Despite not being presented in Figure 3 and Figure 4, the process of identification the buyer satisfaction is also accomplished in the active or passive way. In the former, the buyer informs, through his agent, which products got from the marketplace and informs which is his level of satisfaction with them. In the passive way, the first contact is accomplished by the intermediary agent who will question the buyer agent about buyer's satisfaction.

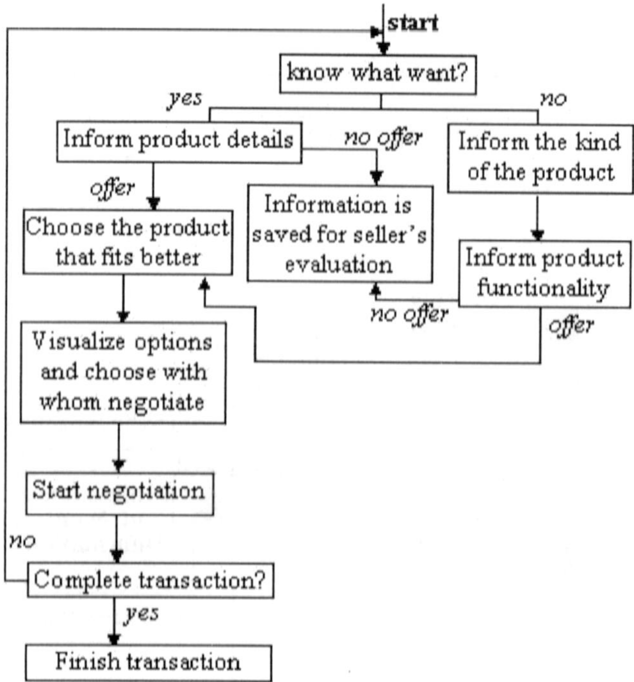

Fig. 3. Buyer agent's perception: active transactional model

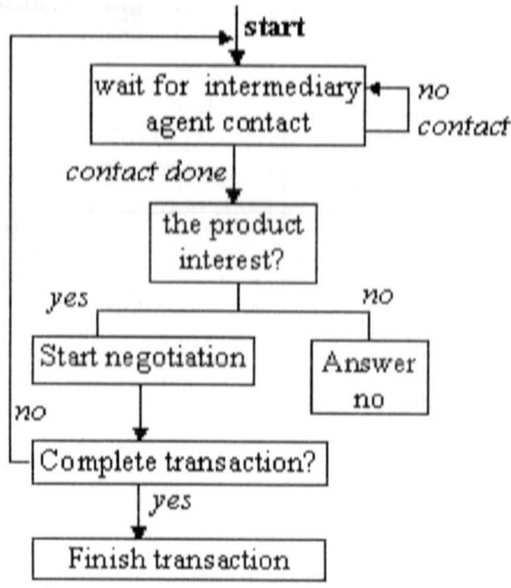

Fig. 4. Buyer agent's perception: passive transactional model

2.2.2 Perception of the Seller Agent

The main interactions of the seller agent with the intermediary agent can happen in an active or passive manner. In the active interaction, the seller agent wishes to "announce" some product. In this case, it informs the detailed data of this product to the intermediary agent, including expiration date of the information. This information base will optimize the search for products done by the intermediary agent. In the passive interaction, the seller agent waits for the contact of intermediary agent, given when the buyer agent requests information about a determined product. Figure 5 presents a transactional active model through the seller agent's perception and Figure 6 presents the transactional passive one.

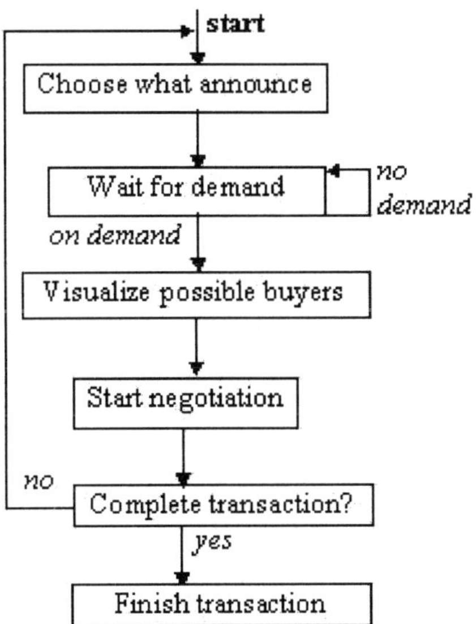

Fig. 5. Seller agent's perception: active transactional model

2.2.3 Perception of Intermediary Agent

The integration between the perceptions of the buyer agent (Section 2.2.1) and the seller agent (Section 2.2.2) is represented by the perception of the intermediary agent. Figure 7 presents the transactional model of the marketplace through the perception of this agent.

In this transactional model, the information recorded when a buyer agent requests some product that does not exist for sale in the marketplace is used in two ways. First, it is used in the product matching that is being announced and buyers that do not find suitable products to their needs. Second, it is used to inform sellers, as a suggestion for sales, which kinds of products exist demand not satisfied in this marketplace.

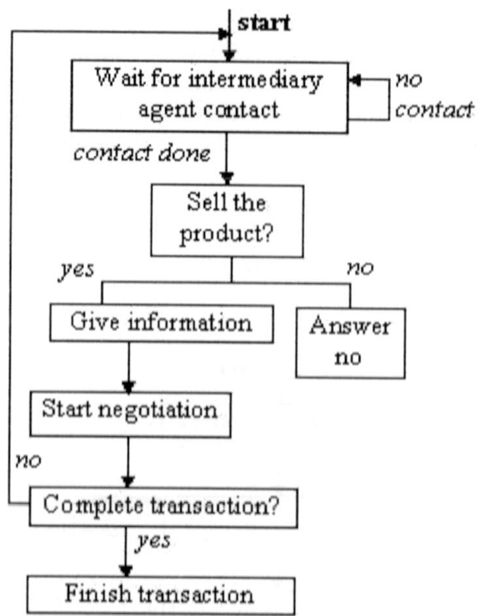

Fig. 6. Seller agent's perception: passive transactional model

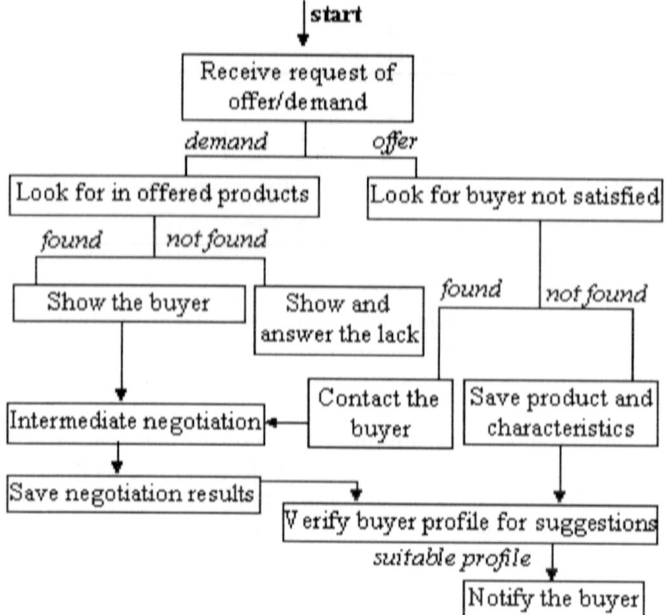

Fig. 7. Intermediary agent's perception: transactional model

2.3 Information Model

One of the roles attributed to the use of pre-constructed ontologies about restrict domains is the sharing of knowledge [7]. Ontologies guarantee, through a common vocabulary of terms and its respective concepts, definitions and relations, axioms and restrictions, the communication at knowledge level among agents. In [7], Gruber presents principles that should be followed in the construction of ontologies to guarantee the maximum quality. They are:

- *Clarity* – In the knowledge definition, it is necessary to have objectivity and define only what is useful for the resolution of the problem. The definition should be independent of social and computation contexts. Formalism can be used in this definition, when the usage of logic axioms is possible. All definition should be documented with natural language.
- *Coherence* – An Ontology should be coherent, that is, the inferences derived from this ontology should be right and logically consistent with the definitions that can be in natural language or axioms.
- *Extendibility* – In the creation of an ontology, extensibility criteria should be added, even the project of this ontology was developed to anticipate the use of a shared vocabulary. The ontology should allow extensions and specialization coherently, without any need to review the theory, that consists in the logical review in searching for contradictions.
- *Minimal encoding bias* – The use of codes should be reduced because agents that share knowledge can be implemented in different systems of representation and representation styles. Generic concepts should be specified, independently of patterns established for measurement, notation and codification. These generic concepts should be limited by clarity.
- *Minimal ontological commitment* – To improve the reusability, only the essential knowledge should be included, building the smallest possible theory about each concept, allowing the creation of new concepts more specialized or instantiated.

Based on these principles and on the methodology for building ontologies presented in [11], the marketplace information model was specified using restrict ontologies to the buying and selling product domain. Therefore, the ontology of products is essential in the definition of this domain. The seller and buyer agents will be able to express their needs through it, while the intermediary agent will be able to associate these needs, allowing commercial transactions.

Ontologies that represent the buyers and sellers and other information pertinent to the marketplace and necessary to the intermediary agent for the accomplishment of its activities are also used.

2.3.1 Basic Model of Product

The basic model of a product is composed by the following information modules:

- Identify – this module identifies the product from their ordinal features;
- Functional features – this module is responsible for identifying the product according to its functionality;
- Required composition – represents the compulsory composition of the product, or which other products it is made from;

- Optional composition – represents the optional compositional of the product, or which other products could be joined to it at the moment of its sale;
- Visual characteristics – as the marketplace environment in question is the Internet, visual means of representing a product have to be taken into consideration;
- Functionality requirements – presents which other products will need to be used together with the product in question.

It is not necessary to describe a product using all the modules above. It is only necessary to specify which modules will be used to represent the product. For example, a buyer who does not know exactly which product he/she is looking for will only use the Functional Features module. Besides, it is possible to use knowledge rules to infer data which can belong to a determined module, even without specifying this module. Figure 8 presents an example of how a product can be described using these ontologies.

```
product_represented_by(functional_features(functionality))
                          ↓
product_represented_by(functional_features(painkiller))
product_represented_by(identify(AAS),
    functional_features(painkiller))
```

Fig. 8. Example of how a product can be described using ontologies

2.3.2 The Models of the Buyer and the Seller

The buyer and seller information models are formed by attributes that are pertinent to each one of these actors and can be classified into dynamic, static/dynamic or static knowledge [8]. Table 4 presents the attributes of these actors classified according to these levels of knowledge.

Table 4. Specific attributes of buyers and sellers

	Buyer	Seller
static knowledge	identification code, name, purchases/sales history	
static / dynamic knowledge	profile, negotiation rules, sellers from whom he/she has already bought.	profile, products, negotiation rules, logistic, clients
dynamic knowledge	product that he/she wants to acquire, intervals of acceptable prices	intervals of acceptable prices, stock

3 Allowing Commercial Transactions: Information Matching

In general, the marketplace activities (Section 2) have one main objective: match the needs of the buyer with the needs of the seller. Each one of these activities can be applied to following situations in the marketplace:

1. The buyer has already defined the product he/she wants and there is offer of it;
2. The buyer has already defined the product he/she wants and there is not an offer of it;
3. The buyer has not defined the product he/she wants yet.

It is important to emphasize that the agents use a synonym dictionary to describe the products in the marketplace. Therefore, one expects that the agent can compare products that have different but synonymous names.

In the first situation, the process of matching is very simple, because, besides the buyer already knows what he really want to buy, there are sellers in the marketplace who offer the wanted product. This way, it will only be necessary the comparison of the product sale characteristics of each seller to present the best options of buying to the buyer. The price, delivery time and ways of payment are some of these characteristics. At this moment, negotiation mechanism can be used. However, as this subject is related to the pricing role of the intermediary, it will not be discussed in this article.

To present the second and third situations the following scenario, whose specific domain is the purchase and sale of medicine, will be used: *"A buyer wants to buy two kinds of medicine. The first has already been determined: VitaminC. The second kind of medicine, the buyer has not determined yet. But he/she knows that it will be used to relieve headaches. In the meantime, two sellers, A and B, are offering medicine in the marketplace (except VitaminC)."*

Since the wanted product by the buyer is *VitaminC* and none of the sellers has this specific product, the intermediary agent should verify if there is a similar product that can be offered to the buyer. To accomplish this, it will use its knowledge base in the search of some product that has the same functionality *VitaminC* has or the same active ingredient (e.g. ascorbic acid) in its composition. Finding this similar product, the intermediary agent will offer it to the buyer agent. Figure 9 shows the example above.

Buyer agent information:

demand (product_represented_by(identify(VitaminC)))

Information that the intermediary agent receives from sellers agents:

offer(product_represented_by(identify(VitaminC), [])

Information in the knowledge base:

product_represented_by(identify(VitaminC),
required_composition(ascorbic acid))

Intermediary agent searches for similar products:

search(required_composition (ascorbic acid))

Search result:

search_result(required_composition (ascorbic acid),
product_represented_by(identify(ExtraVitC)))

Fig. 9. Example of situation 2

The search for the second medicine in the above scenario will be accomplished based on the functionality of the product (it relieves headaches). Knowing about this information, the intermediary agent will verify in its knowledge base which products have this functionality. When these products are found, this information is taken to the buyer agent who will decide which of these products it has interest to buy. Figure 10 shows the example above.

Buyer agent information:
demand (product_represented_by(functionality(headache)))
Intermediary agent searches for products this functionality:
search(functionality(headache))
Search result:
search_result (functionality (headache),
product_represented_by (identify (SuperNoHeadache)))

Fig. 10. Example of situation 3

4 Related Work

The objective of this section is to present some agents or marketplaces based on intelligent agents that were developed to improve the electronic commerce in the net. At the end of this section, some of differences between the approaches of these systems and the approaches used in the proposed marketplace will be indicated.

4.1 BargainFinder

BargainFinder is considered as the first shopping agent for on-line price comparisons [12].

The price comparison began with the information about which product the buyer wanted to buy. With this information, BargainFinder requested the price of nine sellers Web sites, using for this purpose, requests similar as from a Web browser (Figure 11).

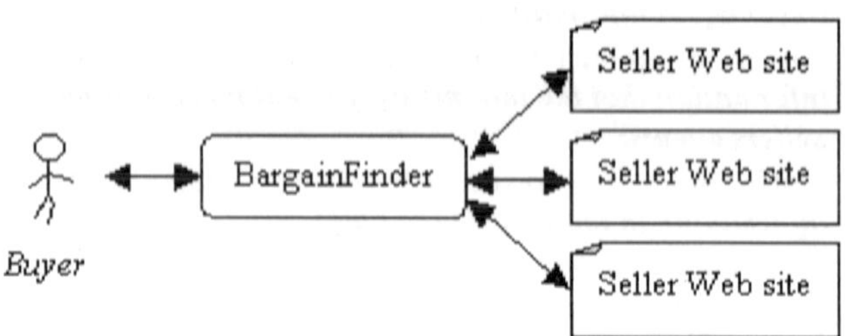

Fig. 11. BargainFinder price comparison

In spite of being a limited system in comparison to other agent system that exist today, BargainFinder raised a series of considerations about the automatic comparison of prices in the Web. One of them is about the resistance of many sellers in taking part of this process of price comparison. This happened because the sellers, which did not want that only their prices were compared through BargainFinder, blocked the access to their Web sites for this agent. The services that aggregate value to the product and normally increase its price were practically ignored by the agent and, consequently, were not considered in the buying decision of the consumer.

4.2 Jango

Jango agent has the same philosophy of BargainFinder (Section 4.1). It allows that price comparison can be based on the information available in the seller Web sites [13].

Jango can be considered an evolution of BargainFinder because it uses an artifice so that its access to the Web sites is not blocked. For this, the requests that are accomplished by Jango to the seller Web sites proceed as if the request were built directly from the browser of any user. This way, the seller Web sites do not distinguish the access that is accomplished by Jango from the others that are accomplished by its users. Afterwards, Jango presents the information obtained in this Web sites so that the consumer can compare the product prices of the sellers.

4.3 Miner

The Miner Family of Web agents is a set of tools whose main objective is to help people in finding information on the Web [15]. The main idea is to bring multiple search and information sources together in one place. The searching is performed by agents working in parallel, collecting answers and unifying them. The Miner Family of Web provides brokerages services that include:

- BookMiner – searches for books in registered Brazilian and international bookstores to match user's specification.
- CDMiner – searches for music titles in Brazilian and international music stores to find the user's preference.

These services work similarly. Each query task can be divided into five main steps, as follows: (1) a user submits a query; (2) The Miner server gets the query and dispatch its agents; (3) each agent queries its target store; (4) each agent receives and parses the query results; and (5) the server unifies, formats and sends the results to the user. Figure 12 presents these steps.

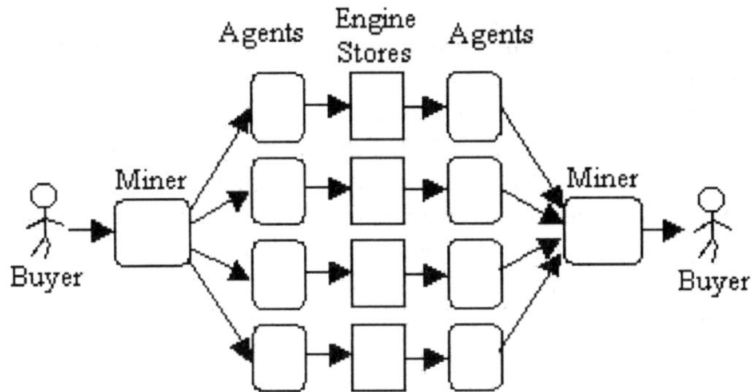

Fig. 12. Miner Family - Steps of a query task

4.4 Tete-a-Tete (T@T)

The agent system T@T provides agents of buying for the buyers and agents of selling for the sellers. These agents interact and negotiate to each other to satisfy the needs of all individuals that are involved (Figure 13) [14].

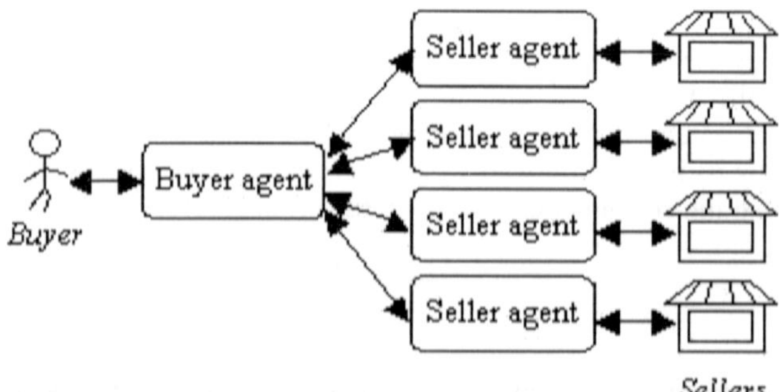

Fig. 13. Tete-a-Tete – Communication between seller and buyer agents

The difference among sellers is accomplished not only based on the price of the products offered. Other dimensions for this evaluation are used, such as, the delivery time, support services, brand and reputation. This guarantees that what is being compared for the buyer is the real value of the product and not only the price of it.

For the seller, T@T becomes the negotiation process automatic. For the buyer, T@T provides assistance during the negotiations offering decision support to determine which seller has better condition of buying. For this, T@T provides an interface that allows the communication of preferences by the buyers and presents which products attend their needs better.

4.5 Kasbah

Kasbah is an online multi-agent system where its users create agents of buying or selling to help in the negotiation process of the product [16]. This way, a user who wants to buy or sell a determined product, creates his agent, gives him strategic directions of negotiation and sends him to a central marketplace of agents.

The objective of this agent is to complete an acceptable business according to the informed strategies. An acceptable business is a business whose defined parameters of buying and selling are in agreement with the defined strategies. Some examples of information that can be defined in these strategies are the interval of acceptable prices of a determined product by the consumer or seller and the time that the agent should use to accomplish a business.

After buyer and seller agents meet having complementary interest, that is, one wants to sell and the other wants to buy the same product, the process of negotiation starts. This process is direct and the only action which is allowed into negotiation protocol is a bid by the buyer agent, without restrictions of time or price, while the seller agent only can answer "yes" or "no" to this bid.

The message exchange happens until the agents get to an acceptable agreement. In the meantime, the bid raise accomplished by the buyer agent is based on the strategy informed by his user, where he identifies which is the degree of the anxiety of the agent: anxious, cool-headed and frugal, corresponding to a linear, quadratic and exponential function, respectively.

4.6 Market Space

Market Space is an open agent-based market infrastructure. Its is based on a decentralized infrastructure model in which humans and machines can get information about products and services, and everyone is able to announce interests to on another [17]. The aims of Market Space is build a marketplace where searching, negotiation and deal settlement is done using agents and is based on models for information and interaction.

4.7 MAGMA

MAGMA is a free-market agent architecture that includes elements required for simulating a real market [18, 19]. Some of these elements are: communication infrastructure, mechanisms for storage and transfer of goods, banking and monetary transactions and economic mechanisms for direct or brokered producer-consumer transactions. The aim of this architecture is provide all essential services to agent-based commercial activities. These services are available through an open-standard messaging API.

MAGMA architecture includes multiple Trader Agents, an Advertising Server and a Bank. Trader Agents are responsible for all their business in the system: buying and selling products and negotiating prices. The Advertising Server provides a classified advertisement service that includes search and retrieval of ads by category. The Bank provides a set of basic banking services that includes checking accounts, lines of credit and electronic cash.

A Relay server was created to facilitate communication between these agents. As these agents communicate to each other through sockets connections, the Relay server maintains all socket connections and routes messages between agents based on unique agent names. The MAGMA architecture is presented in Figure 14.

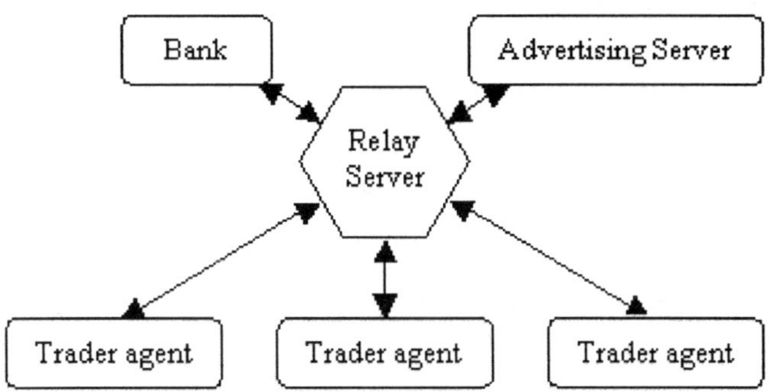

Fig. 14. The MAGMA architecture

4.8 Some Conclusions

Based on the presentation of the systems in the previous subsections, some conclusions can be taken about the differences of approaches used in these systems and in the proposed marketplace.

The first systems presented, BargainFinder (Section 4.1), Jango (Section 4.2) e Miner (Section 4.3), demand that the buyer already knows what he really wants to buy. Besides, the comparison of shopping offers is only based on the price of these products, not considering other variables as the delivery time of the product. The proposed marketplace, besides helping the process of choice of a product by the buyer still allows that other parameters be used in the process of product comparison.

The architectures of T@T (Section 4.4) and Kasbah (Section 4.5) are based on the use of seller and buyer agents. However, it does not foresee the use of intermediary agents as the proposed marketplace. Intermediary agents can be used to aggregate value to the activities offered to buyers and sellers in the marketplace. An example of this activity is the aggregation of consumers that can guarantee scale economy in the marketplace. These two systems offer support to the process of negotiation among buyers and sellers. This functionality was not discussed in the proposed marketplace but is being studied so that it can be used in the future.

The focus of Market Space is the definition of its interaction and information modules. However, these modules were not built using blocks that were specified formally in the conceptual level. The proposed marketplace uses ontologies to share the knowledge among the entities that exist in the marketplace.

One of MAGMA objectives is to cover all the steps of the commercial transaction, including entities that take part in these steps. Besides, the system suggests communication patterns among these entities. In the proposed marketplace, its is also exposed the need that the commercial process can be as automatic as possible. However, some of the activities of the process, as the payment effectuation through credit cards, do not take part in the functions offered by the marketplace. That happens because other systems, developed from initiatives of big enterprises and used a lot with confirmed efficiency, already accomplish these activities. This way the marketplace proposes its integration with these systems.

5 Concluding Remarks

The Internet, with its speed, agility, scalability and wide reach characteristics, can be used to create a wide and open business market. However, the electronic commerce application which are seen in Web do not take advantage of all this potential. It is with the objective to offer efficiency to the process of buying and selling products that this article proposes an electronic marketplace architecture based on intelligent agents and knowledge, contemplating the search and aggregation roles of an intermediary.

The marketplace architecture is in constant evolutions, so that it can adjust better to the needs of the commerce in Internet. Among the foreseen evolutions, some of them can be cited:

- Use of negotiation mechanism, increasing the pricing role of the intermediary;
- Use of trust mechanisms, such as authentication receipts of the transactions accomplished, guaranteeing more reliability to the transactions accomplished in the marketplace;
- Marketplace Adjustment to the other electronic commerce categories, as Business-to-Business one. For this, a study of the behavior of involved entity and how the products are traded among them is being accomplished. With this information, it will be possible the identification of new necessary functions in the marketplace so that it can give support to the needs of this other environment of commercial transactions;
- Adjustment of the intermediary agent so that it can communicate with sellers APIs besides the possibility of communication with seller agents. This initiative will reduce the effort of participation by the seller in this marketplace. It is important to highlight the more consumers and sellers are taking part of the marketplace, the more will be its chances to be a used system in high scale.

Besides these evolutions, the communication with other existent marketplace is also foreseen. For this, it will be necessary to mature the communication and information models that exist in the proposed marketplace.

References

1. Mougayar, W.: Opening Digital Markets. 2nd edn. McGraw-Hill (1998)
2. Bakos, Y.: The Emerging Role of Electronic Marketplaces on the Internet. Communications of the ACM, Vol. 41. No. 8 (1998)
3. Bailey, J. P.: Intermediation and Electronic Markets: Aggregation and Pricing in Internet Commerce. Doctor's Thesis, Computer Science Department, Uppsala University, Sweden (1998)
4. Gruber, T. R.: What is an Ontology?. Knowledge Systems Laboratory, Computer Systems Dept. Stanford University, Stanford, USA (1993)
5. Brazier, F. M. T., Jonker, C. M., Treur, J.: Principles of Compositional Multi-Agent System Development, Proc. of the IFIP'98 Conference IT&KNOWS'98, J.Cuena (ed.), Chapman and Hall (1998)
6. Brazier, F., Keplicz, B. D., Jennings, N. R., Treur, J.: Formal Specification of Multi-Agent Systems: a Real-World Case. In V. Lesser (ed.), Proceedings of the First International Conference on Multi-Agent Systems, ICMAS'95, MIT Press, Cambridge, MA (1995) 25-32. Extended version in International Journal of Cooperative Information Systems, M. Huhns, M. Singh, (eds.), special issue on Formal Methods in Cooperative Information Systems: Multi-Agent Systems, vol. 6 (1997) 67-94
7. Gruber, T. R.: Toward Principles for the Design of Ontologies Used for Knowledge Sharing. In Formal Ontology in Conceptual Analysis and Knowledge Representation, edited by Nicola Guarino and Roberto Poli, Kluwer Academic Publishers (in press). Substantial revision of paper presented at the International Workshop on Formal Ontology, Padova, Italy (1993)
8. Greengrass, E., Sud, J., Moore, D.: Agents in the Virtual Marketplace. Enterprise Application Services (1999)

9. Albers, M., Jonker, C. M., Karami, M., Treur, J.: Albers, M., Jonker, C.M., Karami, M., and Treur, J.: An Electronic Market Place: Generic Agent Models, Ontologies and Knowledge. In H.S. Nwana and D.T. Ndumu (eds.), Proceedings of the Fourth International Conference on the Practical Application of Intelligent Agents and Multi-Agent Technology, PAAM'99. The Practical Application Company Ltd. (1999) 211-228. Earlier version in: Proc. of the Agents'99 Workshop on Agents for Electronic Commerce and Managing the Internet-Enabled Supply Chain (1999) 71-80
10. Mougayar, W.: Theory and Practice Reflections on the Present and Future of Net Commerce. Vol.2, No.3 (1998)
11. Uschold, M., King, M.: Towards a Methodology for Building Ontologies. Workshop on Basic Ontological Issues in Knowledge Sharing, IJCAI'95 (1995)
12. Krulwich, B.: Bargain finder agent prototype. Technical report, Anderson Consulting, http://bf.cstar.ac.com/bf (1995)
13. Doorenbos, R., Etzioni, O., Weld, D.: A Scalable Comparison-Shopping Agent for the World Wide Web. Proceedings of the First International Conference on Autonomous Agents (Agents's 97). Marina Del Rey, CA (1997)
14. Guttman, R., Maes, P.: Agent-mediated Integrative Negotiation for Retail Electronic Commerce. Proceedings of the Workshop on Agent Mediated Electronic Trading (AMET'98), Minneapolis, Minnesota (1998)
15. Almeida, V., Meira, W., Ribeiro, V., Ziviani, N.: A Quantitative Analysis of the Behaviour of a Large Non-Englisg E-Broker. In Proc. of the International Workshop on Advanced Issues of E-Commerce and Web-based Information Systems (WECWIS'99), Santa Clara, CA (1999)
16. Chavez, A., Maes, P.: Kasbah: An Agent Marketplace for Buying and Selling Goods. Proceedings of the First International Conference on the Practical Application of Intelligent Agents and Multi-Agent Technology, PAAM'96, The Practical Application Company Ltd., Blackpool (1996) 75-90
17. Erikson, J., Finne, N., Janson, S.: Market Space: an open agent-based market infrastructure. Master's Thesis. Computer Science Department, Uppsala University, Sweden (1997)
18. Tsvetovatyy, M., Gini, M.: Toward a Virtual Marketplace: Architectures and Strategies. Proceedings of the First International Conference on the Practical Application of Intelligent Agents and Multi-Agent Technology, PAAM'96, The Practical Application Company Ltd, Blackpool (1998) 597-613
19. Tsvetovatyy, M., Gini, M., Mobasher, B., Wieckowski, Z.: MAGMA: An Agent-Based Virtual Market for Electronic Commerce", Applied Artificial Intelligence, vol. 11, no. 6 (1997) 501-523

Appendix: How Activities in the Process of Buying and Selling Are Affected by Internet

Table 5. Examples of how activities of the buyer perspective (Buyer / Seller Model) are affected by Internet

Activities	Affect
Search/Inquire for product	The usage of searching tools available in Internet allows the consumers to look for products easily without demanding they access several Web sites to search for the product they wish.
Discover product	Electronic tools can indicate products that are suitable to the consumer, based on his profile.
Compare products	Electronic tools can also compare competitive products.
Negotiate terms	The negotiation of the terms of buying can be done electronically, not only synchronously but asynchronously as well.
Place order	The buyer can order directly through the Web site of the seller.
Receive acknowledgement	The order acknowledgment can be given directly after order accomplishment, depending on the automatic integration between the Web site and the stock of the seller or institutions that will guarantee the payment.
Initiate payment	Several kinds of payments can be used by consumers (SET, for instance). However, their choice will depend on the available kinds by the seller in his Web site.
Receive product	The consumer can receive his products through the Internet, in case this product be digital. Otherwise, the delivery following can be accomplished through the Web site of the seller.
Request support	The support can be obtained directly in the Web site of the seller, trough Web Call Centers systems, for instance.
Give feedback	From the moment that some kind of relationship is established trough Internet, the consumer begins the process of feedback that can happen actively or passively.

Table 6. Examples of how activities of the seller perspective (Buyer / Seller Model) are affected by Internet

Activities	Benefit
Distribution	Usage of Internet as a channel of distribution where it is possible to have an access not only to the final consumer but to the resellers, as well.
Promotion	The publicity can be accomplished not only in Internet (through banners, search mechanisms, etc.) but in the conventional media, as well (TV, radio, newspapers, magazines, etc.).
Display	Creation of a virtual interface where the consumers will integrate with the seller. Three dimensions and multimedia interfaces can facilitate this communication.
Pricing policy	With the adoption or the virtual environment, besides the consumers have more facility in the access of price and the change of them, the process of stipulation and the bargain of them can be accomplished electronically.
Receive order	The order is placed electronically and it can be integrated to the legacy system of the seller.
Authorize payment	It is possible to interact directly with the financial entities so that the payment acknowledgment can be accomplished automatically, at the moment of placing order.
Schedule order	This activity can be accomplished through automatic integration of the seller with his suppliers.
Build/Retrieve from inventory	The inventory, after the sale transactions, should be consistently according to the withdraws or additions of products.
Ship product	In this activity, the seller system should be integrated to a logistic system that will guarantee the product delivery sold to the consumer. In case the sold product be digital, the distribution can happen in the electronic environment.
Receive payment	The payment reception should happen through the seller's financial institution.
Support products	This activity can be accomplished even the seller does not have a system of selling through Internet. The support can be accessible directly in the seller Web site.
Market research	As the Web allows bigger interaction among sellers and consumers, the sellers can continuously get some consumers' feedback about their needs.

Modelling Broker Agents in Electronic Commerce of Multimedia Products and Services

Isabel Gallego[1] and Jaime Delgado[2]

[1] Universitat Politècnica de Catalunya, Departament d'Arquitectura de Computadors, Campus Nord, Mòdul D6, Jordi Girona 1-3, E-08034 Barcelona, Spain
isabel@ac.upc.es

[2] Universitat Pompeu Fabra (UPF), Departament de Tecnologia, Pg. Circumval.lació 8, E-08003 Barcelona, Spain
jaime.delgado@tecn.upf.es

Abstract. This paper presents the issues related to the different kinds of Broker Agents for electronic commerce. The specificity of electronic commerce of multimedia products and services is considered, proposing a classification of this kind of systems based on different characteristics and levels of complexity. The classification is also based on previous models (functional and architectural) for electronic commerce. Finally, the paper presents some implementations of two applications for electronic commerce of customised products and services in the, respectively, electronic publishing and consultancy sectors, those of the MULTIMEDIATOR and TRADE European projects. The developed systems are classified according to the described levels of complexity, and the main issues and results of the project are introduced.[1]

1 Introduction

Electronic commerce is currently a reality, a business of millions and millions of Dollars or Euros. However, there is still a lot of work to do in research to more and more improve existing systems.

The European Commission is supporting R&D activities in the area of electronic commerce inside different programs, such as ACTS [1]. The authors of this paper have participated in European Union co-funded projects, and contributed to produce guidelines for electronic commerce [2, 3, 4].

Some of the existing work is concentrating on specifying models in which to base future implementations. Developing general models is a hard, and probably useless, task, so it is better to focus on specific kinds of electronic commerce systems. In particular, we are focusing on systems which use the concept of intermediaries, or broker agents, and systems in which the result of the commerce is electronic; i.e., we are concentrating on electronic commerce of multimedia products and services. There are also models that can take different points of view, such as the functional, the architectural and the operational ones, such as those proposed by the authors [5, 6, 7].

[1] This work has been partly supported by the European Commission (TRADE, ACTS project 328) and the Spanish government (TEL98-0699-C02-01).

J. Liu and Y. Ye (Eds.): E-Commerce Agents, LNAI 2033, pp. 61-81, 2001.

Another important concept used in this paper is the distinction between products and services. Currently, most of the existing systems are selling products. We are introducing the concept of electronic commerce of services as an evolution of electronic commerce of products.

At the start of the design of an electronic commerce system, answering some preliminary questions may be useful to identify a first approach to the system. Having at hand different models of electronic commerce systems (Business, Functional, Operational, Architectural, Technological, etc) may be very helpful. As an example, the business and functional models are useful to identify the type of commercial activity, or the entities that are involved and their inter-relationships. On the other hand, the complexity level of the system is closely related to the operational model. In turn, the architectural and technological models may be more relevant in more advanced phases of the design.

Two existing systems, developed in the context of European Commission co-funded projects, are presented. They fall in two of the categories of broker agents described in the paper, showing an example of electronic commerce of products (but an evolution of the current one, consisting on what we call customised products), and an example of electronic commerce of services.

2 Overview of Electronic Commerce Models

There are several standardisation and specification efforts in the area of electronic commerce modelling. Examples are CEN/ISSS (the Information Society Standardisation System of the European Standardisation Committee, previously EWOS, or European Workshop for Open Systems) [8], EBES (European Board for EDI/EC Standardisation) [9], also now cooperating with CEN/ISSS, and industrial fora like OMG [10]. All of them are specifying models and systems for electronic commerce.

It follows a short description of each of the mentioned models. Furthermore, some initiatives of company groups to propose their own models, most of them oriented to payment operations, are described.

2.1 OMG/CommerceNet Model

The Object Management Group's Electronic Domain Task Force (ECDTF) and CommerceNet (EcoSystem: CommerceNet's Architectural Framework for Internet Commerce) work jointly on the standardization and development of a framework for open electronic commerce [10].

The model is based on a layered architecture, the three main layers are:

- Low-level electronic commerce services: payment, semantic data and selection/negotiation.
- Commerce facilities: contract, service management and related desktop facilities.
- Market infrastructure facilities: catalogues, brokerage and agencies

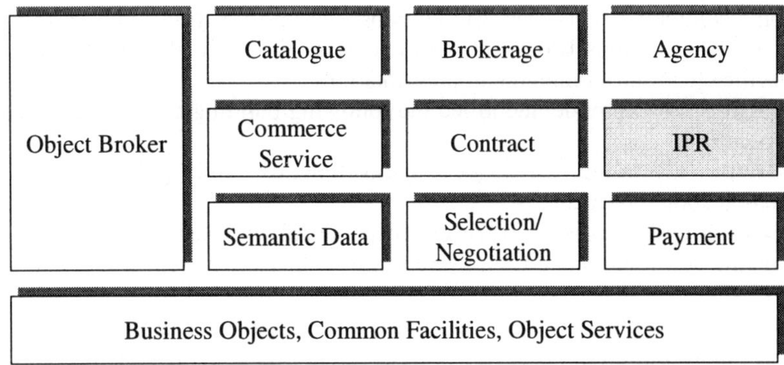

Fig. 1. OMG/CommerceNet Layers of the Architecture Model

Payment Services: Provide a facility that will support and allow for implementation of variety of electronic payment protocols like Secure Electronic Transactions (SET), etc.

Semantic data facility: Commercial service descriptions require a conceptually higher level object model that can be passed between participants in an electronic market. It is also necessary to specify descriptions of services, products, content, etc.

Negotiation facility: Support negotiation selection and configuration of facilities across the independent domains involved in an electronic commerce transaction. Commerce transactions require a common policy and this negotiation facility is necessary to support an agreed macro-policy.

Service management: Describes requirements for an object framework that can be present in commercial services.

Contract facilities: Include specific requirements related with commercial contracts.

Object browser and navigation facilities: Provide desktop facilities including a common connection interface, inspection, presentation and navigation interface, monitoring and progress interfaces.

Catalogue facilities: Provide a framework for portable structured data stores in which service and contracts can be transferred between participants.

Brokerage facility: Allow users to be more focused in dealing with information about commercial services in the global market and introduced two facilities recruiting and forwarding.

Agency facility: Supports general requirements for the standardisation of a point of presence in a marketplace. Establishes a formal access point and public query interface for a player in an electronic marketplace.

2.2 EBES/EWOS (Building Blocks for Electronic Commerce) Model

The European Commission commissioned EBES Electronic Commerce Technical Steering Group (ECTSG) and EWOS Expert Group on EDI (EG EDI) to prepare a report as an input to the Commission's action plan on Electronic Commerce [9]. According to the guidelines provided by the European Commission, this report's focus is to identify standardization, interoperability and legal key issues.

The model presents an electronic commerce scenario decomposed into processes and sub-processes. The subprocesses correspond to the User Business view of electronic commerce. This view can be translated into functions, and these functions can be called Buildings Blocks of the Functional View. Finally, Technology Views are specific electronic commerce implementations.

The EBES/EWOS model identified the following building blocks decomposed into sub-processes:

Marketing: Electronic catalogues (consult/build) and publish/extract/analyse information about products.

Contracting: Order a product (register/accept/cancel) and Replenish stock levels.

Settlement: Select payment, CC payment wallet, Ecash payment wallet and payment reconciliation.

Interface with administrations: Customs reporting and VAT reporting.

Others: Future building blocks are content rating (PICS), IPR (Intellectual Property Rights), personal data (CA, Certification Authority) and Electronic Check.

2.3 EWOS Technical Guide on Electronic Commerce

This document was developed by EWOS Expert Group on EDI to provide a systematic analysis of electronic commerce from the technical perspective [8].

The document analyses different Business Models like the Business to Individual, Business-to-Businessand Business to Public Bodies ones. These business models introduce two different intermediaries: Business Intermediaries and Information Service Intermediaries.

Different business models are developed for each different class of activities:

Marketing: Refer to strategic marketing to selling and purchases, i.e. identifying the best suppliers, or second sources etc.

Contracting: Business is usually carried out under contracts where sellers and buyers fix the conditions of a specific transaction.

Logistics: Delivery of physical or intangible goods.

Settlement: Financial settlement occurring after the receipt of the goods. Define two scenarios: invoicing and payment.

Interfacing to Administration: Public bodies can play the role of sellers and buyers in the Business to Public Bodies model.

Three groups of services are described in the document:

Information Provision Services: Information dissemination, intelligent search, party selection, information production and information indexing/classification.

Party-to-Party Services: Electronic commerce transaction management services and inter-personal services.

Support Services: Directory service, key management and certification services (TTP), security services and internetworking services.

Finally, the document describes five types of data to support the business purpose of an electronic commerce system:

Identification of people: Identify individuals in electronic commerce transactions.

Identification of organisations: Identify business parties in electronic commerce transactions.

Identification of products and items within business services: Coding for product identification (and secure identification) for standardised access to product databases.

Data objects and messages: Define data objects and their association (often as messages) to allow flexibility.
Business process definition: Description of the processes to arrive to a completed business transaction as a number of steps.

2.4 Others Initiatives

There are other initiatives in the area of electronic commerce modelling coming from more industry oriented organisations formed by companies and other institutions. However, their focus is mainly on payment systems. Some of them are described in the following.

OTP (Open Trading Protocols), developed by the OTP Forum specifies a negotiated trade, where it is possible to use different payment protocols [11]. OTP defines OTP Transactions. They are: Purchase, Refund, Value Exchange, Authentication, Withdrawal, Deposit, Offer, Payment, Delivery and Authentication. OTP defines different roles: Consumer, Merchant, Value Acquirer, Deliverer and Customer Care Provider. The OTP entities exchange OTP messages, that are XML documents, according the OTP Protocol.

OBI (Open Buying on Internet), developed by the OBI Consortium focuses on payment and access to electronic catalogues [12].

JEPI (Joint Electronic Payment Initiative) is an initiative of the W3Consortium and is another example of a payment system [13].

SET (Secure Electronic Transaction) is an Internet oriented credit card payment specification developed by VISA and MasterCard [14]. It is probably the most popular initiative.

3 Classification of Broker Agents

The firstly deployed systems for electronic commerce allow users to buy products offered by providers through electronic catalogues. In order to provide more sophisticated features to users, the concept of broker agent started to be introduced. If the number of providers and products increases, the electronic commerce system may become so complex that even more than one intermediary, i.e. broker agent, may be needed in order to offer an efficient enough system.

According to this concept, broker agent based electronic commerce systems may be classified as Uni-Broker (with one centralised broker agent) or Multi-Broker (with a distributed broker structured as several broker agents that collaborate between them).

Focussing on Uni-Broker systems, a second characteristic that may help analysing them is the kind of products on which their business is based. This feature would also allow us to have an idea about the complexity of the system.

The simplest system (First Level) would allow users to buy an existing product offered through a catalogue by a provider. An example would be on-line image shopping over an electronic broker.

A Second Level of complexity in this broker agents classification is allowing users to buy a customised product. In this case, users negotiate with the sellers, through the broker agent, the specific characteristics of a new product starting from already existing products in the providers' catalogue. An example could be the provision of customised video composition from a set of video elements (i.e. images).

It seems reasonable that users and providers of services, in contrast with users and providers of products, would benefit of the advantages of electronic commerce. This is the idea of our Third Level of broker agents. We understand a service as some added value to a product or group of products, such a legal (or professional in general) service, that is provided as a sequence of recommendations to the customer, reports, official documents, and so on, that could be interchanged and managed by electronic means through the network.

Finally, the Fourth Level is reserved for the case in which the system is so complex that there is a need to use more than one broker agent. Multi-broker systems are outside the scope of this paper. Nevertheless, this characteristic is normally transparent for the user, that is provided with a better service in a more efficient way.

Table 1 summarises the basic characteristics of our classification of broker agent based systems.

Table 1. Classification of the Broker Agent Systems for Electronic Commerce

Complexity Level	Type of business
First	Products
Second	Customised products
Third	Services
Fourth	Multi-Broker

Sections 4 and 5 introduce, respectively, our functional and operational models for brokerage based electronic commerce. In every section, after a description of the model, a mapping between its features and the classification of broker agents that we have just presented is done. In particular, for every level of the classification, a table indicates the characteristics values (for the functional model) and the operations (for the operational model) that correspond to the given level.

A similar approach was taken in [15], but mainly based on the OMG Electronic Commerce reference model (see clause 2.1).

4 Functional Model

Several elements can be distinguished in a Functional Model for a system of electronic commerce based on brokerage (we base our description in the model introduced in [7] and in the characteristics introduced in [5]):

- **Buyer:** it includes the users of the system.
  The users can access to the electronic brokerage system in two different ways:
  - Direct Access: if the user previously knows the product to order, the access can be done directly without any browsing or searching.
  - Navigation Access: if the user does not know previously the product or service to be ordered. This mechanism allows to browse and search in the broker information.

The buyer may have the following roles:
- Re-Seller: The buyer will sell the results, as they are, to other users. Brokerage systems are included here.
- Transformer: The buyer will use the results to produce other results.
- End-User: The buyer uses the results directly.

- **Broker:** in this element, one or several broker agents provide the service requested by the buyers, using the services offered by the sellers (Uni-Broker o Multi-Broker agent). An important feature that the broker agent needs to handle is the kind of contract that buyers and sellers subscribe in order to trade. The following cases are possible:
  - No contract: There is no explicit contract, but there are probably some specific rules or an implicit contract.
  - Contract previous: The buyer has previously established a framework contract.
  - Contract per activity: The activity requires the existence of a specific contract and there is no previous contract.
- **Seller:** sellers offer their services through one or more broker agents. In the seller level, the access is similar to that in the buyer level but with more possibilities related to the information about products and services located in the seller system.
  About the results of the commerce (Existence):
  - Pre-Defined: The results of the activity are known since the beginning.
  - Customised: The result of the activity will be a customised product, but clearly identified during negotiation.
  - Events-Dependent: The result of the commercial activity is not necessarily always the same, but it depends on several external events and on intermediate results that may vary from one case to another.

  Regarding the availability of the results (Availability), the options are:
  - Immediate: The results are sent electronically or physically just after the activity.
  - Delayed: The results need some time to be delivered because a predefined action needs to be taken.
  - Negotiated: The results need to be negotiated after the request and before the delivery, because they need to be produced or customised according to the instructions of the buyer
  - Ordered: The request has been made, but the results have not yet been used. In the meantime, there may be modifications of the result depending on certain conditions.
- **Complementary Services:** electronic brokerage requires additional non-specific services, such as electronic security (Certification, Authentication, etc) and payment (electronic or not).
- **Distribution:** the result of the service must be distributed from the buyers to the sellers: this distribution may be electronic over the network or physical, in the general case.

The result of the commercial activity can be something tangible (like a digital picture) or intangible (like a financial investments, tax payments, etc).

Table 2 summarises the characteristics (and their values) of the different elements of the functional view of a broker based electronic commerce system.

Table 2. Functional Model of the Broker for Electronic Commerce

Element	Characteristics (values)
Buyer	Access (Direct/Navigation)
	Role (Re-Seller/Transformer/End-User)
Broker	Number (Uni-Broker/Multi-Broker)
	Contract (No contract/Previous/Per activity)
Seller	Access (Direct/Navigation)
	Existence (Pre-defined/Customised/Events-Dependent)
	Availability (Immediate/Delayed/Negotiated/Ordered)
Distribution	Electronic (Electronic result/No electronic result)
	Result (Tangible/Intangible)
Complementary Services	Payment (Electronic/No electronic)
	Security (TTP / IPR / etc...)

The previous sets of characteristics can be used to differentiate the four levels of broker agents identified in section 3, as it is done in the following sub-sections.

4.1 First Level: Products

The first level (Products) corresponds to the simplest case of electronic commerce, limited to buying pre-defined products, it is enough to have available the characteristics indicated in table 3.

Table 3. Functional Model for Broker Agent in Electronic Commerce for Products (Level 1)

Element	Characteristics (values)
Buyer	Access (Navigation)
	Role (Re-Seller/Transformer/End-User)
Broker	Number (Uni-Broker)
	Contract (No contract/Previous)
Seller	Access (Navigation)
	Existence (Pre-defined)
	Availability (Immediate)
Distribution	Electronic (Electronic result/No electronic result)
	Result (Tangible/Intangible)
Complementary Services	Payment (Electronic/No electronic)
	Security (TTP / IPR / etc...)

4.2 Second Level: Customised Products

The second level corresponds to the case of customised products and it is necessary to add some new features, such as the kind of contract. This is shown in table 4.

Table 4. Functional Model for Broker Agent in Electronic Commerce for Customised Products (Level 2)

Element	Characteristics (values)
Buyer	Access (Navigation)
	Role (Re-Seller/Transformer/End-User)
Broker	Number (Uni-Broker)
	Contract (Previous/Per activity)
Seller	Access (Direct/Navigation)
	Existence (Customised)
	Availability (Delayed/Negotiated)
Distribution	Electronic (Electronic result)
	Result (Tangible/Intangible)
Complementary Services	Payment (Electronic/No electronic)
	Security (TTP / IPR / etc...)

4.3 Third Level: Services

Finally, in the third level (Services) it is necessary to be able to manage the development of the service, that may take some time. This implies, for example, the Event-Dependent value in the Existence characteristic. This is shown in table 5.

Table 5. Functional Model for Broker Agent in Electronic Commerce for Services (Level 3)

Element	Characteristics (values)
Buyer	Access (Direct/Navigation)
	Role (Re-Seller/Transformer/End-User)
Broker	Number (Uni-Broker)
	Contract (Previous/Per activity)
Seller	Access (Direct/Navigation)
	Existence (Events-Dependent)
	Availability (Negotiated/Ordered)
Distribution	Electronic (Electronic result)
	Result (Intangible)
Complementary Services	Payment (Electronic/No electronic)
	Security (TTP / IPR / etc...)

4.4 Fourth Level: Multi-broker

Finally, for Multi-Broker systems, the main peculiarity relies on the Broker and Buyer characteristics, that should take, respectively, the Multi-Broker and Transformer values.

5 Operational Model

The operations related to an electronic brokerage system can be categorised into two types:

- Service-oriented: those that occur during the provision of services to the customers;
- System-oriented: those that provide the users with some added-value system.

We can identify the phases that are carried out generally when a customer requests a product or service to a supplier through an electronic brokerage system.

In the case of the service-oriented phases, we can identify the following sub-phases:

- Service Identification: In this sub-phase, the final user searches and/or asks for services available in the broker system. The user makes a selection in order to identify those services or products that fulfill his interest.
- Service Request: Once the service or product has been selected, the user must perform the formal ordering for the acquisition, with which both parts, seller and buyer, become responsible to fulfill the conditions and statements of an established contract. All the elements that take part in this process need to identify themselves using a reliable authentication mechanism.
- Agreement: If the user has bought a final product that can be delivered in an electronic way, the supplier performs the delivery of the product and the user issues the payment (or takes the responsibility for the future payment). If the item requested was a service, the conditions for the development of the service (service parameters, delivery specifications, etc.) are to be agreed in this point.
- Post-agreement: When the user requests for a customised service, it is necessary to specify a procedure (after the agreement) that allows the follow-up of the service until the final delivery. In this phase, the user can check if the service is being carried out as agreed. If this phase takes place, the payment (whole or partial) may be postponed. There may be a temporal overlapping between the agreement and the post-agreement phases.

In the case of the system-oriented phases, the following sub-phases can be identified:

- Maintenance: It allows the users to access some maintenance services such as automatic software upgrading from the broker.
- Service-Update: The suppliers should be also able to update the information that the broker maintains about them. It should allow to update catalogues and/or to add new offers or services.
- Contract re-negotiation: It allows the customers and suppliers that may have some contractual relationship with the broker, to modify the contract previously established (e.g. to modify the payment conditions).

The next two clauses present some aspects of these phases and sub-phases in more detail. Then, clauses 5.3 to 5.6 map the Operational Model features to the broker classification from section 3.

5.1 Service-Oriented Phases

The following sub-clauses present some concrete aspects of the service-oriented phases described above.

Service Identification. The following list describes some of the most relevant actions associated to the service identification phase. They are mainly based on [7].

SEARCH	The customer can buy products and services. This action is responsible for searching and identifying information about products and services that fit a user description.
BROWSER	The broker agent can provide a form to the users for queries or job requests. This functionality is carried out through the forms mechanism based, for example, in WWW technology.
METADATA	The information about what the different suppliers are able to provide is stored in the broker agent as metadata in a database.
PROFILE	It is possible to define user profiles with information like access rights, supported data formats, etc. This information is stored in a management database.
CATALOGUE	Customers can obtain information about suppliers and services with brochures and forms (for subscription). This information is stored in the broker database.

Other actions identified in this phase are (see [7]): locate, agency, customer and directory services.

Service Request. The following list describes some of the most relevant actions associated to the service request phase. They are mainly based on [7].

CONTRACT	It is possible to manage contracts with the contract management module, providing collaborative contract construction, negotiation, execution, signatures and service plan. The associated information of the contract is stored in the broker management database.

Other actions identified in this phase are (see [7]): brokerage and selection.

Agreement. The following list describes some of the most relevant actions associated to the agreement phase. They are mainly based on [7].

DELIVERY	Manages the delivery of items to the customer. It can support two kinds of delivery, electronic delivery and physical delivery. In some cases, such as in the multimedia information services, it is interesting to provide the possibility to convert the information delivered by the supplier to the format selected by the user.

PAYMENT — Provides a mechanism for doing and monitoring payment, that can be off-line or on-line; in the second case the billing module is involved and this information is stored in the broker management database.

AUTHENTICATION — Provides a mechanism, which allows users to guarantee their identity to a brokerage system by an authentication process.

CERTIFICATION — Supports users identity checking and certification by a certificate.

FEEDBACK — Allows the users to have feedback on a particular action, transaction, and network or system failures. Users can obtain feedback information of the process in course through the broker management database.

Other actions identified in this phase are (see [7]): order and service management.

Post-Agreement. The following list describes some of the most relevant actions associated to the post-agreement phase. This is one of the main contributions, detailed in [7].

CUSTOM SERVICES — This functionality provides the customers with the possibility of obtaining tailored services using, for example, WWW-based technology by filling forms.

SERVICE STATUS — The customers can know the status of all their pending requests. The information is stored in the broker management database.

WORKFLOW — This function provides to the customers with the possibility for following and controls the process until the final, especially if the process is complex.

CUSTOMER UPLOAD — This functionality provides the customers with the possibility to send information to the suppliers, and store it, temporarily, in the broker agent database, e.g. uploading a source document for its translation.

SERVICE POOL — This management function allows the broker agent to queue the different pending requests associated to the services, this information is stored in the broker management database.

AFTER AGREEMENT — Allows users to buy tailored agreed services and to control the operation until the final delivery of the service. When a customer buys a custom service, it is necessary to provide him with functionality to follow up the process until the final delivery.

5.2 System-Oriented Phases

As system-oriented phases, we understand those functionality that can be carried out at any time and independently of the provision of services, and are intended for the maintenance of the system.

Maintenance.

SOFTWARE UPDATING	This functionality allows the users to update the software necessary to access to the broker system.

Service Update.

SERVICE UPDATING	This functionality allows the suppliers to update their offer: new catalogues, discounts, price reductions, etc.

Contract Re-negotiation.

CONTRACT RENEGOTIATION	This functionality allows customers and suppliers to re-negotiate the conditions of their contracts with the electronic broker.

5.3 First Level: Products

It corresponds to the simplest electronic commerce for buying pre-defined products. This implies that the last operation phase (Post-agreement) is not needed. Then, only the first three phases are needed, namely, Service Identification, Service Request and Agreement.

The basic operations in the Service Identification phase are Search, Browser, Catalogue and Customer.

The basic operations in the Service Request phase are Brokerage and Selection.

The basic operations in the Agreement phase are Delivery, Payment, Service Management and Order.

The specific operations associated to the three phases that are needed for broker agents of Level One are listed in table 6.

Table 6. Operational Model for Broker Agent in Electronic Commerce for Products (Level 1)

Service Identification	Service Request	Agreement
Search	Brokerage	Delivery
Browser	Selection	Payment
Catalogue		Service Management
Customer		Order

5.4 Second Level: Customised Products

It corresponds to electronic commerce systems where users may request products adapted to their needs (i.e., customised). This means that the buying process may take some time while the provider is developing or integrating the requested product. This scenario needs a fourth operations phase, called post-agreement, that allows users to follow (and to negotiate, if necessary) the evolution of their buying until the product is finished. This phase was first introduced in [7].

The specified operations associated with Post-Agreement phase are Custom Services, Service Status and After Agreement.

Furthermore, in the Service Identification phase, a series of operations, related to the higher complexity in the storage and retrieval of information, are added. These operations are: Metadata, Profile, Agency and Directory Services.

The specific operations associated to the four phases that are needed for broker agents of Level Two are listed in table 7.

Table 7. Operational Model for Broker Agent in Electronic Commerce for Customised Products (Level 2)

Service Identification	Service Request	Agreement	Post-Agreement
Search	Brokerage	Delivery	Custom Services
Browser	Selection	Payment	Service Status
Catalogue	Negotiation	Service Management	After Agreement
Customer	Contract	Order	
Locate		Feedback	
Metadata		Authentication	
Profile		Certification	
Agency			
Directory Services			

5.5 Third Level: Services

This kind of electronic commerce services includes the possibility of buying services, apart from products. Normally, a service provision consists in the interchange of some products (documents, images, etc.) in a defined order, that may vary depending on external events. At the end of the process, an added value to those products has been generated, that is the service itself.

In the Service Identification, Service Request and Agreement phase, we have, basically, the same operations that in Level Two.

The main difference, in the Post-Agreement phase, is the Workflow operation that allows following and controlling the flow of the service provision, that might be very complex, depending of the specific service.

Furthermore, the Customer Upload operation has been added, since it might be very important in this case to be able to update and interchange information, temporarily stored in the broker agent, between buyers and suppliers.

The specific operations associated to the four phases that are needed for broker agents of Level Three are listed in table 8.

Table 8. Operational Model for Broker Agent in Electronic Commerce for Services (Level 3)

Service Identification	Service Request	Agreement	Post-Agreement
Search	Brokerage	Delivery	Custom Services
Browser	Selection	Payment	Service Status
Catalogue	Negotiation	Service Management	After Agreement
Customer	Contract	Order	Workflow
Locate		Feedback	Customer Upload
Metadata		Authentication	
Profile		Certification	
Agency			
Directory Services			

5.6 Fourth Level: Multi-broker

This kind of electronic commerce systems does not offer new functionality from the user's point of view. We have included this Level Four broker to make evident that, for very complex systems, there is always the possibility of enhancing the system by making it a multi-broker one.

The idea is to make broker agents co-operate in solving complex queries, mange a big amount of providers and/or products or services, etc.

Users of such systems do need to be aware of this complexity, but should get a more efficient view of them.

6 Case Study 1: MULTIMEDIATOR

The ideas presented in this paper have been validated in several real cases. The first one is the ACTS MULTIMEDIATOR (Multimedia Publishing Brokerage Service) project [16] (started in September 1995 and finished in March 1998), that is developing a multimedia brokerage application. The key target of the project is multimedia publishing industry, where multimedia publications developers, the Customers, may need to buy products and services, from the Suppliers, to produce their electronic publications. A basic model for brokerage has been implemented, allowing Customers to easily negotiate with a broker agent the multimedia product they want from the Suppliers, who, in turn, receive orders from the agent and deliver products and services to it. For this purpose, a database containing information on products (that may lead to customised products) to sell is included in the broker. Suppliers are responsible for keeping up to date the information on that database. In this case the brokerage service is provided by one only agent and therefore not distributed.

In MULTIMEDIATOR, the communication is always between the users' site and the broker agent (there is not direct communication of a given user with other users). Customers connect to the broker when they want to look for (and, eventually, buy) products. On the other hand, the broker agent accesses suppliers when a product has been bought, or they connect to the agent when they want to update the information about their offers. Figure 2 illustrates how the system works. More information can be found in [16, 17].

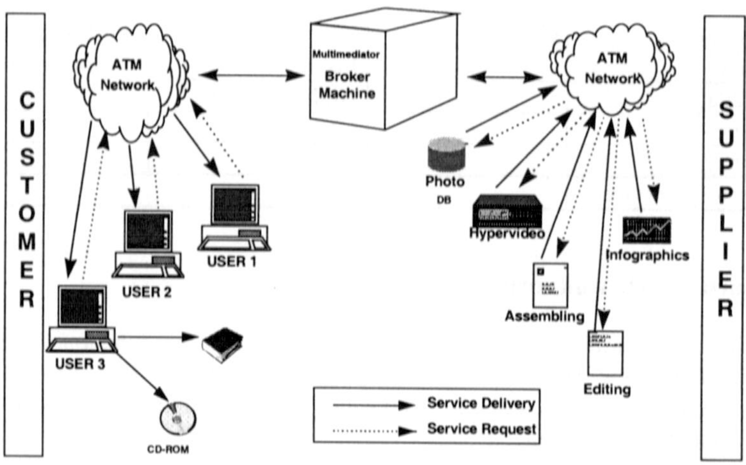

Fig. 2. MULTIMEDIATOR Scenario

Mapping the broker levels specified in section 3 into the MULTIMEDIATOR features, it turns out that this fits into the Level Two; i.e., this broker agent is a second step in the classification of brokers (see customised video composition scenario in Section 8).

7 Case Study 2: TRADE

Following with the classification of broker agents, we then started with the implementation of a broker agent that fits into the Level Three of our classification. This is being done in the TRADE (TriAls in the Domain of Electronic commerce) project [18, 19], that started in March 1998 and finished in March 2000.

TRADE (also an European Commission co-funded project in the ACTS programme [1]) has implemented, apart from other things not relevant here, a distributed system for the lawyer and administrative consultant professionals to offer legal and administrative services by electronic means. Customers can contract these kinds of services. Then, this is a clear example of electronic commerce of multimedia services, i.e., Level Three broker agent.

7.1 Main Features

The main component of the system is a service agent that acts as a simple broker between suppliers and customers. The TRADE agent has the basic functionality of a broker, as to select a supplier or to store temporarily the information interchange among customer and suppliers. The real commerce takes place between the customers and the agent and between the agent and the suppliers. Although there is no direct electronic communication between customers and suppliers, as in a normal broker situation, customers and suppliers interact between them without the broker avoiding the disclosure of their identities. Furthermore, the TRADE agent could be even exploited by one provider itself.

The architecture of the system is illustrated in figure 3. More information on the TRADE applications presented here can be found in [18, 19, 20].

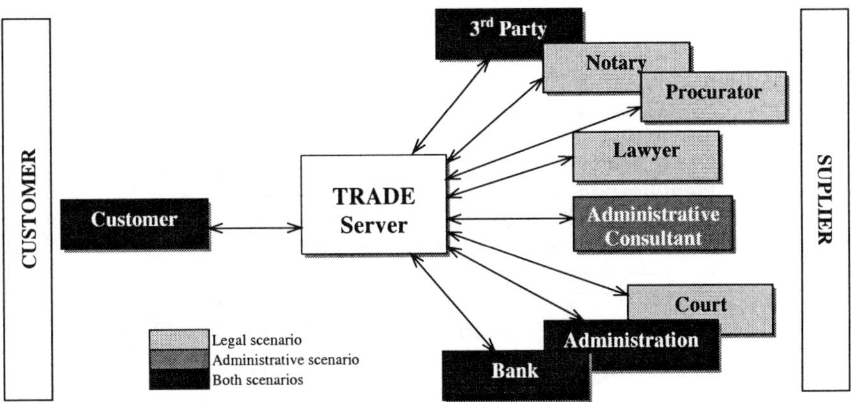

Fig. 3. Architectural Model of the Legal and Administrative Scenarios in TRADE

Lawyer and administrative consultants offer their services through the TRADE server in two different scenarios (Legal and Administrative)

Following the client-server paradigm in both scenarios, the TRADE Service Agent corresponds to the server and all other constituents to the clients (see figure 3). The TRADE server centralises all interchanges done by the clients, also named actors. These can be: customers, lawyers, administrative consultants, notaries, procurators, courts, administrations, 3rd parties, etc. The activity in these scenarios is basically a document and information interchange in a specific order between the actors. In the legal scenario, the lawyer is the actor that controls the correct operation of the interchanges (legal cases) between him and the other actors. In the administrative scenario, the actor who controls the interchanges (administrative cases) is the administrative consultant (see Administrative and Legal scenarios in section 8).

The server contains all information about documents and information to interchange, the actors that have to take part, and the interchange order (workflow rules). It allows lawyers or administrative consultants to carry out all case steps.

8 Scenarios

This clause provides descriptions of three scenarios where the ideas presented in the Operational Model (section 5) are reflected. The phases carried out during the processes are identified and illustrated in real scenarios of the MULTIMEDIATOR and TRADE projects.

8.1 Administrative Scenario (Level 1)

The first scenario presents the provision of a typical administrative service, such as a VAT three-monthly return handling, or a National Insurance medical fitness or sick leave handling in the TRADE project. An important characteristic of the administrative services in this scenario (in comparison with the legal services scenario of the TRADE project) is that normally each case has a specific treatment and normally always the same.

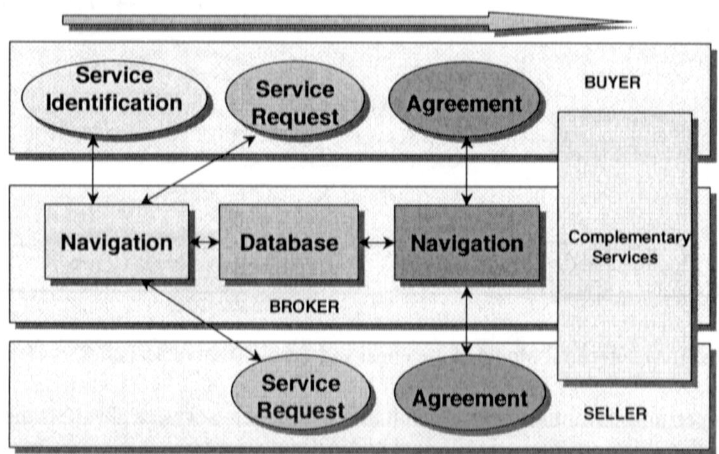

Fig. 4. TRADE: Administrative Scenario (Level 1)

If we only consider this Administrative Scenario from TRADE, then we could consider these very simple service as equivalent to the Level One broker agent, i.e., the electronic commerce of pre-defined products, since providing most of the administrative services is like selling pre-defined products, with the specificity that the values of the attributes Existence (see the functional model in section 4) should be Pre-defined and Availability should be Immediate.

Figure 4 illustrates the functional model and the operational model (phases of operations) in the case of the administrative scenario of the TRADE project, where Navigation and Database are architectural building blocks of the broker element, and the big arrow is the time axis.

8.2 Customised Video Composition Scenario (Level 2)

The second scenario corresponds to a customised video composition in the MULTIMEDIATOR project. In this scenario, a customer can order the creation of a video resulting from the composition of a set of video elements (MPEG4 video objects, for example) that have been selected by the customer in a video object catalogue. In the selection process, the customer can select the objects that will be included in the video, and their characteristics (placement, repetition, etc.). The supplier will then compose a video sequence using a MPEG4 composition tool and will deliver the resulting video to the customer. This is a scenario in which the customer buys a service whose results will be delivered later, after the service is carried out. The customised video composition scenario of the MULTIMEDIATOR project is an example of the Level Two broker agent.

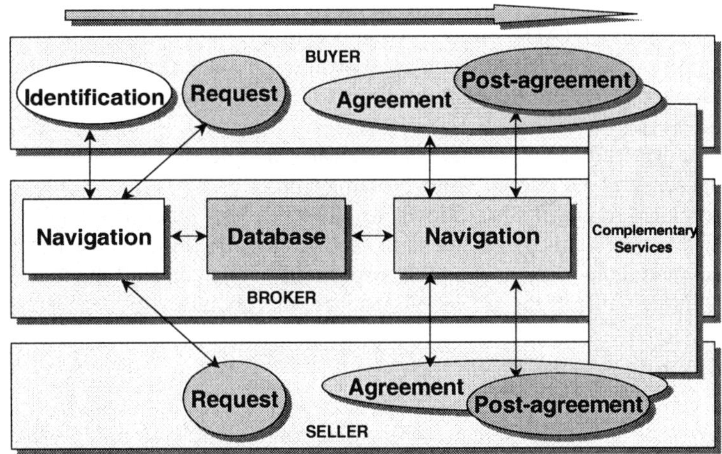

Fig. 5. MULTIMEDIATOR: Customised Video Composition Scenario (Level 2)

Firstly, the customer browses the catalogues of video services offered by the brokerage level (*service identification phase*). Once the service has been selected (*selection*), customer and supplier negotiate the contract (*contract*) and the video is ordered. In this case, the elaboration of a video is requested, and various aspects, such as the delivery time, must be agreed (*service request phase*). This is one of the main differences between this scenario and the previous one.

In this scenario, the agreement and post-agreement phases overlap in time; for example, payment is post-poned until the final video delivery.

After the ordering of the service (*order*), in the *post-agreement phase*, users (customers and suppliers) can perform the customisation of the service (*custom services*). Customers can also find out the status of the pending services (*service status*, *service pool*). This is another significant difference from the previous scenario.

Once the supplier has delivered the final video product (*delivery*), the user proceeds to the payment as agreed in the contract (*payment*). The customer can follow up the development of the service (*service management, feedback*). For guaranteed payment, users need to be authenticated and transactions must be carried out securely.

The final video may be in MPEG4 format (if the customer is able to process it) or it can be converted to any other video format, such as MPEG1 or MPEG2 (*delivery*). In this case, the *delivery* action includes customisation of the information format depending on the characteristics of the user.

Figure 5 illustrates the functional model and the operational model (phases of operations) in the case of the customised video composition scenario of the MULTIMEDIATOR project. In this case, it is necessary to introduce the post-agreement phase (see the operational model in section 5) and the most important characteristics are the values of the attributes Existence, that should be Customised, and Availability, that should be Delayed or Negotiated (see the functional model in section 4).

8.3 Legal Scenario (Level 3)

The third scenario presents a typical legal service provision, such as a Dismissal or a Divorce case, in the TRADE project. An important characteristic of the legal services in this scenario is that normally each legal professional decides the steps to follow in the legal service provision depending on the case. The evolution of a legal case uses to be different in every case.

Then, the TRADE legal scenario is a clear example of electronic commerce of multimedia services, i.e., Level Three broker agent.

The previous figure 5 also allows to illustrate the functional and operational models in the case of the legal scenario of the TRADE project (see functional and operational models in sections 4 and 5, respectively). We can find the most important difference in the value of the attribute Existence, that should be Event-Dependent.

9 Conclusions

As we have seen in section 2, the existing electronic commerce models that we have analysed, give us little information about the complexity of the system and about the influence of its commercial activity on the system design. In this paper, we present our own brokerage based electronic commerce models, and we relate them to their commercial activity and their characteristics. This has allowed us to characterise the electronic commerce systems complexity with their functional and operational models, and to establish a classification. As a result of this, we have got to the conclusion that the design of an electronic commerce system may start with the identification of the kind of goods to be sold. These goods may belong to three main big groups: products, customised products and services. We can also see electronic commerce systems for these groups of goods as an evolution (starting from systems for handling products, and finishing with systems for handling services), in which we advance from one to the next one by adding some functionalities and operations.

Then, this paper has presented different kinds of broker agents for electronic commerce. Based on the developed models and on the implementation of two different electronic commerce systems, one for selling customised products and a second one for selling services, the evolution of the needed characteristics of the broker agents has been used to develop a classification of broker agents.

The first level corresponds to the systems currently deployed, while the second one, that corresponds to our first implementation (the MULTIMEDIATOR project) is a first evolution by adding some new features, such as the customisation of the multimedia products to sell. A next step leads us to the third level of broker agents, where services are sold. This is offered in our second implementation (the TRADE project).

Previous work on modelling of brokerage based systems has been the starting point for this classification of their evolution.

A next step, not considered in the paper, would be related to the implementation of multi-broker systems, where several broker agents co-operate to provide better features to users.

References

1. ACTS (Advanced Communications Technology and Services) Web Page, http://www.infowin.org/acts/
2. ACTS SIA Guideline 3 "Enterprise Models of Electronic Brokerage" Edited by S. Plagemann and J. Hands. Version 1.6, September 1997
3. MULTIMEDIATOR Document A0096/UPC/DAC/PI/I/031/a1 "Contribution to SIA Guideline 3", May 1997
4. MULTIMEDIATOR Document A0096/UPC/DAC/PI/I/038/a1 "Application and Middleware functions for electronic brokerage – A MULTIMEDIATOR contribution to SIA-G3", September 1997
5. Delgado J., Gallego I. and Acebrón J.J. "Electronic Commerce of Multimedia Products", 7th IFIP/ICCC Conference on Information Networks and Data Communications (INDC'98), 1998 Aveiro (Portugal). ICCC Press, ISBN 1-891365-03-7
6. Delgado J., Gallego I. and Polo J. "Electronic Commerce of Multimedia Services" 7th International Conference on Multimedia Modeling (MMM'99) 4-6 October 1999, Ottawa, Ontario (Canada). World Scientific, ISBN 981-02-4146-1
7. Gallego I., Delgado J. and Acebrón J.J. "Distributed Models for Brokerage on Electronic Commerce", International IFIP Working Conference Trends in Electronic Commerce (TREC'98), 3-5 June 1998, Hamburg (Germany). Springer, ISBN 3-540-64564-0
8. EWOS/ETG 066: "EWOS Technical guide on electronic commerce". September 1996
9. EBES "Building Blocks for Electronic Commerce", October 1997. http://www.cenorm.be/ebes/
10. OMG Electronic Commerce Domain Task Force "EC-DTF Reference Model", http://www.osm.net/ec-dtf/working.html
11. IOTP "Internet Open Trading Protocol", http://www.otp.org
12. OBI "Open Buying on the Internet", http://www.supplyworks.com/obi/
13. JEPI "Joint Electronic Payment Initiative", http://www.w3.org/Ecommerce/specs/
14. SET "Secure Electronic Transaction", http://www.visa.com or http://www.mastercard.com
15. Martí R. and Delgado J. "Definition of Service Levels for Electronic Brokerage Applications", Intelligence in Services and Networks (IS&N'98), May 1998. Springer, ISBN 3-540-64598-5
16. Martí R. and Delgado J. "Use of WWW technology for Client/Server Brokerage Applications in MULTIMEDIATOR", Intelligence in Services and Networks (IS&N'97), May 1997. Springer, ISBN 3-540-63135-6
17. MULTIMEDIATOR Web Page, http://www.ac.upc.es/multimediator/
18. TRADE Legal and Administrative applications Web Page, http://www.mtg.es/trade/
19. TRADE Web Page, http://trade.cosi.it/
20. Llorente S. and Delgado J. "Legal and Administrative Services through Electronic Commerce", 7th International Intelligence in Services and Networks Conference (IS&N'2000), 23-25 February 2000, Athens (Greece). Springer, ISBN 3-540-67152-8

A Brokering Protocol for Electronic Trading

Kwang Mong Sim[1] and Raymond Chan[2]

[1]Department of Information Engineering,
Chinese University of Hong Kong, Shatin, NT, Hong Kong.
kmsim@ie.cuhk.edu.hk
[2]Department of Computing,
Hong Kong Polytechnic University,
Hung Hom, Kowloon, Hong Kong.

Abstract. This paper explores the use of information agents for partially automating some of the activities of information brokering in e-commerce. In this paper, the issue of matching buyers' and sellers' profiles is viewed as a kind of connection problem. A connection algorithm that matches advertisement of buyers and requests from sellers based on pre-specified multiple criteria was devised and implemented. The connection algorithm mainly consists of: *selection of requests and advertisement*, and *evaluation and filtering of connected advertisement and requests*. Ideas of the connection approach are realized in a testbed on securities trading consisting of a society of information agents (a *broker agent*, a *recommendation agent* and a *record agent*) and trading agents (*buyer* and *seller agents*) that communicates via a blackboard database. In addition, an information *brokering protocol* was devised and implemented to structure the interactions and information exchange among agents in the testbed. The protocol does not assume that connections of advertisements and requests can always be made. When the broker agent fails to match requests and advertisements, the recommendation agent proactively pushes e-mail recommendations to potential trading agents by tracing previous transaction profiles. A series of experiments that were carried out shown favorable results in executing the protocol.

Keywords: agent-mediated e-commerce, information agent, information brokering, multi-agent system

1 Introduction

Given the unprecedented surge in information sources globally the demand for acquiring valuable and strategic business information for (electronic) trading has been ever increasing. In particular, the difficulty of finding information about trading partners in the global business arena accentuates the need for electronic intermediaries to assist, navigate, and mediate the invocation of these services. This paper explores the issues of engineering a society of agents that partially automate the task of connecting buyers and sellers trading electronically.

J. Liu and Y. Ye (Eds.): E-Commerce Agents, LNAI 2033, pp. 82-105, 2001.

Objectives : The goals of this research are to:

1. design and implement an algorithm that connects buyer and seller agents
2. devise a brokering protocol for specifying and structuring the interactions among electronic intermediaries and trading (buyer and seller) agents
3. design and engineer a testbed that models and simulates some of the activities of information brokering in electronic trading

In section 2, the main highlight of this research: an approach for connecting buyer and seller agents is exposed. The overall architecture of the agent-based brokering testbed (consisting of a *broker agent*, a *record agent*, a *recommendation agent*, *buyer agents* and *seller agents*) is explicated in section 3. Section 4 describes the broker protocol and explicates stages of interaction and information exchange among agents in the testbed. Examples of executions of the various information agents are given in section 5. Some experimental results and evaluation are illustrated in section 6. In section 7, the testbed is compared with some extant agent-based brokering systems. Section 8 concludes this paper.

2 Connecting Buyers and Sellers

While issues of the connection problem in the domain of resource and task allocation have been addressed by Smith [4], this research explores the issues of matching profiles of buyers and sellers in electronic trading. In the *contract net protocol* [4], nodes coordinate their activities through contracts to accomplish specific goals. *Contracting* involves an exchange of information between interested parties, an evaluation of the information by each member from its own perspective, and a final agreement by mutual selection. Contracts are elaborated in a top-down manner. At each stage, a *manager* node decomposes its contracts into subcontracts to be accomplished by other *contractor* nodes. This process involves a bidding protocol based on a two-way transfer of information to establish the nature of subcontract and to determine which node will perform a particular subcontract. Nodes allocate tasks in the following stages:

1. A manager forms a task to be allocated.
2. The manager announces the existence of the task.
3. Available nodes evaluate task announcement.
4. Suitable nodes submit bids for task.
5. The manager evaluates bids.
6. The manager awards contracts to the most appropriate node.
7. The manager and contractor communicate privately during contract execution.

Much like allocating resources (agents) to tasks in the contract net protocol, connections of buyers and sellers are based on a set of predefined selection criteria that is domain specific. In this research the process of connecting buyers and sellers are carried out in three stages: *selection*, *evaluation* and *filtering*.

Selecting buyers and sellers. This stage compares requests from buyers and advertisements from sellers. In selecting buyers (sellers) for an advertisement (request) two selection policies are used. The algorithm prefers to select:

1. buyer and seller agents with profiles and preferences that are closely matched
2. buyer (seller) agents that have not been previously connected to other seller (buyer) agents

While criterion (1) provides *focus decisions* [4] to connect trading partners with profiles and preferences that coincide, criterion (2) bears some resemblance in realizing the property of *balanced loading* in the contract net protocol. In the contract net protocol, focus decision is achieved by effective selection of tasks for allocation to nodes and by effective selection of knowledge sources for execution of tasks. Effective resource allocation is achieved by balancing the computational load among the nodes.

For example, in the domain of securities trading, the stock type (for example, Asian Bank's Stock) specified in a buyer's request that matches the stock name/type specified in a seller's advertisement (for example, Hang Seng Stock Index) satisfied criterion (1). Criterion (2) ensures that every trading agent has quite uniform (albeit, not necessarily equal) opportunity of being connected to other trading partners.

Evaluating Buyer and Seller Agents. In this stage the utility of each of the connection of trading partners is determined. The utility U is a multi-attribute function that consists of a list of domain specific attributes $<a_1 \ldots a_n>$. The utility of a connection C_i is defined as :

$$U(C_i) = \sum_{j=1..n} w_j \times a_j \quad (1)$$

where w_j is a coefficient of arbitrary value.

For example, in the domain of securities trading, the utility is a function of price (**P**), volume (**V**) and desirability (**D**) with values from 1 (very poor) to 10 (very good). **D** is determined by analyzing the transaction histories of a trading agent. In evaluating trading agents, the factors that contribute to higher rating (desirability) may include: the numbers of previously successful transactions and the payment records of the traders (that is, the traders deliver payment in time).

The utility function for securities trading is defined as follows:

$$\mathbf{U} = w_1 \times \mathbf{P} + w_2 \times \mathbf{V} + w_3 \times \mathbf{D} \quad (2)$$

Values of **P**, **V** and **D** ranges from 0 to 1 with the following interpretations:

1. A smaller difference between buying and selling price results in a higher value of **P**
2. A smaller difference between buying and selling volume results in a higher value of **V**
3. A trading agent with larger number of previous successful transactions receives a higher value of **D**

Filtering: This stage filters out connections in two steps. The first step drops connections with **U** lower than a pre-defined cut off point β that is an adjustable parameter. If the number of connections after the first step is larger than the expected number of responses specified in the transaction profiles, the second step selects and filters out connections with the lowest ratings. This filtering process ensures that users are given more desirable connections.

To realize the ideas of the connection algorithm and to provide an electronic infrastructure for bolstering information brokering, an agent-based information testbed (section 3) and a brokering protocol (section 4) were designed and implemented.

3 An Agent Based Information Brokering Testbed

The agent-based information brokering testbed (shown in figure 1) consists of a society of intermediary or information agents (the broker agent, the record agent and the recommendation agent) and trading agents (buyer agents and seller agents) using a blackboard database as a central repository. The features and functions of the testbed include:

- *enabling buyers to post requests and sellers to post advertisements*
- *connecting buyers and sellers* (see descriptions in section 2)
- *maintaining and documenting user profiles*
- *documenting successful connections*
- *making recommendations to potential buyers or sellers.* In addition to making connection between buyers and sellers, the testbed also has a mechanism for making recommendation to potential buyers or sellers.

The above features are bolstered by a society of agents described below:

Buyer Agent: Buyer agents provide user interface to the users of the testbed. They post or requests to or withdraw requests from the blackboard, view results of each request, and make purchase decisions.

Seller Agent: Seller agents are similar to buyer agents but act on behalf of human sellers.

Broker Agent: The broker agent connects buyer and seller agents together using the connection algorithm described in section 2. In addition, it manages and controls the transactions and accesses to the blackboard. Examples and details of its executions are given in section 5.

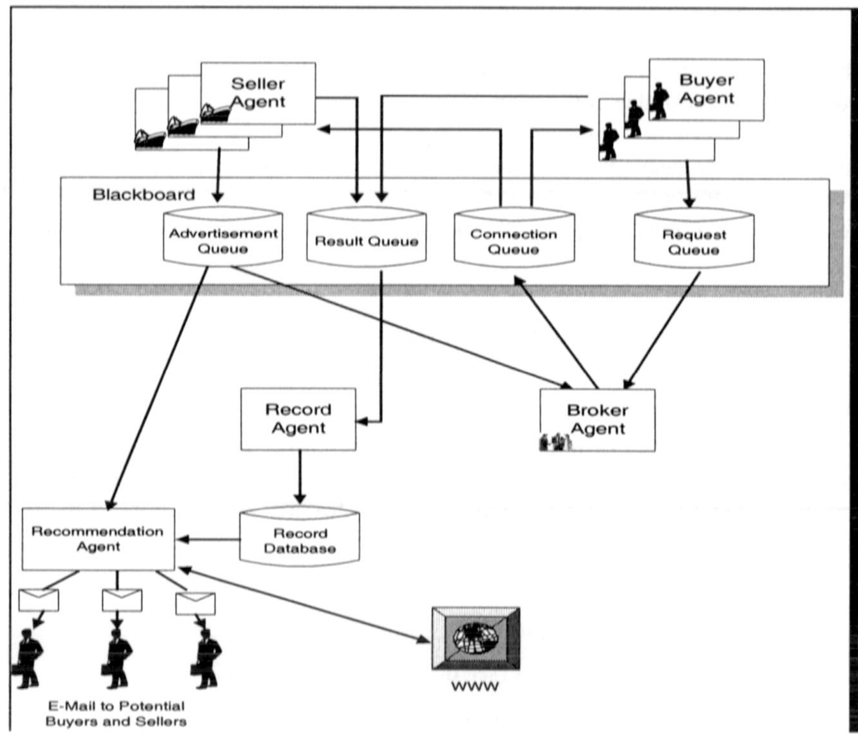

Fig. 1. An Agent-based Information Brokering Testbed

Record Agent: The record agent documents and records the transaction histories of users in the record database. Using the information in the database, user profiles can be traced and determined.

Recommendation Agent: By accessing documented transaction histories, the recommendation agent proactively seeks potential buyers (sellers) when there is no matching sellers (buyers) or when the buyer to seller (seller to buyer) ratio is too large. Employing this 'push' technology, recommendations are sent to potential trading partners via e-mail.

Blackboard Database: The blackboard accepts (1) requests from the buyer agents in the request queue and (2) advertisements from the seller agents in the advertisement queue. It is used to record buyer to seller connection information from the broker agent in the connection queue, and the transaction results and user satisfaction from the buyer and seller agents in the result queue.

4 An Information Brokering Protocol

While the testbed provides an electronic infrastructure for the information and trading agents, the brokering protocol specifies the interactions and information exchange among the information and trading agents. The stages of the brokering protocol are listed as follows:

1. Buyers send *requests* and sellers send *advertisements* to the broker agent to specify their profiles and preferences. Buyers and sellers may also withdraw requests or advertisements previously sent. Buyers' specifications may include the type of products (for example, stocks of banks) and the broker agent attempts to match them with actual product names based on information stored locally. Sellers' specifications may include the product name (for example, stocks of Citi-Bank).

2. The broker agent attempts to connect buyers and sellers (see section 2) by matching the specifications of requests and advertisements. It determines the rating of each connection made and filters out those with rating lower than a predefined cut off point. Multiple connections for a request or an advertisement are also possible.

3. The protocol does not assume that connections can always be made. If advertisements (requests) with matching specifications cannot be found, the recommendation agent proactively "pushes" e-mail recommendations to trading agents by accessing the record database to determine their profiles and transaction histories. For selecting advertisements/requests, the recommendation agent prefers to contact trading agents:
   a) with the largest number of successful transactions,
   b) that have most recently completed a transaction (that is, sold/bought a similar product/service).

   The e-mails may contain additional information of the stock or the company found using Internet search engines.

4. Buyers and sellers review connections made by the broker agent. In this stage if connections for a request (advertisement) has not been made, it will be placed in the request (advertisement) queue, awaiting connection in future cycles.

5. Buyers and sellers complete the transaction. In this stage, trading agents can either take or reject recommendations made by the broker agent. They can also provide feedback to the brokering testbed by indicating their satisfaction level. Users' satisfaction will be used as one of the evaluation criteria of the agent-based information brokering testbed.

5 Information Agents at Work : Brokering and Recommendation

This section presents examples of executions of various information agents. The operations and user interfaces of these agents are illustrated by stepping through a buying and selling experience that consists of the following steps :

- Step 1 : Buyer agents create new requests
- Step 2 : Seller agents create new advertisements
- Step 3 : The broker agent connects requests and advertisements
- Step 4 : The recommendation agent attempts to find potential buyers or sellers if connections are not found in step 3
- Step 5 : Seller and buyer agents review connection results and confirm transactions if connections are found in step 3
- Step 6 : The record agent stores completed transactions in the record database

For ease of exposition, it is assumed that the request, advertisement and connection queues are initially empty while the record database contains five records. There are three seller agents and two buyer agents issuing advertisements and requests as shown in table 1 :

Table 1. Input data used for demonstrating the operation of the testbed

Agent	Name	Adv / Req ID	Stock	Volume	Price	Expected Response
Buyer 1	chan	21	1001	2000	70	2
Buyer 2	ho	22	2002	900	10	1
Seller 1	lee	11	1001	2000	100	1
Seller 2	cheung	12	1001	1800	80	1
Seller 3	wong	13	1001	1500	130	1

Step 1 : Buyer agents create new requests

In the testbed, there is a Trading Agent User Interface (as shown in figure 2) that provides functions for both buyers and sellers to :

1. submit new requests,
2. submit new advertisements,
3. review connection results for requests,
4. review connection results for advertisements,
5. withdraw previously submitted requests, and
6. withdraw previously submitted advertisements.

Fig. 2. Trading agent user interface

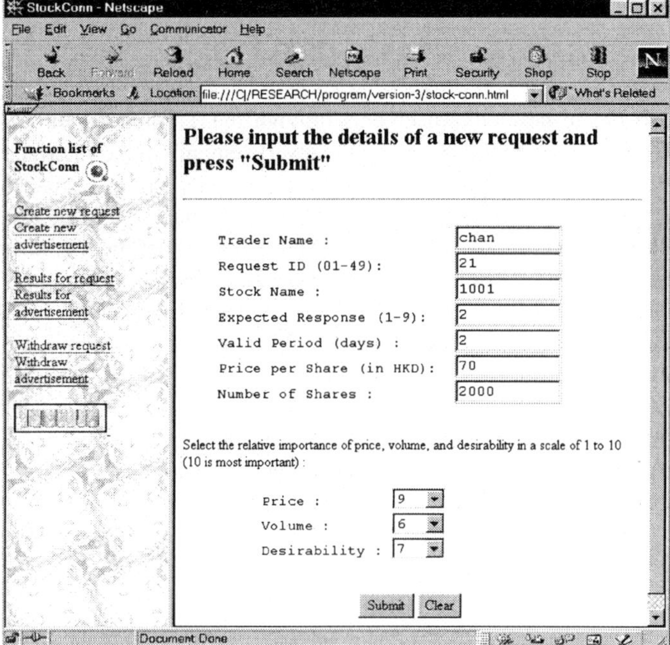

Fig. 3. Create new request window

For trading of stocks, it is likely that a trader will act as a buyer and also a seller. Hence, the single user interface approach in the testbed simplifies user operations for issuing and reviewing requests and advertisements.

By selecting the "Create new request", buyers can input transaction details and submit new requests to the system as shown in figure 3. In figure 3, a buyer "chan" creates a new request for 2000 shares of stock 1001 at an expected price of $70 per share wishes to have two recommendations from the broker agent. The request will be valid for 2 days starting from the date of creation. In addition to having a request ID for future reference, the buyer can then specify his preference by giving weighting to price, volume, and desirability (see section 2) to indicate the amount of emphasis placed on the three attributes. In figure 3, the buyer gives higher weighting to price and desirability than to volume. This information will be used by the system to evaluate and determine the utility of a connection (see section 2).

Using the graphical interface of the Broker Agent, the content of the request queue can be reviewed. Figure 4 shows that two new requests (as shown in table 1) were added to the request queue. In figure 4, the "Expected Resp" column shows the number of expected response specified by the buyer, and the "Conn Resp" column indicates that there is currently no connection being recommended by the broker agent. The "Assigned" column equals 'N' indicates that connection result for this request is not yet available for retrieval.

Step 2 : Seller agents create new advertisements

Sellers can create new advertisements through the Trading Agent User Interface (see figure 2). By selecting the "Create new advertisement" in the interface, sellers can input transaction details and submit new advertisements to the testbed as shown in figure 5. In figure 5, a seller agent "lee", having 2000 shares of stock 1001, wishes to sell the stock at a price of $100 per share. One recommendation is expected from the broker agent and the advertisement will be valid for 3 days from the date of creation. When creating an advertisement, the seller does not need to specify the weighting of price, volume, and desirability because this information will be provided by the buyer for evaluation of connections.

By selecting the "Submit" button, the advertisement is added into the advertisement queue which will be processed by the broker agent. The content of the advertisement queue can be reviewed using the broker agent interface as shown in figure 6. Figure 6 shows the content of the advertisement queue after adding the three new advertisements (as shown in table 1). The "Expected Req", "Conn Req", and "Assigned" columns bear the same meaning as those in the request queue described in step 1.

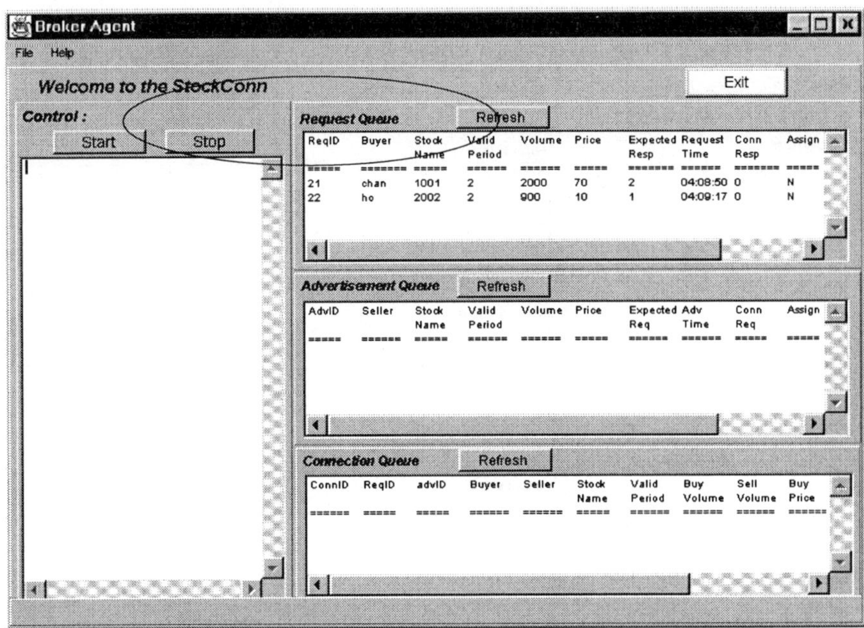

Fig. 4. Listing of the request queue showing two new requests

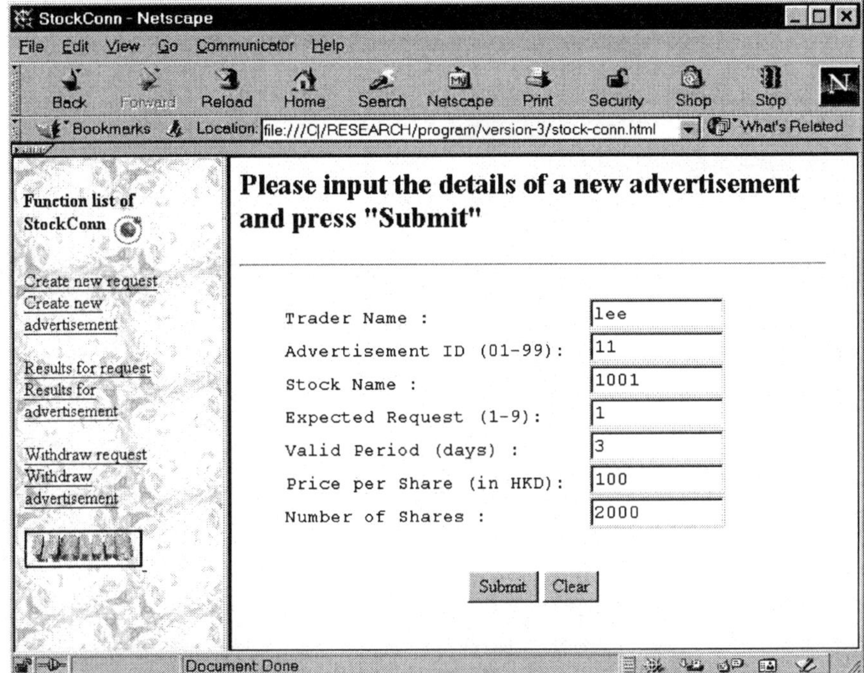

Fig. 5. Create new advertisement window

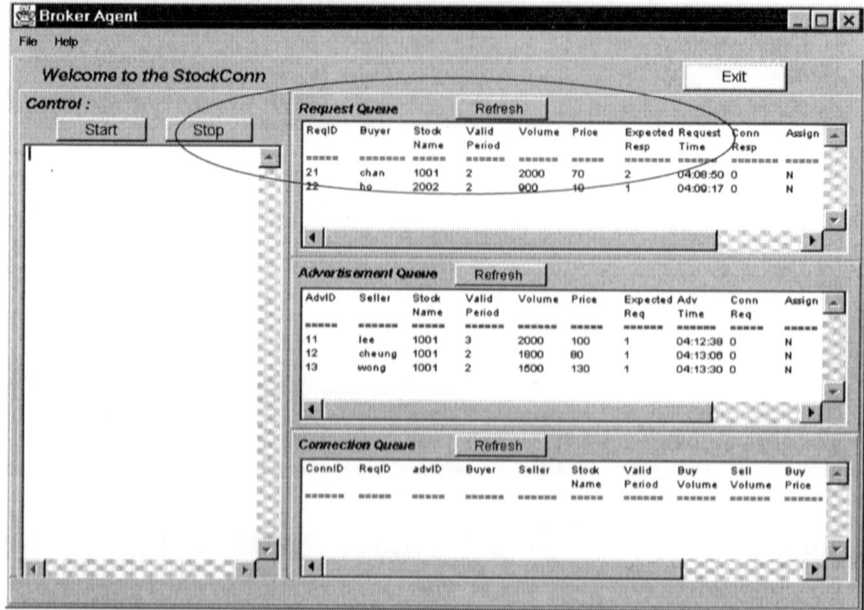

Fig. 6. Listing of the advertisement queue showing three new advertisements

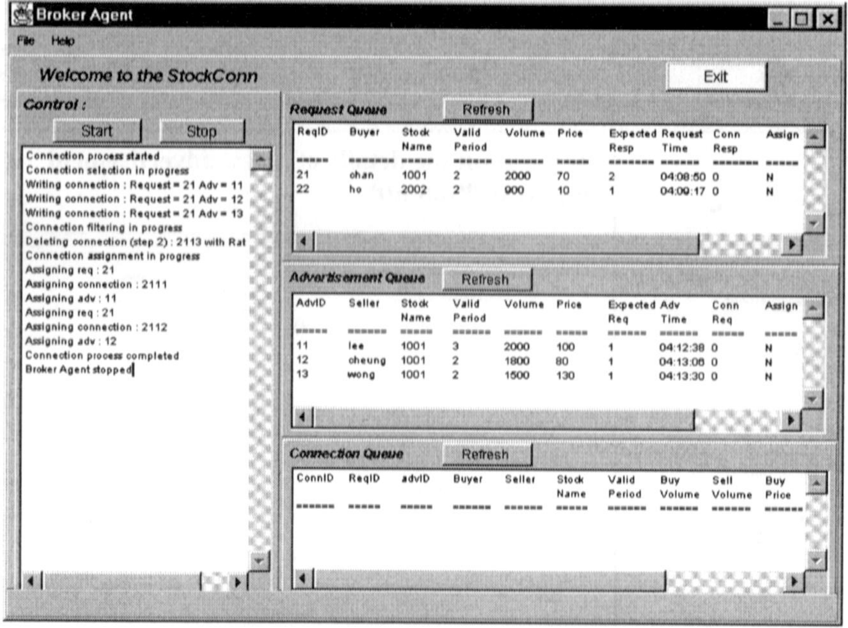

Fig. 7. Execution log of the broker agent

Step 3 : The broker agent connects requests and advertisements

The broker agent connects advertisements and requests according to the connection algorithms that consist of four stages (selection, evaluation, filtering, and assignment) as described in section 2. The system provides a broker agent interface (as shown in figure 7) that allows system administrators to :

1. start and stop the executions of the broker agent,
2. review the execution log of the broker agent, and
3. browse the contents of the request, advertisement, and connection queues.

The execution log of the broker agent contains information about the current state of the broker agent, connections being created or filtered, and requests or advertisements being assigned.

The right hand side of figure 7 shows the content of the request, advertisement, and connection queues before the execution of the broker agent. There are two requests created in step 1 and three advertisements created in step 2 waiting for connection (see table 1). The connection queue is empty before the connection process commences.

The execution log of the broker agent on the left hand side of figure 7 shows the four stages for the connection process as depicted in section 2. During the *selection stage*, the request from "chan" and the advertisements from "lee", "cheung" and "wong" are selected because of similar profiles (stock name 1001). Three connections (between "chan" and "lee", "chan" and "cheung", and "chan" and "wong") are formed and written into the connection queue. No connection is found for request from "ho" because there is no advertisement with similar profile (stock name "2002"). During the *evaluation stage*, the utility (or rating) for each connection is calculated according to the utility function described in section 2. Figure 8 shows the content of the connection queue with utilities calculated after the evaluation stage.

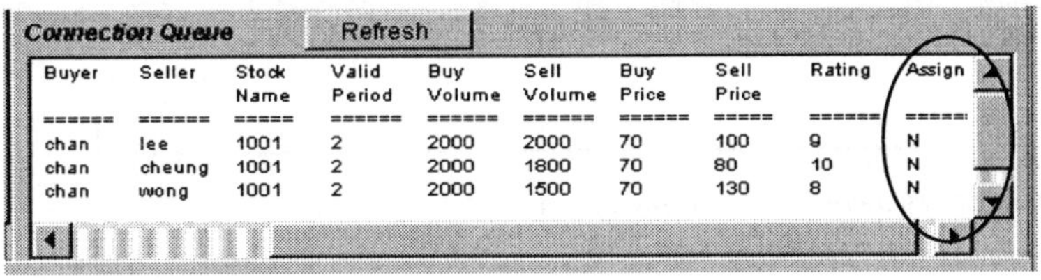

Connection Queue   Refresh

Buyer	Seller	Stock Name	Valid Period	Buy Volume	Sell Volume	Buy Price	Sell Price	Rating	Assign
======	======	=====	======	======	======	======	=====	======	=====
chan	lee	1001	2	2000	2000	70	100	9	N
chan	cheung	1001	2	2000	1800	70	80	10	N
chan	wong	1001	2	2000	1500	70	130	8	N

Fig. 8. Content of the connection queue after evaluation stage

Since buyer "chan" is expecting only two recommendations, the two connections with highest utilities are selected and the rest are deleted during the *filtering stage* (see section 2). Therefore, connection between "chan" and "wong" (with rating 8) is deleted after the filtering stage and the content of the connection queue is shown in figure 9.

Connection Queue Refresh

Buyer	Seller	Stock Name	Valid Period	Buy Volume	Sell Volume	Buy Price	Sell Price	Rating	Assign
chan	lee	1001	2	2000	2000	70	100	9	N
chan	cheung	1001	2	2000	1800	70	80	10	N

Fig. 9. Content of the connection queue after filtering stage

The *assignment stage* marks the completion of the connection process and makes the connection results available for retrieval by corresponding buyers and sellers. The "Assigned" column in the three queues after assignment stage (as shown in figure 10) indicates that buyer "chan", and sellers "lee" and "cheung" can now review their connection results. However, since no matching advertisement is found for buyer "ho" and the connection between "chan" and "wong" is filtered out, chan's request and wong's advertisement will remain in the system to be processed in the next cycle of connection.

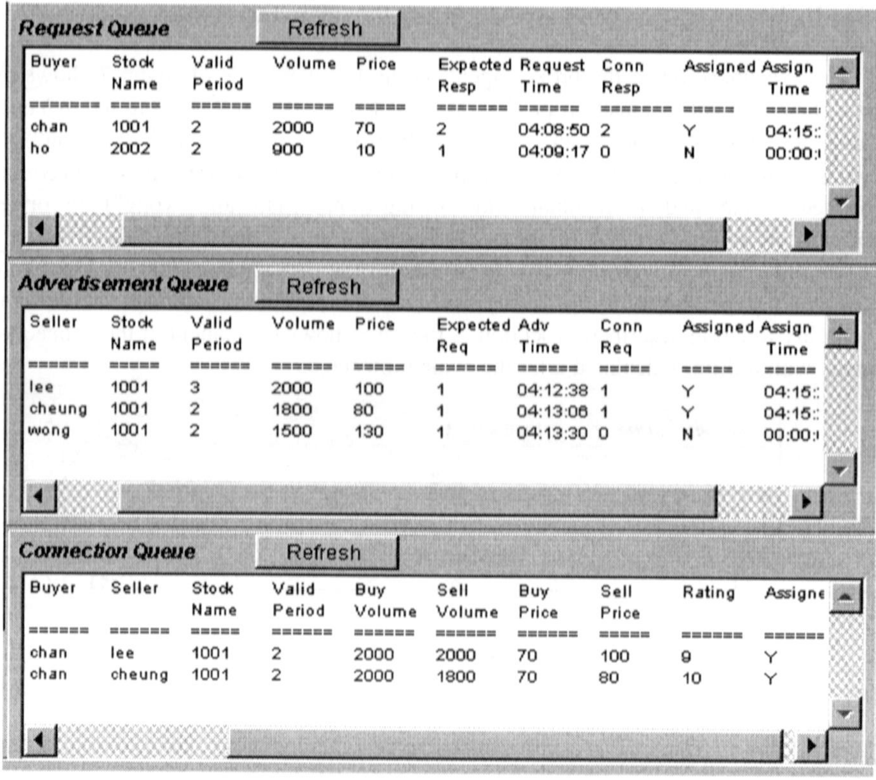

Request Queue Refresh

Buyer	Stock Name	Valid Period	Volume	Price	Expected Resp	Request Time	Conn Resp	Assigned	Assign Time
chan	1001	2	2000	70	2	04:08:50	2	Y	04:15::
ho	2002	2	900	10	1	04:09:17	0	N	00:00:!

Advertisement Queue Refresh

Seller	Stock Name	Valid Period	Volume	Price	Expected Req	Adv Time	Conn Req	Assigned	Assign Time
lee	1001	3	2000	100	1	04:12:38	1	Y	04:15::
cheung	1001	2	1800	80	1	04:13:06	1	Y	04:15::
wong	1001	2	1500	130	1	04:13:30	0	N	00:00:!

Connection Queue Refresh

Buyer	Seller	Stock Name	Valid Period	Buy Volume	Sell Volume	Buy Price	Sell Price	Rating	Assigne
chan	lee	1001	2	2000	2000	70	100	9	Y
chan	cheung	1001	2	2000	1800	70	80	10	Y

Fig. 10. Content of the request, advertisement, and connection queue after assignment stage

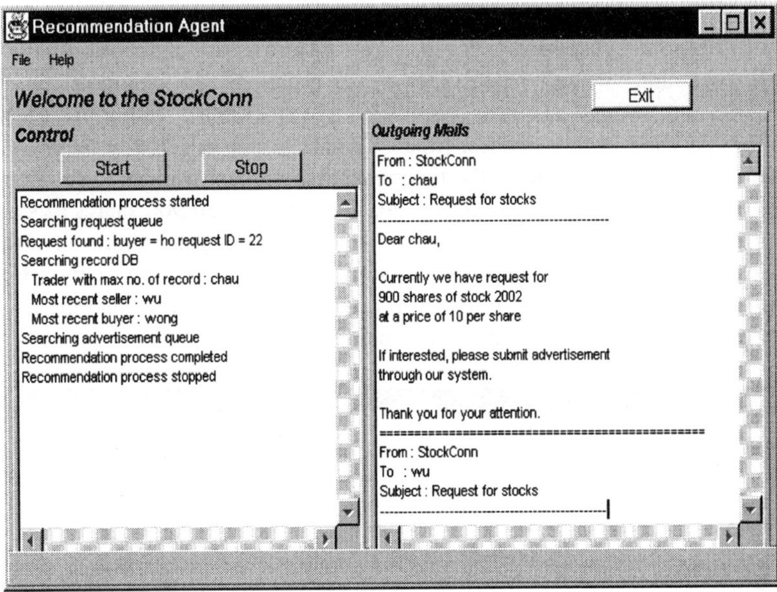

Fig. 11. Recommendation agent interface showing execution log and outgoing e-mails

Step 4 : The recommendation agent finds potential buyers or sellers if connection not found in step 3

The recommendation agent in the testbed, based on the transaction history stored in the record database, proactively seeks potential buyers and sellers when there is no matching trading partners for a request or advertisement (see also section 4). The system provides a recommendation agent interface (as shown in figure 11) that allows system administrators to :

1. start and stop the executions of the recommendation agent,
2. review the execution log of the recommendation agent, and
3. browse the contents of outgoing e-mails sent by the recommendation agent.

The execution log of the recommendation agent contains information about the current state of the recommendation agent, unmatched requests or advertisements, and potential buyers or sellers being selected. The contents of outgoing e-mails include : sender, recipient, subject, volume and price of stocks requested or available.

Since the request from buyer "ho" created in step 1 is still outstanding, the recommendation agent attempts to find potential sellers for "ho" using the following criteria (see also section 4) :

1. trader with the largest number of successful transactions, or
2. trader that has most recently completed a transaction.

By referencing information in the record database in figure 16, trader "chau" matches criterion (1) because he has the most (four) transaction records of stock 2002. Traders "wu" and "wong" match criterion (2) because "wu" has most recently sold stock 2002 and "wong" has most recently bought stock 2002 with a price lower than the price specified in ho's request (trader "chau" is not selected because he already matches criterion (1)). Hence, the recommendation agent decides to send e-mails to "chau", "wu" and "wong" to see if they are interested to sell 900 shares of stock 2002 at a price of $10 per share. If they are interested, they can submit advertisements through the trading agent user interface (similar to step 2). The execution log of the recommendation agent is shown on the left hand side of figure 11 and the contents of outgoing e-mails are shown on the right hand side.

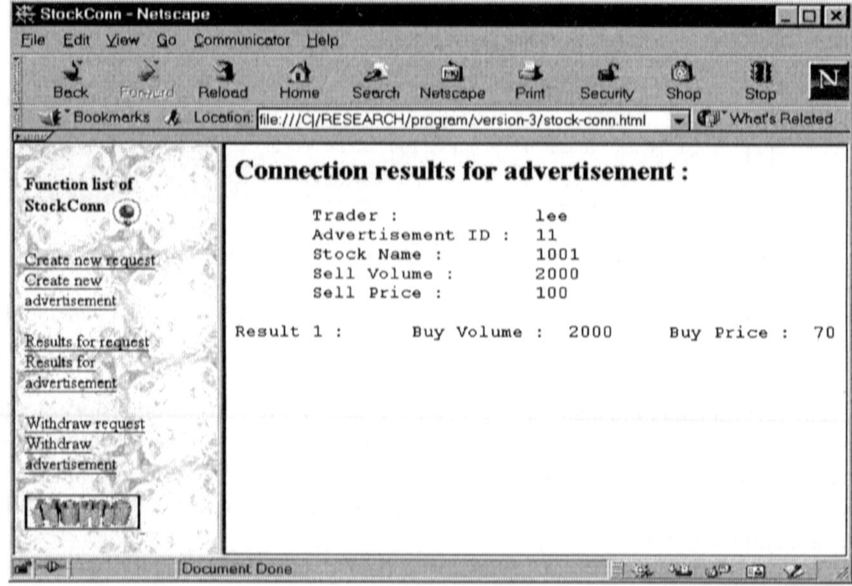

Fig. 12. Connection result for seller "lee"

Step 5 : Seller and buyer agents review connection results and confirm transactions if connections found in step 3

Using the trading agent user interface (see figure 2), buyers and sellers can review connection results recommended by the broker agent. Sellers (buyers) can select the "Results for advertisement" ("Results for request") and input an advertisement (request) ID to retrieve connection results from the system. Figure 12 shows the connection results for seller "lee" and figure 13 for seller "cheung". The personal information of the buyer, for example name, is hidden in figures 12 and 13 to protect the privacy of the buyer.

For buyer "chan", there are two connections recommended by the broker agent as shown in figure 14. In figure 14, the personal information of the seller is hidden and similarly the privacy of the seller is protected by the system.

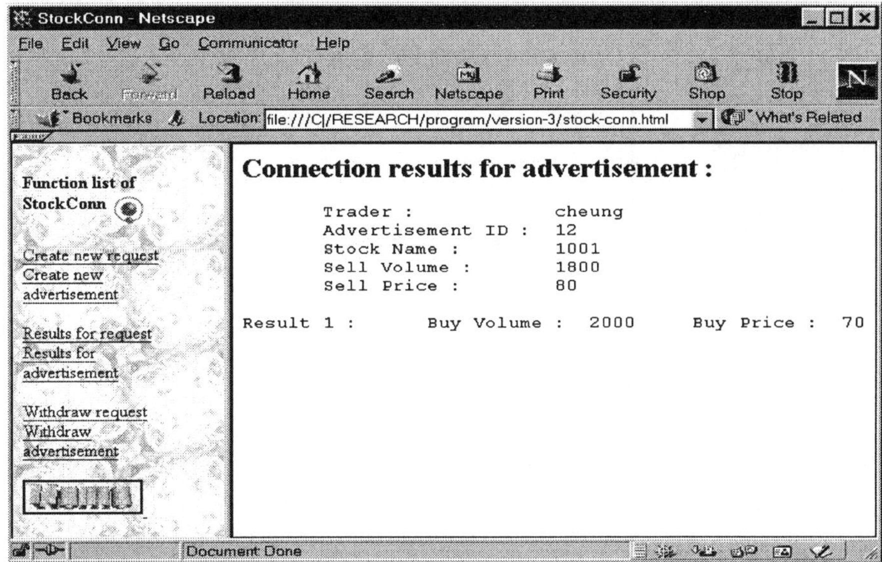

Fig. 13. Connection result for seller "cheung"

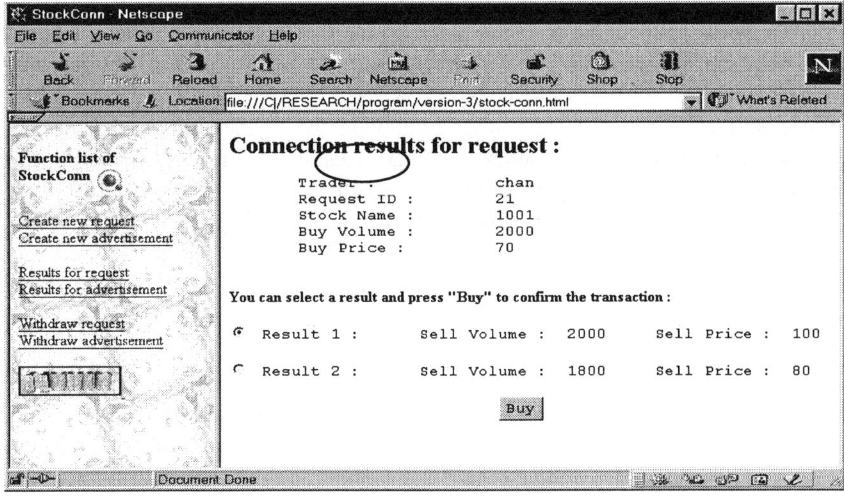

Fig. 14. Connection result for buyer "chan"

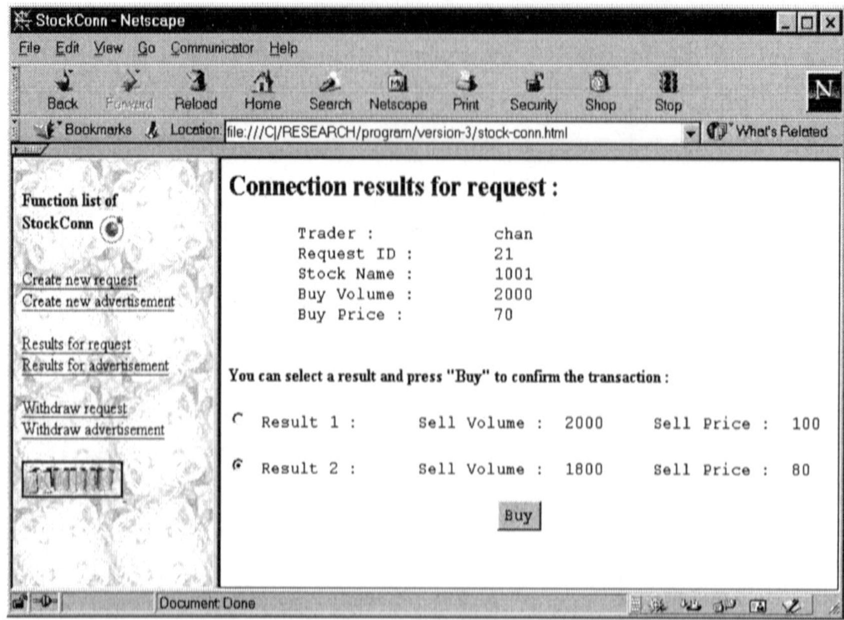

Fig. 15. Buyer "chan" chooses to buy from the second result

In the testbed, buyers can decide whom to buy from and transactions are initiated by buyers instead of sellers. Since negotiation between buyers and sellers is currently not supported by the testbed, buyers must agree on the price offered by sellers. Number of shares being traded in a transaction is the minimum of offering and requesting volume.

For example, if buyer "chan", after reviewing the connection results, decides to complete the transaction with seller "cheung" (result 2 in figure 15), a transaction between "chan" and "cheung" on 1800 shares of stock 1001 at a price of $80 per share will be initiated and subsequently processed by the testbed.

Step 6 : The record agent stores completed transactions in the record database

The record agent in the testbed documents and stores successful transactions in the record database. Such information will be used by the broker agent in determining the desirability of users and by the recommendation agent in determining potential buyers or sellers. The system provides a record agent interface (as shown in figure 16) that allows system administrators to :

1. start and stop the executions of the record agent,
2. review the execution log of the record agent, and
3. browse the contents of the record database.

The execution log of the record agent contains information about the current state of the record agent and transactions being written into the record database. The contents of the record database are stored and displayed in chronological order of transaction date and time. As shown in figure 16, before the execution of the record agent, there were five records in the record database.

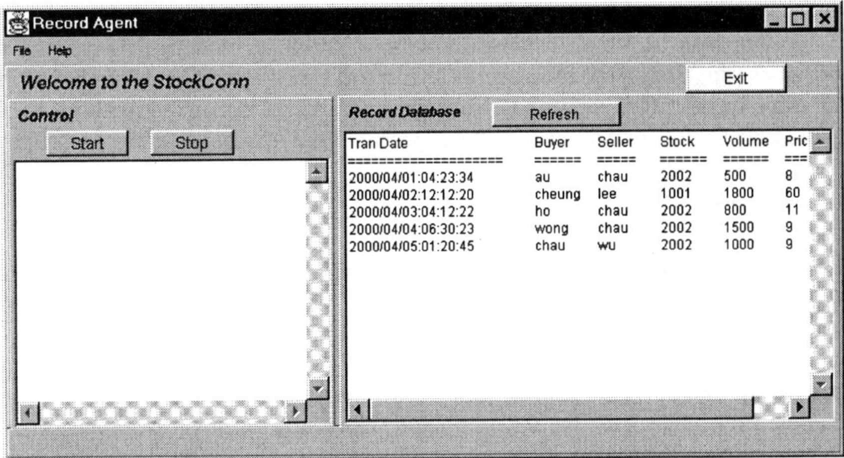

Fig. 16. Record agent interface showing original content of the record database

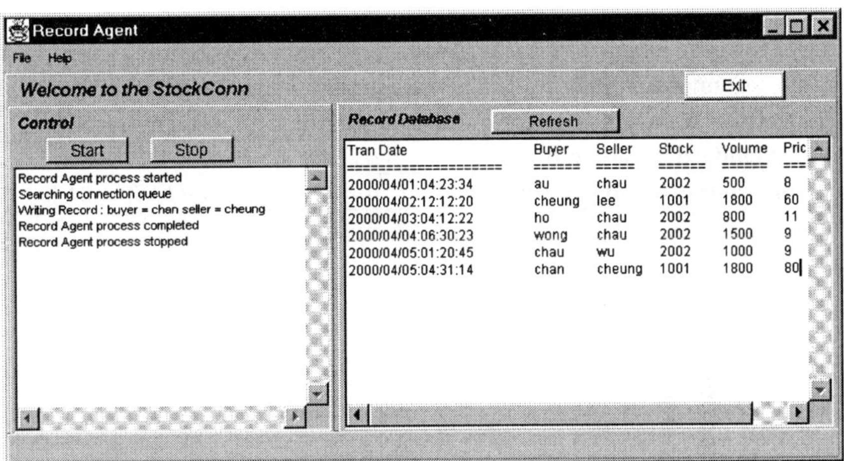

Fig. 17. Record agent interface showing execution log and the new transaction record

With the execution of the record agent, the completed transaction (from step 5) between buyer "chan" and seller "cheung" on 1800 shares of stock 1001 with a price of $80 per share was added into the record database. The record agent also performed housekeeping of corresponding entries in the request, advertisement, and connection queues. The execution log of the record agent and the content of the record database after the completion of the record agent process is shown in figure 17. Figure 17 shows that one record was added into the record database.

6 Experimentation and Evaluation

The performance of the testbed was determined using several parameters, including the rate at which requests and advertisements are generated and the number of buyer and seller agents. Two representative experiments in the domain of securities trading are presented below to demonstrate the approach taken in evaluating the testbed.

6.1 Experiment One: Average Connection Time

In the first experiment, the performance of the testbed was examined by measuring the average time used in making connections for buyers and sellers. The average connection time and the standard deviation of fifty connections were recorded. Fifty requests and fifty advertisements were generated by 5 buyer agents and 5 seller agents respectively. Each buyer (seller) agent generates one request (advertisement) every minute. The connection time for each request and advertisement were measured and shown in figures 18 and 19 respectively. The mean and standard deviation of connection time were in table 2. The results showed relatively stable average connection time with relatively small standard deviation.

Table 2. Average Connection Time

Connection time	Requests	Advertisements
Mean χ	= 21.8 seconds	= 22.5 seconds
Standard deviation σ	= 5.4 seconds	= 5.0 seconds
% of requests within $(\chi \pm \sigma)$	= 41 / 50 = 82 %	= 42 / 50 = 84 %

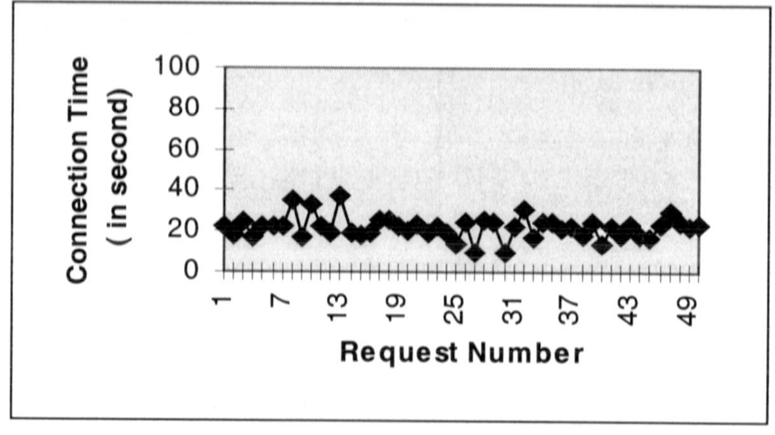

Fig. 18. Result of experiment 1 (request connection time)

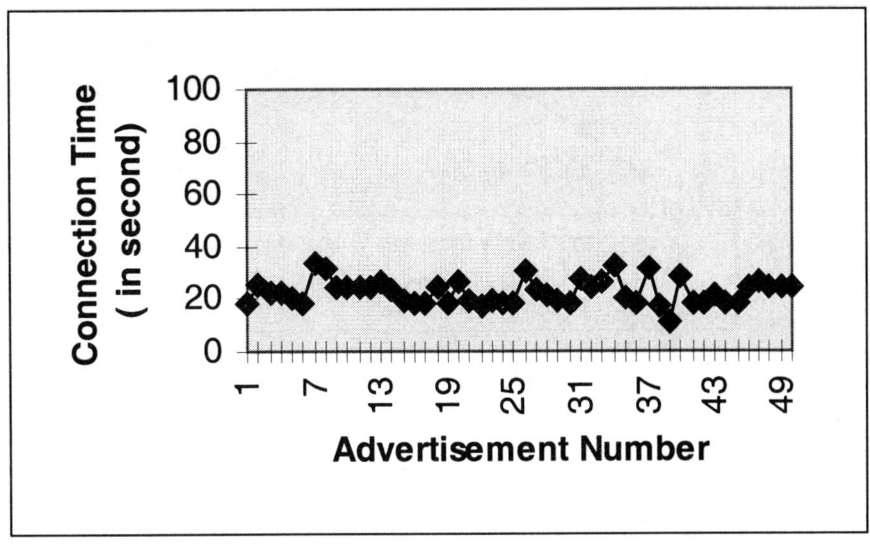

Fig. 19. Result of experiment 1 (advertisement connection time)

6.2 Experiment Two: Users' Satisfaction

In the second experiment, the relationship between user satisfaction and time was studied. User satisfaction (U_s) is a function of ΔP (the percentage difference of buying and selling price), ΔV (the percentage difference of buying and selling volume) and Δ C (the percentage difference of expected number of responses and the number of connections recommended). U_s is mapped to a scale from 0 to 99.

In part 1 of experiment 2, the average buyer satisfaction for 20 requests was measured at 20 seconds interval from 40 seconds to 200 seconds. Advertisements were generated by 9 seller agents. Each seller agent generated one advertisement in 20 seconds. The connection parameters including price and volume in each request and advertisement were generated randomly. The results were shown in figure 20. In part 2 of experiment 2, the average seller satisfaction of 20 advertisement was measured. Requests were generated by 9 buyer agents with same rate as in part 1. The result was shown in figure 21. Both the results of part 1 and part 2 showed an increase of U_s when the time for making connections increased. The experiments showed that given reasonable amount of time (about 200 seconds), the system was able to connect buyers to sellers with an almost complete user satisfaction. It only took about 80 seconds before a high user satisfaction (80) can be achieved.

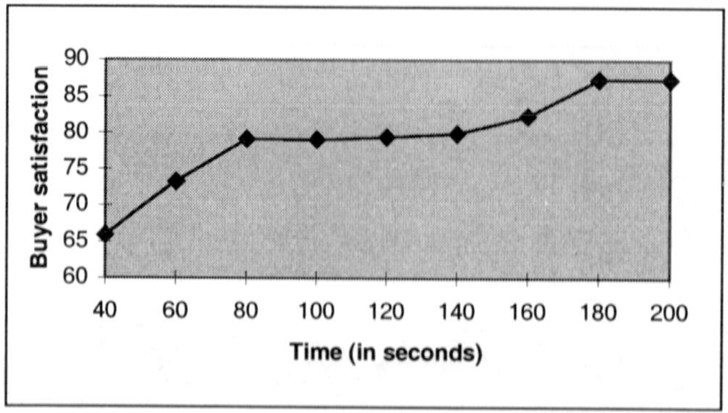

Fig. 20. Result of experiment 2 part 1

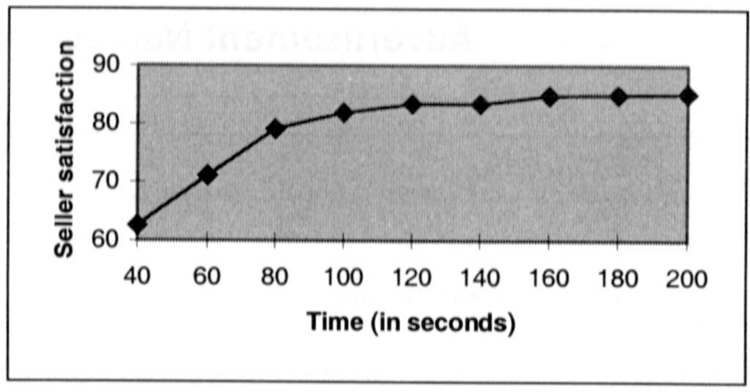

Fig. 21. Result of experiment 2 part 2

7 Related Work

The information brokering protocol in this paper bears some resemblance to the Contract Net Protocol (CNP) [4] in the way that both protocols are used to solve the connection problem. While the CNP provides a mechanism for structuring high-level interactions between nodes for co-operative task executions, the information brokering protocol defines high-level interactions between buyers, sellers, and the information agents in a brokering process. However, unlike the CNP, the information brokering protocol does not assume that connections will always be made.

Some of the extant brokering systems that are similar to this research include Andersen's Bargain Finder [1], FAST Broker from University of Southern California [3], Firefly from Firefly Inc.[5], and WARREN multi-agent portfolio management system from Carnegie Mellon University [2].

Andersen's Bargain Finder is one of the first agent-based systems to provide online price comparison shopping on the Internet and it supports the merchant brokering stage in the Consumer Buying Behavior (CBB) model [6] which consists of: need identification, product brokering, merchant brokering, negotiation, purchase and delivery, and product service and evaluation. It allows users to type in the name of a compact disc (CD) or music group and search on-line stores for the lowest prices available. Bargain Finder looks up its price from at least nine different merchant web sites using web browser-like requests. With Bargain Finder, on-line shoppers can browse the displays, listen to samples and read the liner notes before purchasing a CD. Agents are then invoked to find the on-line store with the best price. It was developed to demonstrate the impact of electronic commerce on the retail industry. Similar to the broker agent in this research, Bargain Finder also provides connection services. In particular, it provides service to on-line stores for the lowest price of compact disc available. Unlike the broker agent, Bargain Finder is a matchmaker that makes comparison solely on price while the broker agent considers multiple factors when making connections.

FAST is a purchasing agent with rapid access to a large number of distributors and manufacturers. Customers send quote requests and orders to FAST via electronic mail in a pre-defined format. The communications between FAST and its customers make use of either standard forms (templates) developed by FAST for quotes or orders, or the industry standard for Electronic Data Interchange, X12. FAST identifies vendors that carry the requested items and contacts them to obtain quotes. As quotes accumulate, they are sent to the customer via E-mail. The customer may then order through FAST via E-mail. FAST places the order with the vendor who ships directly to the customer. Just like the brokering system in this research, FAST is a broker system providing connection services. However, FAST does not perform comparison among advertisements. Hence, users need to manually compare and decide which advertisement is more appropriate.

Firefly from Firefly Inc. [Firefly] is a system that can help users find information relevant to their interests in the areas of music, movies and web sites. Firefly recommends products through an automated "word-of-mouth" recommendation mechanism called "collaborative filtering". Firefly can recommend to the users artists or recordings based on some knowledge of their interests. It does this by exploiting patterns it finds among users. Users enter their profiles to the system by listing the music they like and dislike. When a user asks for recommendations, the system searches for other users with similar interests. The system then checks for music they are interested in that the user does not seem to know about and recommends that music to the user. Firefly is a recommender that supports only the product brokering stage of the CBB model while the brokering system in this research supports both the product and merchant brokering stages. However, unlike the recommendation agent in this research, Bargain Finder, FAST and Firefly do not automatically initiate recommendations for users when connections for appropriate trading partners cannot be found.

WARREN from CMU is a multi-agent system for the management of financial portfolios. It experiments with several design constraints and related models of middle agents including brokering and matchmaking. Like the broker agent, WARREN keeps track of the current state of the situation, environment, and user information needs. Unlike the recommendation agent and record agent, WARREN does not 'push' information to users with reference to the transaction history and currently available products and requests in the system. Table 3 compares and summarizes the characteristics of the above related systems and the brokering system in this research.

Table 3. Comparison of systems discussed in section 7

	Bargain Finder	FAST	Firefly	Warren	This research
System nature	matchmaker	broker	recommender	information monitor	broker
Main objective	online price comparison	rapid access to distributors	Product ecommendation	financial portfolio management	connection service
Provide connection service	4	4	8	8	4
Product brokering	8	8	4	N/A	4
Merchant brokering	4	4	8	N/A	4
Initiate recommendation	8	8	8	4	4

8 Conclusion and Future Work

The agent-based brokering system exposed in this paper partially solves the connection problem in the product brokering and the merchant brokering stages of e-commerce. The design and engineering of the brokering system that consists of user interfaces, the broker agent, the record agent and the recommendation agent was briefly introduced. The structure of the broker agent and the approach of making connection based on multiple factors were described. In this paper, the stages of the broker protocol that define the brokering process were outlined. Finally, favorable results from the two experiments show that the system has relatively good performance. As part of an on-going research initiative, further experiments will be performed to evaluate different properties of the system (such as focus decision and balanced loading). Some of these results are reported in [7].

References

1. Andersen, Bargain Finder: *http://bf/cstar.ac.com/bf/.*
2. Decker K., Sycara, K. and Zeng, D.: Designing a Multi-Agent Portfolio Management System, *http://www.cs.cmu.edu/~softagents/papers/cikm95.ps*, 1995.
3. FAST Broker, Information Sciences Institute of the University of Southern California (ISI): *http://info.broker.isi.edu/l/fast.*
4. Smith, Reid G.: The Contract Net Protocol: High-Level Communication and Control in a Distributed Problem Solver. In: *IEEE Transaction on Computer*, vol. C-29, no. 12, pp 1104-1113, 1980.
5. Firefly, Firefly Inc. *http://www.firefly.com.*
6. Guttman, Robert H., Moukas, Alexandros G., and Maes, Pattie: Agent-mediated Electronic Commerce: A Survey. In: *Knowledge Engineering Review,* June 1998.
7. Sim, K.M. and Chan, R.: A Brokering Protocol for Agent-based E-commerce. Submitted to *IEEE Transactions on Systems, Man, and Cybernetics.*

Price Formation in Double Auctions*

Steven Gjerstad[1], John Dickhaut[2]

[1] T. J. Watson Research Center
IBM Corporation
Route 134, Kitchawan Road
Yorktown Heights, NY 10598

[2] Carlson School of Management
University of Minnesota
Minneapolis, MN 55455

Abstract. We develop a model of information processing and strategy choice for participants in a double auction. Sellers in this model form beliefs that an offer will be accepted by some buyer. Similarly, buyers form beliefs that a bid will be accepted. These beliefs are formed on the basis of observed market data, including frequencies of asks, bids, accepted asks, and accepted bids. Then traders choose an action that maximizes their own expected surplus. The trading activity resulting from these beliefs and strategies is sufficient to achieve transaction prices at competitive equilibrium and complete market efficiency after several periods of trading.

1 Introduction

The double auction (DA) is one of the most common exchange institutions, used extensively in stock markets such as the New York Stock Exchange, commodity markets such as the Chicago Mercantile Exchange, and in markets for financial instruments, including options and futures. The prevalence of this institution can be traced to its operational simplicity, efficiency, and to its capacity to respond quickly to changing market conditions. Nevertheless, the DA is a persistent puzzle in economic theory. How is information which is held separately by many market participants – in the form of privately known reservation values and marginal costs – quickly and accurately coordinated through the trading process in order to reach the competitive equilibrium (CE) price and allocation?

In the double auction, any seller may at any time (during a specified trading period) submit an offer that is then observed simultaneously by all buyers and sellers. Similarly, any buyer may submit a bid which is observed by the other

* "Price Formation in Double Auctions" by Steven Gjerstad and John Dickhaut from *Games and Economic Behavior*, Volume 22, 1-29, ©1998 by Academic Press, reprinted by permission of the publisher.

J. Liu and Y. Ye (Eds.): E-Commerce Agents, LNAI 2033, pp. 106–134, 2001.

buyers and by the sellers. When a buyer's bid is acceptable to some seller, that seller may then accept the buyer's bid, and a trade is executed between the buyer whose bid was accepted and the seller who accepted this bid. Similarly, buyers may accept a seller's offer at any time.

Market experiments have established that transaction prices converge quickly to a competitive equilibrium price in the DA for a wide variety of market environments. Experimental investigation of trader behavior and market performance in the DA began with Smith [12]. Smith induced supply and demand conditions by giving buyers a redemption value for each unit of an abstract commodity purchased, and by giving sellers a cost for each unit of this abstract commodity sold. Buyers receive surplus equal to the difference between their redemption value and the purchase price negotiated with a seller, and sellers receive surplus equal to the difference between the purchase price paid by the buyer and their unit cost. Since reservation prices – and therefore supply and demand conditions – are known to the experimenter when this procedure is employed, the procedure makes possible comparison between experimental outcomes and theoretical predictions. The basic result observed in these experiments is that prices do converge quickly to within a few cents of competitive equilibrium prices in markets with stationary supply and demand. Smith and many other economists in the 35 years since his initial studies have also documented features of the path of convergence to equilibrium in a variety of market environments. For surveys and interpretation of these experimental results, see Plott [11] and Smith [13].

Models of trader behavior in the DA have been constructed by several authors, including Easley and Ledyard [3], Friedman [4], Gode and Sunder [7], and Wilson [14]. Although these models have furthered understanding of the interaction of individual behavior and institution in the DA, we provide a model that accounts for several important regularities of double auction data that no one of the previous models predicts or replicates in simulations. For comparison of the predictions of the last three models with properties of experimental data, see Cason and Friedman [1], [2].

We model individual behavior of sellers and buyers in a continuous DA and demonstrate that the persistent puzzle of convergence to CE prices and allocations in the DA can be resolved with traders whose information processing and strategy choices are simple and intuitive. For each possible bid each buyer forms a subjective belief that some some seller will accept her bid. The buyer then determines which bid will maximize her own expected surplus. Similarly, each seller determines which offer will maximize his expected surplus. Subjective beliefs are formed using only observed market activity, including bids, offers, and accepts of bids and offers. This procedure does not require any knowledge of the types (costs and valuations) of other buyers and sellers; in fact, traders in this model do not even have beliefs about the types of others. Nevertheless, this behavior results in efficient allocations, and convergence of transaction prices to within a few cents of CE prices within several periods of trading. In addition, these beliefs respond quickly to changes in market conditions, such as shifts in market demand or supply.

The organization of the paper is as follows. The model is formulated in Section 2. Simulations of the model are shown and some important statistical properties of these simulations are reported in Section 3.3. Section 4, the conclusion, summarizes the relationship between our model and experimental data.

2 The Model

Like most forms of market organization, the double auction is an informationally decentralized system. Our model emphasizes this structure in order to give a more compelling answer to Hayek's question: How is privately held information coordinated through the market process? Hurwicz, Radner, and Reiter [8] have shown that in general equilibrium environments, even with non-convexities, there are simple and intuitive forms of market organization and bidding behavior (which they call the B process) that lead to Pareto optimal outcomes. Gjerstad and Shachat [6] construct a map between partial equilibrium environments of standard market experiments and general equilibrium economies. In this paper, we develop a model of informationally decentralized bargaining for these environments which results not only in Pareto optimal outcomes, but also results in substantial stability of transaction prices. Our bargaining model, together with the general equilibrium interpretation of the environments considered here, results in a model of learning competitive equilibrium in a class of general equilibrium environments.

In this section, we describe the elements of a microeconomic system, interpret the double auction environment and institution within this framework, and construct an informationally decentralized model of trader behavior for these environments in the double auction institution.

The double auction is an example of a *microeconomic system* as in Hurwicz [9] and Smith [13]. The primary features of a microeconomic system are the *environment* $\mathbf{e}$, consisting of the characteristics of the economic agents, and the *institution* $\mathbf{I}$, which includes the messages that traders may send to one another, the allocation rules, and the adjustment process rules. A microeconomy is an economic system $\mathbf{S} = (\mathbf{e}, \mathbf{I})$ – together with behavioral actions β^i for market participants – as shown in figure 1.

The environment $\mathbf{e}$ consists of a set $\mathcal{A} = \{1, 2, \ldots, n\}$ of agents, and for each agent i characteristics $\mathbf{e^i}$ consisting of that agent's preferences, technology, and endowment. The environment is then $\mathbf{e} = \prod_{i \in \mathcal{A}} \mathbf{e^i}$. The institution $\mathbf{I}$ consists of a message space M^i for each agent, an adjustment process rule specifying the sequence of agent messages, and an outcome function or allocation function $h(m_t) = (h^1(m_t), h^2(m_t), \ldots, h^n(m_t))$, where $m_t = (m_t^1, m_t^2, \ldots, m_t^n) \in M_t = \prod_{i \in \mathcal{A}} M_t^i$ is the vector of agents' messages.

According to Smith ([13], p. 930)

> "We want to measure messages because we want to be able to identify the behavioral modes, $\beta^i(e^i, I)$, revealed by the agents and test hypotheses derived from theories about agent behavior."

When an environment $\mathbf{e}$ and an institution $\mathbf{I}$ are specified in a market experiment, and an outcome $\mathbf{X}$ is observed, the only elements remaining to be specified are the behavioral actions $\{\beta^i(H_t \,|\, \mathbf{e^i}, \mathbf{I})\}_{i \in \mathcal{A}}$, where H_t is the history of activity observed by agents through time t. The focus of the research in this paper is to specify forms of behavior $\{\beta^i(H_t \,|\, e^i, \mathbf{I})\}_{i \in \mathcal{A}}$ that are consistent with observations $\mathbf{X}$ from exchange environments $\mathbf{e}$ when the institution $\mathbf{I}$ is the double auction. We now describe a representation of the double auction in terms of this framework.

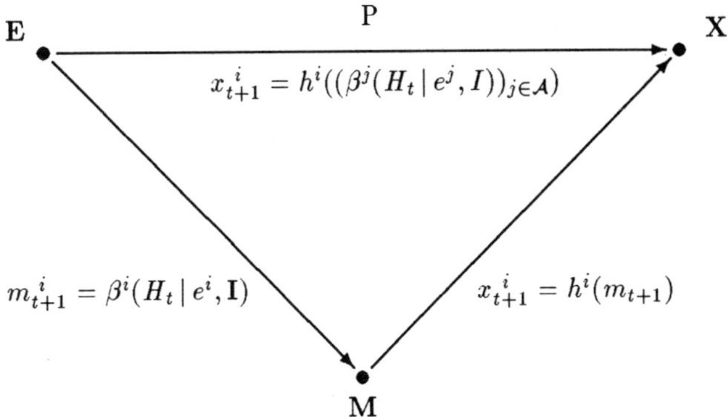

Figure 1: A microeconomic system.

2.1 Environment

In the double auction market environments we consider, there are two goods: an experimental currency X and a fictitious commodity Y. Our theory addresses the case of markets with the set of traders partitioned into a group I of sellers and a group J of buyers. Both types of agents (sellers and buyers) are assumed to have preferences over monetary rewards that are monotonically increasing.

Seller $i \in I$ has a vector of induced unit costs $c_i = (c_i^1, c_i^2, \ldots, c_i^{m_i})$ for production of an abstract commodity. Here c_i^1 is the cost to seller i of the first unit sold, c_i^2 the cost of the second unit, and so on. We index the cost of each unit because the model of trader behavior is developed for traders who frequently sell (or purchase) multiple units. The gain to seller i on his k^{th} unit sold is the difference $\pi^k_{s,i}(p_k, c_i^k) = p_k - c_i^k$ between the price p_k received from a buyer for that unit, and the cost c_i^k at which the unit is produced. If seller i sells $\mu_i \leq m_i$ units at prices $p_1, p_2, \ldots, p_{\mu_i}$, then the utility to this seller is $U_{s,i}\left(\sum_{k=1}^{\mu_i}(p_k - c_i^k)\right)$, where $U_{s,i}(\cdot)$ is monotonically increasing.[1]

Gjerstad and Shachat [6] show that the cost vector of each seller $i \in I$ is dual to a technology which is described by a production function $f_i(x)$. Let $\bar{x}_{s,i} \geq \sum_{\iota=1}^{m_i} c_i^{\iota}$. A seller with an endowment $\omega_{s,i} = (\bar{x}_{s,i}, 0)$ will have sufficient

[1] In Section 2.4.7, where sellers' strategies are formulated, we assume that seller i attempts to maximize surplus on each of his m_i units separately and in sequence.

currency (the input good) to produce each of the m_i units for which he has finite cost. Then characteristics of seller i are described by the vector $\mathbf{e^{s,i}} = (f_i, \omega_{s,i})$. In example 1 below, we carry out this construction for one seller in a market experiment.

Buyer $j \in J$ has a vector of unit valuations $v_j = (v_j^1, v_j^2, \ldots, v_j^{n_j})$, where v_j^1 is the redemption value for the first unit acquired, v_j^2 is the redemption value for the second, and so forth. Buyer j has an endowment $\bar{x}_{b,j}$ of trading currency that is sufficient to purchase each unit at a price up to the redemption value of the unit, i.e., $\bar{x}_{b,j} \geq \sum_{l=1}^{n_j} v_j^l$. Monetary rewards for buyers are the difference $\pi_{b,j}^{\,l}(p_l, v_j^l) = v_j^l - p_l$ between the redemption values of units purchased and the price p_l paid to a seller. If buyer j purchases $\nu_j \leq n_j$ units at prices $p_1, p_2, \ldots, p_{\nu_j}$ the monetary gain from trading for buyer j is $\sum_{l=1}^{\nu_j} (v_j^l - p_l)$, and the utility of this monetary gain is $U_{b,j}\left(\sum_{l=1}^{\nu_j} (v_j^l - p_l)\right)$, where $U_{b,j}(\cdot)$ is monotonically increasing.

For any vector of valuations v_j, Gjerstad and Shachat [6] show that there is a quasi-linear utility function $u_j(x, y) = x + v_j(y) - \bar{x}_j$ and an endowment $\omega_j = (\bar{x}_j, 0)$ such that the demand for good X by this buyer is v_j. The characteristics of buyer j are then $\mathbf{e^{b,j}} = (u_j, \omega_{b,j})$. In example 1, we carry out their construction for one buyer in a market experiment.

We describe the environment of an induced cost and valuation experiment by the collection

$$\mathbf{e} = \{(f_i, \omega_{s,i})\}_{i \in I} \cup \{(u_j, \omega_{b,j})\}_{j \in J}.$$

Example 1 Figure 2 shows supply and demand conditions for market trading experiment 3pda01 run in the experimental lab at the University of Arizona by Vernon Smith and Arlington Williams. In this market there are four buyers, each with positive valuations for three units, and four sellers, each with finite costs for three units. The vector of buyers' valuations is

$$\begin{aligned} v &= \{\{3.30, 2.25, 2.10\}, \{2.80, 2.35, 2.20\}, \\ &\quad \{2.60, 2.40, 2.15\}, \{3.05, 2.35, 2.30\}\}. \end{aligned}$$

The vector of sellers' costs is

$$\begin{aligned} c &= \{\{1.90, 2.35, 2.50\}, \{1.40, 2.45, 2.60\}, \\ &\quad \{2.10, 2.30, 2.55\}, \{1.65, 2.35, 2.40\}\}. \end{aligned}$$

Since buyer j with redemption value v_j^l makes a monetary gain at any purchase price $p < v_j^l$, and since buyers' preferences are assumed monotonically increasing in monetary gain, this buyer is willing to pay any price up to v_j^l for the lth unit purchased. Therefore, the demand shown in figure 2 is determined by arraying the buyers' redemption value vectors. Supply is obtained analogously.

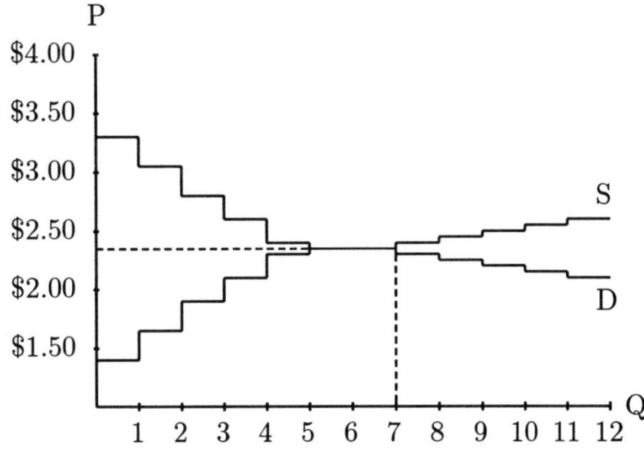

Figure 2: Supply and demand conditions for market experiment 3pda01.

The diagram on the left of figure 3 shows the production function $f_1(x)$ that is dual to the cost vector $c_1 = \{1.90, 2.35, 2.50\}$ for seller 1 in this market, where

$$f_1(x) = \begin{cases} x/1.90, & 0 \le x \le 1.90; \\ (x+0.45)/2.35, & 1.90 < x \le 4.25; \\ (x+0.75)/2.50, & 4.25 < x \le 6.75; \\ 3, & 6.75 < x. \end{cases} \tag{1}$$

We assume that seller 1 has an endowment $\omega_{s,1} = (\bar{x}_{s,1}, 0)$ where $\bar{x}_{s,1}$ is large enough to produce all three units. It is easy to verify that the supply of a cost minimizing producer with the production function f_1 will be 0 units if the price is below 1.90, 1 unit if the price is between 1.90 and 2.35, and so on, so the seller's vector of unit costs is dual to the production function in equation (1). The characteristics of seller 1 are then $\mathbf{e^1} = (f_1, \omega_{s,1})$.

The diagram on the right of figure 3 shows two indifference curves for buyer 1 whose vector of unit valuations is $v_1 = \{3.30, 2.25, 2.10\}$. For buyer 1, define the valuation function v_1 by

$$v_1(y) = \begin{cases} 3.30\,y, & 0 \le y \le 1; \\ 2.25\,y + 1.05, & 1 < y \le 2; \\ 2.10\,y + 1.35, & 2 < y \le 3; \\ 7.65, & 3 < y. \end{cases} \tag{2}$$

If we assume that buyer 1 has the endowment $\omega_{b,1} = (\bar{x}_{b,1}, 0) = (7.65, 0)$ and that the utility function of buyer 1 is $u_1(x, y) = x + v_1(y) - 7.65$, then the lower indifference curve in figure 3 corresponds to $u_1 = 0$ and the upper one to $u_1 = 1$.

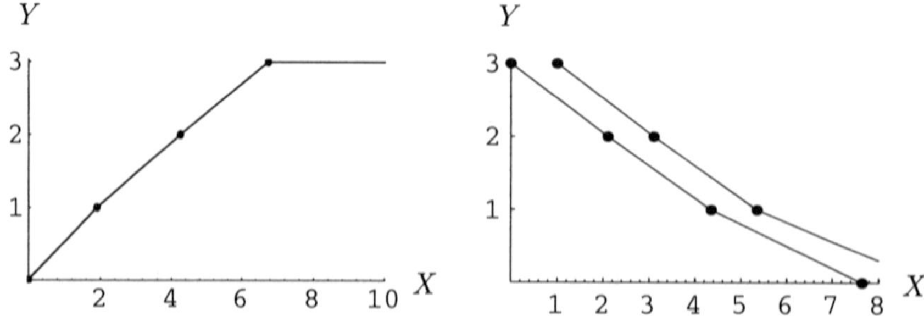

Figure 3: Production function (left) and indifference curves (right) corresponding to costs for seller 1 and values for buyer 1 in example 1.

If the production functions and endowments of the remaining 3 sellers and the utility functions and endowments of the other 3 buyer are constructed in this way, then the environment is $\mathbf{e} = \{(f_i, \omega_{s,i})\}_{i=1}^{4} \cup \{(u_j, \omega_{b,j})\}_{j=1}^{4}$. In what follows, we refer to this market as the symmetric market design.

Trading periods

A typical laboratory market experiment involves trading over several periods. Each seller has costs induced for the trading period, and each buyer has valuations induced. A buyer's valuation for a unit remains in effect throughout the trading period or until the buyer transacts that unit. After a unit is transacted, the seller's cost and the buyer's valuation for the unit just transacted are removed from the supply and demand schedules, trading continues, and this process proceeds until there are no more surplus enhancing trades remaining, or until time expires in the trading period. At the conclusion of a trading period, the costs and valuations are reinitialized – possibly at different amounts – in the subsequent period. In market experiment 3pda01 the supply and demand conditions in figure 2 were employed in each of nine trading periods, each lasting 300 seconds.

2.2 Institution

In the double auction sellers post ask prices, and buyers post bids. The message space defines the set of allowable messages for each agent. In this paper, we consider the double auction with a bid-ask spread reduction rule (defined below).

In effect, this produces restrictions on agents' messages as a function of some previous messages of other agents. In a microeconomic system, adjustment process rules specify the set of allowable messages for each trader, the time when exchange of messages begins, a transition rule governing the sequencing and exchange of messages, and a stopping rule. The DA imposes no restrictions on the sequencing of messages: any trader can send a message at any time during the trading period. Allocation of units is by mutual consent between any buyer and seller. If a seller's ask is acceptable to a buyer then a transaction is completed when the buyer takes (accepts) the seller's ask. Similarly, a buyer's bid may be accepted by a seller.

Definition 1 (Message space) Let $\tilde{N} = \{x : x = \frac{n}{100} \text{ for } n \in N\}$. Seller i at time t has a message space $M_t^{s,i}$ where $M_t^{s,i} \subset \{i\} \times \{0\} \times \tilde{N}$. Buyer j has a message space $M_t^{b,j}$ where $M_t^{b,j} \subset \{0\} \times \{j\} \times \tilde{N}$.

Definition 2 (Asks) An ask a by seller i is an amount which seller i is willing to accept from a buyer as payment for a unit of the commodity being traded. To submit an ask of a, seller i sends the message $(i,\ 0,\ a)$.

Definition 3 (Bids) A bid b by buyer j is an amount that buyer j is willing to pay to some seller for a unit. Buyer j submits this bid by sending the message $(0,\ j,\ b)$.

Definition 4 (Spread reduction rule) The lowest ask in the market at any time is called the outstanding ask and is denoted oa. At any time sellers may place an ask $a \in \tilde{N}$ with $a < oa$. The highest bid is called the outstanding bid ob, denoted ob. At any time, buyers may make a bid $b \in \tilde{N}$ above the outstanding bid. The outstanding ask oa and outstanding bid ob define the bid-ask spread $[ob, oa]$. In markets with a *spread reduction rule* all bids and asks must fall in the bid-ask spread.

Note that in a double auction with the bid-ask spread reduction rule, any ask that is permissible must be lower than the current outstanding ask, so each new ask either results in a trade or it becomes the new outstanding ask. A similar remark applies to bids.

Definition 5 (Acceptance) If seller i sends the message $(i,\ 0,\ a)$ and holds the outstanding ask $oa = a$, then a take of oa by buyer j is an agreement by j to purchase a unit from seller i at the transaction price $p = oa$. Buyer j accepts the outstanding ask oa by sending the message $(0,\ j,\ b)$ where $b \geq oa$. Similarly, if the outstanding bid ob is held by buyer j', then a take of ob by seller i' is an agreement by i' to sell a unit to buyer j' at the transaction price $p = ob$.

2.3 Observed history (Outcome)

Example 2 (Messages and histories) For the market of example 1, depicted in figure 2, if the first action in the period is an offer of 3.00

by seller 3 we indicate this with the message $m_1 = (3,\ 0,\ 3.00)$. Suppose that the next action is a bid of 3.00 by buyer 1, which we indicate with the message $m_2 = (0,\ 1,\ 3.00)$. At this point a trade is completed between seller 3 and buyer 1 at the price 3.00. We indicate the history of these two messages by the list

$$\begin{aligned} H_2 &= \{h_1, h_2\} \\ &= \{(3,\ 0,\ 3.00), (3,\ 1,\ 3.00)\}. \end{aligned}$$

Note that in H_2 the triple h_2 unambiguously denotes an accept by buyer 1 of the offer of 3.00 made with message 1 by seller 3, because seller 3 holds the outstanding offer of 3.00, which is the transaction price. (See 'Accept of oa' in definition 6.)

Definition 6 (Histories) After n messages have been sent, there is a history H_n of length n comprised of n ordered triples. For each message $m_{n+1} = (m_{n+1,1},\ m_{n+1,2},\ m_{n+1,3})$, one of six cases will hold.

Invalid ask or bid A message $m_{n+1} = (i, 0, a)$ is not valid if $a \geq oa$. An invalid ask will not be included in the history. In effect, the institution ignores messages that violate the spread reduction rule. Similarly, a message $m_{n+1} = (0, j, b)$ is not valid if $b \leq ob$.

No ask outstanding If no ask has been made since the last transaction, then there is no outstanding ask, and any ask $a \in \tilde{N}$ is valid. If in addition $m_{n+1,\,3} > ob$, then $h_{n+1} = m_{n+1}$.

No bid outstanding Similarly, if no bid has been made since the last transaction, then there is no outstanding bid, and any bid $b \in \tilde{N}$ is valid. If $m_{n+1,\,3} < oa$, then $h_{n+1} = m_{n+1}$.

Accept of *ob* If $m_{n+1,1} \neq 0$ and $m_{n+1,3} \leq ob$ then seller $m_{n+1,1}$ is making an offer at or below ob, so m_{n+1} is an accept of ob. The buyer's identity is found by looking back in H_n and finding the last h_k with $h_{k,2} \neq 0$, that is $k^* = max\{k : h_{k,\,2} \neq 0\}$. Then $(h_{n+1,1},\ h_{n+1,2},\ h_{n+1,3}) = (m_{n+1,1},\ h_{k^*,2},\ ob)$.

Accept of *oa* If $m_{n+1,2} \neq 0$ and $m_{n+1,3} \geq oa$ then m_{n+1} is an accept of oa (by buyer $m_{n+2,2}$). The seller's identity is found by looking back in H_n and finding $k^* = max\{k : h_{k,\,1} \neq 0\}$. Then $(h_{n+1,1},\ h_{n+1,2},\ h_{n+1,3}) = (h_{k^*,1},\ m_{n+1,2},\ oa)$.

Improving ask or bid If $m_{n+1,3} \in (ob, oa)$ then m_{n+1} is either an improving ask, or an improving bid, and $h_{n+1} = m_{n+1}$.

2.4 Behavior

2.4.1 Frequencies of takes

As noted in Section 2.1, sellers attempt to maximize $\pi^k_{s,i}(p_k,\ c^k_i)$ and buyers attempt to maximize $\pi^l_{b,j}(p_l,\ v^l_j)$. Since asks or bids must be accepted in order to result in a transaction, we take the point of view that sellers will maximize *expected* surplus myopically, where the expectation is taken relative to beliefs $p(a)$ that an ask a will be accepted by some buyer. These beliefs are formed on the basis of observed market data (as described in Section 2.4.2). Similarly, buyers are assumed to maximize expected surplus myopically, where the expectation is taken relative to beliefs $q(b)$ that a bid b will be accepted by some seller.

When traders form their belief, the history that they consider is restricted to those messages that lead up to the last L transactions, where $L \in \{0, 1, 2, \ldots\}$. The parameter L is the memory length of traders. Note that the number of messages remembered and the clock time elapsed within the traders' memory may vary, while the number of trades completed within the traders' memory does not vary (once L trades have occurred). The next definition provides a procedure for truncating the history, so that beliefs can be constructed using the data within the traders' memory. The procedure for constructing beliefs using this (truncated) history is described in Section 2.4.2.

Note 1 We will work with the vector H_n, although traders do not have access to all the information in H_n. Traders know their own asks or bids, but do not know the identity of the trader making other bids or asks. Information about identities is not used in the formation of beliefs or strategies, so use of H_n is made only to avoid complicating notation.

Definition 7 (Remembered history) Let $\mathcal{H}_n$ be the space of possible history vectors of length n. Given $H_n \in \mathcal{H}_n$, we make the following definitions.

Trade function For a vector H_n, define a function $T : \mathcal{H}_n \mapsto \{0,1\}^n$ by setting $T_k(H_n) = I_{\{h_{k,1} \cdot h_{k,2} > 0\}}(h_k)$. Then each component T_k of T indicates whether a trade occurred in the k–th element of the history.

Number of trades Let $x = (x_1, x_2, \ldots, x_n)$. For each n, define $S_n : \{0,1\}^n \mapsto N$ by $S_n(x) = \sum_{k=1}^{n} x_k$. Then $S_n(T(H_n))$ is the number of trades resulting from the first n messages.

Remembered history Let L be the memory length of a given trader. For fixed n and H_n, to simplify notation, let $S = S_n(T(H_n))$. Let n' be the position of trade $S - L$ if $S > L$, and let $n' = 0$ if $S \leq L$. Define $\tilde{H}_n^{(L)}$ by $\tilde{H}_n^{(L)} = \{h_{n'+1}, h_{n'+2}, ..., h_n\}$.

Deletion of *oa* and *ob* from history Let $n'' = \max\{k : T_k(h_k) = 1\}$, i.e., n'' is the index of the most recent trade. Let n^* be the index of the lowest (most recent) ask in the vector $\{h_{n''+1}, ..., h_n\}$. Let n_* be the index of the highest bid in the vector $\{h_{n''+1}, ..., h_n\}$. Note that if $T_n(h_n) = 0$, then $h_{n,3}$ is either the outstanding ask or the outstanding bid, as a consequence of the spread reduction rule, and if $T_n(h_n) = 1$ then there is no outstanding bid and no outstanding ask. If $T_n(h_n) = 0$ and $h_{n,1} = 0$, then $h_{n,3}$ is the outstanding bid. If $h_{k,1} \neq 0$ for some $k \in \{n'' + 1, \ldots, n - 1\}$, then $n^* \neq \emptyset$ and we define $H_n^{(L)}$ by $H_n^{(L)} \equiv \{h_{n'+1}, h_{n'+2}, \ldots, h_{n^*-1}, h_{n^*+1}, \ldots, h_{n-1}\}$. That is, $H_n^{(L)}$ is $\tilde{H}_n^{(L)}$ with

h_{n^*} and h_{n_*} removed. This is done because it is not known at time n if the outstanding ask or bid will be accepted. The other case – where $h_{n,3}$ is the outstanding ask – is treated similarly. Then $H_n^{(L)}$ is the history remembered by traders with memory length L who observe the history H_n.

Set of asks and bids Let $D_n^{(L)}$ be the set of all asks and bids that have been made in $H_n^{(L)}$, i.e., $D_n^{(L)} \equiv \bigcup_{k \in \{n'+1,\ldots,n\} \setminus \{n_*,n^*\}} \{h_{k,3}\}$.

Definition 8 (Ask frequencies) For each $d \in D_n^{(L)}$, let $A(d)$ be the total number of asks that have been made at d, and let $TA(d)$ be the total number of these that have been accepted. Let $RA(d) \equiv A(d) - TA(d)$ be the rejected asks at d.

For $A(d)$, the counting procedure is as follows. For each $k \in \{n'+1, ..., n\} \setminus \{n_*, n^*\}$, if $h_{k,3} = d$, $h_{k,1} \neq 0$ and $h_{k,2} = 0$, then $A(d)$ is incremented by one. If $h_{k,3} = d$ and $T_k(h_k) = 1$, then h_k is either a taken ask or a taken bid. To determine which is the case, find $m^* = \min\{m \geq 1 : h_{k-m,3} = h_{k,3}\}$. If $h_{k-m^*,1} \neq 0$, then $A(d)$ and $TA(d)$ are incremented by one. The rejected asks at d are given by $RA(d) \equiv A(d) - TA(d)$.

Definition 9 (Bid frequencies) For each $d \in D_n^{(L)}$, let $B(d)$ be the total number of bids that have been made at d, and let $TB(d)$ be the total number of these that have been accepted. Let $RB(d) \equiv B(d) - TB(d)$. The interpretations and counting procedures for $B(d)$, $TB(d)$, and $RB(d)$ are analogous to those described in definition 8 for asks.

At each time during a market, the proportion of asks at $a \in D$ that have been accepted is

$$\check{p}(a) = \frac{TA(a)}{A(a)}$$

whenever $A(a) > 0$. The proportion of bids at $b \in D$ that have been accepted is

$$\check{q}(b) = \frac{TB(b)}{B(b)}$$

whenever $B(b) > 0$.

In stationary market environments these empirical frequencies show substantial regularity: $\check{p}(a)$ tends to be a decreasing function of a and $\check{q}(b)$ tends to be an increasing function of b.

Note 2 In what follows, the sets of asks and bids is frequently denoted D, with the subscripts and superscripts omitted. When traders have finite memory, that will be noted. After n messages have been sent, the relevant set of asks and bids is $D_n^{(L)}$ and the relevant history is $H_n^{(L)}$.

2.4.2 Beliefs

While the frequencies $\check{p}(a)$ and $\check{q}(b)$ tend to be monotonic when the number of asks and bids is large, there is more variability in small samples. For this reason, it is useful to work with a modification of these summary statistics.

Modification of $\check{p}(a)$ is made by taking the point of view that if an ask $a' < a$ is rejected then had that ask been made at a it would also have been rejected. This assumption is made because $a > a'$ and is therefore less appealing to buyers than a', which was rejected. Similarly, if ask $a' > a$ was made and taken, then that ask would also have been taken if it were made at a. Also, if a bid $b' > a$ is made, then an ask $a' = b'$ would have been taken if it had been made (the assumption being that this ask of a' would be acceptable to the buyer who bid b'). This heuristic – and an analogous one for buyers' beliefs – are formalized in the next two definitions.

Definition 10 (Sellers' beliefs) For each potential ask $a \in D$, define

$$\hat{p}(a) = \frac{\sum_{d \geq a} TA(d) + \sum_{d \geq a} B(d)}{\sum_{d \geq a} TA(d) + \sum_{d \geq a} B(d) + \sum_{d \leq a} RA(d)}. \tag{3}$$

Then $\hat{p}(a)$ is the seller's belief that an ask amount a will be acceptable to some buyer. We assume that sellers always believe that an ask at $a = 0.00$ will be accepted with certainty, and that there is some value $M > 0$ such that $\hat{p}(M) = 0$.

The notation of equation (3) is simplified by the following definitions. Let $TAG(a) = \sum_{d \geq a} TA(d)$, $BG(a) = \sum_{d \geq a} B(d)$, and $RAL(a) = \sum_{d \leq a} RA(d)$. These are the taken asks greater than or equal to a, the bids greater than or equal to a, and the rejected asks less than or equal to a, respectively. Then equation (3) may be rewritten as

$$\hat{p}(a) = \frac{TAG(a) + BG(a)}{TAG(a) + BG(a) + RAL(a)}. \tag{4}$$

Definition 11 (Buyers' beliefs) For each possible bid $b \in D$, define

$$\hat{q}(b) = \frac{\sum_{d \leq b} TB(d) + \sum_{d \leq b} A(d)}{\sum_{d \leq b} TB(d) + \sum_{d \leq b} A(d) + \sum_{d \geq b} RB(d)}. \tag{5}$$

We assume that buyers always believe that $\hat{q}(0.00) = 0$ and that there is some value $M > 0$ such that $\hat{q}(M) = 1$.

As in definition 10, to simplify notation in equation (5) we introduce functions $TBL(b) = \sum_{d \leq b} TB(d)$, $AL(b) = \sum_{d \leq b} A(d)$, and $RBG(b) = \sum_{d \geq b} RB(d)$. These are the taken bids less than or equal to b, the asks less than or equal to b, and the rejected bids greater than or equal to b. Then

$$\hat{q}(b) = \frac{TBL(b) + AL(b)}{TBL(b) + AL(b) + RBG(b)}. \tag{6}$$

With the specification of seller's beliefs in definition 10, the belief function $\hat{p}(a)$ is a monotonically decreasing function of a (proposition 1). The argument of $p(\cdot)$ is the price that the seller asks, and the value of $p(\cdot)$ at a represents the seller's assessment of the probability (belief) that an offer at a will be accepted by some buyer. It is reasonable to expect that seller's beliefs are monotonic: this captures the intuition that a trader who has seen an ask of a rejected should decrease the belief that a will be accepted later, and decrease the belief that an ask at any value greater than a will be accepted. The buyers' belief function has an analogous property: $\hat{q}(b)$ is a monotonically increasing function of the bid b.

2.4.3 Spread reduction rule and beliefs

The spread reduction rule has the effect of making the probability of a take for an ask $a \geq oa$ equal to 0 (where oa is the outstanding offer from definition 4). We denote this modification of $\hat{p}(a)$ by $\tilde{p}(a)$, where $\tilde{p}(a) = \hat{p}(a)$ if $a < oa$, and $\tilde{p}(a) = 0$ if $a \geq oa$. Similarly, $\tilde{q}(b) = 0$ for all b with $b \leq ob$. These facts are incorporated into traders' beliefs in the following definition.

Definition 12 Let $\tilde{p}(a) = \hat{p}(a) \cdot I_{[0,oa)}(a)$ for each $a \in D$. That is $\tilde{p}(a) = \hat{p}(a)$ if $a < oa$ and $\hat{p}(a) = 0$ if $a \geq oa$. For all $b \in D$, let $\tilde{q}(b) = \hat{q}(b) \cdot I_{(ob,M]}(b)$.

2.4.4 Cubic spline interpolation

The belief functions in definition 12 are defined on the set D of all offers and bids within the trader's memory. These beliefs are extended to the positive reals using cubic spline interpolation. For each successive pair of data points $(a_k, \tilde{p}(a_k))$ and $(a_{k+1}, \tilde{p}(a_{k+1}))$, we construct a cubic equation $p(a) = \alpha_3\, a^3 + \alpha_2\, a^2 + \alpha_1\, a + \alpha_0$ passing through these two points with the following four properties:

1. $p(a_k) = \tilde{p}(a_k)$;
2. $p(a_{k+1}) = \tilde{p}(a_{k+1})$;
3. $p'(a_k) = 0$;
4. $p'(a_{k+1}) = 0$.

These four conditions generate the four equations represented in matrix equation (7) below. The coefficients α_j are obtained as the solution to the equation

$$\begin{bmatrix} a_k^3 & a_k^2 & a_k & 1 \\ a_{k+1}^3 & a_{k+1}^2 & a_{k+1} & 1 \\ 3\,a_k^2 & 2\,a_k & 1 & 0 \\ 3\,a_{k+1}^2 & 2\,a_{k+1} & 1 & 0 \end{bmatrix} \begin{bmatrix} \alpha_3 \\ \alpha_2 \\ \alpha_1 \\ \alpha_0 \end{bmatrix} = \begin{bmatrix} \tilde{p}(a_k) \\ \tilde{p}(a_{k+1}) \\ 0 \\ 0 \end{bmatrix}. \tag{7}$$

The function $q(b)$ is defined similarly from $(b_k, \tilde{q}(b_k))$ and $(b_{k+1}, \tilde{q}(b_{k+1}))$.

2.4.5 Monotonicity of beliefs

The function $\hat{p}(a)$ defined in Section 2.4.2 is monotonically non-increasing. That is, as the ask a is increased, $\hat{p}(a)$ – the belief that an ask a will be accepted – is non-increasing in a. Similarly, $\hat{q}(b)$ is non-decreasing in b: buyers believe higher bids are more likely to be accepted. These results are proven in propositions 1 and 2. This monotonicity property is extended successively to $\tilde{p}(a)$, $\tilde{q}(b)$, $p(a)$, and $q(b)$ in propositions 3 – 6.

Proposition 1 For all $a_1 \in D$, $a_2 \in D$, with $a_1 < a_2$, $\hat{p}(a_1) \geq \hat{p}(a_2)$.

Proof Let $G(a) = TAG(a) + BG(a)$. Note that $G(a_2) \leq G(a_1)$ and $RAL(a_1) \leq RAL(a_2)$ because $a_1 < a_2$. Multiplying these two inequalities results in

$$G(a_2)\,RAL(a_1) \leq G(a_1)\,RAL(a_2). \tag{8}$$

Now add $G(a_2)\,G(a_1)$ to both sides of inequality (8) and from this sum factor out $G(a_2)$ from the left side of the equation and factor $G(a_1)$ out of the right side, then divide both sides of the resulting inequality by $[G(a_1) + RAL(a_1)]\,[G(a_2) + RAL(a_2)]$ to get $\hat{p}(a_1) \geq \hat{p}(a_2)$. ■

Proposition 2 For all $b_1 \in D$, $b_2 \in D$, with $b_1 < b_2$, $\hat{q}(b_1) \leq \hat{q}(b_2)$.

Proof The proof is similar to the proof of proposition 1. ■

Proposition 3 The functions $\tilde{p}(a)$ is non-increasing.

Proof Since $\tilde{p}(a) = \hat{p}(a)\,I_{[0,oa)}(a)$, and since $\hat{p}(a)$ is non-increasing, $\tilde{p}(a)$ is also non-increasing. ■

Proposition 4 The functions $\tilde{q}(b)$ is non-decreasing.

Proof The proof is similar to the proof of proposition 3. ■

Proposition 5 Let $a_1 \in D$ and $a_2 \in D$, with $a_1 < a_2$. Then $p(a)$ is non-increasing on (a_1, a_2).

Proof The belief function $p(a)$ is given by $p(a) = \alpha_3\,a^3 + \alpha_2\,a^2 + \alpha_1\,a + \alpha_0$ on the interval (a_1, a_2), where the coefficients α_j are given by the solution to equation (7). The slope of $p(a)$ on this interval is

$$p'(a) = 3\,\alpha_3\,a^2 + 2\,\alpha_2\,a + \alpha_1. \tag{9}$$

The coefficients α_3, α_2, and α_1 can be obtained from equation (7) by Cramer's rule. Substitution of these values into equation (9) results in

$$p'(a) = \frac{6\,(a_2 - a_1)\,(p(a_1) - p(a_2))}{(a_2 - a_1)^4}\,(a - a_1)\,(a - a_2).$$

Note that $a_2 - a_1$, $p(a_1) - p(a_2)$, and $(a_2 - a_1)^4$ are all non-negative. Since $a - a_1 > 0$ and $a - a_2 < 0$ on (a_1, a_2), it follows that $p(a)$ is non-increasing on (a_1, a_2). ■

Proposition 6 The belief function $q(b)$ is non-decreasing.

Proof The proof is similar to the proof of proposition 5. ■

2.4.6 Monotonicity of optimal ask in cost and optimal bid in valuation

The expected surplus maximizing ask is monotonically increasing in the cost parameter c. The following example illustrates this idea, and the proposition following the example proves this property.

Example 3 Assume the beliefs of a take given ask a are:

$$p(a) = \begin{cases} 1.0, & a = 10, \\ 0.8, & a = 11, \\ 0.6, & a = 12, \\ 0.3, & a = 13. \end{cases}$$

If sellers in a DA market have costs c = 5, c = 6, ..., c = 11, there will be expected surplus functions for each of these sellers as shown in table 1. In table 1, the expected surplus maximizing asks are underlined and exhibit the non-decreasing property of the optimal ask as cost increases, for fixed beliefs $p(a)$.

Table 1. Expected surpluses for traders with beliefs in example 3.

		Cost						
		5	6	7	8	9	10	11
	10	5.0	4.0	3.0	2.0	1.0	0.0	—
Ask	11	4.8	4.0	3.2	2.4	1.6	0.8	0.0
	12	4.2	3.6	3.0	2.4	1.8	1.2	0.6
	13	2.4	2.1	1.8	1.5	1.2	0.9	0.6

The following proposition shows that the optimal ask for a seller when beliefs are $p(a)$ is non-decreasing in the cost parameter. An analogous result is stated for the relation between buyers' valuations and their optimal bids.

Proposition 7 Let c_1 and c_2 be cost parameters with $c_1 < c_2$, and let the ask values $\{a_1^1, a_1^2, \ldots, a_1^m\}$, $\{a_2^1, a_2^2, \ldots, a_2^n\}$ be the sets of maximizers of $\pi(p,\, c_1)$ and $\pi(p,\, c_2)$, respectively. Let

$$a_1 = \max\{a_1^1, a_1^2, \ldots, a_1^m\}$$

and let

$$a_2 = \min\{a_2^1, a_2^2, \ldots, a_2^n\}.$$

Then $a_1 \leq a_2$.

Proof Assume $a_2 > a_1$. Notice that for each a_1^i that is a maximizer of $\pi(p, c_1)$,

$$p_1(a_1^i) = \frac{(a_1 - c_1) \cdot p(a_1)}{a_1^i - c_1}.$$

Similarly, for each a_2^i that maximizes $\pi(p, c_2)$,

$$p_2(a_2^i) = \frac{(a_2 - c_2) \cdot p(a_2)}{a_2^i - c_2}.$$

Extend the functions p_1 and p_2 to functions f_1 and f_2 on the sets (c_1, ∞) and (c_2, ∞) by writing

$$f_1(a) = \frac{(a_1 - c_1) \cdot p(a_1)}{a - c_1}$$

and

$$f_2(a) = \frac{(a_2 - c_2) \cdot p(a_2)}{a - c_2}.$$

Note that f_1 and f_2 are branches of hyperbolas on their respective domains. Define the point α implicitly by setting $f_1(\alpha) = f_2(\alpha)$. It is easy to see that α exists and $\alpha \in (c_2, \infty)$. Solving the equation $f_1(\alpha) = f_2(\alpha)$ for α results in

$$\alpha = c_2 + \frac{(c_2 - c_1)(a_2 - c_2)\, p(a_2)}{(a_1 - c_1)\, p(a_1) - (a_2 - c_2)\, p(a_2)}.$$

The denominator of the second term on the right is positive since $(a_1 - c_1)\, p(a_1)$ is the maximum expected surplus for a trader with cost c_1 and $(a_2 - c_2)\, p(a_2)$ is the maximum for a trader with cost c_2, where $c_2 > c_1$. The numerator is positive also, so $\alpha \in (c_2, \infty)$. (Of course, this depends on the traders each having some ask with positive expected surplus, but this is the only case of interest.)

Either $a_2 < \alpha$ or $a_2 \geq \alpha$. In the case of $a_2 < \alpha$ it will be shown that

$$(a_2 - c_1)\, p(a_2) > (a_1 - c_1)\, p(a_1).$$

Since a_1 is the largest maximizer of $\pi(p, c_1)$, and since we have assumed that $a_2 > a_1$, a_2 may not be a maximizer of $\pi(p, c_1)$. This establishes the contradiction.

For all $a \in (c_2, \alpha)$,

$$\frac{(a_2 - c_2)\, p(a_2)}{(a - c_2)} > \frac{(a_1 - c_1)\, p(a_1)}{(a - c_1)}.$$

This holds in particular for $a = a_2$:

$$\frac{(a_2 - c_2)\, p(a_2)}{(a_2 - c_2)} > \frac{(a_1 - c_1)\, p(a_1)}{(a_2 - c_1)}$$

or

$$p(a_2) > \frac{(a_1 - c_1)\,p(a_1)}{(a_2 - c_1)}.$$

Now multiply each side in the above inequality by $(a_2 - c_1)$ to get

$$(a_2 - c_1)\,p(a_2) > (a_1 - c_1)\,p(a_1).$$

This contradicts the fact that a_1 is expected surplus maximizing for a seller with cost c_1, so $a_2 \geq \alpha$.

A similar argument shows that $a_1 \leq \alpha$.

Combining these two inequalities gives the desired result:

$$a_1 \leq \alpha \leq a_2. \blacksquare$$

Proposition 8 Let v_1 and v_2 be valuations with $v_1 < v_2$. Suppose that the bid values $\{b_1^1, b_1^2, \ldots, b_1^m\}$ is the set of maximizers of $\pi(p,\, v_1)$ and let $\{b_2^1, b_2^2, \ldots, b_2^n\}$ be the set of maximizers of $\pi(p,\, v_2)$. Let

$$b_1 = \max\{b_1^1, b_1^2, \ldots, b_1^m\}$$

and let

$$b_2 = \min\{a_2^1, b_2^2, \ldots, b_2^n\}.$$

Then $b_1 \leq b_2$.

Proof The proof is similar to the proof of the previous proposition. ■

2.4.7 Expected surplus maximization

When attempting to sell his k^{th} unit, seller i with cost $c_i^k < oa$ may make an offer $a \in [0,\, oa)$ which results in expected surplus $E[\pi_{s,i}^{\;k}(a,\, c_i^k)] = (a - c_i^k) \cdot p(a)$. The maximum expected surplus of seller i for the sale of this unit[2] is

$$S_{s,i}^{\;k} = \max\{ \max_{a \in (ob,\, oa)} E[\pi_{s,i}^{\;k}(a,\, c_i^k)], 0\}. \tag{10}$$

Similarly, if buyer j with valuation v_j^l for her l^{th} unit bids $b \in (ob,\, \infty)$, this results in expected surplus $E[\pi_{b,j}^{\;l}(b,\, v_j^l)] = (v_j^l - b) \cdot q(b)$. The maximum expected surplus on this unit for buyer j is

$$S_{b,j}^{\;l} = \max\{ \max_{a \in (ob,\, oa)} E[\pi_{b,j}^{\;l}(b,\, v_j^l)], 0\}. \tag{11}$$

[2]Seller i with cost vector $c_i = \{c_i^1,\, c_i^2,\, \ldots,\, c_i^{m_i}\}$ faces the problem of choosing a sequence of asks or accepts to maximize $\sum_{k=1}^{m_i}(p_i^k - c_i^k)$, where p_i^k is the purchase price received for unit k. We assume that the seller will attempt to maximize the surplus of each unit in sequence, independently of other units. In addition to simplifying the strategy choice, this is consistent with the myopic formulation of strategy choice. A similar remark applies to buyers.

2.4.8 Timing of messages

Let t be the parameter for time within a trading period. Let T be the length of the trading period and let $t_\kappa \in [0, T)$ be the time of of the κth offer, bid, or acceptance of an offer or bid. At time t_κ let $T^\kappa_{s,i}$ be the random variable that specifies the time which seller i would allow to elapse before sending a message; let $T^\kappa_{b,j}$ be the random variable that specifies the time which buyer j would allow to elapse before sending a message.

We assume that $T^\kappa_{s,i}$ is exponentially distributed, and that the parameter $\alpha_{s,i}$ in the distribution of $T^\kappa_{s,i}$ depends only on the maximum expected surplus $S^k_{s,i}$ of seller i (from equation (10)) of seller i, on the length T of the trading period, and on t_κ, the time elapsed in the trading period. We write this dependence as $\alpha_{s,i} = f_{s,i}(S^{\,k}_{s,i}; t_\kappa, T)$. Similarly for buyers $\beta_{b,j} = f_{b,j}(S^{\,l}_{b,j}; t_\kappa, T)$. Then the probability that seller i' will be the next trader to send a message in the market is

$$\begin{aligned} p_{s,i'} &= \frac{f_{s,i'}(S^{\,k}_{s,i'}; t_\kappa, T)}{\sum_{i\in I} f_{s,i}(S^{\,k}_{s,i}; t_\kappa, T) + \sum_{j\in J} f_{b,j}(S^{\,l}_{b,j}; t_\kappa, T)} \\ &= \frac{\alpha_{s,i'}}{\sum_{i\in I}\alpha_{s,i} + \sum_{j\in J}\beta_{b,j}}. \end{aligned} \tag{12}$$

Equation (12) indicates that the probability that seller i' is the next to send a message is equal to the parameter $\alpha_{s,i'}$ of seller i' divided by the sum of the parameters of all agents. This is shown in the following proposition.

Proposition 9 If $T^\kappa_{s,i}$ and $T^\kappa_{b,j}$ are independent exponentially distributed random variables on $[0, \infty)$ with parameters $\alpha_{s,i} = f_{s,i}(S^{\,k}_{s,i}; t_\kappa, T)$ and $\beta_{b,j} = f_{b,j}(S^{\,l}_{b,j}; t_\kappa, T)$, i.e.,

$$Pr\{T_{s,i} < t\} = 1 - e^{-\alpha_{s,i}\cdot t},$$

then the probability that seller i' will be the next trader to send a message is $p_{s,i'}$, where $p_{s,i'}$ is given by equation (12).

Proof Consider, for example, seller 1. Let

$$T_{s,-1} = \min_{i>1, j\geq 1}\{T_{s,i}, T_{b,j}\}.$$

This random variable is exponentially distributed with parameter

$$\alpha_{s,-1} = \sum_{i>1}\alpha_{s,i} + \sum_{j\geq 1}\beta_{b,j}.$$

Then the probability that seller 1 is the next seller to move will be the probability that $T_{s,1} < T_{s,-1}$, i.e.,

$$\begin{aligned} p_{s,1} &= Pr\{T_{s,1} < T_{s,-1}\} \\ &= \int_0^\infty \int_0^u \alpha_{s,1}\cdot e^{-\alpha_{s,1}\cdot t}\cdot \alpha_{s,-1}\cdot e^{-\alpha_{s,-1}\cdot u}\, dt\, du \\ &= \frac{\alpha_{s,1}}{\alpha_{s,1} + \alpha_{s,-1}}. \end{aligned} \tag{13}$$

After substitution of the definitions of $\alpha_{s,1}$ and $\alpha_{s,-1}$, the expression in equation (13) is the same as equation (12) for $i' = 1$. ■

There are two reasons for defining the timing of each trader's message as an exponential random variable. The first is an important conceptual issue: with this formulation, the mechanism is informationally decentralized, in that the information about each trader's surplus is not held by any agent. Each trader's timing decision is independent of any (unobserved) characteristics – such as costs or valuations – of other traders. The second issue is empirical. With this formulation, the timing of bids and asks is testable within the model, and it is possible to compare the timing data for various specifications of the functions $f_{s,i}(S^k_{s,i}; t_\kappa, T)$ and $f_{b,j}(S^l_{b,j}; t_k, T)$ with timing data from experiments. It should be noted that the arguments of $f_{s,i}(\cdot)$ may be any data observed by or known to seller i. In the formulation above, the surplus $S^k_{s,i}$ is a summary statistic derived from the information privately held by and publicly observed by seller i.

The specifications of $f_{s,i}(S^k_{s,i}; t_\kappa, T)$ and $f_{b,j}(S^l_{b,j}; t_\kappa, T)$ used in the simulations reported in Section 3 are

$$f_{s,i}(S^k_{s,i}; t_\kappa, T) = S^k_{s,i} \cdot \frac{T}{(T - a\, t_\kappa)} \tag{14}$$

and

$$f_{b,j}(S^l_{b,j}; t_\kappa, T) = S^l_{b,j} \cdot \frac{T}{(T - a\, t_\kappa)} \tag{15}$$

where $a \in (0,\, 1)$.

This specification has been chosen to reflect two empirical observations about timing of bids and offers in experimental markets. There is strong positive rank-order correlation between buyers' valuations and the order that buyers purchase units, and strong negative rank-order correlation between sellers' costs and the order that units are sold. In the formulation above, buyers with high valuations will have higher maximum expected surplus, and will therefore have a larger parameter $\beta_{b,j}$ for the timing decision. Since the expected time until buyer j sends a message is proportional to the reciprocal of $\beta_{b,j}$, buyers with high valuations will tend to send messages more frequently and will trade earlier. Similarly, sellers with low cost will trade earlier. The second observation is that trading activity is typically concentrated at the beginning of the trading period, when many high surplus units are traded, and toward the end of the period. The term $\frac{T}{(T - a\, t_\kappa)}$ in equations (14) and (15) is consistent with these observations, since high surplus units will trade earlier, but as $t_\kappa \to T$, this term approaches $\frac{1}{(1-a)}$ and low surplus units will be traded toward the close of each period if a is near 1.

Though the model is formulated so that timing data can be obtained and examined, we have followed the reduced form in equation (12) in simulations and generated messages without the time stamp.

Example 4 (Beliefs, surplus, and timing) Consider again the market of example 1. In example 2 we discuss the first two messages sent in experiment 3pda01, which result in the history $H_2 = \{(3,\, 0,\, 3.00), (3,\, 1,\, 3.00)\}$.

The set of bids and offers D where the beliefs $\hat{p}(a)$ and $\hat{q}(b)$ are calculated is $D = \{3.00\} \cup \{0.00, 10.00\}$. The values of $\hat{p}(a)$ at these three points are $\hat{p}(0.00) = 1.0$, $\hat{p}(3.00) = 1.0$, and $\hat{p}(10.00) = 0.0$. The values of $\hat{q}(b)$ at these 3 points are $\hat{q}(0.00) = 0.0$, $\hat{q}(3.00) = 1.0$, and $\hat{q}(10.00) = 1.0$. Since there is no outstanding ask or bid, the spread reduction rule has no effect, so $\tilde{p}(a) = \hat{p}(a)$ for all $a \in D$ and $\tilde{q}(b) = \hat{q}(b)$ for all $b \in D$. Finally, the belief functions $p(a)$ and $q(b)$, shown in figure 4, are

$$p(a) = \begin{cases} 1, & 0 \leq b \leq 3.00; \\ \frac{1}{343}\left(100 + 180x - 39x^2 + 2x^3\right), & 3.00 \leq b \leq 10.00; \\ 0, & 10.00 \leq b, \end{cases} \tag{16}$$

and

$$q(b) = \begin{cases} \frac{1}{27}\, x^2\,(3 - 2\,x), & 0.00 \leq b \leq 3.00; \\ 1, & b > 3.00. \end{cases} \tag{17}$$

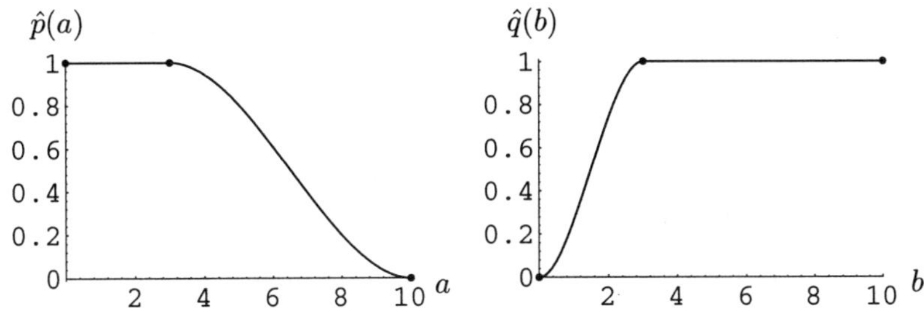

Figure 4: Sellers' beliefs (left) and buyers' beliefs (right) after trade in example 3.

After the trade between seller 3 and buyer 1 in this example the lowest cost units of sellers 1 – 4 are 1.90, 1.40, 2.30, and 1.65, respectively. The highest unit values for buyers 1 – 4 are 2.25, 2.80, 2.60, and 3.05. The expected surplus maximizing bids and offers and the maximum expected surplus for each agent is easily determined from these values and costs and the belief functions in equations (16) and (17). The values of the maximum expected surplus for buyers 1 – 4 are 0.38, 0.66, 0.55, and 0.81. For sellers 1 – 4, the values of maximum expected surplus are 2.55, 2.91, 2.27, and 2.73. As a result, given the formulation of the timing of messages in equations (14) and (15), in our model an offer will be more than 4 times as likely as a bid with this history. Even if the next message is an offer, the expected surplus of sellers will continue to be greater than expected surplus for buyers, and there is high probability of a series of decreasing offers. As a result, the next transaction price is likely to move toward the market equilibrium of 2.35.

3 Simulations

While the formation of traders' beliefs, their choices of strategies, and the timing of messages are simple and intuitive, the dynamics of the model are complex due to the non-stationarity of beliefs and the probability distribution over the timing of agents' messages. As a result, analytic characterization of properties of the model are difficult to obtain. For this reason, much of the evidence presented on performance of the model is from simulations. It may be possible to obtain analytic results on asymptotic convergence of prices to an approximate equilibrium, but asymptotic convergence alone does not provide information about the path. For the important question of the path of convergence to equilibrium, simulations are a useful tool for investigating properties of this model.

3.1 Criteria

The primary objective of this section is to demonstrate that prices and allocations in our model converge to the competitive equilibrium price and allocation. To identify the effect on convergence to competitive equilibrium of the belief formation and strategy choice defined in Section 2.4, we compare the outcomes of simulations of our model to the "Zero-intelligence trader" (ZI) model of Gode and Sunder [7], which has no belief formation or learning. [3] By convergence of the sequence of prices we mean that for some $n_0 \geq 1$, each element of the sequence $(p_n)_{n=n_0}^{N}$ of transaction prices is "close to" p_e, the competitive equilibrium price. This condition is met if the mean absolute deviation of transaction price from equilibrium price is small, so we measure convergence using this statistic. Of course, convergence to competitive equilibrium implies convergence to a Pareto optimum, so we also test this weaker condition. With efficiency measured as the ratio of surplus extracted by agents to total surplus possible, we find that in simulation of the model, market allocations are nearly efficient (over 99.9% of possible surplus is extracted after several periods of trading), and prices are close to competitive equilibrium prices. Note that while we do not examine the market allocation directly, the outcome is a competitive equilibrium if and only if the transaction prices are the competitive equilibrium price *and* the allocation is Pareto optimal, and we do establish that these two conditions hold (approximately) in simulations of our model.

3.2 Environments

Throughout this section, we consider a market design with four sellers each with finite unit costs for 3 units, and four buyers, each with positive unit valuations for 3 units. The unit costs and valuations for the design we consider are given in example 1 of Section 2.1 and are depicted in figure 2 (and also on the left

[3] In this model, sellers make offers which are random and uniformly distributed on the interval $[c, M]$, where c is the seller's cost, and M is some upper bound on their set of possible choices. Buyers make bids that are uniformly distributed on $[0, v]$, where v is the buyer's valuation.

column of figure 5). We report statistics from seven laboratory market experiments reported initially in Ketcham, Smith, and Williams [10] and statistics from 100 simulations of our model with the same environment parameters. Finally, in order to demonstrate that our model is capable of responding to shifts in market conditions, we show the results of a simulation in which the market design described above is employed through 5 periods of trading, and then for the remaining five periods of the simulation, each unit cost and unit valuation is increased to amounts 0.50 above those employed in periods 1 – 5.

3.3 Evaluation

The only free parameter in the model is the memory length of traders. We report simulations with memory length $L = 5$. For short memory lengths $(L \leq 3)$ the outcomes are unstable. For long memory lengths $(L \geq 8)$ the outcomes are similar to those with intermediate memory lengths $(4 \leq L \leq 7)$, but computation time increases significantly. It should also be noted that beliefs change more slowly in markets with shifts in supply and demand if memory length is long, so traders with intermediate and short memory length will adapt to changes in market conditions more quickly.

Efficiency The sum of consumers' and producers' surplus provides a convenient measure of efficiency for these markets. We evaluate the surplus obtained by traders in the market divided by the maximum surplus available to determine the efficiency of trade. Table 2 summarizes efficiency statistics from the seven lab markets, from 100 simulations of our model, and from 100 simulations of the ZI model. This table shows that our model attains higher efficiency than both the laboratory experiments and the ZI model simulations.

Table 2. Efficiency statistics from simulations of models and from lab data.

Periods evaluated	Symmetric Markets	Model Simulations	ZI Model Simulations
First two periods	0.907	0.9982	0.968
Entire experiment	0.959	0.9991	0.968
Last two periods	0.970	0.9992	0.967

Convergence The diagrams in the left column of figure 5 show graphs of the supply and demand conditions for the symmetric market 3pda01. On the right side of that figure in the top row is a graph of the sequence of transaction price through the 9 periods of trading in this laboratory market. In that figure, the equilibrium price is shown as a solid line across the diagram. Prices from each of the nine trading periods are separated by a vertical line, and the number of transactions in each period is indicated at the bottom of the diagram below the vertical line that indicates the end of the trading period. A simulation of our model under the same supply and demand conditions is shown on the right side of figure 5 in the center row. Price sequences from lab experiments with this design (as in the top of figure 5) and from simulations with this market design (as in the center row of figure 5) both converge quickly to prices near the competitive equilibrium price and an equilibrium quantity of trade typically occurs in each period.

The belief functions $p(a)$ and $q(b)$ shown in figure 6 are produced using data from the the end of the second period of the simulation of figure 5 using definitions 10 and 11 of Section 2.4.2. In this graph, a seller's belief that ask a will be accepted by a buyer is shown for each ask from 2.32 to 2.38; buyers' beliefs are shown for bids from 2.30 to 2.36.[4] These belief functions are monotonic (see propositions 5 and 6), so the value of the sellers' belief is $p(a) = 1$ for all $a < 2.33$ and it is 0 for all $a > 2.38$. With this belief function, and with myopic surplus maximization, the optimal ask is approximately 2.33 for any seller with unit cost below 2.30. The buyers' belief functions in this case have a similar property: the optimal bid for a buyer with valuation of 2.40 or greater is 2.35. At the beginning of each period, the sellers' costs are 1.90, 1.40, 2.10, and 1.65 and the buyers' valuations are 3.30, 2.80, 2.60, and 3.05 so the the first action at the beginning of the third period will be either an ask of 2.33 or a bid at 2.35. We see in the center row of figure 5 that the first transaction price is 2.35 in period 3 of this simulation: the belief functions and strategy choice described frequently produce transactions at equilibrium, even from the beginning of the trading period.

The figures on the bottom row of figure 5 shows a simulation of the ZI model in the symmetric market environment. While the ZI traders attain high efficiency in this market design, that model does not result in the formation of equilibrium prices. In the ZI model, there is no belief formation process. As a result there is no convergence of transaction prices to equilibrium, as the diagram on the right side of the bottom row in figure 5 clearly shows.[5] In table 3, the mean absolute deviation of transaction price from equilibrium price is shown for 100 simulations of the ZI model in the symmetric market design.[6] This statistic is also shown for 100 simulations of our model[7] and for the seven lab markets. These data

[4]Note that the range from the lowest cost to the highest valuation in this market is 1.40 to 3.30, with an equilibrium price of 2.35; beliefs are focused in a narrow range around the equilibrium price.

[5]Gode and Sunder [7] (p. 129) argue that "By the end of a period, the price series in budget constrained ZI trader markets converges to the equilibrium level almost as precisely as the price series from human trader markets does." In the ZI simulation of figure 5, final trades in 8 of 10 periods are within 0.10 of equilibrium. We apply a definition of convergence which is more demanding and conforms more closely to the intuitive notion of convergence of market prices. We argue that prices in a stable market environment converge if after several periods, the mean deviation of all trades from equilibrium is small. By this criterion, the ZI model does not converge to equilibrium.

[6]Although the mean absolute deviation in the last two periods of the ZI model simulations is less than in the first two periods, this is not the result of convergence. The price sequence in each period constitutes a draw from the same distribution.

[7]The timing specification employed in the simulations is given in equations (14) and (15).

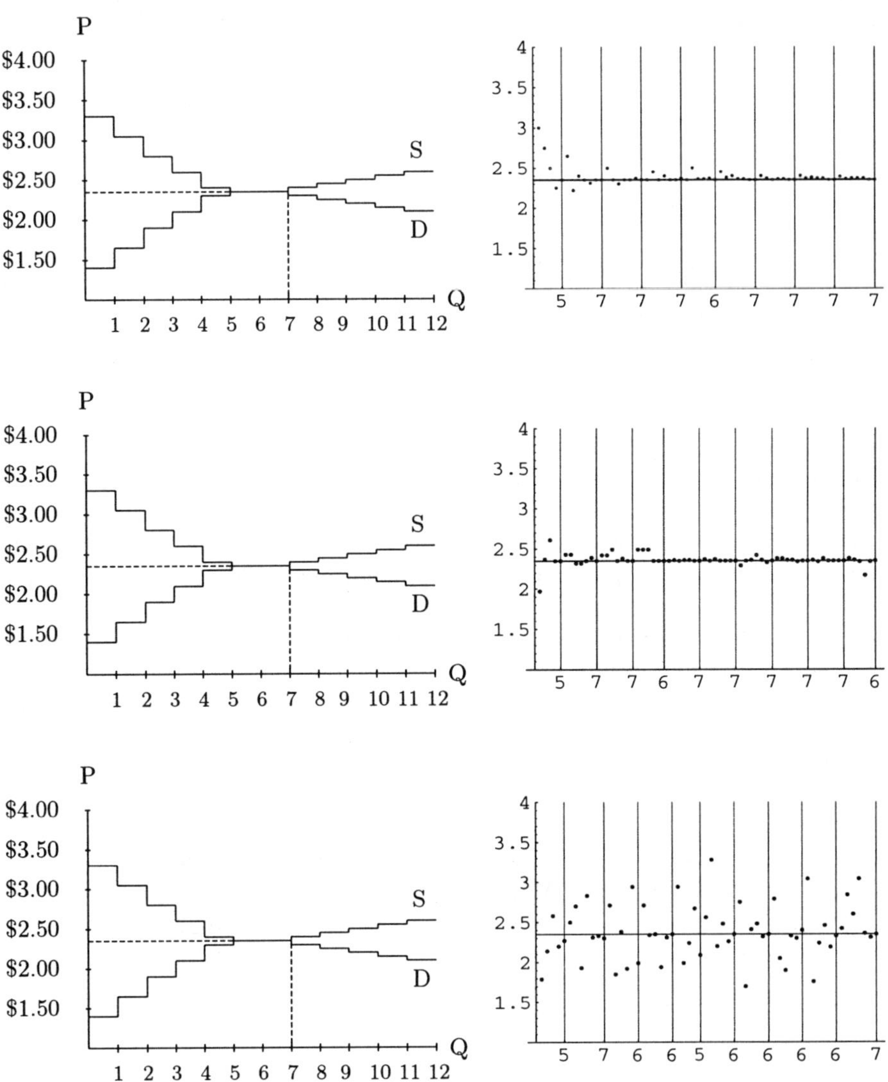

Figure 5: Supply and demand conditions (top left) and transaction prices (top right) for market experiment 3pda01; for a simulation of market 3pda01 (center) and for a ZI simulation of market 3pda01 (bottom).

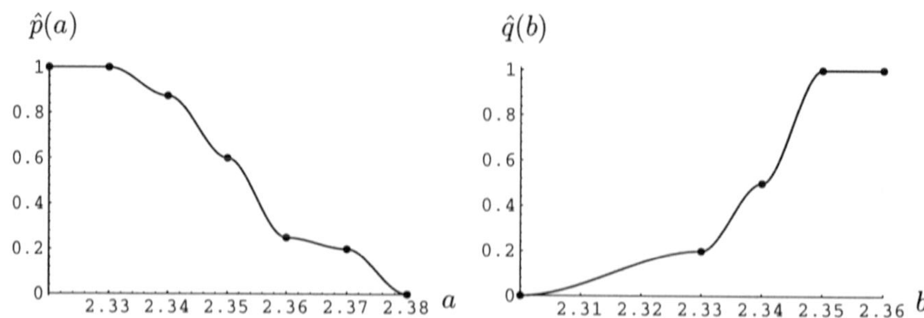

Figure 6: Sellers' beliefs (left) and buyers' beliefs (right) after five periods of trading in simulation of market 3pda01.

(and the ZI simulation graph at the bottom of figure 5) show that the ZI model does not result in convergence to competitive equilibrium. The behavior in our model does produce convergence to approximate equilibrium prices after several periods of trading. The contrast between the outcome of the simulations of the ZI model and of our model identify the effect on market convergence of belief formation and myopic surplus maximization in our model. From the graphs and the statistics, it is clear that this effect is substantial. Moreover, data on mean absolute deviation in table 3 show not only that our model converges to within a few cents of the equilibrium price, but that the rate of convergence is similar to – though initially slightly faster than – that found in laboratory experiments.

Table 3. Convergence statistics from simulations of models and from lab data.

Periods evaluated	Symmetric Markets	Model Simulations	ZI Model Simulations
First two periods	0.101	0.077	0.276
Entire experiment	0.050	0.045	0.237
Last two periods	0.022	0.040	0.209

Shifting conditions The diagram on the left of figure 7 shows two sets of supply and demand conditions. The lower set, shown with thicker lines labeled S and D, is identical to the supply and demand conditions in figure 2 and figure 5. If after several periods of trading, buyers have each valuation increased by 0.50 and sellers have the cost of each unit increased by 0.50, then the new supply and demand are those shown with thinner lines in figure 7. The equilibrium quantity of trade and the total surplus are unaffected by this shift, but the

In one alternative tested, all agents with positive surplus were equally likely to send a message. This resulted in higher variance in transaction prices and in more instability in the outcomes.

equilibrium price increases from 2.35 to 2.85. Since expectations focus near the original equilibrium after several periods of trading (see figure 6), the dynamics of movement to the new equilibrium can be examined by considering this type of market. The sequence of transaction prices from a simulation of our model in this type of market – with the shift occurring after 5 periods of trading – is shown on the right side of figure 7. From periods 6 through 10 in this market the equilibrium price is 2.85. In the simulation shown, convergence to the original equilibrium occurs by the end of period 2. Beginning in period 6, the equilibrium price shifts up 0.50. By the end of period 7 transaction prices establish near the new equilibrium price. This simulation shows that in the model developed here, traders respond to shifting market parameters, and prices quickly adjust to a new equilibrium.

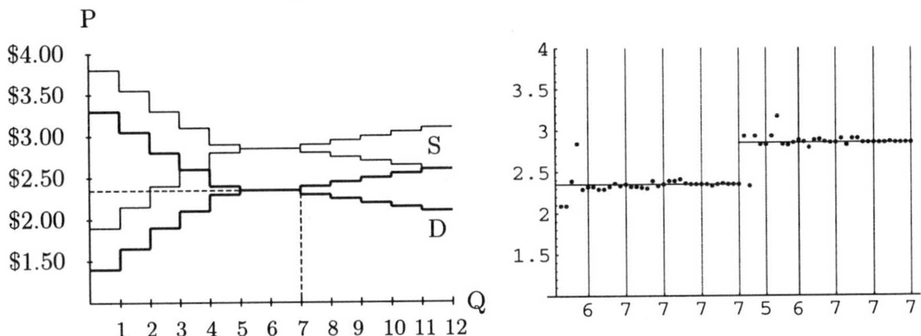

Figure 7: Supply and demand conditions and transaction prices for a simulation of a market with a supply and demand shift.

3.4 Boundaries on performance

Though we have developed a model that simultaneously converges to competitive equilibrium prices, produces efficient outcomes, and responds quickly to altered market conditions, we want to indicate direction for improvement in the outcomes of the bargaining behavior developed in our model. We do so by describing a distinctive feature of price sequences from experimental markets.

We split the sequence $(p_n)_{n=1}^N$ into two subsequences, one consisting of those exchange prices $(p_n)_{n\in N_s}$ which were initially proposed by the selling side of the market, and the other consisting of the transaction prices $(p_n)_{n\in N_b}$ which were proposed initially by the buying side. We provide evidence that in laboratory experiments, the mean of $(p_n)_{n\in N_s}$ is greater than the mean of $(p_n)_{n\in N_b}$. Yet in simulations of our model, this pattern is reversed. This observation allows us to evaluate behavior in the model and uncover a key difference between the behavior of laboratory subjects and behavior in the model, providing direction for further research on bargaining behavior in DA markets.

Table 4. Price sequence and subsequence means in symmetric markets.

Market	p_e	$\overline{p} - p_e$	$\overline{p_a} - p_e$	$\overline{p_b} - p_e$
3pda01	\$2.35	\$0.04	\$0.12	\$0.01
2pda17	\$6.20	\$0.03	\$0.07	\$0.00
2pda20	\$6.20	\$0.06	\$0.12	\$0.01
2pda21	\$5.30	−\$0.03	−\$0.01	−\$0.04
2pda24	\$4.70	\$0.02	\$0.04	−\$0.02
2pda47	\$6.35	−\$0.03	−\$0.01	−\$0.05
2pda53	\$7.55	\$0.00	\$0.01	−\$0.02
Mean	—	\$0.01	\$0.05	−\$0.02

In laboratory trading experiments, there is a clear difference between mean prices of trades initiated by sellers and those initiated by buyers. For example, in the seven symmetric markets we consider, table 4 shows the market equilibrium price for each of these experiments in column 2 and the mean difference of transaction price from the equilibrium in column 3. Column 4 shows the mean difference between the transaction price and equilibrium price for all trades initially proposed by sellers. Column 5 shows the same statistic for all trades initially proposed by buyers. Note that in each of these seven experiments, the transactions initiated by sellers have a higher mean price than those initiated by buyers. Two additional data sets – one involving over 11,000 trades – are examined in Gjerstad [5] and this is a feature of all markets in both data sets considered there. In simulations of our model we find that this feature is reversed, and as a result, we are able to discern a difference between the bargaining behavior of laboratory subjects and behavior in the model.

Consider again the belief functions $p(a)$ and $q(b)$ shown in figure 6. In the description of the beliefs in these graphs in Section 3.3, we note that at the beginning of a period, sellers in this market with these beliefs will all have an optimal offer of 2.33 and buyers' optimal bids will all be 2.35. At the beginning of the third period, the first action will be either an ask of 2.33 or a bid at 2.35. Suppose that the first action is a bid of 2.35. As a result of the spread reduction rule, buyers' bids must be greater than 2.35. A bid of 2.36 would result in expected surplus $(v_j^1 - 2.36) \cdot 1$ for each of the four buyers in this market. Since the distribution of costs and valuations at the beginning of each period in this market is symmetric, and since the probability of each trader being the next to send a message is equal to that trader's proportion of total surplus (see proposition 9), the probability that a buyer will send the next message is approximately 0.50, so that the probability of two consecutive bids is approximately 0.25, and in this case the price will be above the equilibrium price. In general, the distribution of absolute deviations from equilibrium is approximately geometric, since a low price results from a sequence of asks and a high price results from a sequence of bids. Recall that in table 4, the transactions initiated by the selling side typically are above equilibrium, so the simulations and the laboratory markets lead to the opposite result in this respect.

While this is a subtle feature of DA data, a model which eliminates this difference would capture fine aspects of bargaining behavior and would represent progress in modeling behavior in this institution.

4 Conclusions

In this paper we have defined beliefs for agents in a double auction market which are generated endogenously on the basis of observed market activity. An agent's choice of an action depends only on these beliefs and on that agent's private information about their own costs or valuations. Agents who adopt the simple bargaining strategy of myopic expected surplus maximization employing these beliefs trade at prices which converge quickly and accurately to within several cents of the market equilibrium price and reach the competitive allocation. These beliefs and strategies are flexible enough to respond quickly to changes in supply and demand conditions.

Laboratory market experiments dating back 35 years have demonstrated that human subjects quickly and reliably reach competitive equilibrium outcomes. The model developed in this paper demonstrates that this capability of double auction market participants to reach competitive equilibrium outcomes may result from simple, intuitive information processing and strategy choice. Since we know that laboratory subject operate with limited information processing capabilities and boundedly rational strategy choices, this finding resolves, at least for the class of environments considered here, the puzzle Hayek posed.

References

[1] Cason, T.N., Friedman, D.: An Empirical Analysis of Price Formation in Double Auction Markets. In: Friedman, D., Rust, J. (eds.): The Double Auction Market: Institutions, Theories, and Evidence. Addison-Wesley (1993) 253-283

[2] Cason, T.N., Friedman, D.: Price Formation in Double Auction Markets. Journal of Economic Dynamics and Control **20** (1996) 1307-1337

[3] Easley, D., Ledyard, J.: Theories of Price Formation and Exchange in Double Oral Auctions. In: Friedman, D., Rust, J. (eds.): The Double Auction Market: Institutions, Theories, and Evidence. Addison-Wesley (1993) 63-97

[4] Friedman, D.: A Simple Testable Model of Price Formation in the Double Auction Market. Journal of Economic Behavior and Organization **15** (1991) 47-70

[5] Gjerstad, S.: Price Formation in Double Auctions. Ph.D. Thesis. University of Minnesota (1995)

[6] Gjerstad, S., Shachat, J.: The General Equilibrium Structure of Bargaining Models and Market Experiments. IBM Research Report RC 21812 (2000)

[7] Gode, D., Sunder, S.: Allocative Efficiency of Markets with Zero Intelligence Traders: Market as a Partial Substitute for Individual Rationality. Journal of Political Economy **101** (1993) 119-37

[8] Hurwicz, L., Radner, R., Reiter, S.: A Stochastic Decentralized Resource Allocation Process: Part I. Econometrica **43** (1975) 363-393

[9] Hurwicz, L.: On Informationally Decentralized Systems. In: McGuire, C.B., Radner, R. (eds.): Decision and Organization University of Minnesota Press, Minneapolis (1972) 297-336

[10] Ketcham, J., Smith, V.L., Williams, A.W.: A Comparison of Posted-Offer and Double Auction Pricing Institutions. Review of Economic Studies **LI** (1984) 595-614

[11] Plott, C.: Industrial Organization Theory and Experimental Economics. Journal of Economic Literature **XX** (1982) 1485-1527

[12] Smith, V.L.: An Experimental Study of Competitive Market Behavior. Journal of Political Economy **LXX** (1962) 111-137

[13] Smith, V.L.: Microeconomic Systems as an Experimental Science. American Economic Review **72** (1982) 923-955.

[14] Wilson, R.B: On Equilibria of Bid-Ask Markets. In: Feiwel, G.W. (ed.): Arrow and the Ascent of Modern Economic Theory. New York University Press, New York (1987) 375-414

Negotiating Agents in Manufacturing Decision Making Processes

P.W. Lei[1*], M.I. Heywood[2], and C.R. Chatwin[3]

[1*]University of Macau, FBA, MACAO, fbapwl@umac.mo
[2]Dalhousie University, Faculty of Computer Science, Halifax, Nova Scotia, B3H 1W5 CANADA, mheywood@cs.dal.ca
[3]University of Sussex, *iims*, Falmer, Brighton, East Sussex. BN1 9QT. UK
[*] indicates corresponding author.

Abstract. Real-time decision making for on-the-spot orders is considered using a novel distributed agent architecture. The order agents will have the ability to perform multi-stage negotiation using continuous double auction market-based model representing resources as producers and orders as customers. Qualitative information of resources and order requirements is captured in a Quality Function Definition (QFD) decision table. The QFD decision table also provides the interface for the agent to evaluate objectives, attributes and user preferences relating to resources and order requirements. This directs the negotiation against the most applicable resources at each stage through the market. In particular, the agents can learn from experience and adapt to the market change. The operation of such a system is illustrated within a garment industry application context.

Keywords: Intelligent Systems, Artificial Intelligence and Information Systems

1. Introduction

A shift in emphasis in the management of discrete production processes from achieving economies of size to realising economies of scope has required a corresponding change to the manufacturing planning and control activities. The manufacturing environment is no longer dominated by the identification of an optimal schedule over a planning horizon, as derived from an estimated projection of the next periods' demand. Instead reduced development and lead-times, diversification of product portfolios and increased market competition has shifted the emphasis of the production control process towards real-time scheduling in which just-in-time practices predominate. Furthermore, increases to the complexity associated with scheduling in production environments capable of manufacturing diverse ranges of products in 'customer driven' sizes, makes the real-time operation of production control activities much more significant. Finally, the increasing use of local area networks to link what were previously islands of automation into the manufacturing enterprise, means that it is now feasible to perform production planning and control in a decentralised/ distributed fashion, thus avoiding bottlenecks and the brittleness associated with centralised systems.

J. Liu and Y. Ye (Eds.): E-Commerce Agents, LNAI 2033, pp. 135-153, 2001.

The specific approach proposed to address the above manufacturing scenario focuses on the combination of three techniques: the global control of a distributed scheduling process may be provided for by way of an Optimised Production Technology systems perspective; the efficiency of the scheduling activity is a function of the ordering heuristics employed; and a combination of market modelling and fuzzy-neural reinforcement learning enables autonomous agents to provide the basis for a decentralised autonomous scheduling system.

In the following sections we begin by detailing related works (section 2) and the specific methodology employed here (section 3). Section 4 describes how a fuzzy decision matrix is used to capture user preferences. In section 5 the details of the Continuous Double Auction market are described and the relation between market, learning system and agent goals. Results demonstrating the action of the market model are presented in section 6, with section 7 concluding the paper.

2. Background

Intelligent agents have recently become the focus of significant research effort, both nationally and internationally, resulting in annual conferences in the area (e.g. [1]). However, a large quantity of work with intelligent agents has focused on the application of deontic logics to control agent interaction in terms of the logical expression of belief, commitment and goals. The approach taken by this research uses a second, less well investigated methodology based on "market based control" [2, 3]. This takes the form of either game theoretic or economically motivated market models. Game theoretic formulations were popularised by Rosenschein and Zlokin [4] and Maynard Smith [5]. In the latter case a biologically motivated concept of optimal (evolutionary stable) strategies was proposed. This has been placed on a more rigorous footing by Sverrir Olafsson (AA&T/ BT laboratories) through an interpretation in terms of Nash equilibrium which ensures that local solutions are not pursued at the decrement of the overall objective [6]. In particular Olafsson has identified sufficient conditions for stable convergence [7] and demonstrated applications in task distribution for heterogeneous processor systems [8]. An alternative approach, or be it resulting in a similar solution, uses a completely economic formulation from the outset, with no restriction to non co-operative interaction. Wellman in particular has championed the use of tatonnement in the method of General Equilibrium, a framework for market models composed from: producers (defined in terms of a technology), customers (defined in terms of utility) and goods (the items traded) [9, 10]. Specific enhancements to the original theory include adaptation to enable implementation in terms of a decentralised system and sufficient conditions to avoid oscillation [11]. This approach, however, tends to focus on the modelling of flows; that is applications in which the problem is modelled as a continuum. When applied to discrete problems, as in this case, the method is generally unstable or does not map easily to the domain [12, 13]. In particular a strict synchronisation between auctioneer and agents is required. The clearing price is only available once all the agents have bid, hence leaving the process open to manipulation by competing agents. Finally, the one shot clearing process used by Wellman assumes a complete mathematical description of their respective utility functions [13]. A more appropriate approach is that of the Double Action Market. This method concentrates on providing a model of the auction activity itself. Needless to say the method was initially developed by the economic community for investigating the dynamics of monetary markets [14, 15]. However, it is beginning to see application in other areas in which the problem is distributed and consists of multiple conflicting priorities [13, 16].

Within the context of intelligent agents as applied to the control of manufacturing systems, most published material employs the Contract Net protocol first suggested by Smith [17]. This system uses a recursive bidding process (sealed bid auction) in which a task (customer order) enters the production process and initiates a bidding cycle with production processes capable of fulfilling the root activity of the bill-of-materials. On identification of a successful candidate process, the same activity is repeated between each production process representing sub-assemblies and the associated 'assembly stage' (already allocated as part of the previous bidding cycle). At some point the leaf nodes of the bill-of-materials are reached. These then inform the original initiating agent, after which an assessment of the overall schedule is made. If this is unsatisfactory then the 'money', 'priority', 'endowment' etc. may be reallocated in order to improve the schedule. On identification of a suitably constrained schedule, a 'purchase-order' is released and the relevant capacities committed by the contributing agents assignment (denotes authorisation of the contract). Specific recent examples of this methodology include that at the Industrial Technology Institute (USA) [18], Purdue University (USA) [19], Cincinnati University (USA) [20] and Loughborough University of Technology (UK) [21]. In each case the stated rational is to achieve robust control and organisation of large industrial processes through local co-operative behaviour of interacting entities (representing resources and requirements). We note, however, that the Contract Net framework only makes use of the negotiation/ arbitration abilities of the agents during competition for each production task, and not over the span of the schedule. No attempt is made to explicitly represent time. That is, the bidding process is only a general framework against which ad-hoc interpretations are used to identify task allocations. In terms of production control systems used in practice, we also note that the method is most synonymous with a pull or just-in-time system. A more intuitive approach would be to instigate a distributed scheduling system against the most constrained (bottleneck) resources; the Optimised Production Technology(OPT) system context.

Optimised Production Technology, OPT is an approach designed to help a company make money and improve its performance in terms of net profit, return on investment and cash flow. It is mainly concerned with the efficient scheduling of resources [22]. The objectives are to maximise throughput, minimise inventory and minimise operating expenses. There are several main concepts involved in OPT. First, operational measures. Second, bottlenecks, as applied to high volume, fairly stable environments. Third, batching - separating process and transfer batches. Fourth, concentration on the control of the bottleneck resources. Fifth, scheduling of the bottleneck to its maximum capacity, using the bottleneck schedule to derive the delivery dates. Sixth, sychronisation of other operations with the bottleneck schedules. It is operated under the assumptions that the bottlenecks are relatively stable and the demand is statistically stable. Also employers will and can follow the schedule. Bottlenecks should be loaded to 100% of their capacity, by definition, but constraints need to be finitely controlled to meet management objectives and will not necessarily be loaded to 100%.

Optimisation of the schedule span either implies that a global representation of the plan exists (undesirable as this represents a return to the centralised planning context) or that the agents are able to apply expert knowledge locally to achieve global objectives. Knowledge associated with this latter scenario is generally expressed in the form of scheduling heuristics. These have been a topic of study by the research community for a number of years, with particular emphasis on improving the performance of centralised automated planning systems based on constraint satisfaction algorithms. The Constraint Satisfaction Problem (CSP) basis for solving scheduling problems involves the instigation of a 'depth-first backtrack' search over the various combinations of variables (tasks)/ values (start times) for the production planning periods under consideration. When the combination of variables/ values does not give rise to a satisfying schedule, then backtracking takes place; removing the last branch from the analysis. Naturally this is an NP complete problem, the solution speed of which is significantly effected by the order in which variable/ value combinations are applied. Heuristics employed to speed this process take two general forms; those used to constrain the search space, and those used to rank the order of variable/ value selection. The former, generally referred to as techniques for consistency enforcing, are sufficient for defining when a valid schedule exists. They are, at best, only able to supply limited information regarding what the most economic corrective action at any stage of the scheduling process may be. The second form of heuristic, an ordering heuristic, are used to indicate which task should be applied next (variable ordering) and the respective time line allocation (value ordering). It is these heuristics which have most significance during the formulation of a schedule/ plan with a minimal amount of backtracking. Unfortunately, they are also the most computationally intensive to evaluate in their own right. Sadeh and Fox review the current state-of-the-art in ordering heuristics. By doing so, better definitions for the purpose of the ordering heuristics are identified, and some new more efficient methods are derived for their identification [23]. However, this is still a centralised approach to scheduling, in which the evaluation of the various metrics constitutes the majority of the computational overhead. With this project we use the aforementioned market based paradigm to conduct the variable ordering activity, with the value ordering process performed using a neural-fuzzy systems perspective. That is to say, a learning system is employed by the respective task and resource agents to identify application specific scheduling strategies (correspond to cost functions based on make-span minimisation and utilisation maximisation respectively).

With respect to the identification of user preferences and system state it is necessary to provide an interface with the ability to represent both a local customer orientated description of management objectives and a general overview of the plan condition. In the former case, the method of Quality Function Definition (QFD) has received wide spread interest. The system represents a symbolic management matrix format for representing trade-offs in multifaceted decision problems. The ensuing decision matrix represents the problem in terms of objectives, attributes and preferences. Prasad [24, 25] demonstrates how the QFD framework may be employed to aid production planning problems involving the selection of most applicable activity for improving production throughput/ balance etc. Previous work has demonstrated how QFD matrices naturally support the use of fuzzy metrics and are therefore applicable to performing quantitative-to-qualitative transforms between the present plan condition and customer identified requirements [26].

3. Methodology

As indicated above, the approach used to achieve robust planning processes subject to uncertain demand patterns is composed of three elements: a framework for global control and management; local ordering heuristics; and a user interface incorporating QFD techniques for capturing preferences of the user. Global control and stability is maintained by basing the operation of the agent flow on the Optimised Production Technology (OPT) framework. Such a global framework is necessary in the first instance in order to ensure that communication efficiency is maintained. There are constraints on parameters such as the routing, availability of tools, capacity and communication infrastructure. This is also reflected in product information such as a bill-of-materials, in this case constraining the number of candidate processes against which bidding is elected. Furthermore, preferences are also reflected in the specification of the 'ideal' recipient. Secondly, an OPT perspective is explicitly used to ensure that scheduling is initiated against the most constrained process(es) first. That is to say, there is no benefit in beginning the scheduling process against the root (or leafs) of the bill-of-materials if these do not represent the most contested resources. By enforcing such a basis the most 'difficult' problems are identified and solved first — a heuristic forming a central tenet to the OPT methodology. Furthermore, this enforces a 'submissive' relationship between processes with a higher bottleneck ranking and those with greater temporal freedom. Once a task is scheduled at a bottleneck process, the global scheduling schema favours the manipulation of less contested resources. If scheduling within the required time frame is not possible, however, an activity synonymous with (distributed) backward chaining is instigated. Finally, under time-out conditions, as specified by the administrator, the system alerts the user to any processes which where not scheduled within the target time frame; along with the closest available schedule. The opportunity then exists for the user to relax constraints sufficiently to allow instigation of such a schedule (preferred relaxation's may of cause be specified from the outset and incorporated within the initial scheduling activity).

The observation regarding bottleneck processes, however, implies that the location of such critical resources are known *a priori*. To ensure this is the case, and encompass the case of temporal variation in the critical resources, monitoring agents are included within the suit of management tools to collect statistics regarding global production parameters. These instigate automatic updating of the record of bottleneck activities. By doing so, changes to the plant dynamics resulting from process breakdowns or dynamic changes in the product mix (customer orientated production) are naturally incorporated into the scheduling system. This activity also aids the collection of timely information regarding performance degradation. For example, drift in process times may indicate the need for maintenance, whilst consistent association of bottlenecks with a specific process will aid management decision making regarding future investment policies. Finally, the management system will also enable timely tracking of individual tasks, with delays highlighted and assessment of the effectiveness being possible on a part-by-part basis.

Most of the technical details of the proposed methodology are concerned with satisfying the requirements of the agent-based heuristics governing the scheduling process. The methodology used is based on general observations made regarding the significance of variable and value ordering heuristics [23]. However, rather than requiring a centralised system to perform this activity on the basis of measurements made by remote sensor systems, the scheduling activity is itself conducted across the network of resources. Such a perspective is employed in order to: avoid high costs of a centralised scheme for real-time scheduling; provide the basis for a robust control architecture; and make use of the inherent parallelism in the decentralised approach to production planning. As indicated above, a constraint logic programming framework is employed to describe the nature of the scheduling process. This process has generally been performed using a classical branch and bound context. However, as highlighted by Sadeh and Fox [23] the order in which variables (tasks) and values (times) are allocated has an over-riding influence on the efficiency of the scheduling process. Variable ordering heuristics associate resources with tasks. We employ a market agent methodology of this activity, detailed in section 5. This allows us to arbitrate robustly between many tasks (or customers) and a typically lower number of resources (or producers). Furthermore, by using an approach based on double auction markets, costs characterising the present utilisation of each resource or immediate resource preferences are included in the arbitration, e.g. the significance of set-up time. The utilisation and task preferences are themselves characterised at the customer and producer agents respectively.

Value ordering heuristics are effectively responsible for identifying a suitable temporal position for a task at a specified target resource. The objective of such a heuristic is therefore to quantify the degree of constraint associated with each position in the space of possible allocations. Furthermore, this should also encompass any increase to the down-stream tightness to the available temporal positions. Traditional approaches to this requirement include the use of Maximal Spanning Graphs or probabilistic models such as those identified by Sadeh and Fox [23] or Dechter and Pearl [27]. Each of these methods, however, requires a Herculean data collection and processing within the context of a centralised implementation. The approach taken here makes use of: local statistics about the scheduled process; fuzzy heuristics regarding temporal move operators; and reinforcement learning. As indicated above, bottleneck information is used to classify resources in terms of the degree of contention experienced. Those resources with least contention are subject to most re-organisational efforts about points identified in the most constrained resources. Conflicting temporal allocations are resolved from an iterative rescheduling perspective using a reinforcement learning perspective [28]. Central to the success of this approach is the encoding of suitable feature vector information. This was previously achieved by the use of statistics characterising the state of the production process. Moreover, the method may be extended by using *a priori* information, as defined by a set of fuzzy rules. Examples include task priority, temporal ratio and change frequency [29].

As indicated in section 2, a QFD framework is used in order to describe the temporal rules used during the value ordering process. This supports the expression of one constraint against another and prioritisation of different objectives, e.g. set-up time reduction at constrained and unconstrained resources. Furthermore, if the learning process adapts the initial user specified configuration, direct interpretation of the new associations is provided. Past experience with the QFD framework indicates that the system may naturally be implemented using a combination of Microsoft Excel and Visual Basic [26].

4. Garment Industry Application Context

Small to medium sized enterprises make up a considerable component of the garment industry. In order to remain competitive, however, these enterprises have came under increasing pressure to accept smaller orders but at an increasing regularity and uncertainty. A single human expert planning by hand can no longer fulfil the real-time solution of such a dynamic problem. The objective of this research is to investigate the appropriateness of autonomous agents and market models to aid the expert in solving problems of this form.

The manufacture of even a simple garment for example, a T-shirt, involves a multitude of manufacturing processes: design, marking, cutting, screen-printing, etc. As for the sewing process, there are several machines available, many with different capabilities or present tooling. This results in a situation where the status of the resources is very dynamic as well as the order list. In order to present the proposed solution to this problem consider the case of the fuzzy membership functions of three machines, m1 m2 and m3, see table 1 and three prospective jobs, j1, j2 and j3 see table 2. The capabilities of the respective machines and present state are described in terms of a fuzzy set, as derived from the corresponding QFD matrix. A fuzzy set is a set without a crisp boundary. That is, the transition from "belonging to a set" to "not belonging to a set" is gradual, and this smooth transition is characterised by membership functions that gives fuzzy sets flexibility in modelling commonly used linguistic expressions, such as "the water is hot" "the temperature is high". This theory gives more flexibility to describe the status of agent. Whereas classical set only provides 0(no) or 1(yes) answer. Useful information will be scarified. Agents representing the three prospective jobs also have a set of membership functions, this time denoting their respective requirements, where this is again derived from characterising QFD matrices. As each job agent visits the resource agents (by visit we imply a heterogeneous as opposed to a centralised organisation of resources), job agents assess the degree of overlap between their requirements and the services offered by each machine (moreover job agents may also be allowed to retain historical information regarding the most applicable resources, hence constraining the matching processes). At the end of this process, the respective job agents have a short list of the most applicable resources.

Table 1. Fuzzy triangle values of machine agents, m1 , m2 and m3

Condition	m1	m2	m3
Timing	2,3, 4	14 ,15, 16	8 ,10, 13
Speed	13,14 ,15	6 ,7 ,8	7 ,8 ,9
Capability	4 ,5 ,6	8 ,10 ,11	15, 16 ,17

Table 2. Fuzzy triangle value of job agents, j1 , j2 and j3

Requirement	j1	j2	j3
Timing	1, 3, 4	7, 8, 9	14, 15, 17
Speed	5, 7, 9	16, 17, 18	2, 5, 6
Capability	9, 10, 11	20, 23, 24	1, 2, 3

4.1 Fuzzy Quality Function Definition

QFD matrix (the house of quality) is a decision matrix that provides the means for inter-functional planning and communication [24, 25]. It provides the interface for an agent to evaluate task objectives, attributes (elements which the agent may manipulate) and preferences (different views/ measures of the objectives). The components of QFD matrix are depicted in figure 1.

	Attributes	Priorities
Objectives	Capture Relationship Between Attributes and Objectives	Weighting On the Objectives
	Result (Ranking)	

Fig. 1. The components of QFD matrix

From the context of the garment industry, for example, the QFD matrix for a job agent's 'objectives' are the characteristics of machines such as speed and tooling/functionality. The 'attributes' are the number of available machines[1]. The 'priorities,' i.e. preferences of the job agent towards the machines, are shown in the 'weighting on the objectives' column, where this indicates which objectives are more important. A metric distance is employed to capture the 'relationship between attributes (machines) and objectives'. This will be discussed in the next section. To evaluate the relationship between 'relationship between attributes and objectives' and 'weighting on the objectives', multi-objective decision making is applied, where this is again detailed below. The outcome is the ranking of attributes i.e. machines. As the result, the job agents are able to locate its favorable machine according to their own preferences.

---

[1] By 'available machines,' all machines of type 'sewing' and not presently broken down are implied.

4.2 Metric Distance

The process of comparing the degree of similarity between the requirements of the order agent and the available resources, as represented by resource agents, is provided through the concepts of Fuzzy maximising sets [30] and a distance metric [31]. Specifically, the QFD matrix provides a ranking of the various competing resources in terms of multi-dimensional membership functions. The ideal situation would be the case of perfect overlap between agent requirements and available resource for at least one resource agent. In practice job agents may have to wait for a resource to become available or accept a compromise solution in which some of the requirements are not satisfied. This information is captured in two ways. In the first case attribute membership functions may not overlap at all. In this case we desire the nearest solution, hence a distance metric is employed. In the second case several resource agents may be able to offer a degree of match, hence overlap between membership functions. In this case the concept of a maximising set is employed by the job agent to select the most robust solution.

A metric distance is defined as the distance between job and machines in terms of the distance between their centre of gravity and the overlapped area of maximizing set as job agent matches with machine agent. The distance between the centre of gravity measures the fulfillment of the job agent's requirements. The closer machine means that it meets most of the requirements whereas a more distant one means that it meets part of the requirements. However the suitability of machine agent is not measured. So the overlapped area of maximising set is required to measure the suitability. The higher the overlapped area implies the higher suitability. As the result, the metric distance not only measures the fulfillment of requirements but also the suitability of a machine for a job. Specifically,

$$F(x,y)=[\ 0.5y\ ]^{(2-d)} \text{ and } d = (2\,/\,(1 + \exp(-2.5(x\text{-}0.5)))) \tag{1}$$

where x is the membership function of center of gravity and y is the membership function of maximum set. Such a function is illustrated in figure 2. Whereas the concept of a maximising set is employed in preference to the traditional approach of merely selecting the maximum overlap. Here we are interested in identifying the overlap between membership functions, which exists for the widest region. In doing so we avoid cases in which two membership functions overlap with a maximum value but only for a very small region. Such a solution implies that there is very little if any leeway for adjusting the agreement say up or down a planning time line.

More formally a maximising set, M, for some function, f, in X (the domain) is specified as the fuzzy sub-set of X which maximises a *region* about some point x [30], or

$$\mu_M(x) = \frac{Sup(f) + Inf(f) - f}{Inf(f)} \tag{2}$$

where μ_M is the membership function of the maximising set; *Sup(f)* is the supremum operator; and *Inf(f)* is the infimum operator.

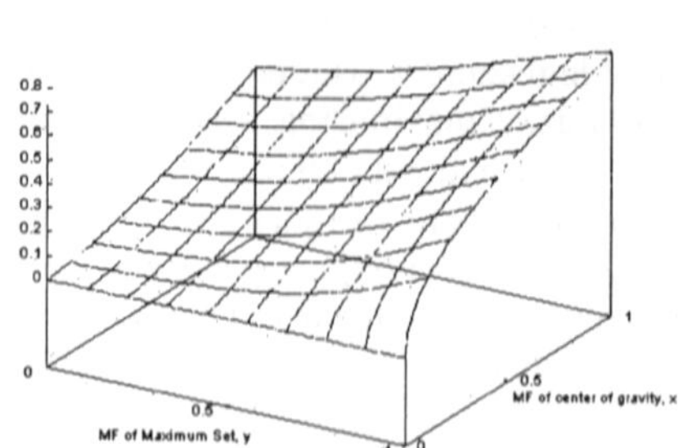

Fig. 2. Max set, y and the center of gravity, x

In figure 3, the much larger triangles represent the machine agents, m1, m2, and m3 and job agent j2. The small triangles within m1, m1 and m3 are the maximum set as job agent, j2 matches the machine agents. J2 will obtain the higher value in the maximum overlapping area with m3 as it has the shorter distance from m3. Obviously j2 will choose m3 in terms of machine timing. However j2 has two other objectives. What will the job agent, j2 choose in term of capability? In figure 4, the job agent, j2 will face a dilemma in choosing the right machine. The job agent, j2 receives the highest value in the maximum overlapped area with machine, m2 while machine, m3 is much closer to it. In fact, which machine is most suitable? Here a distance function is adapted to measure metric distance in terms of the maximising set and distance, figure 2. When concerning speed, the job agent, j2 will choose the machine, m1, figure 5. It turns out that the job agent, j2 will choose different machines to accomplish the objectives. In reality, the job agent can choose only one machine. How can job agents to select the suitable machine in satisfying the objectives? It is resolved by Multiobjective Decision Making.

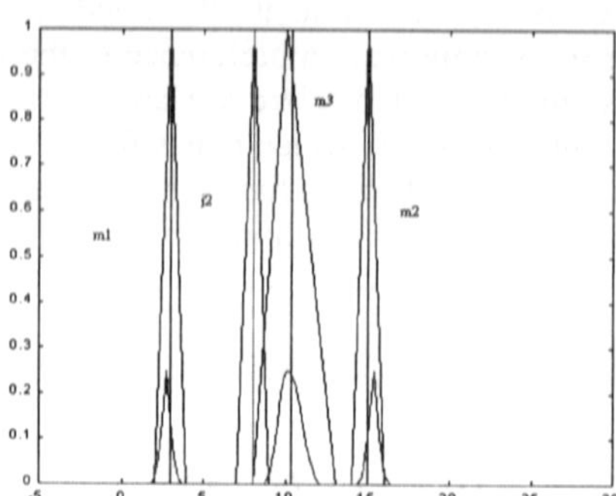

Fig. 3. j2 evaluates machines' time

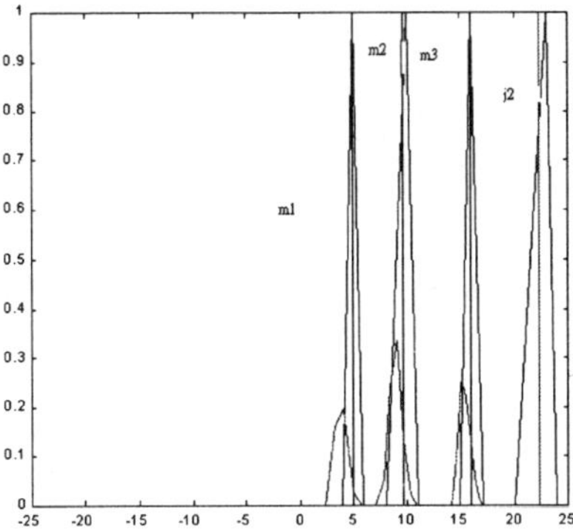

Fig. 4. j2 evaluates machines' capability

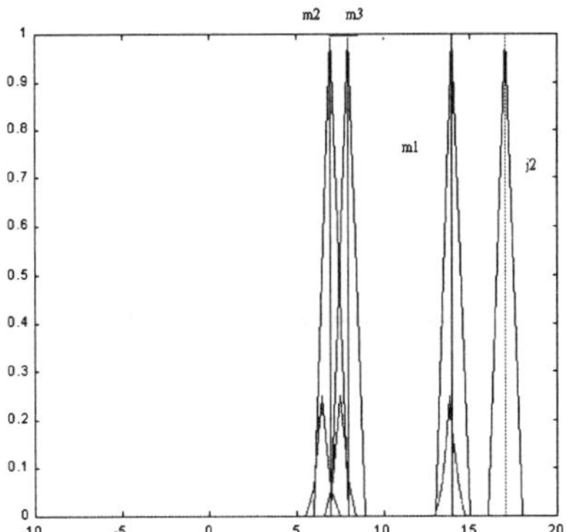

Fig. 5. j2 evaluates machines' speed

4.3 Multiobjective Decision Making

Decisions are often made in an environment where more than one objective function governs constraints on the problem, and each objective is relatively important. A job agent faces the same dilemma in the selection of machines. The relative importance of each of the objectives is reflected in agent's preferences P as shown in table 3, 4 and 5. To evaluate how well each preference satisfies each objective and to combine the weighted objectives into an overall decision function in a plausible way, a multiobjective decision making model is applied [32]. The model takes the joint intersection of *r* decision measures composed from an objective and a corresponding preference,

$$D = \bigcap_{i=1}^{r} \left(\overline{b_i} \cup O_i \right)$$

where b_i is the preference of the *i*-th objective and O_i is the corresponding objective. The optimum solution, a^*, is that which maximises D, hence letting $C_i = \overline{b_i} \cup O_i$;

enables the definition of a suitable membership function, $\mu_{C_i}(a) = \max\lfloor \mu_{\bar{b}_i}(a), \mu_{O_i}(a) \rfloor$. The membership function of the maximising solution is therefore,

$$\mu_D(a^*) = \max_{a \in A} \lfloor \min(\mu_{C_1}(a), \mu_{C2}(a), ..., \mu_{Cr}(a)) \rfloor$$

Table 3. The preference of Job agent, j1

Objectives	m1	m2	m3	Pref.
Speed	0.7867	0.4495	0.8572	1
Timing	0.7279	1	0.9682	0.2
Capability	0.7817	0.9995	0.7279	0.6
Ranking	0.7817	0.4495	0.7279	

Table 4. The preference of Job agent, j2

Objectives	m1	m2	m3	Pref.
Speed	0.8174	0.7279	0.9277	0.6
Timing	0.9287	0.7279	0.7607	0.8
Capability	0.7279	0.6823	0.9063	0.3
Ranking	0.7279	0.7	0.7607	

Table 5. The preference of Job agent, j3

Objectives	m1	m2	m3	Pref.
Speed	0.4495	0.7847	0.9020	0.4
Timing	0.7080	0.9503	0.9198	0.6
Capability	0.9498	0.8545	0.7279	0.8
Ranking	0.6	0.7847	0.7279	

By way of example, let job agent, j1 's relative rating towards objectives: speed, timing and capability is 1, 0.2 and 0.6 respectively see table 3. The columns 2, 3 and 4 indicate the metric distance of each machine from job agent, j1. The m1's ranking value is calculated by applying multiobjective decision making as follows:

$$
\begin{aligned}
&(0.7867 \cup 0) \cap (0.7279 \cup 0.8) \cap (0.7817 \cup 0.4) \\
&= 0.7867 \cap 0.8 \cap 0.7817 \\
&= 0.7817
\end{aligned}
$$

The same method is applied to the rest of agents. As a result, a preference ranking, the relative importance of each machine to the job agent, j1 is obtained. The machine m1 has the highest ranking. Again and again, the same method is applied to other job agents. After ranking the machines, the job agent, j2 favours machine agent, m3 see table 4 and the job agent, j3 favours machine m2 see table 5. The job allocation is completed if we distribute m1 to j1, m3 to j2 and m2 to j3 based on preference. The result of this process is the identification of a set of applicable resources. Moreover these will typically be many jobs, which may have the same preference towards the same machine. Thus a continuous double auction market is deployed in resources allocation.

5. Market Model

As a job agent has identified the applicable resource agent, it will negotiate with competing jobs in order to obtain resources. This process is modelled as a double auction market. Job (customer) and resource (producer) agents will bid in the market. Traders i.e. agents are allowed to make offers to buy or sell and to accept other traders' offers at any moment during a trading period. In such a way, the information controlling the decision-making process is decentralized. Also, the market operates as a game of incomplete information, since traders generally do not know each other's preferences. The only centralised entity is the market institution representing the trading clearing house. Such an institution is duplicated for each type of goods exchanged. This corresponds to different machine types in the garment industry example. The market institution is also responsible for enforcing a set of rules determining the legitimacy of the various bids and messages, such as the how and when specific traders transact, given their chosen messages [15]. In this particular case the following rules are employed [13],

```
1. MarketSale Price is defined as the minimum sale price
   received by the market auctioneer.

2. Market Bid price is the maximum bid price received by the
   market auctioneer.

3. For every sale agent enquiry
    IF sale <= MarketBid
    THEN transaction performed at bid price, remove
    quantities traded from  Bid and Sale agents
    ELSE IF sale < MarketSale
    THEN MarketSale = Sale

4. For every bid agent enquiry
    IF  bid <= MarketSale
    THEN transaction performed at Sale price, remove
    quantities traded from Bid and Sale agents
    ELSE IF bid < MarketBid
    THEN MarketBid = Bid
```

The negotiating agents are coordinated through a continuous double auction market. In the next section, we will show how individual negotiating agent set his/her MarketBid/MarketSale.

5.1 Continuous Double Auction Market

The model employed is that of a Continuous Double Auction market in which agents are provided with 'cash' and 'shares' which together constitutes the wealth of an agent [15]. Agents determine how much to bid or sell (the volume, v) based on the previous market performance/ experience, the forecasted value of the market at the next period, and their progress towards their overall objective (e.g. maximising utility in the case of resource agents and minimising makespan in the case of job agents). To begin with agents have one of two intentions, $E_i(t)$, either to participate within a market or not. Thus,

$$E_i(t) = \begin{cases} 1 & \textit{to bid} \\ 0 & \textit{no participation} \\ -1 & \textit{to sell} \end{cases} \text{ step.}$$

where i is the agent index and t is the time step.
Wealth of agent i at time step t, $w_i(t)$, is expressed as,

$$w_i(t) = c_i(t) + s_i(t)\tilde{p}(t)$$

where $c_i(t)$ and $s_i(t)$ is the current levels of cash and shares owned by the agent and $\tilde{p}(t)$ is the market price as determined by the market institution, see below.

The wealth of such an agent therefore varies depending on whether it buys (a job agent) or sells (a resource agent). Thus in the case of a job agent, a transaction is governed by the following relationship [15],

$$IF\ c_i(t) \geq v_i(t)p(t) \text{ (i.e. test for sufficient resources to pay for the transaction)}$$

$$THEN\ w_i(t+1) = \{c_i(t) - v_i(t)p(t)\} + \{s_i(t) + v_i(t)\}\tilde{p}(t+1)$$

In the case of the selling agent then the corresponding relation takes the form [15],

$$IF\ s_i(t) \geq v_i(t) \text{ (i.e. test for sufficient resources to pay for the transaction)}$$

$$THEN\ w_i(t+1) = \{c_i(t) + v_i(t)p(t)\} + \{s_i(t) - v_i(t)\}\tilde{p}(t+1)$$

In each case p(t) represents the previous market price or the price actually paid for the shares by the agents, whereas the current market price $\tilde{p}$ represents the price quoted by the market institution for the present round of trading. This price is manipulated by the institution to attract sufficient buyers and sellers for transactions to be granted. Thus market price is defined by the ratio between the total volume of bids, D(t), and sales, S(t), or

$$\tilde{p}(t+1) = \begin{cases} \tilde{p}(t) + \delta & \textit{if } D(t) + \varepsilon > S(t) \\ \tilde{p}(t) & \textit{if } D(t) = S(t) \\ \tilde{p}(t) - \delta & \textit{if } D(t) < S(t) + \varepsilon \end{cases}$$

where δ is a fixed constant representing the minimal change in market price, and ε is a tolerance applied to the market institution in question, to avoid the requirement for an exact mach between the number of resources and jobs.

The objective of the agents is therefore to define the volume traded such that their overall objective is satisfied. This problem is interpreted as a prediction problem. That is to say, agents make a prediction regarding the next market price or rather their action at the next market, such that their overall objectives (as defined by the QFD matrices) are satisfied. To this end the volume transacted is proportional to the difference between the proposed action, $F_i(t)$, and market price, or

$$v_i(t) = |F_i(t) - \tilde{p}(t)|$$

The estimation of $F_i(t)$ by the agent therefore represents an indirect control problem, well suited to the capabilities of reinforcement type learning based on neural or evolutionary computational techniques [33].

6. Results

Based on the AAA model, a market based agent can set his/her MarketBid or MarketSale according to his/her own preference and interpretation on the market information. By way of an illustrative example we first base the agents prediction, $F_i(t)$, on a simple linear model, taking inputs from the previous transaction volumes and market prices, p. For this experiment, the MarketSale price is fixed to the relation 40 + 20* sin (pi*t*1/250), the trend of predicted price movement will move in the same way as the MarketSale price see figure 6. As the result, agents learn to estimate the transaction price following the same trend see figure 7. The error in predicting the future price is in equilibrium in the long run seeing figure 8. Thus the market based agents demonstrate the ability to learn strategies.

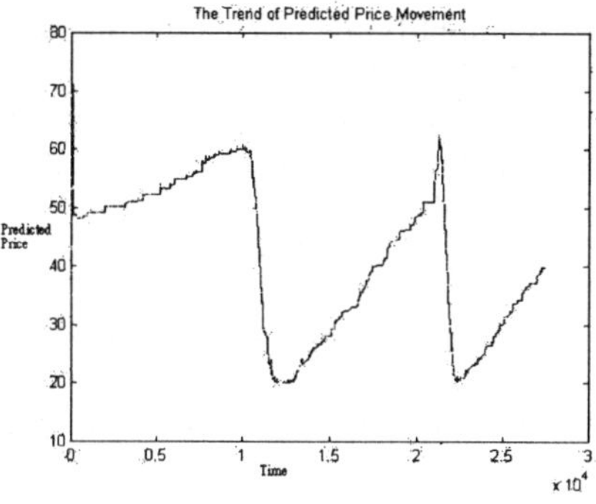

Fig. 6. The trend of Predicted Price

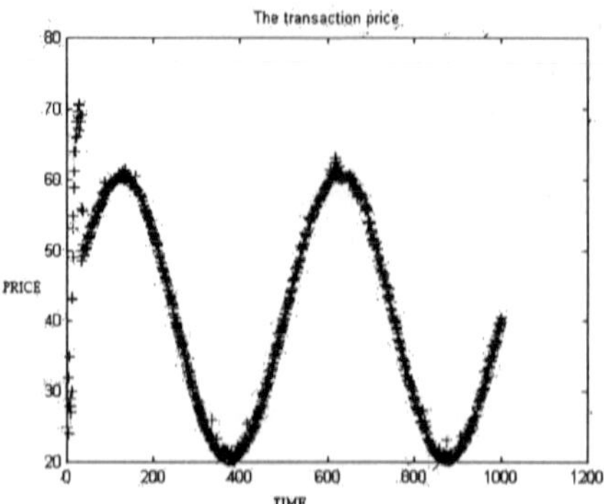

Fig. 7. The movement of transaction price

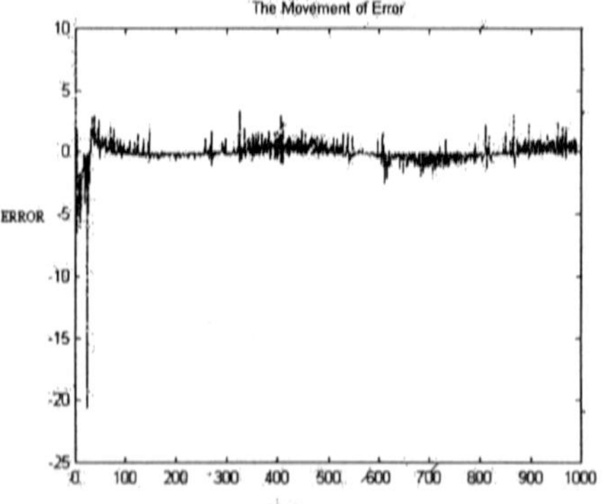

Fig. 8. The error in predicting the price

Each job agent is unique in his/her wealth (job value) and preference ranking towards individual machine. The job agents' wealth are to be 100, 200, 300 for j1, j2, and j3 respectively. In order to simplify the calculation, the preference of machine to accept any job is to be 0.6449, 0.8998, 0.8216 for m1, m2 and m3 respectively. In our situation, each machine represents the market for that kind of machine. Totally there are three different markets for job agents to participate. A job agent will participate the machine market for bidding only if his/her preference is greater than 0.5. If the preference is less than 0.5, this implies that the machine is unsuitable for the job agent.

The job agents now set the MarketBid based on his/her unique characteristics, i.e. preference, wealth and own interpretation about the historical market information. And the machine agents also set the MarketSale. After the trading in three different markets, the job agent, j2 wins the bid in market, m1 and m3 while the job agent, j3 wins the bid in the market, m3. The job agent, j1 lost the bidding though he/she has the higher ranking to the market, m1. It is because the value of job agent, j1 is 100 while the job agent, j2 is 200. During the transaction, the job agent, j2 will choose one of the markets, m1 and m3 and j3 will choose m2. The job agent, j1 will readjust the bid and participate the markets again until it finds the match. In this way, resources are effectively distributed according to individual agent's unique wants and needs see figure 9.

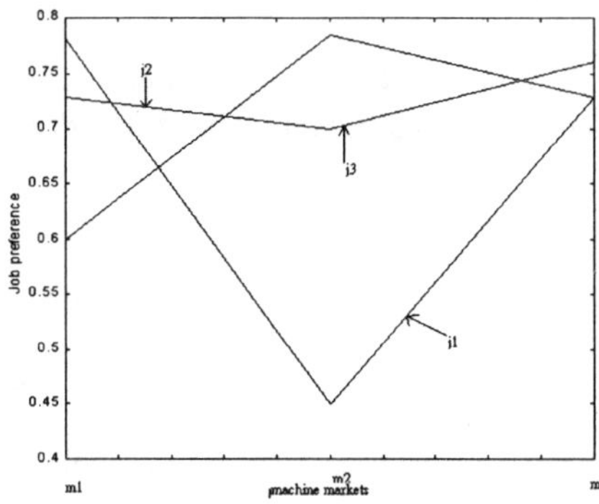

Fig. 9. Jobs' pref. to each machine

7. Conclusion

The distributed agent architecture of a real-time decision making system for order planning in a garment industry application is proposed. There are four design objectives to be emphasized. First, the order requirements and resource capabilities are summarised using a QFD decision matrix approach. This captures the information in a structured and visual format. Moreover the methodology is naturally applicable to a fuzzy decision making context. Second, the similarity between order objectives and available resources is expressed in terms of a distance metric rather than purely in terms of a maximum overlap value alone. This process provides a ranked list of the most suitable resources for each order. Third, a double auction market is to coordinate negotiation between jobs competing for the same set of resources. Fourth, the negotiating agents have the ability to learn from past experience and adapt to the market change. Future work will address the chaining of the above process across multi-stages of the planning process and assess the robustness of the overall system under different resource constraints.

In this simple model, we illustrate that an agent has the ability of predicting price based on the historical price and transaction volume. In a dynamic market however, many factors such as interest rate will have impact on the market price too. Much work has to be done to make agent more intelligent to cope with multivariable so that they can act in a wise way like a human expert in a distributed environment. Evolutionary computation may be a promising solution to this.

References

[1] Intelligent Agents Series, 1-5; Lecture Notes in Artificial Intelligence, Sub-series of Lecture Notes in Computer Science, Volumes 890, 1037, 1193, 1365, 1555, Springer-Verlag, 1995-1999.

[2] Huberman B.A., (ed) The Ecology of Computation, Elsevier Science Pub, isbn 0-44-70375-6, 1988.

[3] Clearwater S., (ed) Market based control: A paradigm for distributed resource allocation, World Scientific, isbn 9-810-22254-8, 1996.
[4] Rosenschein J.S., Zlotkin G., Rules of Encounter: Designing Conventions for Automated Negotiation among Computers, MIT Press, isbn 0-262-18159-2, 1994.
[5] Maynard Smith J., Evolution and the theory of games, Cambridge University Press, 1989.
[6] Olafsson S., "Resource allocation as an evolving strategy," Evolutionary Computation, 4(1), 33-55, 1996.
[7] Olafsson S., "Self Adaptive Network Utilization," IWANNT'97.
[8] Olafsson S., "A General Model for Task Distribution on an Open Heterogeneous Processor System," IEEE Transactions on Systems, Man and Cybernetics, 25(1), pp 43-58, 1995.
[9] Wellman M.P., "A market-orientated programming environment and its application to distributed multicommodity flow problems," Journal of Artificial Intelligence Research, 1 pp 1-23, 1993.
[10] Wellman M.P., "A computational market model for distributed configuration design," Artificial Intelligence for Engineering Design, Analysis and Manufacturing, 9, pp 125-133, 1995.
[11] Hu J., Wellman M.P., "Self-fulfilling bias in multi-agent learning," 2nd Int. Conf. On Multi-agent Systems, pp 118-125, 1996.
[12] Masson P., "Progressive equilibrium markets in discrete process allocation problems — A tutorial," *iims*, School of Engineering, tr-sus-iims-970829, 1997.
[13] Rajan V., Slagle J.R., Dickhaut J., Mukherji A., "Decentralised Problem Solving Using the Double Auction Market Institution," *Expert Systems with Applications*, 12(1), pp 1-10, 1997.
[14] Friedman D., "A simple testable model of double auction markets," *Journal of Economic Behaviour and Organisation*, 15 pp 47-70, 1991.
[15] H. A. Wan and A. Hunter, " On Artificial Adaptive Agents Models of Stock Markets", Simulation 68:5,729-289, May 1997.
[16] Ledyard J.O., Porter D., Rangel A., "Using Computerised Exchange Systems to Solve an Allocation Problem in Project Management," Journal of Organisational Computing, 4(3), 271-296, 1994.
[17] Smith R.G., "The Contract Net Protocol: High level communication and control in a distributed problem solver," IEEE Transactions on Computers, 29(12), pp 1104-1113, 1980.
[18] Parunak H.V.D., "Manufacturing experience with the contract net," Research Notes in Artificial Intelligence: Distributed AI, Chapter 10, (ed) Huhns M.N., Morgan Kaufmann, isbn 0 273 087778 9, 1987.
[19] Lin G.Y.-J., Solberg J.J., "Integrated shop floor control using autonomous agents," IIE Transactions, 24(3), pp 57-71, 1992.
[20] Baker A.D., "Metaphor or reality: A case study where agents bid with actual costs to schedule a factory," Chapter 8 in [3].
[21] Tilley K.J., "Machining task allocation in discrete manufacturing systems," Chapter 9 in [3].
[22] Jones G., Roberts M., "Optimised Production technology (OPT)", Chapter 2, isbn-1-85423-072-7, IFS Publications, UK, 1990.

[23] Sadeh N., Fox M.S., "Variable and value ordering heuristics for the job-shop scheduling constraint satisfaction problem," Artificial Intelligence, 86, pp 1-41, 1995.
[24] Prasad B., "Product Planning Optimisation using Quality Function Deployment", in Artificial Intelligence in Optimal Design and Manufacturing, Chapter 5, Dong Z., (ed), Prentice Hall, ISBN 0130375403, 1994.
[25] Prasad B., "JIT quality matrices for strategic planning and implementation," Int. J. of Operations and Production Management, 15 (9), pp 116-142, 1995.
[26] Dagersten N., Heywood M.I., Chatwin C.R., "Batch process control using QFD matrices and simulation," Production Planning & Control, 9(4), pp 335-348, 1998.
[27] Dechter R., Pearl J., "Network based heuristics for constraint satisfaction problems," *Artificial Intelligence*, 34, pp 1-38, 1988.
[28] Heywood M.I., Chan M.-C., Chatwin C.R., "Application of SRV reinforcement learning neural networks to batch production rescheduling," Proc. of the Inst. of Mechanical Engineers, Pt B — Journal of Engineering Manufacture, vol 211, pp 591 – 603, 1997.
[29] Liu, J.-S., "Collective Problem Solving through co-ordination in a society of reactive agents," CMU RI TR 94-23, Robotics Institute, Carnegies Mellon, Pittsburgh, 1994.
[30] Zadeh L. A., " Maximizing Sets and Fuzzy Markoff Algorithms", IEEE Transactions on Systems, Man, and Cybernetics – Part C: Applications and Reviews, Vol., 28, No. 1, February 1998.
[31] Heywood M.I., Zincir-Heywood A.N., Chatwin C.R. "Digital Library Query Clearning using Prioritised Clustering and Fuzzy Decision Making," Information Processing & Management, 36: (4) 571-583 , July 2000.
[32] Yager R., "A new methodology for ordinal multiobjective decisions based on Fuzzy Sets," Decision Science, 12, pp 589-600, 1981.
[33] Paraskevopoulos V., Heywood M.I., Chatwin C.R., "Modular SRV Reinforcement Learning Architectures for Non-linear Control," International Journal of Intelligent Control and Systems, 1999.

Evaluating Resource Bundle Derivatives for Multi-agent Negotiation of Resource Allocation

Lars Rasmusson*

Swedish Institute of Computer Science
Box 1263, S-16429 Kista, Sweden
Lars.Rasmusson@sics.se

Abstract. Consider continuous negotiations where the goal is to obtain exactly one complete bundle of resources and there exists alternative bundles that solve the task. This paper presents a market-based model of this negotiation that does not require commitment and decommitment during the negotiation phase. A negotation goal is represented by a graph, called a resource network. Goals are achieved by obtaining resources along one path in the graph. The resource network model can be applied to electronic commerce with agents trading bandwidth in all-or-nothing deals, and for agents that want to combine simple goods into more complex goods.

1 Introduction

The agent design problem is the problem of how to write programs that act as helpers for a specific user. The help provided may consist of individualized search for information in large data sets such as the web, automation of repetitive tasks such as negotiating meeting times, coordination of the use of common resources with other people, doing the bidding for the user in computer-mediated auctions, etc.

An agent is of course always "just a program", but by calling it "agent" one emphasizes the wish to design a flexible open-system component that the user interacts with on a high level. The user supplies goals rather than a task list, and leaves specific details (such as locating relevant information servers and deciding with whom to interact) up to the agent.

The need for and benefit of agent programs increases when programs can communicate with information sources and other agents on remote computers. A number of execution platforms, agent communication languages, class libraries for common tasks, such as maintaining user models, exchanging data or meta data (plans, protocol descriptions, etc.) have already been developed to simplify the task of programming flexible, efficient and inter-operable agents.

Computer algorithms using market-based resource allocation started with decentralized algorithms by [2,3,6,10]. Perspectives on the limits of market-based

* This work was supported by a grant from NUTEK, the Swedish National Board for Industrial and Technical Development.

J. Liu and Y. Ye (Eds.): E-Commerce Agents, LNAI 2033, pp. 154–165, 2001.

systems are discussed in [5,11]. Bandwidth markets are a hot topic, see for instance [1,7]. A recent proposal for a combinatorial auction is described in [9].

This paper outlines a way to design parallel negotiation over bundles in a way that does not require the agent to reserve or lock some resources during the negotiation phase. The idea is to trade the components in the bundle in a continuous market, and also support a liquid and functioning derivatives market. By casting the agent decision problem into a market based problem, it is possible to evaluate the value of an action numerically, something that is difficult or impossible in traditional negotiation where one uses commitment and decommitment. This paper does not address how to decide which bundles that are required, nor do we focus on implementation on a particular execution platform.

We begin by defining the task structure that specifies the goals of an agent and enumerate a set of agent types that need to be implemented for an efficient market. Next we define the problem of negotiating over multiple resources in parallel in multiple markets. We go on to formulate the agent's task as the problem of insuring itself against risk during the trading period. We arrive at an expression for the value of a network option, the option needed for agents using the resource network structure. This could be used for instance for agents that trade bandwidth capacity, and who need to use the capacity to set up routes. Finally, we show that the value of the option can be expressed in a recursive formulation, assuming that prices are normally distributed (not necessarily independent) and discuss some different techniques available for evaluating the expression, numerically and analytically.

2 Agents

In the context of this paper, an *agent* is a program that acts to maximize the payoff for its *client* through negotiations with other agents or clients. Typically a client is a human user, and the payoff is measured in net cash income or increase in utility. In many negotiation cases, clients are indifferent to each others' payoffs, meaning that the payoff of one client is not a function of the payoffs of another client.[1] We can then express the task of the agent to obtain as much profit as possible.

An agent system consists of

- *agents* representing clients,
- *resources*, each one owned by one agent,
- *offers* to exchange resources,
- *goals* for the agents to achieve,
- *payoff/valuation functions* to order the goals.

Depending on the properties of these entities, we may have market-based systems, cooperative/non-cooperative behavior, self-interested behavior, etc.

[1] This is not the case for *games*, situations where the performance is measured *relative to the performance of others*, i.e. when one agent's profit is another agent's loss.

Resources can be modeled in many different ways. For instance, they can have a number of attributes that have to be negotiated over. Here, we assume that all the details of the resources have been standardized, so that to "normal" resources with different attributes are here represented as two different kinds of resources. So the resources are the "atoms" of the negotiation. The preferences over different attributes are instead represented in the payoff function (see below).

Messages with commitments to exchange resources are what changes the state of the agent system. Much agent work have consisted in describing the communication that is used to discover which resources one is willing to place offers for. In this paper, we assume we already have sufficient knowledge about the resources and the alternatives to be able to create the resource network. A *negotiation* is an interaction where two or more parties exchange offers to exchange resources until a mutually satisfying offer is found.

Most generally, goals are "desirable states of the world", and they usually require the agent to find which actions to perform and then which resources it requires to be able to achieve those actions. In this scenario, we assume that the agent has figured out which resources it needs to fulfill it's task, so a task can be completely specified by a set of resources. However, there may be alternative ways of performing a task, each of which requires a different set of resources. Therefore, we represent a task with a set of sets of resources, each of which is one particular solution to the task.

Some "states of the world" may be more preferable than others, so some sets of resources will be less valuable than others to the agent. If the agent is to be able to make a rational choice of which tasks to perform it needs a function that assigns a value to each solution of the task. For instance, the task t_2 = "buy a car" may give the payoff function for agent 5 the values

$$u_5(t_2, \{\text{Ferrari}\}) = 10000$$
$$u_5(t_2, \{\text{Volvo}\}) = 5000$$
$$u_5(t_2, \{\text{skate-board}\}) = 0$$

The goal for the agent a is to get the resources

$$R = \bigcup_i s_i, i \neq j \Rightarrow s_i \bigcap s_j = \emptyset$$

that maximize

$$\sum_i u_a(t_i, s_i)$$

where the solution sets s_i to the tasks t_i have to be disjunct since no resource may be used to solve more than one goal. If the agent does not already have the resources needed, it must negotiate with other agents to exchange resources. If one wants the agent to economize with the resources given to it by the user, one of its tasks should be to get the currency resource.

We suggest that this negotiation can be performed in a market based infrastructure. The resources are exchanged for some specific resource class used as currency. Resource offers are represented as options on bundles of resources, and since they can be priced, the agent can get the value on the price of a commitment. The agent framework we suggest will require the following agent roles (each agent can take on one or more of these at the same time):

- **exchange agents** which establish a secondary spot market for a particular resource class by relaying offers between traders,
- **trading agents** which represent clients with goals in terms of resource networks,
- **arbitrage agents** which exploit arbitrage opportunities, and thereby establish the arbitragelessness of markets,
- **institution agents** which provide network options, and
- **market-maker agents**which provide liquidity to derivative markets.

3 Resource Networks

A resource class is a set of resources the client considers completely interchangeable, and thereby may be negotiated over as a set, i.e. traded at an exchange.

The resource network definition: For the agent, solving the task is equal to obtaining one resource in each node on a path from the start node to the end node. Each node contains the relevant parameters for specifying the resource class (temporal, quantitative, or other, constraints). The resource network structure is implied by solutions to $u(t, s) > 0$. (The resources in those tasks that have a payoff greater than zero build up a path.)

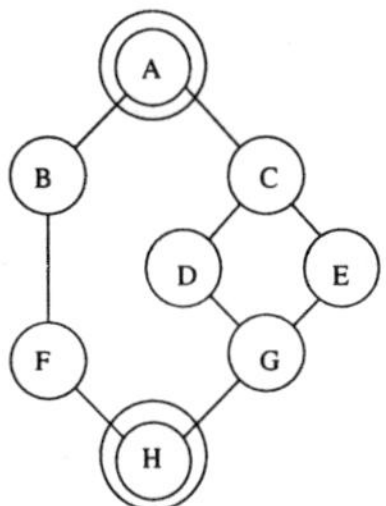

Fig. 1. The path A-B-F-H may represent the solution "Airport cab", "Broadway ticket", "Flight to N.Y.", "Home from airport cab". The path A-C-D-G-H may represent "Airport cab", "Canberra flight", "Diving trip", "Go sightseeing", "Home from airport cab". The second path has the alternative solution where D is replaced for E, an "Excursion in the desert". For all other combinations, the payoff $u(t, s)$ is zero.

A resource network can be used to express the task for the ubiquitous travel agent. To arrange a holiday trip, the agent has to book a flight, reserve a hotel, arrange sightseeing tours and dinners, all according to the client's interests and needs. Finally it will call a cab to get the client to the airport in time.

For each of the different subtasks there exists a variety of solutions. The solutions may partially overlap, and the set of solutions may be represented in a resource network where each node represents a resource class.

Another scenario is where the client wants to watch a film over a computer network. To guarantee good transmission quality, it is necessary to reserve some of the capacity in each of the routers on the path from the video server to the client.

Two kinds of difficulties arise when trading for resources in a resource network: disjunctions and conjunctions. In disjunctions, need one resource or another, but do not benefit from getting both. In conjunctions, you need to get a set of resources, but you do not benefit from getting a subset.

To understand the risk with disjunctions, lets consider the problem where an agent wants to acquire one of two resources, while having a specified time to negotiate. In a spot market, traded resources are exchanged immediately ("on the spot"). An agent that needs a resource at a future time t faces in a spot market continuously the problem of estimating whether the price will go down between now and t. In the case where there are alternatives and the agent has managed to obtain one resource the agent also has to estimate whether the the price of the alternative will decrease below the price of the obtained resource. In other words, the agent's marginal payoff is insecure.

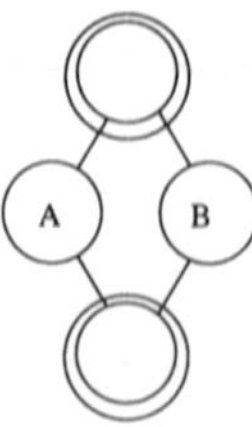

Fig. 2. The agent wants to buy either A or B and have it at a future time t.

Risk related to conjunctions occurs if an agent requires resources of several resource classes at once, and it must trade on several markets in parallel. When the agent holds a set of resources, it faces two risks, that prices go up for the remaining resources, or that prices go down for the possessed resources. Of these two, the former is more problematic, since then the total cost of getting all the resources may be higher than the limit set by the client (via the payoff function).

The task of a trading agent with a resource network is in a market reduced to finding the shortest, i.e. lowest cost path from source to destination, bid for the resources while reducing the risk of obtaining a bad end result.

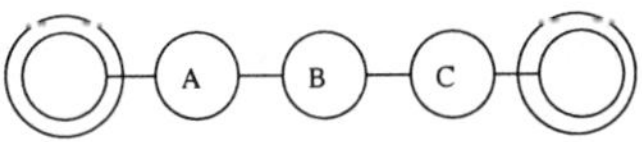

Fig. 3. The agent wants to buy all of A, B and C and have them at a future time t, but not just some of them.

4 Risk Reduction via Hedging

As we saw, an agent trading resources in a resource network takes a risk during the trading phase. A common approach used in non agent-based trading is to buy an insurance against the risk of price movements. The theory in this area is well developed and could be used in agent systems [4]. The two suggestions by the theory of market risk are *diversification* and *hedging*, of which hedging seems to be the most appropriate for our needs. To hedge a set of resources, one acquires another set of resources such that their price fluctuations cancel out. An agent may simply watch the movements and measure the correlation between prices of different resources to find suitable hedging candidates.

To hedge a portfolio with other resources is expensive and may be inefficient since the correlation may be low. More efficient is to hedge the risk during the negotiation with some derivate resources. A derivative is an intangible resource which value can be derived from the values of other resources, hence its name. Since its price is a function of the underlying resources, the correlation with the underlying resource is very high. Also, since contracts can be specified on large volumes of resources, the covariance of the prices can be arbitrarily large.

The mathematical theory of derivative pricing is well developed. It is usually based on assumptions such as *arbitragelessness* of markets and requirements such as the possibility of *short selling*. Arbitragelessness means that it is not possible to buy a set of resources for less than for what it can be sold. Short selling means that it is allowed to sell a resource that one does not have, provided that one eventually will deliver the resource, so it is a kind of future. To guarantee arbitragelessness, "arbitrage agents" should constantly watch for arbitrage opportunities and exploit them.

The simplest form of hedging consists of obtaining resources such that all first order partial derivatives of the resources equal to zero. For instance, to momentarily hedge one unit of resource r with an option o on the same resource, one should get $-1/(\frac{\partial o}{\partial r})$ units of o. (If the amount is negative, one should sell the option.) To hedge a complex portfolio w with the options o_i on resources r_i one should (if one ignores price correlations) obtain $(\partial w/\partial r_i)/(\partial o_i/\partial r_i))$ units of o_i for all i.

The cost of solving the task equals the cost of the resources plus the cost of setting up the hedge. The latter may be both positive or negative, since some hedges allow that the agent itself sells derivatives. An efficient agent should use techniques making this "insurance cost" as small as possible.

It may be quite computationally and communicationally expensive for each agent to hedge its resources. Instead of hedging itself, an agent could offer an *institution agent* to sell it a specialized option that captures the intention of its resource network. The role of the institution agent would be similar to that of a financial institution, such as a bank or an insurance company, which sells specialized, or "exotic", options for their customers on demand. In the resource network structure that agents have to deal with, the exotic option would consist of an option to buy one of any of the paths form source to destination for a fixed price.

One beneficial property of this design is that the market gets the ability to replan in real time. In the design where agents hedge their resources individually, they buy a set of resources and hold on to them, only compensating for their personal risk of loss. If the hedging strategies of the institutional agents are efficient, they will possess the resources for the least expensive path when it is time for the trading agent to exercise the option. Therefore, the resource allocation is able to adapt to resource demands that arrive after the start of a particular allocation task.

5 Market Liquidity

An exchange agent profiting on the traded volume wants there to be interested traders on both sides, i.e. liquidity. Liquidity is vaguely defined as how much prices are affected by trading. Causes of low liquidity are lack of immediacy and thickness, i.e. when it is difficult to find someone to trade with, and when only small volumes are offered at each price. In both cases, traders must bid far off from the current price to be able to finish a deal. A commonly used indirect measure of liquidity is the standard deviation of the price, where a low value signifies high liquidity. The issue of liquidity also arises in the design of an agent system, when we decide which resources that should be traded.

A naïve approach to a market for a demand network is to create one market for each pair of nodes, see [12]. In the case of $R = \{A, B, C, D\}$ we would create the markets $\{A, B, C, D, AB, AC, AD, BC, BD, CD\}$. Speculating agents buy two resources and offer the combination at a third market. This is clearly infeasible for larger networks, as each market would be very thin (cause 2 of illiquidity above), and a lot of resources would be held in buffers, causing a virtual demand that will generate prices away from "rational" prices.

By limiting trade to the resources in R plus a derivative market on carefully selected derivatives we have a better chance of getting liquidity. The cost compared to only using a spot market is the added complexity that the agents have to deal with when trading derivatives too.

To provide immediacy, exchanges may allow "market-maker" agents to trade for a lower transaction fee in return for being required to at all times give simultaneous buy and sell offers which price difference is less than a certain amount. This (together with some of the mathematical properties of options) implies that when someone wants to trade, the exchange is always guaranteed to find a matching offer that is not too far away from the theoretical option price. Since market-makers have low transaction costs, they may easily exploit arbitrage opportunities, and thereby help establishing arbitragelessness.

6 The Network Option for Bandwidth Markets

To create agents for a specific domain, we must design suitable options that capture the structure of the payoff function $u(\ldots)$ of the agents. Agents trading telecom bandwidth have the task of buying capacity in a number of nodes or routers so that they can establish a connection between two sites. They are indifferent to the actual path they receive (assuming that latency is not a major factor). To implement an institution agent for this domain, we must develop an expression for the value of an option to buy one of any path in a network. Note that for the institution it is obviously best to always deliver the least cost path since it is only paid a fixed price anyhow.

The value of the option on the time it may be exercised is

$$w_0 = max(0, min(P_1, \ldots, P_n) - X)$$

where P_i is the cost of buying all the resources on path i and X is the price for which the path may be bought. Obviously, if it is cheaper to buy the resources on the spot market, that is preferable to the agent, and the option is worthless to the agent, and the option is worthless.

The costs of the paths may be correlated, and this correlation depends on the specific network structure and traffic model.[2] This correlation must be estimated by the agents, and it may be represented in a correlation matrix, Σ. The estimated expected prices M must also be computed. M will typically be a function of the current prices, and Σ an estimation based on the historical distribution of the prices.

We denote the probability for a specific outcome of prices $f(p_1, p_2, p_3, \ldots, p_n)$. Assuming that the resource prices are linear drift and diffusion Ito-processes ($dS = \mu S dt + \sigma S dW$), one can show that this distribution should be a multivariate distribution of sums of log-normal variables. If we approximate this distribution with a log-normal distribution $lognorm(M, \Sigma)$, we can express the expected value of the option under the risk neutral measure

$$E[w_0] = \int_{-\infty}^{\infty} \cdots \int_{-\infty}^{\infty} max(0, min(p_1, \ldots, p_n) - X) f(p_1, \ldots, p_n)\, dp_1 \ldots dp_n$$

Since we use a risk neutral measure for the resource prices, the value of an option with a time t to the exercise time is

$$w_t = e^{-rt} E[w_0]$$

where r denotes the continuous risk free interest rate, the return rate one can get with probability 1, like the bank account interest rate.

Since the $max(\ldots)$ expression always will be zero when any p_i is less than X, we can move up the lower integration limit to X. We can further assume that the p's are ordered, for instance by $i < j \Rightarrow p_i < p_j$ if we write $E[w_0]$ as the sum over all permutations Γ, since they are disjunct.

$$E[w_0] = \sum_{\gamma \in \Gamma} E[w_0]_\gamma$$

2 The traffic model specifies who wants network capacity, when and where to.

Since the second argument of $max(0, ...)$ is always greater than zero, and $min(p_{\gamma(1)}, ..., p_{\gamma(n)}) = p_{\gamma(1)}$ we can rewrite the equation (dropping the cumbersome $\gamma(i)$ notation.)

$$E[w_0]_\gamma = \int_X^\infty \int_X^{p_n} \cdots \int_X^{p_2} (p_1 - X) f(p_1, \ldots, p_n) dp_1 \ldots dp_{n-1} dp_n$$

By recursively using Bayes' rule $P(A, B) = P(A|B)P(B)$ we can split $f(\ldots)$ into a product

$$f(p_1, p_2, \ldots, p_n) = f(p_1|p_2, \ldots, p_n) f(p_2|p_3, \ldots, p_n) \ldots f(p_{n-1}|p_) f(p_n)$$

and expand

$$E[w_0]_\gamma = \int_X^\infty f(p_n) \int_X^{p_n} f(p_{n-1}|p_n) \ldots \int_X^{p_2} f(p_1|p_2, \ldots, p_n)(p_1 - X) dp_1 \ldots dp_{n-1} dp_n$$

since $f(p_n)$ does not contain $p_1, \ldots, p_{n-1}$ and we can move it and the other terms of the integral. One benefit of this formulation is that if $f(p_1, ..., p_n)$ is the density function for a normal distribution, then so is $f(p_1|p_2, \ldots, p_n)$.

7 Evaluation of the Network Option

7.1 Numerical Evaluation

This integral unfortunately has no simple analytical solution for $n > 2$. Milton [8] discusses a method for evaluating the integral using multidimensional quadrature.

Another way to evaluate complex integrals that has become increasingly popular during the last decade is to use numerical methods like Monte-Carlo integration.

Monte-Carlo integration of a function $f(x)$ uses sampling of the function to estimate the integral from the observation that

$$\int_a^b f(x)dx = lim_{n\to\infty} \frac{1}{n} \sum_{i=1}^n f(s_i), s_i \in U[a, b]$$

where s_i are drawn i.i.d. from a uniform distribution $U[a, b]$. If $f(x) = g(x)h(x)$ in the interval $[a, b]$, where

$$\int_a^b h(x)dx = 1$$

then we can improve the convergence speed of the integration by sampling $g(s)$ with s drawn from a distribution H with density function $h(x)$.

$$\int_a^b f(x)dx = lim_{n\to\infty} \frac{1}{n} \sum_{i=1}^n g(s_i), s_i \in H$$

This is exactly what we can do in the formula for $E\lfloor w_0 \rfloor_\gamma$ above, since the functions $f(p_i|\ldots)$ all satisfy the requirement for $h(x)$.

The Monte-Carlo technique may be extended for multivariate distributions, but even with the above improvement the convergence is slow, making it costly to compute the value of the option.

Another approach is to use a multinomial tree evaluation of the option. This method also suffers severely of large growth for problems of high dimensionally since the branching factor increases exponentially with the number of resource classes.

7.2 Analytical Approximation

An analytical solution of the integral seems to be impossible since it involves integrating over *Erf(x)*. However, if we can show that the value of the option can be expressed in simpler terms for which we can find a good approximation, that implies that if we would be able to evaluate the price of the option very fast.

There might exist a converging series expansion of the terms in the integral such that an approximation of the integral is possible to express in a closed form. If so, it would be possible to evaluate the price of a network option very rapidly.

We note that we can write the integral recursively

$$\begin{aligned} I_0(p) &= p - X \\ I_i(p) &= \int_X^p I_{i-1}(p_i) f(p_i|p_{i+1}, \ldots, p_n) dp_i \end{aligned}$$

and thus we can write the value of the network option as

$$E\lfloor w_0 \rfloor_\gamma = I_n(\infty)$$

If the price changes follow a normal distribution[3], $f(p_i|\ldots)$ is of the form $ke^{h(p_1,\ldots,p_n)}$, where $h(\ldots)$ is a polynomial in $p_1, \ldots, p_n$.[4] The Taylor series of an exponential of that form (not shown here) is

$$f(\ldots) = g(p_i, \ldots, p_n) e^{h_2(p_{i+1},\ldots,p_n)}$$

so the integral I_i of a function on the form above is

$$\begin{aligned} I_i &= \int g(p_i, \ldots, p_n) e^{h(p_i,\ldots,p_n)} dp_i \\ &= e^{h_2(p_{i+1},\ldots,p_n)} \int g_2(p_i, \ldots, p_n) dp_i \\ &= g_3(p_{i+1}, \ldots, p_n) e^{h_2(p_{i+1},\ldots,p_n)} \end{aligned}$$

which is of the same form as the integrated function, but without p_i. Recursion shows that we could iterate this step, for instance doing the Taylor expansion

[3] this is approximately true when t or r are small

[4] This can be worked out from the definition of the multivariate distribution.

around the center of the integration interval, until we have an analytic approximation of the integral. Since it would be a polynomial in $p_1, \ldots, p_n$, it would be very fast to evaluate on a computer. By keeping track of the error terms we may even get a bound on the error.

The weakness with this approach is that the error of the Taylor series increases rapidly as we leave the region around point where we developed the series. If the error term does not even tend towards zero if we leave it too much, we cannot get a better approximation even by expanding the series further. One way to circumvent this problem could be to partition the integration interval into N pieces and doing N expansions around the center of each small interval. An open issue is to find a better series development for the integral.

8 Summary

We describe a way to model agents as self-interested actors on a market, and give a framework for reasoning about their actions. The agents are equipped with a set of resources which they exchange to another set of resources according to the client user's specification. Our idea is to declare the client's requests as a network of resources that must be acquired along one path by the agent. This model can express both traditional agent programming examples such as the travel agent, as well as market-based bandwidth reservation negotiation for a computer network. In the latter case, the resource network is equal to the topology of the computer network.

Although suitable for many scenarios, resource networks are yet not so suited for domains where utility functions depend on the obtained volume, or where the resources have too many parameters and constraints for them to be seen as members of a class. The alternatives to resource nets are generally search, and one-to-one negotiating, which can be very inefficient for complex tasks.

We propose the use of derivatives to create hedged portfolios to coordinate parallel bidding and reduce trading risk, and institutional agents which provide "network options", options on the min value of a set of sums of correlated lognorm-distributed price processes. The formula for the option value is given, and shown to be of a nice recursive structure which implies that if we can approximate this substructure efficiently, we can evaluate the price of the option very fast. The derivation assumes that resources are liquid enough for assuming that the market is enough like the financial market to allow for risk-neutral evaluation.

We have so far not a good approximation function for the option price, and the current way to evaluate the option seems to be by using Monte-Carlo techniques.

References

1. Aspnes J., Azar Y., Fiat A. Plotkin S. and Waarts O., On-Line Routing of Virtual Circuits with Applications to Load Balancing and Machine Scheduling, Journal of the ACM, vol. 44, no. 3, (1997), pp. 486–504.

2. Davis R. and Smith R. G., Negotiation as a Metaphor for Distributed Problem Solving, Artificial Intelligence, 20 (1983), pp. 63–109.
3. Ferguson D., Yemini Y. and Nikolaou C., Microeconomic Algorithms for Load Balancing in Distributed Computer Systems, Proc. of DCS, (1988).
4. Hull J. C., Options, Futures, and Other Derivatives, Prentice Hall, (1997).
5. Hurwicz L., The Design of Mechanisms for Resource Allocation, Richard T. Ely Lecture, American Economic Association, vol. 63, no. 2, (1973), pp. 1–30.
6. Kurose J. F., A Microeconomic Approach to Decentralized Optimization of Channel Access Policies in Multiaccess Networks, Proc. of the 5th Int. Conf. On Distributed Computer Systems, Denver Co., (1985).
7. Lazar A. A. and Semret N., Spot and Derivative Markets for Admission Control and Pricing in Connection-Oriented Networks, Technical Report CU/CTR/TR 501-98-35, Dept. of Electrical Engineering, Columbia University, (1998).
8. Milton R. C., Computer Evaluation of the Multivariate Normal Integral, Technometrica, 14 (1972), pp. 881–889.
9. Sandholm, T. An Algorithm for Optimal Winner Determination in Combinatorial Auctions, Proc. of IJCAI'99, (1999.), pp. 542–547.
10. Waldspurger C. A., Hogg T., Huberman B., Kephart J. O. and Stornetta W. S., Spawn: A Distributed Computational Economy, IEEE Trans. on Software Engineering, vol. 18, no. 2, (1992).
11. Walsh W. E., Wellman M. P., Wurman P. R. and MacKie-Mason J. K., Some Economics of Market-based Distributed Scheduling, 18th Int. Conf. on Distributed Computing Systems, (1998).
12. Wellman M., A Market-Oriented Programming Environment and its Application to Distributed Multicommodity Flow Problems, Journal of Artificial Intelligence Research, 1 (1993), pp. 1–23.

Conversational Speech Biometrics

Stéphane H. Maes, Jiří Navrátil, and Upendra V. Chaudhari

IBM T.J. Watson Research Center Rt. 134, Yorktown Heights, NY, USA
{smaes,jiri,uvc}@us.ibm.com

Abstract. This paper discusses a new modality for speaker recognition - conversational biometrics - as a high security voice-based authentication method for E-commerce applications. By combining diverse simultaneous conversational technologies, high accuracy transparent speaker recognition becomes possible even in channel or environment mismatches. For speaker identification over very large populations, we combine dialogs to reduce the set of confusable speakers and text-independent speaker identification to pin-point the actual speaker. Similarly, dialogs with personal random or predefined questions are used to perform simultaneously knowledge-based and acoustic-based verifications of the user. Adequate design of the dialog allows to tailor the ROC curves to the needs of most applications. We demonstrate the conceptual advantages using our telephony prototype. Users familiar with the system can log into the system with 0.8% or 1.3% false rejection and ca. $5 \cdot 10^{-12}\%$ or $2 \cdot 10^{-6}\%$ false acceptance rates in about 40 sec or 20 sec respectively which is an impressive result as compared to purely voice-print based authentication.

1 Introduction

With the rapid development of automated applications for finances and E-commerce and in the context of the evolving internet and wireless communication technology, the importance of reliable, high-security, and non-intrusive methods for personal authentication has been growing significantly. Today, the quality of these methods plays an essential role for the acceptability and ease of use of the target applications. Many modalities and techniques have been applied to achieve the task of authentication, ranging from retina scans to finger prints. In this paper, a particular modality is of interest - the voice. This modality has a unique advantage over other biometrics by relying on speech, the primary vector of communication and is especially important in applications such as telephony dialog systems where it is a natural and, besides the touchtone keypad, also the only communication means. By extracting appropriate features from a person's voice the uniqueness of the physiology of the vocal tract and the articulatory properties can be captured to a high degree and can serve the purpose of authentication. Speaker recognition technology analyzing and modeling the voice prints has been a major research effort for the past decades, today gradually reaching maturity. Despite impressive results multiple unknown factors in the acoustic speaker recognition still exist: unicity, uncooperative speakers, robustness etc. Multiple commercial systems are already available, in most cases, however, as field prototypes or secondary systems. Text-constrained methods which

J. Liu and Y. Ye (Eds.): E-Commerce Agents, LNAI 2033, pp. 166–179, 2001.

are technically more simple and achieve higher accuracies, are prone to fraud by recorded speech or using future-generation speech synthesizers which can mimic the target person. Text-constrained methods are also intrusive and therefore can not be closely integrated within an application dialog flow: either the speaker recognition is performed as a separate process or it is performed once in the business logic, but it is not an underlying process or always invokale option. Text-independent systems, on the other hand, are technically more challenging, and the accuracy rates may be somewhat lower compared to text-depedendent systems, but they open new perspectives and application possibilities. In particular these methods are non-obstrusive. As a result they can be closely integrated within a dialog, run in parallel, contribute to the dialog flow or application business logic and be invoked at any time. In general, the voice-print recognition accuracy tends to deteriorate in adverse acoustic conditions, such in the telephony environment which introduces highly variable and unknown transducer properties to the source speech. Hitherto, the problems of robustness and accuracy have been major obstacles for deploying voice-print based speaker recognition for remote authentication applications. In this paper a concept of combining two authentication modalities, the voice-print and the speaker's knowledge is presented that allows for flexible identification and verification with a high degree of security: a concept called Conversational Speech Biometrics [16,17]. The following sections detail on the principles of this concept and its both functional components: the speaker and the speech recognition technologies. Corresponding application scenaria together with a description of a prototype implementation in the telephony environment and experimental result are presented. We show that the speech biometrics is a powerful framework for remote authentication which enables speech, as a single communication modality, to serve as a primary security key for a wide range of applications.

2 Conversational Biometrics

Classical authentication relies on one of these three items: what you own, what you are and what you know. Key or card-based systems characterize what you own. PIN and password based systems rely on what you know. Voice passwords have been proposed: utterance verification for access control and password compliance [22,15,13]. Biometrics and in particular speaker recognition rely on what you are. The new approach of speech biometrics or conversational biometrics [17] employs text-independent speaker recognition to acoustically identify or verify answers from the user in dialog with the system. The questions addressed to the user can be randomly selected, follow a pre-defined sequence or follow a business logic. With this approach, user verification and identification rely on acoustic recognition and on the content of the answers to the questions. Beyond eliminating the problem of prerecorded speech and increased security, this combination has many application-related advantages as will be discussed later.

2.1 Acoustic Speaker Recognition

The speaker recognition problem can be divided into four different functional modi:

- *Speaker identification*, aiming at determining the identity of a speaker based on his or her voice. The speakers are already enrolled in the system. No identity claim is provided. If the set of speakers to be identified is restricted to be the enrolled speakers, we speak of closed-set identification. The ability of the system to also detect unknown speakers extends the task to so-called open-set speaker identification.
  In terms of biometrics, speaker identification is a "many-to-many" recognition task. The decision alternatives are equal to the size of the enrolled speakers (+ 1 in open-set case). Therefore, the accuracy of speaker identification degrades as the size of the speaker population increases.
  Besides classical speaker identification, some extensions exists with added functionality of providing N-best lists or confidence scores. In the former case, a speaker identification system returns a sorted list of N identities that match the best the current speaker. The latter case rather implies that the identifier will produce a confidence level for each enrolled speakers that he or she matches the current speaker. Open set speaker identification requires rejection features that can usually be directly used for verification purposes. The recognition rates for closed-identification range from ca. 95% for small populations (100 speakers) to 70-90% for large populations (few thousands of speakers) based on 3-5 sec telephony-quality speech [6].
- *Speaker verification*, a task of verifying the identity claim of a speaker based on his or her voice.
  In terms of biometrics, speaker verification is a "one-to-many" recognition task. In contrast to speaker identification, the accuracy of speaker verification does not directly depend on the population size. However, as it is typical in biometrics, the estimate of this accuracy depends on the representation of the population samples used to evaluate the accuracy. In contrast to other biometrics, these estimators also strongly depend on the channel effects and noise corruption of the signal. As mentioned above, speaker recognition performances vary dramatically from matched conditions (same type of microphone, channel characteristics and background noise) to mismatched conditions.
  Besides classical speaker verification, we must also mention extensions where instead of hard accept or reject decisions, confidence levels are returned. Typical performances, represented as equal-error-rates, lie between 2 and 5% for 2-4 sec telephone-quality speech. [6]
- *speaker classification*, performing the speaker recognition over an unknown number of unknown (unenrolled) speakers. Usually, it means to be able to detect speaker changes, also called speaker separation, and index the resulting segments according to the identity.
  This function is specifically speech related. Only portions of the concept are met in other biometrics. However, the capabilities that it offers to distinguish between different undeclared successive users of a system may also be implemented with other biometrics.

- *speaker enrollment.* In order to recognize the user based on his or her voice, samples of the user's voice need to be acquired and the speaker model (voice-print) created. Often, the models used for speaker identification differ from those used for speaker verification. By analogy to fingerprints, voice-prints refer to the minimum set of characteristics of a speaker required to create the speaker models used for identification and verification. Voice-prints are algorithm-dependent.
  Similarly to speech recognition, the principle here is that there is no better enrollment data than more data! The more data available for a speaker the more accurate the resulting voice-prints. Especially if this data can be collected over multiple mismatched conditions representative of the actual mismatches experienced during recognition. [5]

Further on, the task complexity can be distinguished w.r.t. the type of vocabulary presented in the enrollment and during the recognition. Text-dependent and text-constrained recognition restricts the words to be spoken to a certain small set, e.g. a password (global or user-selected), or a digit string. Similarly, text-prompted systems restrict the input utterance whereby the words to be spoken are generated by the system itself, which reduces the chances of using prerecorded speech. Finally, the text-independent speaker recognition offers most freedom as for the use of vocabulary and belongs to the technically most demanding tasks. As for the conversational speech biometrics the text-independency is an essential feature as it allows for analysis of all the user-application conversation regardless of whether related or unrelated to the act of authentication, e.g. as a continuous background listener.

The literature on voice-print modeling and recognition comprises areas of template-matching, statistical modeling and artificial neural networks [1,8,19, 9,12,10,11,4,16]. Our speaker recognition engine is based on structured speaker modeling using Gaussian mixture models in all four functional modi listed above [3,5,2,6]. Depending on the text-modus, the voice-prints are created in the enrollment stage from the user's speech transformed to a sequence of feature vectors and collected over several different channels. Typically, the amount of enrollment speech ranges between 30 and 120 sec. The incoming speech is internally segmented into specific phonetic units on multiple levels of granularity (e.g. phone level, phone-class level, global level) using speaker-independent Hidden Markov Models. The Gaussian mixtures are with diagonal covariances and are initialized with estimates from a global, speaker-independent model (seed) in order to alleviate the problem of data sparseness, which strongly applies with the enrollment amounts mentioned above. For each model grain unit a linear feature transform is estimated so as to minimize the loss of likelihood mass due to the diagonal covariance assumption. During the test, a likelihood measure between the test utterance and the voice-print is calculated as the accumulated maximum observation probability of the feature vectors over all granularity levels and their associated units [6]. Whereas the identification consists of calculating the test likelihoods based on all models of enrolled speakers, the verification is posed a hypothesis test with a discriminant function calculated as a likelihood-ratio test. In the hypothesis test the target speaker's likelihood is obtained from the target voice-print and the non-target speaker hypothesis is represented by the likelihood of a certain number of competing models (cohorts). The cohorts are determined either in the enrollment or on-the-fly during the test. Combining both methods the identification and the verification, also the open-set identification task can be performed in order to detect (and to reject) unknown speakers.

Typical performance rates measured for telephone-quality speech for the described speaker recognition engine, using 30 sec speech for enrollment and ca. 3-5 sec utterances for testing. On a population of 100 speakers the identification error is 4.8% and increases to 10.0% with a larger population size consisting of 1000 speakers [6]. The text-independent verification performance measured in the operating point of equal level of false acceptances and false rejections (equal error rate) for 3 sec tests is ca. 2.0%. Fusion with additional decisions based on algorithms to be disclosed elsewhere can further reduce this number to 1.2% These values will also be used for estimating the performance of the overall speech biometrics system in connection with the experiments described in section 3.

2.2 Speech Biometrics: Integration of Speaker Recognition and Speech Recognition

Consider the system described in figure 1, which simultaneously performs speech recognition and speaker recognition on the input utterances. The audio stream is provided to the acoustic front-end as isolated utterances (command and control mode or answers to a directed dialog) or as a continuous stream. The front-end captures the audio and extracts the acoustic features (e.g. MFCC). The

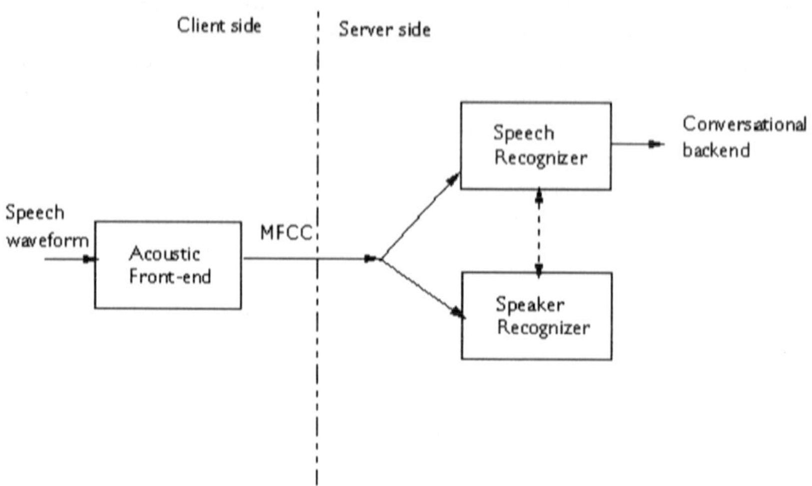

Fig. 1. Integration of speech and speaker recognition engines.

features can be further compressed using the algorithm described in [21]. Note that the acoustic features can be shared by the speech recognition engine and any post processing system (e.g. natural language understanding module [20]). In networked applications, where the acoustic front-end can be on the client side while the other conversational functions are performed on the server side, sharable features allow one data stream at data rates as low as 4 to 5 kb/s, quite suitable for wireless modem connections. On embedded systems, only one signal processing task is performed. This reduces the CPU, memory and power requirements. The feature stream is then split up between the speech recognition engine and the text-independent speaker recognition engine.

Besides numerous advantages for speaker adaptation in the speech recognition engine and command disambiguation, the integrated framework offers the basis for implementing the conversational speech biometrics (CSB) concept. Simultaneous speech recognition and text-independent speaker verification can be used for continuous access control. For example, in a command and control application or directed dialog, each command or transaction request can be executed only upon verification of the speaker. The verification can be performed on a continuous streaming input, on a command by command basis or on a set of utterances. This also provides continuous background monitoring capabilities to certify that no speaker change took place during a transaction, or after the authentication.

Obviously, such integration of the speaker recognition capability allows transparent recognition in a non-obstrusive manner to the user and the transaction. Also, since it is well known that with more data a more robust recognition can be achieved, it is particularly advantageous to postpone recognition decisions later in the transaction when a final decision is required.

Speech biometrics, as we originally called it [16] requires a close integration of the text-independent engine with the entire conversational system. As illustrated in figure 2 conversational systems consist of speech recognition, speech synthesis, natural language understanding, natural language generation and dialog management [20,7]. Indeed, the dialog management now carries a conversation with the speaker aimed at automatically identifying a cooperative user or verifying a claimant.

Conversational identification consists of a dialog that reduces the set of confusable speakers handled by the speaker identification engine, assuming cooperative users. For example, an IVR (Interactive Voice Response) system interrogates the speaker as follows:

- *"What is your name"*
- I am John Doe
- *"What city are you calling from?"*
- I am in Manhattan
- ...

By now, out of the pool of millions of users enrolled in the system, the dialog has reduced the set of candidates to a subset for example smaller than say twenty to fifty speakers. If the sub-set is still bigger the dialog can continue. Text-independent speaker identification can now benefit from the reduced number of

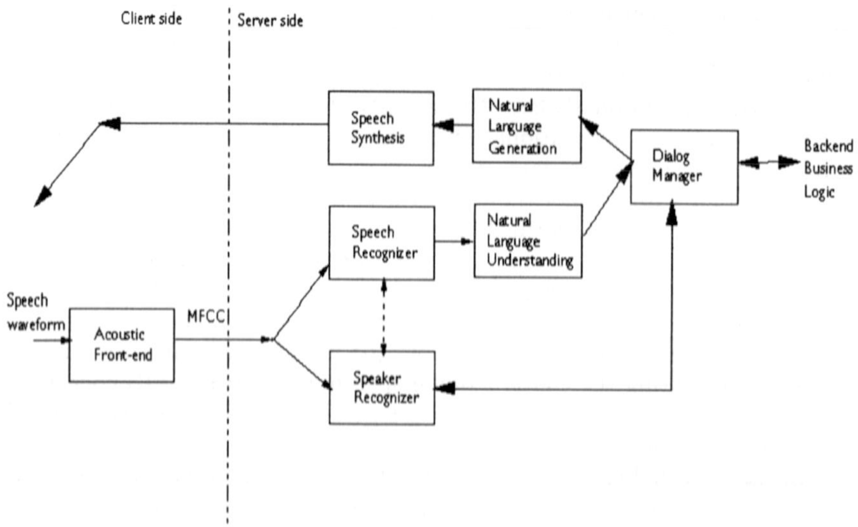

Fig. 2. Conversational biometrics architecture.

candidates and can perform identification or generate a N-best candidate list [17].

Conversational verification consists of a dialog to perform a knowledge-based verification of the person in parallel with the acoustic-based verification. It is a powerful mechanism to combat the limitations still inherent to speaker verification systems. Consider an automated phone banking application driven by an IVR. The following dialog takes place:

- *"What is your mother's maiden name?"*
- My mother's name was Doe1
- *"What is your favorite color?"*
- I like red
- ...

The questions can be randomly generated out of information collected during enrollment or they can be dynamically generated based on past transactions history. With an appropriate recovery dialog the false rejections can be reduced to an arbitrary level.

It has been shown empirically [23] that this method allows authentication based on information that is easy to remember for the enrolled user, while at the same time being hard to guess. These "cognitive" passwords are easy to remember because they are based on factual events regarding the user and on his or her opinions. While some of these data are known to others, the amount of unrelated information is large. It was thus observed that only a small fraction of this information could be guessed, even by persons of close relationship to the enrolled user. In comparison, standard passwords, which are conventionally alphanumeric strings that are either user generated or randomly constructed, were difficult to remember and insecure by virtue of the steps users took in order to be able to remember them. Speech biometrics provides an additional benefit by leveraging information in the acoustic signal to make the overall system even more robust.

The described verification scenaria can be exercised and are applicable to virtually all E-commerce transactions with users acting in networks with voice or mixed voice-data connections. One example is a CSB verification that follows a transaction request previously completed in a purely data-based network connection. The verification is achieved by creating an automated voice connection from the network to the user terminal, typically a mobile phone, in order to carry out a CSB session. CSB and the steadily growing number of mobile-phone terminals, their convergence with the internet involving a variety of applications such as banking and shopping, represent a particularly attractive basis to establish a universal voice-supported user authentication modality.

The following items summarize the advantages of the concept:

- improved system robustness against impostors
- system flexibility in carying out the authentication, e.g. adaptive length of a verification session dialog dependent on a voice-print confidence, extensibility to indentification and speaking style adaptation/recognition
- possibility of continuous voice-print enrollment. Unlike the purely voice-print-based systems, the CSB is able to handle new types of channels without a-priori voice enrollment by first backing off to verbal verification with subsequent voice-print creation
- continuous verbal information collection (enrollment)
- transparency and non-obtrusivity with respect to business-logic dialog

3 Implementing CSB: The Voice Identification and Verification Agent

The practicability and performance of the CSB concept has been studied by implementing the principles described above in the telephony environment and measuring the performance on an authentication task with real speech. In this framework, an application-independent module was developed [18] that incorporates a natural-language-enabled part for the verbal information verification, so-called Verbal Identification and Verification Agent (VIVA), and the speaker recognition engine (see Section 2.1 engine for the voice-print analysis.

The VIVA system (see Fig. 3) has a client-server architecture and is suitable for various applications and plattforms because of its independence in terms of maintaining own databases and handling dialogs. The architecture consists of the following functional parts (Fig. 3) 1) the VIVA server which handles requests for verbal verification sessions and maintains the database records, 2) the VIVA client interface, 3) the speech biometrics module which interacts with both the user and the application via a speech and a proprietary interface respectively. Further on this module requests sessions from the VIVA server, triggers the voice-print analysis, processes and combines both results. For the communication

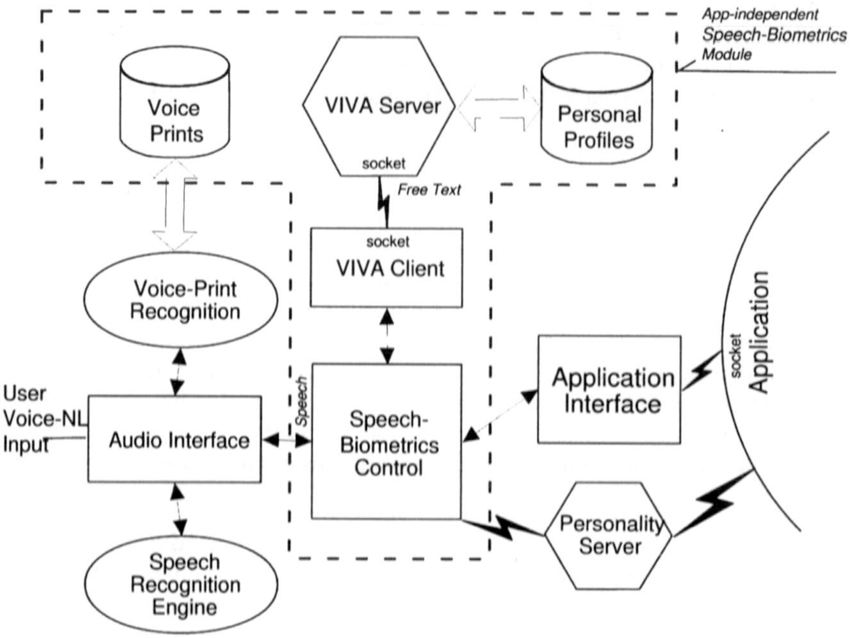

Fig. 3. VIVA overview.

between a VIVA client and the server a proprietary protocol was introduced involving the notion of a verification "session" and "interview." An interview represents an elementary dialog consisting of a small number of questions given a security policy. The policy can be defined as the ratio of the maximum number of questions and the minimum number of correct answers per interview. Within one session, multiple interviews with varying policies can be opened which allows for adapting the session length to the current voice-print match confidence. The questions asked within one session are generated so as to prevent repetitions across interviews and also to guarantee for sufficient security by an appropriate topic coverage, e.g. there will be at least one password question among questions about family, hobbies, or favourite colors.

The typical procedure looks like the following: The application creates an instance of the CSB VIVA module when the user tries to log on (e.g. an incoming call is detected). The VIVA then takes over the control and first tries to obtain the user's ID claim. This is achieved through a direct prompt or using an identification procedure based on voice and verbal information. In our implementation the claim ID is a digit string (extension number). If the user does not explicitly specify this number and issues commands to the application directly, the VIVA suspends the speech command and starts determining the claim in a short dialog using an open-set acoustic speaker identification. In case of an unsuccessful identification the user is prompted for the claim number explicitly. Using the claim ID the speech biometrics control creates a verification session and an initial interview with the VIVA server. Questions generated by the server are synthesized for the user and user's response is decoded using the IBM ViaVoice Telephony engine [7]. Appropriate vocabularies and grammars are switched by the biometrics control module on a question basis according to the current topic. Decoded answer is returned back to the server for evaluation. In parallel, the control module collects the audio data in a buffer. Once the security policy for the open interview is satisfied the server returns a positive result and closes the verbal interview (session remains still open). The control module triggers the voice-print verification based on the the collected audio and subsequently decides whether to accept the speaker, or to continue the verification session by creating an additional interview, or possibly to reject the speaker due to too many unsucessful interviews (incorrect or ambiguous answers) or a too poor acoustic match.

After this initial verification, if closed positive, the control is given back to the application. The instance of the CSB module may be terminated if the application does not require any further authentication or may remain instantiated. In the latter case the speech biometrics control creates a listener associated with the audio stream and collects the speech from the regular user-application communication. Then, a voice-print re-verification can be requested from the application at any time (especially before committing crucial operations) thus achieving continuous speaker tracking and detecting potential speaker changes.

The VIVA system supports an automated user enrollment via HTML for the knowledge database and a telephone voice collection for the acoustic information.

3.1 Experimental Results

It is obvious that accuracy of both the speaker and the speech recognition has an impact on the false rejection rate of the overall CSB system. Inaccurately decoded answers containing wrong or no values will be considered as incorrect by the VIVA server. The overall false rejection (FR) rate of the CSB system resulting from the acoustic FR $P_{FR}(X)$ and the FR due to erroneous-dialog with probability $P_{FR}(\mathcal{D})$ (both conditioned on the acoustic and dialog analysis and assuming correctly formulated answers by the user in the dialog) within an interview can be estimated as [17]:

$$\begin{aligned} P(FR(X)) &= P_{FR}(X) + P_{FR}(\mathcal{D}) - P_{FR}(X, \mathcal{D}) &\quad (1)\\ &= P_{FR}(X) + P_{FR}(\mathcal{D}) - P_{FR}(X)P_{FR}(\mathcal{D}) &\quad (2)\end{aligned}$$

in which the the acoustic voice-print performance and the rejection rate due to dialog errors are seen statictically independent. The corresponding false acceptance (FA) rate of the CSB is written as

$$P(FA(X)) \propto P_{FA}(X)\frac{1}{M_q^k} \quad (3)$$

where $\frac{1}{M_q^k}$ stands for the expected perplexity of k questions with M_q possible answers which approximates the probability of false acceptance in a dialog due to a correct random guess of an impostor as well as due to a speech recognition error. In general, it is possible to apply various policies to combine the outcomes of both the acoustic-based and the dialog-based match. For example, using the information about the quality of the current acoustic channel the decision might rely more on the verbal part of the verification without causing a too high false rejection due to poor acoustic channel. In fact, the equations (2) and (3) represent an upper bound for the FR and a lower bound for the FA respectively. In the case of N questions in an interview and a *minimum* required number of k correct answers the dialog error obeys the binomial distribution

$$P_{FR}(\mathcal{D}) = \sum_{l=N-k+1}^{N} \binom{N}{l} p_{err}(q)^l \; (1 - p_{err}(q))^{N-l} \tag{4}$$

whereby $p_{err}(q)$ is the probability of a question answered incorrectly (assuming topic independence). However, in the reported experiment an interview policy was implemented such that the interview is closed already when the $l = N-k+1$ incorrect answers are detected. Thus the dialog error calculation (4) must take the variable interview length into account as a probability of observing the l-th error and ending the interview:

$$P_{FR}(\mathcal{D}) = \sum_{n=l}^{N} \binom{n-1}{l-1} p_{err}(q)^l (1 - p_{err}(q))^{n-l} \tag{5}$$

where $l = N - k + 1$.

To estimate the dialog recognition error a data collection was carried out [18] on speakers who were asked to answer 25 speech biometrics questions to several topics: digits, years, cities, states, colors, hobbies and favourite food. some of the speakers were acquainted with the system, the rest were first-time users. The attribute perplexity varied from topic to topic. M_q in (3) was dependent on the question topic: ranging from 20 (colors) over ca. 50 (years) to $> 10^6$ for digit strings. It has to be noted that no exact value of the real attribute perplexity can be determined because 1) the natural-language-part of the FSG adds a certain perplexity and can catch some out-of-vocabulary values by decoding them as non-value words, i.e. the decoding is open-set (the same applies to statistical NL modeling), 2) the perplexity of certain attributes, e.g. years, is reduced by their meaning and predictability in real context. The overall answer correctness, defined as containing the correct answer without insertions of multiple incorrect values due to erroneous recognition, was 11.3% ranging from 0% for hobbies to 15% for cities and states. Note that empty answers (i.e. containing no relevant atribute values) were considered as incorrect (representing ca. 5-8% of the answers) which might be potentialy recovered by an apppropriate dialog, thus reducing the $P_{FR}(\mathcal{D})$ in (3). For the experienced users the answer error rate was less than 5%. Further experimental details can be found in [18].

For the calculations in Table 1 an equal-error-rate (EER) of the acoustic speaker recognition 2.0% and the realistic question perplexities $1/2.10^4$ for digits, and 1/50,or 1/20 as representative values for other topics were used, assuming that in an interview with $k = 3$ there is one question for each of these perplexities, for $k = 4$ additional 1/50 and for $k = 5$ additional 1/20 factors were taken.

The Table 1 shows FA and FR rates for various security policies in which the first parameter stands for the maximum number of questions to be asked and the second for minimum number of correct answers. Allowing a small number of the answers to be incorrect prevents too high false acceptance due to speech recognition errors.

Table 1. False acceptance and rejection rates for various interview policies. Calculated for an acoustic EER=2.0% (*OP*timistic rows calculated for system-acquainted users with $p_{err}(q) = 0.05$ and an ac. FR=1.0%).

Policy	FA %	FR %	Avg. Interview length in sec.
3-2	$2\ 10^{-6}$	5.1	20
5-4	$5.0\ 10^{-12}$	11.9	35
5-3	$1.0\ 10^{-7}$	3.2	30
6-5	$1.0\ 10^{-13}$	15.8	45
6-4	$5.0\ 10^{-12}$	4.2	40
3-2 *OP*	$4.0\ 10^{-6}$	1.7	20
6-4 *OP*	$1.0\ 10^{-11}$	1.2	40

Smaller FR can be obtained by decreasing the acoustic FR (1.0%) entailing a higher FA rate (4.0%) and by assuming that users familiar with the system achieve $p_{err}(q) = 0.05$ (last two "optimistic" rows in Table 1). The acoustic EER might also be lower in reality, even though 2.0% was assumed in this calculation, especially for longer interviews where the amount of collected speech exceeds 3 sec the EER will be roughly halvened, reducing the overall error rates correspodingly. Further improvements of the acoustic EER to 1.2% (or roughly 0.6 and 2.4% for the optimistic operating poing), as mentioned earlier, change the last two rows to $FA/FR = 2.2\ 10^{-6}\%/1.3\%$ and $FA/FR = 5.5\ 10^{-12}\%/0.8\%$ for the policies 3-2 and 6-4 respectively.

4 Conclusion

We have demonstrated the advantages of integrating speaker recognition and conversational systems to implement conversational biometrics. Appropriate design of the application allows to perform simultaneous content/knowledge-based recognition with high accuracy even in challenging conditions or over very large populations.

The results obtained using our telephony prototype prove the feasibility and robustness of the CSB concept. Users familiar with the system can log into the system with 0.8% or 1.3% false rejection and ca. $5 \cdot 10^{-12}\%$ or $2 \cdot 10^{-6}\%$ false acceptance rates in about 40 sec or 20 sec respectively which is an impressive result as compared to purely voice-print based authentication.

The concept of Conversational Speech Biometrics makes speaker recognition for the first time deployable for high security applications as a primary security system even with today's technology - a claim that can't be made with other speaker recognition technology.

References

1. Atal B. S.: Automatic recognition of speakers from their voices. *Proc. IEEE*, 64:pp. 460–475 (1976).
2. Beigi H. S. , Maes S. H. , Sorensen J. S. , and Chaudhari U. V.: A hierarchichal approach to large-scale speaker recognition. In *Proc. Eurospeech* (1999).
3. Beigi H. S. M. , Maes S. , and Sorensen J. : A frame-based statistical method for speaker recognition. In *Proc. RLA2C*, Avigon, France, (1998).
4. Campbell J. : Automatic speech and speaker recognition, advanced topics. In Lee et al. [14].
5. Chaudhari U. V. , Beigi H. S. , and Maes S. H.: Multi-environment speaker verification. In *Proc. AutoID*, (1999).
6. Chaudhari U.V. , Navrátil J. , and Maes S.H.: Multi-grained data modeling for speaker recognition with sparse training and test data. In *Proc. of the International Conference on Spoken Language Processing (ICSLP)*, Beijing, (2000). submitted.
7. Davies K. and al.: The IBM conversational telephony system for financial applications. In *Proc. Eurospeech*, (1999).
8. Doddington G. R.: Speaker recognition - identifying people by their voices. *Proc. IEEE*, 76(11):pp. 1651–1664, (1985).
9. Farell K.R. , Mammone R.J. , and Assaleh K.T.: Speaker recognition using neural networks and conventional classifiers. *IEEE Trans. on Acoustics, Speech, and Signal Processing*, 2(1):194–205, (1994).
10. Furui S. : Automatic speech and speaker recognition, advanced topics. In Lee et al. [14].
11. Furui S. : Recent advances in speaker recognition. In Bigun J. , Chollet G. , and Borgefors G. , editors, *Proc. Audio- and Video-based biometric person authentication*, pages 237–252. Springer-Verlag, (1997).
12. Furui S. and Sondhi M. , editors: *Advances in speech signal processing*. Marcel Dekker, New York, NY, (1991).
13. Kimball O. , Schmidt M. , Gish H. , and Waterman J. : Speaker verification with limited enrollment data. In *Proc. Eurospeech*, volume 2, pages 967–970, (1997).
14. Lee C.-H. , Soong F. K. , and Paliwal K. K. , editors: *Automatic speech and speaker recognition, advanced topics*. Kluwer Academic Publishers, Norwell, MA, (1996).
15. Li Q. , Juang B.-H. , Zhou Q. , and Lee C.-H.: Verbal information verification. In *Proc. Eurospeech*, volume 2, pages 839–842, (1997).
16. Maes S. H. and Beigi H. S.: Open Sesame! Speech password or key to secure your door. In *Proc. ACCV*, (1998). invited paper.
17. Maes S.H.: Conversational biometrics In *Proc. of the European Conference on Speech Communication and Technology (EUROSPEECH)*, Budapest, Hungary, (1999).

18. Navrátil J. , Kleindienst J. , and Maes S.H.: An instantiable speech biometrics module with natural language interface: Implementation in the telephony environment. In *Proc. of the International Conference on Acoustics, Speech, and Signal Processing (ICASSP)*, Istanbul, Turkey, (2000). IEEE.
19. O'Shaughnessy D. : Speaker recognition. *IEEE ASSP Magazine*, 3(4):pp. 4–17, (1986).
20. Papineni K. A. , Roukos S. , and Ward R. T.: Free-flow dialog management using forms. In *Proc. Eurospeech*, (1999).
21. Ramaswamy G. and Gopalakrishnan P. : Compression of acoustic features for speech recognition in network environments. In *Proc. ICASSP*, volume 2, pages 977–980, (1998).
22. Rosenberg A. E. and Parthasarathy S. : Speaker identification with user-selected password phrases. In *Proc. Eurospeech*, volume 3, pages 1371–1374, (1997).
23. Zviran M. and Haga W.J.: User authentication by cognitive passwords: An empirical assessment. *IEEE*, (1990).

Secure Communication for Secure Agent-Based Electronic Commerce Applications

Joris Claessens, Bart Preneel, and Joos Vandewalle

K.U.Leuven ESAT-COSIC
Kardinaal Mercierlaan 94, 3001 Heverlee, Belgium
joris.claessens@esat.kuleuven.ac.be
http://www.esat.kuleuven.ac.be/~joclaess/

Abstract. Although electronic commerce is a relatively new concept, it has already become a normal aspect of our daily life. The software agent technology is also relatively new. In the area of electronic commerce, software agents could be used for example to search for the lowest prices and the best services, to buy goods on behalf of a user, etc. These applications involve a number of security issues, such as communications security, system security, and application security, that have to be solved. This paper describes how communications security is added to a lightweight agent framework. Secure agent-based electronic commerce applications require communications security services. Adding these services is a first basis and an important enabler for the framework in order to be used for secure electronic commerce applications.

1 Introduction

Money is a very important aspect of our modern society. We are confronted with several kinds of money in our daily life. Besides ordinary cash, electronic payment systems are nowadays commonly used. On the Internet, commerce itself is done electronically as well. People can buy books, compact discs, and even cars; flights can be booked at several airlines; music can be bought on-line directly from a producer, and downloaded in digital format; etc.

Currently most electronic transactions are executed manually, i.e., by going to the particular web site, selecting what is wanted, and entering a credit card number (if this particular payment mechanism is used) in order to pay. However, the concept of software agents can be used for electronic commerce to automate these tasks. Software agents will help people for example to find the lowest prices and the best services. They will also be able to pay without user intervention. Of course, as these applications involve electronic payments, other sensitive operations to be performed, and confidential information to be exchanged, a number of security issues have to be solved first.

The contribution of this paper to this area can be summarized as follows: a lightweight agent framework is secured, making it (partially) suitable for secure agent-based electronic commerce applications. In the next section, the security aspects with respect to agent-based electronic commerce applications are briefly

J. Liu and Y. Ye (Eds.): E-Commerce Agents, LNAI 2033, pp. 180–190, 2001.

discussed. Thereafter, background information on the SSL/TLS protocol – which is used for providing communications security – is given. The impact of Java on the system security aspect is then explained. In Sect. 5, the unsecured lightweight agent framework is presented, together with the different approaches that were taken to provide communications security. Further comments and achievements are given and discussed in Sect. 6. Finally, related work and alternative approaches for providing secure communication are described in Sect. 7.

2 Secure Agent-Based Electronic Commerce Applications

Without giving a formal definition, a software agent is a very generic term for a piece of software that can operate autonomously, and that helps facilitate a certain task. Software agents can communicate, they often have learning capabilities, and they can sometimes travel from one computer to another computer (they are called mobile agents in that case). When agents are used in electronic commerce, a number of security aspects arise. These aspects are communications security, system security, and application security.

Communications security. A first important security aspect is communications security. The messages exchanged between software agents or between a software agent and its owner, can be confidential, or can contain sensitive information. Software agents and their owners should be able to detect whether the messages are tampered with. They should be able to verify whom they are communicating with, and that the messages they receive are really originating from that entity. A communication infrastructure of an agent framework should therefore provide the following services: data confidentiality, entity authentication, and data authentication (meaning data origin authentication and data integrity).

System security. Especially for mobile agents, system security is a second important security aspect. When agents can travel from host to host, hosts should be protected from malicious agents. For example, agents should not be able to consume all the host's resources, and to steal information stored on the host. On the other hand, agents (or at least the information they carry with them) should be protected from malicious hosts and from other possibly malicious agents. In this way, mobile agents do not need to completely trust in advance the environment they are going to travel to.

Application security. In the context of this paper, the communications security aspect only involves basic security services. These services are not sufficient for most electronic commerce applications. For electronic commerce, security services such as non-repudiation and access control are required as well. Non-repudiation of origin and receipt ensures that agents (or their users) cannot deny having agreed upon an electronic contract; access control is applied when information is not available to everyone.

Note that these different security aspects are not entirely independent. For communications and application security purposes, the communicating parties will need cryptographic keys. Mobile agents will have to carry these keys with them. Therefore the communications and application security services will be completely dependent of the level of system security that is provided.

3 Secure Communication through SSL/TLS

Secure Sockets Layer (SSL) is an end-to-end security protocol, that provides entity authentication, data authentication, and data confidentiality at the 'socket' level. It was an initiative of Netscape Communications. There are two versions of the protocol: 2.0 and 3.0. SSL 2.0 contains a number of security flaws which are solved in SSL 3.0. The SSL 3.0 protocol was adopted by the IETF Transport Layer Security (TLS) working group, in which it is now standardized as the TLS 1.0 protocol [2] (some minor modifications to SSL 3.0 were made).

SSL 2.0, SSL 3.0 and TLS 1.0 provide the same security services in conceptually the same way. Therefore in this paper, "SSL/TLS" will be used to refer to these three protocols. However, the use of the TLS 1.0 protocol is preferred to SSL 3.0, and the use of SSL 2.0 is discouraged.

SSL/TLS is situated underneath the application layer. Therefore it can be used to secure the communication of any application. However, it is commonly known as the protocol that is being used to secure the communication between web browsers and web servers.

The Handshake protocol and the Record layer protocol are the two most important parts of the SSL/TLS protocol. The Record layer protocol provides the communications security services. Symmetric key cryptography is used: data confidentiality by encrypting the messages, and data authentication by adding a MAC (Message Authentication Code). In addition, it is foreseen that the Record layer provides data compression too, although no compression algorithm has been defined yet. In the beginning of a communication session, the Handshake protocol is performed. Public key cryptography is here used to authenticate the participating entities, and to exchange the cryptographic session keys that are needed for encryption and calculating MACs. The cryptographic algorithms that are going to be used, are negotiated as well.

SSL/TLS depends on a Public Key Infrastructure. Participating entities should have a public/private key pair and a certificate (unless there is no need for authentication). An additional – but not less important – aspect is the trust issue. Participating entities have to decide which certificates to trust (and for what purposes), and which not to trust. Root certificates (the certification authorities' certificates that are needed to verify the certificates of the entities) should be securely distributed in advance (e.g., on the World Wide Web, root certificates are shipped with the browsers).

4 Java and System Security

Java is a platform-independent object-oriented programming language developed by Sun [12]. Java code runs on a virtual machine. The virtual machine on its turn, has to be implemented using platform-specific code, or can be directly provided by hardware (e.g., Java card and ring). Java is rather easy to learn and to work with, and this is probably one of the reasons for the fact that the lightweight agent framework is easy to learn and to use (see further).

An important aspect of the language is the Java security model, i.e., the sandbox model. Applets (pieces of Java code that run within a browser environment) run inside a sandbox, and have limited privileges. They cannot for example read/write files on the local hard disk, and they cannot open network connections to other machines than the one they are originally downloaded from. In Java 2, every piece of code runs in a sandbox, and the borders of this sandbox – the security restrictions for that piece of code – can be defined differently based on who digitally signed the code. It is also impossible for a Java application to read the contents of other memory locations than the ones reserved for the application itself. To some extent, the Java security model already provides a partial solution for the system security aspects of a software agent framework.

A second important aspect of the Java programming environment is the provision of cryptographic functionality through the Java Cryptography Extension [13]. These cryptographic services are of course very important with respect to the communications security issues in a software agent framework.

5 Securing a Lightweight Agent Framework

The focus of this paper is on securing – in the sense of communications security – a lightweight software agent framework. The lightweight agent framework is first described. How communications security is added using a Java SSL/TLS library is then discussed.

5.1 Lightweight Agent Framework

A Java-based agent framework for multi-agent applications, has been designed and implemented at the University of Linköping, Sweden [9]. A minimalistic approach has been used. The design goal was a small and simple framework that is easy to learn and to use, and at the same time generic and extensible. The agent framework provides agent communication and agent autonomy facilities to developers of agent applications.

There are two different kinds of agents within the framework. An *Agent* can send and receive messages, and it can act autonomously. A *System Agent* manages a system of agents. It keeps track of the agents in the system, handles communication, and provides support for agent autonomy.

The PingServer application is a very basic example, included in the package, that shows how to use the framework. Only the part of the code, important for agent communication, is given here. The same code will be extended in the next sections to show where exactly security is added into the framework, and how it affects an agent application.

PingServer.java:
```
SystemAgent system = new SystemAgent(4042);
Agent agent = new PingServerAgent();
system.addAgent(agent);
```

SystemAgent.java:
```
MessageServer server = new MessageServerSocketImp(port);
```

MessageServerSocketImp.java:
```
ServerSocket serverSocket = new ServerSocket(port);
Socket socket = serverSocket.accept();
```

First, a System Agent has to be setup, that will send and receive messages on a specific port (in this case 4042). Then, the actual Agent application is started, and is registered with the System Agent. The PingServerAgent does nothing more than sending back the messages it receives. The MessageServer class handles the communication between the agents. Different implementations of this class can be used. The MessageServerSocketImp implementation is used, which performs the communication via standard TCP sockets.

5.2 Java SSL/TLS Library

The communication between agents in the lighweight agent framework can be socket based. As SSL/TLS offers the necessary services for securing this communication, and as the framework is implemented in Java, a Java SSL/TLS library should be used.

IAIK-iSaSiLk [7] is an example of a Java implementation of the SSL version 3.0 and TLS version 1.0 protocol. It operates on top of the IAIK-JCE implementation of the Java Cryptography Extension. Ideally, when securing an application using iSaSiLk, the only modification of the existing Java code, is replacing all occurrences of 'Socket' by 'SSLSocket'. Additional code has to be added for setting up the security parameters of the SSL'ed socket (a so-called security context).

Communications security can now be added in different ways, as shown in the following two paragraphs.

5.3 Transparent Security

In a first approach, security is added in a completely transparent manner towards the actual agent application. The MessageServerSocketImp implementation is replaced by the MessageServerSSLSocketImp implementation. Within MessageServerSSLSocketImp, security is established. All parameters are stored in one context class (different classes for server and client contexts), which has to be passed when opening a secured socket.

PingServer.java:

```
SystemAgent system = new SystemAgent(4042);
Agent agent = new PingServerAgent();
system.addAgent(agent);
```

SystemAgent.java:

```
MessageServer server = new MessageServerSSLSocketImp(port);
```

MessageServerSSLSocketImp.java:

```
SSLServerContext serverContext = new SSLServerContext();
SSLServerSocket serverSocket =
     new SSLServerSocket(port,serverContext);
SSLSocket socket = serverSocket.accept();
```

Security is completely transparent for the agent application. Note that the PingServer agent application did not need to be changed. When using SSL/TLS, this might be an ideal situation. However, the agent application cannot setup the security parameters, and has to use the ones offered by the system.

5.4 Security Interface towards Application Agents

In the next approach, the agent application is provided with a basic interface to setup the security parameters. The parameters are setup using the appropriate methods of the Java SSL/TLS library, and they are stored in a server or client context. This context is passed when setting up the System Agent, and the communication (note that either the server context or the client context is passed when constructing the System Agent, depending on the agent being a server or a client application; the other context variable remains null).

SecurityAwarePingServer.java:

```
SSLServerContext serverContext = new SSLServerContext();
serverContext.setEnabledCipherSuites(cs);
serverContext.setRSACertificate(chain,
     SSLKeyStore.getPrivateKey(0,0));
serverContext.setTrustDecider(trustDecider);
SystemAgent system =
     new SystemAgent(4042,serverContext,null);
Agent agent = new PingServerAgent();
system.addAgent(agent);
```

SystemAgent.java:

```
MessageServer server = new MessageServerAgentAware-
     SSLSocketImp(port,serverContext,clientContext);
```

MessageServerAgentAwareSSLSocketImp.java:

```
SSLServerSocket serverSocket =
     new SSLServerSocket(port,serverContext);
SSLSocket socket = serverSocket.accept();
```

In this example, the following security parameters are setup: the SSL/TLS cipher suites, a selection of cryptographic algorithms the server wants to use; a certificate, which contains the name of the server and an RSA public key, and which is digitally signed by a trusted third party (certification authority); the RSA private key that belongs to the RSA public key in the certificate; and last but not least information that is needed for deciding who (not) to trust.

Note that, as in the previous approach, again all agents depending on the same system agent, use the same SSL/TLS tunnel, with the same security parameters. This is not surprising as also in the original unsecured framework, there is only one socket connection per system agent, shared by all agents that depend on this system agent.

6 Further Comments and Achievements

Some further comments can be made with respect to the approach that has been presented in the previous sections.

6.1 Security

Only communications security has been addressed. For most electronic commerce applications, application security is also needed. System security is desired in general, and moreover it plays an important role for both communications and application security in particular.

System security. Server and client system agents need to access their private key (for SSL/TLS key exchange and entity authentication). In a typical environment, these keys are stored on the local disk, encrypted with a symmetric key derived from a pass phrase (in a more advanced setup, smart cards would be used). When agents are manually started up, users can type in the pass phrase to unlock the key. When (system) agents are automatically started up (e.g., by other agents), the keys either have to be stored in cleartext, or the pass phrase has to be hard coded in the agent software. It is clear that there is a link between communications security and system security. When agents are mobile, it becomes much more difficult. In a complete transparent approach, one set of keys per host could be used, as part of the infrastructure. Mobile agents could use these keys then to establish secure connections back to the originating host. Mobile agents and hosts should mutually trust each other in that case, as agents do not want malicious hosts to tamper with their communication, and as hosts do not want malicious agents to steal the private host keys. Mobile agents could carry their own cryptographic keys to the host. An important problem then is how the agent should protect these keys from possible malicious hosts and from attackers on the network (a discussion of possible solutions for this falls out of the scope of this article).

Application security. The SSL/TLS enabled software agent framework only provides communications security services. These only serve as a first basis, and for secure agent-based electronic commerce applications, application-level security is needed (e.g., non-repudiation). This will also involve cryptographic keys, and therefore there will be again a link with the system security issues.

6.2 Performance

Establishing the server and/or client security context appears to require a lot of time. When a secure connection is established, an SSL/TLS handshake has to be performed, which also causes overhead. In addition, all communication is cryptographically secured. There is thus certainly a decrease in performance compared to the original unsecured framework. Without giving detailed measurements, some reflections can be made on this decrease. On a normal workstation or personal computer, encrypting and protecting the authenticity of the messages does not cause a noticeable performance decrease. Since the connections between the system agents remain open (for a certain period of time), the decrease in performance only occurs in the beginning. Therefore the decrease is relatively smaller when the communication frequency is high and/or the message size is large. When using small mobile devices, the decrease could be a problem, especially due to SSL/TLS's use of public key cryptography during the handshake.

6.3 Other

Primary goals of the framework. It is important to check whether the primary goals of the framework (simplicity, small code size, ...) are still maintained in the secured framework. Although the secured framework is still rather simple and easy to learn and to use, the code size is certainly not as small anymore, especially not if one takes into account the complete SSL/TLS and cryptography libraries. However, the current code size is not optimized, and it is for example possible to exclude all unnecessary algorithms and utilities from these libraries.

Application-independence. SSL/TLS is considered to be an application-independent protocol, situated at the transport layer. In many SSL/TLS enabled applications, this is not clear. For example, some browsers and web servers implement SSL/TLS as part of the application. Within our secured framework, the real applications are situated on top of the agent 'transport layer', and are not aware of SSL/TLS (except for setting up the security context, which can be omitted when using the completely transparent approach). Note that if SSL/TLS is completely transparent, applications cannot for example decide for themselves who (not) to trust.

6.4 Achievements

The work described in this paper focused on the communications security aspect. By adding the SSL/TLS protocol, the lightweight agent framework now provides three communications security services: (system) agent authentication, data authentication, and data confidentiality. As seen in Sect. 2, two other important security aspects with respect to agent-based electronic commerce applications are system security and application security. As mobile agents are not possible within the lightweight framework at this moment, the system security aspect is of less importance. Note that when the framework would be extended with mobility functionality, a Java implementation already provides a first level of system security (as explained in Sect. 4). Especially for mobile agents, system security plays an important role in the communications security aspect as well. For example, agents will need cryptographic keys to communicate securely. How will these keys be protected when the agents are traveling to other hosts? As we focused on the agent framework, we did not work on agent applications, and therefore we did not cope with application security. For the time being, this is left for the developers of agent applications. Note again that in the case of mobile agents, system security is important for application security, for the same reasons as it is important for communications security.

7 Related Work and Alternative Approaches

Security in other agent frameworks. A number of alternative (Java-based) agent frameworks exist: Aglets [8], JATLite [11], to name a few of them. These frameworks all have their software agent specific features. Just as with the original lightweight agent framework, communications security does not seem to be an important issue in many of these frameworks. However, system security (at least the host protection part) has mostly being thought of in case of mobile agents: the agent code is digitally signed in order to be able to identify the owner, access restrictions are assigned to the agent based on the owner's identity, and the code is executed in a secure execution environment (see e.g., [1]).

Mobile agents and security. A substantial amount of work has been done in the area of mobile agents and security. Especially with respect to system security, some interesting solutions were presented in the past.

To protect a host against possibly malicious mobile agents, a secure execution environment can be used (e.g., the Java sandbox). Necula and Lee use an alternative approach of Proof-Carrying Code, with which one host can determine whether or not program code provided by another host is safe to install and execute [15].

It seems to be a very difficult task to protect a mobile agent from a possibly malicious host. An obvious solution is to require that an agent (or its critical code) should be run on trusted and/or neutral servers. However, some more advanced techniques would allow an agent to be run on a non-trusted host. Riordan and Schneier propose to construct keying material from certain classes of environmental data [16]. In this way, agents could receive encrypted messages, that they would only be able to decrypt if some environmental conditions were true. Hohl creates a black box out of an original agent [6]. This black box performs the same work as the original agent, but since the code is obfuscated, a minimum amount of time is required by an attacker to figure out what exactly is being done by the agent. Vigna proposes a mechanism that allows an agent owner, by using cryptographic traces, to check if the agent was correctly executed [18].

Other SSL/TLS implementations. There are many other Java SSL/TLS libraries that could be used instead of the IAIK iSaSiLk one. The Java Secure Socket Extension (JSSE) [14] is Sun's own package that provides SSL/TLS support. Due to export restrictions, it is however not possible [June 2000] to download a JSSE version with domestic-grade encryption outside the U.S. and Canada (although export regulations have become less strict, and are almost absent).

Security at other layers. In this article the SSL/TLS protocol is chosen to provide communications security services. These services are provided at the transport layer. There are alternative security protocols and frameworks that could be used instead to provide these (and, in case of application layer, more) services.

IPSec [3] provides communications security at the network layer. When participating hosts are trusted and IPsec enabled, agents could rely on the completely transparent IPsec communications security services provided by the infrastructure.

Instead of securing the communication channel (that has been established by the system agent), the messages themselves (that are exchanged by the agents) could be secured. He and Sycara take this approach in [5] by defining security extensions for the Knowledge Query and Manipulation Language (KQML) [4], a language used in some frameworks for constructing agent messages. A standardized application-level security framework, such as Kerberos [10] or SESAME [17] could be integrated. (Note that when communications security is added at the application layer, agents can be subscribed to the same system agent, while working with different security parameters and cryptographic keys.)

8 Conclusion

An existing Java-based lightweight software agent framework has been (partially) enabled for secure electronic commerce applications. The framework provided agent communication and agent autonomy facilities to developers of agent applications. A Java implementation of the SSL/TLS protocol was used to secure the communication facility. Communications security is one important aspect in software agent security in general. Other important aspects are system security and application security. System security is important when mobile agents are involved. In that case, it is also very relevant for communications security. Using Java already provides some system security, namely a certain level of protection of the host against a malicious agent. More research is needed in the area of protecting an agent against a malicious host. The work in this paper focused on the framework level, and therefore application security has to be built in by the developers of secure agent-based electronic commerce applications.

Acknowledgements. This work has been done during a short research visit at the Laboratory for Intelligent Information Systems (IISLAB), Linköping University, Sweden. The first author wants to thank Prof. Nahid Shahmehri of IISLAB for the inviting him to her research group. This article is a revised version of the paper that was published in the Proceedings of the Workshop on Agents in Electronic Commerce (WAEC'99). This workshop was organized as part of the

First Asia-Pacific Conference on Intelligent Agent Technology (IAT'99, Hong Kong, December 14-17, 1999). The authors want to thank the (cross-)reviewers for their valuable and constructive comments.

References

1. Dartmouth College. D'Agents. http://agent.cs.dartmouth.edu/
2. Dierks, T., Allen, C.: The TLS Protocol Version 1.0. RFC 2246 (1999)
3. Doraswamy, N., Harkins, D.: IPSec The New Security Standard for the Internet, Intranets, and Virtual Private Networks. Prentice-Hall (1999)
4. Finin, T., Labrou, Y., Mayfield, J.: KQML as an agent communication language. In: Bradshaw, J. (ed.): Software Agents (1997)
5. He, Q., Sycara, K. P.: Towards a Secure Agent Society. ACM AA'98 Workshop on Deception, Fraud and Trust in Agent Societies (1998)
6. Hohl, F.: Time Limited Blackbox Security: Protecting Mobile Agents From Malicious Hosts. In: Vigna, G. (ed.): Mobile Agents and Security. LNCS 1419, Springer-Verlag (1998)
7. IAIK. Java crypto software. http://jcewww.iaik.tu-graz.ac.at/
8. IBM. Aglets. http://www.trl.ibm.co.jp/aglets/
9. Kindborg, M., Åberg, J., and Shahmehri, N.: A lightweight agent framework for interactive multi-agent applications. In: Proceedings of Fourth International Conference on the Practical Application of Intelligent Agents and Multi-Agents (1999) http://www.ida.liu.se/~mikki/PAAM99/
10. Kohl, J., Neuman, C.: The Kerberos Network Authentication Service V5. RFC 1510 (1993)
11. Stanford University. JATLite. http://java.stanford.edu/
12. Sun Microsystems. Java. http://java.sun.com/
13. Sun. Java Cryptography Extension (JCE). http://java.sun.com/products/jce/
14. Sun. Java Secure Socket Extension (JSSE). http://java.sun.com/products/jsse/
15. Necula, G., Lee, P.: Safe, Untrusted Agents Using Proof-Carrying Code. In: Vigna, G. (ed.): Mobile Agents and Security. LNCS 1419, Springer-Verlag (1998)
16. Riordan, J., Schneier, B.: Environmental Key Generation Towards Clueless Agents. In: Vigna, G. (ed.): Mobile Agents and Security. LNCS 1419, Springer-Verlag (1998)
17. SESAME. https://www.cosic.esat.kuleuven.ac.be/sesame/
18. Vigna, G.: Cryptographic Traces for Mobile Agents. In: Vigna, G. (ed.): Mobile Agents and Security. LNCS 1419, Springer-Verlag (1998)

MA/LMA Architecture for Dealing with Malicious Agents in Agent-Mediated Electronic Markets

Ding Peng, Shi Jun, Sheng Huan Ye, and Liming Lu

ICHI Lab, Department of Computer Science, Shanghai Jiaotong University
Shanghai, China, 200030
DingPeng@ichi.sjtu.edu.cn Shi-j@cs.sjtu.edu.cn
HySheng@mail.sjtu.edu.cn lml@ichi.sjtu.edu.cn

Abstract. This paper describes and discusses the malicious agent issues in the agent-mediated electronic markets. We define the malicious agents as software agents that have malicious purpose. Malicious agents can do harm in various ways, such as attacking normal agents, disordering deals, cheating users, stealing intimate information, wasting resources, destroying the markets and so on. We compare the malicious agents with PC viruses in four aspects: originations, actions, means of propagation & infection and speed of propagation & infection. In our opinion, malicious agents are more harmful than the common PC viruses in some measure. We proposed the MA and LMA architecture to deal with the problem described above. Besides, some agent transaction protocols are also presented to show how the MA and LMA architecture works. In the last of this paper, we give some implementation considerations as the foundation for further developments.

1. Introduction

Over the last few years, there have been intense works on the area of mobile agents. The general workflow of a mobile agent system is as this: (1) a client device sends an itinerant agent to some other clients or servers (2) When the itinerant agent reaches a server, it is delivered to an agent execution environment called Agent Meeting Point (AMP). (3) The AMP inspects the itinerant agent's external wrapper authentication credentials. (4) The agent computes in the server (5) After complete the task, it comes to other server or comes back. [1].

The idea of dispatching a program for remote computing is not new. Milling described an executable script that could be dispatched among networks of mini-computers to permit distributed, real-time processing [2]. Telesript mobile scripting language was deployed for an initial set of services on AT&T public PersonaLink network [3]. The HotJava web browser offered by Sun Microsystem can retrieve programs from WWW and execute it on the local machine [4]

Some researchers applied knowledge representation techniques to agent –agent communications, for instance, Knowledge Query and Manipulation Language (KQML) [5], Knowledge Interchange Facility (KIF) [6].

J. Liu and Y. Ye (Eds.): E-Commerce Agents, LNAI 2033, pp. 191-205, 2001.

In recent years, the mobile agent technology was widely studied, developed and applied by the academia, industries and business. One typical application of mobile agent is the agent-mediated electronic market where there is an open space for transactions between agents. The principle is similar to the AMP describe before. [7]

In order to give the reader a concept basis for our later presentation, we describe the typical operation process of the agent-mediated electronic market here (1) The customer delivers a customer agent to the open space (2) The supplier delivers a supplier agent to the open space (3) The two agents meet in the open space and negotiate with each other. (4) The customer agent sends an order to the supplier agent (5) The supplier agent delivers goods after it received the order. Some examples of the current agent-mediated electronic markets could be found in AuctionBot (http://auction.eecs.umich.edu), Kasbah (www.media.mit.edu/~guttman/research/kasbah)

It is obvious that the security issue is one of the important problems in such kind electronic markets. Loureiro and his co-workers described a protocol to prevent the data collected by mobile agents from going to some potentially malicious host [8]. Romao discussed the security issues related to the usage of mobile agents in the operation environments to which their owners have to bound and proposed a proxy certificating mechanism to deal with this problem [9]. Yi spent efforts on integrating the software agent technology with the cryptographic technology to realize safe electronic transactions for a series of online interdependent purchases [10].

Some pioneers addressed their opinions on security issues in mobile agent systems as this: (1) It is impossible to hide everything within an agent without the use of cryptography.

(2) It is impossible to communicate secretly with a large, anonymous group of electronic markets.

(3) It is impossible to prevent agents from tampering by malicious markets unless trusted hardware is available in it.

If every market were equipped with such a trusted processor, only agents that have valid credentials and signatures would be allowed to run on it. But current such hardware and related software are expensive and not readily available [11]

(4) It is impossible to verify with complete certainty that an entering agent is not a virus [12].

In fact, the problem of writing a program that can decide the correct behavior of another program is unsolved yet. Trusting an agent means trusting every program that ever had writing access to it. Although well-designed access controls and hierarchical authentication services could reduce the danger, it seems there are no completed solutions in spite how carefully the market is implemented.

Preventing the agent from being attacked by the malicious servers or AMPs attracts many researchers' interests. Some related works could be found in [8] [13] and [14].

But on the other side, how to prevent the agent or the market from being attacked by malicious agent is also an interesting and important issue in mobile agent systems.

We could see that the malicious agent can do harm to two objects, one is the normal agent and the other is the market. Different kinds of attacking strategies are available, for example, stealing the sensitive data, wasting the resources, modifying the user accounts, deleting important files, jamming network traffics, even worse, destroying the markets.

The mobile agents can travel easily from one market to another, so that it can propagate very quickly in the open Internet as the network viruses can do. Recently, the virus named "I love you" infects tens of thousand machines in the Internet within only six hours. We think that the malicious agent could be more harmful than "I love you" in some circumstances. We will address the reasons in the next section.

We believe that the malicious mobile agent issue is an important security problem in agent-mediated electronic markets, so that we spent some efforts on discussing and finding a way to deal with it.

This paper is organized as this. We describe the malicious agents issue in the agent-mediated E-Markets in section 2. The abstract model, the definitions and actions of the malicious agents and the comparison between the malicious agents and the PC viruses are presented in detail. In section 3, the core element of this paper: the MA and LMA architecture is proposed and some agent transaction protocols are also addressed. We give our implementation considerations in section 4 for further developments.

2. The Malicious Agents Issue in the Agent-Mediated E-Markets

2.1 The Abstract Model of Agent-Mediated Electronic Markets

Firstly, we abstract the fundamental elements in the general agent-mediated electronic market so that the readers may have a clear mind on where they are starting. Most of the current agent-mediated electronic markets are consisted of three kinds of elements: Customer agents, Supplier agents and Broker agents. We show it in fig 1. The E-Market is the place where these three types of agents meet, negotiate and deal.

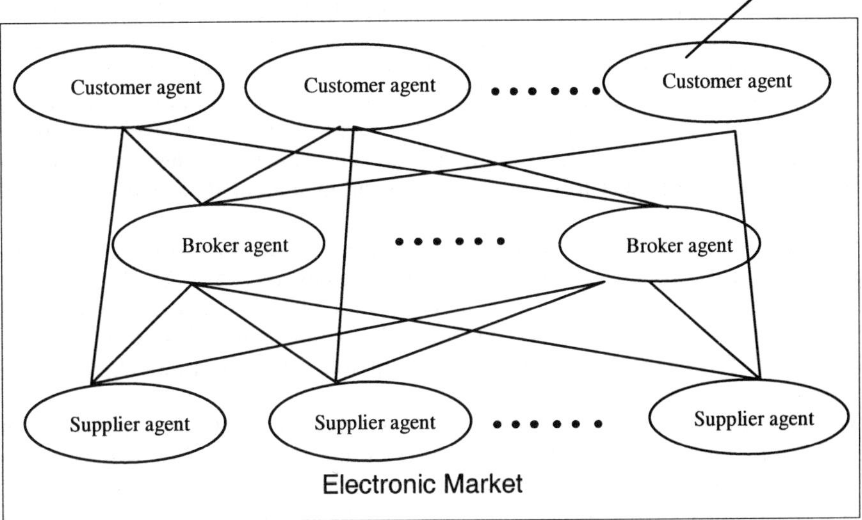

Fig. 1. The Abstract Model of Agent-Mediated Electronic Market

The E-Market should be supervised by some authorized organizations so that it can improve its reputation

All the users are request to create agents and assign transaction tasks to each of the agents at first. In this step, the users tell their agents the property of the transaction, for example, the desired price, the period of dealing, etc.

Then users dispatch their agents to the E-Markets respectively. The customer agents and the supplier agents negotiate with each other in the E-Market directly or though the broker agents based on the demands required by their owners. If two requirements do not meet, the customer agents will raise their payment and supplier (broker) agents will lower their price until there is a meet or go to a certain limitation. The two kinds of agents will send reports to their owner's after the transactions complete.

The competitions between the broker agents and the supplier agent and the agents' executions in some unknown principals require more careful security schemes. It is obvious that security issues play an important role in this style of electronic market. How important it is has not been recognized yet. But we are sure that the users will not be interested in such an E-Market if there are no any security mechanisms within it. Some security problems are identification, authorization, privacy, confidence, and integrity etc. We try to define, analysis, discuss the malicious agents problem in detail, as we are especially interested in it.

2.2 The Definition of the Malicious Agents in E-Markets

We define the malicious agent as a "software entity that has malicious purpose " When the term 'agent' appeared many years before, there was no a widely acknowledged definition. Here we adopt Wooldridge's definition " an agent is a computer software that is *situated* in some environment, and that is capable of *autonomous action* in the environment in order to meet its design objectives".

Based upon this definition, we formalized the agent as a set of purpose, action and effect. It is clear that our definition of malicious agent resides in the level of purpose. If one agent is created for doing harm to the environments (other agents or E-Markets), we could say that it is a 'malicious agent' in spite of its actual actions and effects.

To be clearer, let us have a look at an example. A user wants to destroy an E-Market so he programs an agent and delivers it to the desired E-Market. But the agent has not do any bad things in the market at last because of various reasons, perhaps the agent was not programmed well, or the market has a strong defense. Now the question is: can we call this agent a malicious one? The answer is yes, because the purpose of this agent is malicious.

We could see in the description above that whether an agent is malicious or not depends on its purposes rather than on its actions and effects. In fact, there are two types of malicious agents, one is the original malicious agent created by malicious users and the other is the hijacked agent created by normal users but hijacked by malicious users.

2.3 The Actions of the Malicious Agents

After we finished the definition, we will discuss some things on this issue: who create it? How to create it? How does it act? What is the effect? How to defend it?

The consumers, brokers and suppliers, are able to create such malicious agents for various reasons, for example, to steal valuable information, to cheat other agents, to destroy the market and so on. The second origination is the E-Market itself. This kind of E-Market is a malicious server that can create agents with malicious code. As agents can travel from one market to another, that it is possible for a malicious server to build and dispatch some malicious agents to other markets to do bad things. The third origination is the crackers who are interested in attacking computer systems and it is obvious that the E-Market is a good target for their assaulting.

The malicious agent has a segment of malicious codes that can replicate, broadcast and spasm over the Internet. Besides, it is able to do some more things, such as attacking normal agents, disordering deals, cheating users, stealing privacy information, wasting resources and destroying the markets. We will use some more place to describe these actions so that the readers would have a better understanding about our works.

Attacking normal agents is perhaps the most popular skill that a malicious agent uses to do harmful things. Normal agents are the core elements in an E-Market and all the transaction among customer agents, broker agents and supplier agents should be fair. But it is obvious that some users want to break the fair business rule to get more benefit. They can construct malicious agents to attack normal agents by many ways, such as decrypting the password, flooding the message and manipulating. If a malicious agent can get the dealing information, the desired price and modify them to make an unfair transaction if it decrypts the target agent's password. Message flooding is the way that the malicious agents use to send a large amount of unmeaning information to the normal agents who will be slumped in a mess. Manipulating is an approach to lead the normal agents to some hard condition. For example, a malicious agent tries to negotiate with a normal agent repeatedly, so that the normal agent has to waste its resources in insignificant things.

Disordering deals is another approach that a malicious agent may adapt. The normal deals in an E-Market should obey some rules, such as meeting rules, negotiation rules, ordering rules and so on. It is easy for a malicious agent to disturb the transaction, for instance, it can sell goods in an unimaginable low price although it doesn't own such goods at all. Many customer agents will come and deal with it because software agents are not reasonable enough as human beings to tell the truth of the price. After all these customer agents 'successfully' makes a deal, they will deliver the orders to the malicious agent. But actually, the malicious agent has no such low price goods, so that all the operations that the customer agents do are wasteful. At the same time, other normal supplier agents are deprived of the chances to make deals, because their price is 'too high' from the point of view of the supplier agents. As business transaction is 'profit-oriented', selling goods in an unimaginable low price will cause a 'transaction storm', which will be a disaster in the E-Market.

Cheating users is perhaps not so widely used by the malicious agents because users do not directly involve in the transaction within a market. Different E-Markets have different strategies so that some E-Markets may allow the user to get into the transactions. This gives the malicious agent chances to face up the user directly. For example, some suppliers may create malicious agents who can provide incorrect information to the user so that the users may go to the wrong direction when they make decisions.

Stealing privacy information. Customer agents and supplier (broker) agents make deals in the E-Market, so that some privacy information, such as the initial price, the desired price, the period of deals, the user's individual information, some market information, are of essential importance. If a malicious agent found a way, it can use these materials to do many bad things, such as to deliver this privacy information to the Internet, to annoy the user, to let the user's competitor know it.

Destroying the E-Markets is the most grievous effect that a malicious agent can cause. We could see that some bad actions are wasting resources, deleting files, destroying software system, even worse, and ruining the hardware. Some PC viruses have this ability. The malicious agent's effects are even more serious in some measures. As for PC, if some viruses ruin its operation system (Windows, Linux), it can be repaired by re-setup the system. Although the important data was destroyed, the lost is no more than individual materials in most of cases. But as the E-Markets are opened to the public, so that losing a group of people's materials is no less than an earthquake in this situation.

2.4 Comparison between the Malicious Agents and the PC Viruses

Maybe PC virus is the most powerful attacking tool that has destroyed countless machines in world since it exist tens of years before. Could the malicious agents be regarded as one kind of the viruses? Or are there any differences between the malicious agents and the viruses?

It is interesting to compare the malicious agent with the viruses, so that we can some significant results. We'd like to discuss this issue based upon four parameters: the origination, the damage, the means of propagation & infection and the speed of propagation & infection. Table 1 shows it.

The *Origination* defines the place where the malicious agents and the viruses come from. Consumers, merchants, markets builders and crackers are able to program their own malicious agents and dispatch them to the E-Markets. Software engineers, system administrators and crackers are those who usually create PC viruses. In many PC application systems, users have no right to create their own software and put them to the system. As the E-Markets admit the users to create their own agents, so that it gives the common users the chances to construct their own malicious agents. It shows that the malicious agents have a larger sphere of origination.

The *Actions* indicates the behaviors of the malicious agents and the viruses. We have mentioned above that the malicious agents usually do harmful things in these ways: attacking normal agents, disordering deals, cheating users, stealing privacy information, destroying systems. In the other hand, PC viruses usually cause users mad by wasting resource (memories, disk spaces, CPU time, etc), erasing important files, modifying vital data, and destroying systems (operation system, even worse, the hardware). We can see that the behavior of malicious agents is different from that of the PC viruses in many aspects.

The *Means of propagation & infection* defines the way that the malicious agents and the PC viruses broadcast themselves. The malicious agents can infect other agents when they meet and negotiate, and can propagate to some other E-Markets by traveling. In the other side, PC viruses can not infect the other software and propagate to other systems without the assistance of the users, such as coping floppies, running infected codes, downloading software, receiving email and etc. In other words, malicious agents infect other systems and propagate *actively* while the PC viruses infect other systems and propagate *passively*. It seems that malicious agents are harder to control than viruses.

The last is the *Speed of propagation & infection*. There are no any experiments that show the comparison of the speed of propagation and infection between the malicious agents and the PC viruses. Here we'd like to discuss this issue and reason out the result by our common knowledge. We think that the malicious agents can infect other systems and propagate more quickly than the PC viruses can do due to different reasons. The first one is that the PC viruses have to be active before they infect others, while malicious agents are always active in the markets. In a PC system, if the viruses' files reside in the hard disk and have not active in the running system, they have no any chance to infect other files. The second one is that the PC viruses cannot propagate to other systems without the assistance of the users, while the malicious agents can migrate freely to other markets. The malicious agents are autonomic entities that can go to anywhere according to their willing, so that we believe that it is possible for the malicious agents to propagate to and infect more than thousands of markets in a few minutes.

Table 1. Comparison between the malicious agents and the PC viruses

	Malicious agents	PC viruses
Origination	Created by consumers, merchants, market builders crackers	Created by software engineers, system administrators, crackers
Actions	Attacking, disordering, cheating, stealing, destroying	Wasting resources, erasing files, modifying data, destroying system
Means of propagation & infection	Migration, meeting, negotiation	Coping files, running infected codes, downloading software, receiving emails
Speed of propagatio & infection	Fast	Medium

3. MA and LMA Architecture for Dealing with the Malicious Agents Issue

We propose here dynamic transaction-oriented authorization schemes in which we used a trusted third party (certificate authority) for all security events. In this paper we use a two-level market authorities architecture to deal with the malicious agents so that it can improve the efficiency and provide more assurances. Fig 2 shows the architecture

3.1 The MA and LMA Architecture

The core element of this architecture is the Market Authority (MA) and the Local Market Authority (LMA). MA is the root authority organization that supervises all the events in each E-Market who has its own LMA that supervises the actions of each agent within it.

The basic idea of our schemes is that all the agents are only authorized the least capability in a certain period of time. Each agent should have the shot-lived transaction certificate and the key that are issued by its owner and LMA.

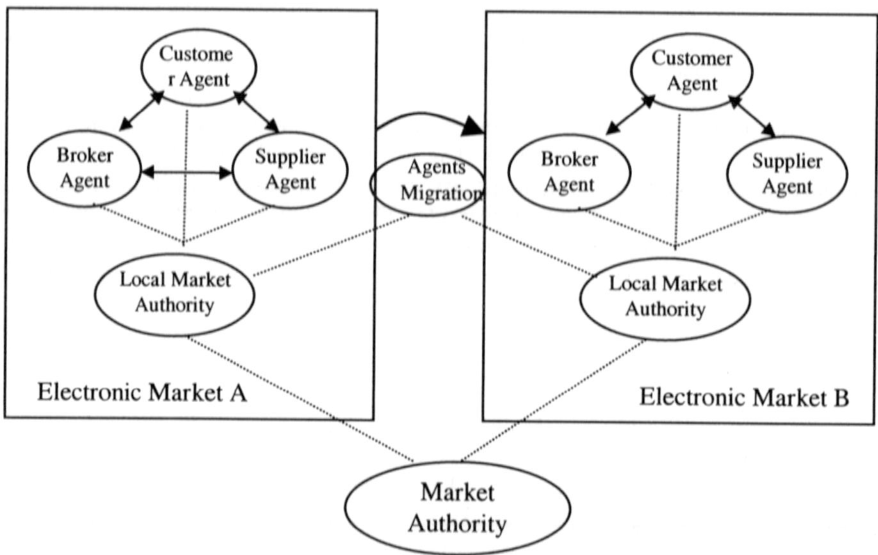

Fig. 2. The MA and LMA Architecture for Dealing with Malicious agents issue in E-Markets

We mentioned in the previous sections that the malicious agents are created by two kinds of users: (1) the E-Markets builders (2) the common users (customers, brokers, and suppliers). Now let us see how the MA and the LMA prevent malicious agents from being created by these two kinds of users and how the malicious agents can be restricted in E-Markets. We give the assumption here that there are only a few malicious E-Market builders and the malicious agents are much more. Our schemes rely on certain cryptographic primitives.

For markets builders. If the builders of some E-Market want their markets opened to the public, they have to apply to the MA and provide enough materials to demonstrate their abilities. The MA checks the materials and decides whether or not to distribute the rights to the builders. This could prevent a lot of the vicious engineers from building illegal E-Markets to cheat users. The operation of the legal markets is under the supervision of the MA.

For common users. Common users (the owners of customer agents, broker agents or supplier agents) are some individuals or some organizations. They are required to register in the LMA of a home E-Market before they can build agents to do the transactions. Then the MA distributes the users' public keys, private keys and certificates for signing their deals in the local E-Markets. The certificates are the identification to the E-Markets when they log in. The LMA will check the user's validity and credit records. The users can enter the E-Markets to do business after they passed the evaluation performed by the LMA based upon some standards

For normal agents. The users are request to authorize their agents with transaction certificates and keys to the LMA. A single agent has no rights to preserve its owner's private key. The "TransactionType" item defines the style of the transactions that the agent's keys can be applied to. It is described by a list of {purchase x units of product y at price p/ unit}. The "Capability" item is consisted of the limitation of the transaction types that the agents can deal with, the set of legitimate opposing party of transactions, whether or not can sign contact. The users generate a secret transaction key for its agent, specify its expiry date, encrypt [key, expiry date] pair with LMA's public key and sign them. The key is only known to the LMAs of the E-Market where the agents do transactions. The user creates a unique identifier for his agent using a pseudorandom generator. The user sends these data and his certificate that was encrypted with the LMA's public key to the LMA who will check the validity of received data, signs it and send back to the user after encrypted them using the user's public key. After then the agents have the legal transaction ability.

3.2 Some Agent Transaction Protocols in the E-Markets

After we shown our MA and LMA architecture in the previous section, it is time to describe some protocols that play an important role in guaranteeing the safe agents transactions in the E-Market.

U→LMA: PLMA [CERT (U), ID (A_{U1}), TransactionType$_{AU}$, Capability$_{AU}$,
SINGU (H (CERT (U), ID (A_{U1}), TransactionType$_{AU}$, Capability$_{AU}$))]
LMA→U: PU [T_C, SIGN$_{LMA}$ (T_C, SING$_U$ (H (CERT (U), ID (A_U),
TansactionTypeAU, Capability$_{AU}$)))
U→A_U: CERT (U), ID (A_U), TansactionType$_{AU}$, Capability$_{AU}$, T_C,
SINGU (H (CERT (U), ID (A_U), TansactionType$_{AU}$, Capability$_{AU}$)),
SIGNLMA (T_C, SING$_U$ (H (CERT (U), ID (A_U), TansactionType$_{AU}$,
Capability$_{AU}$))) *// Transaction certificate of agent A_U, denoted by*
TransactionCertificate (A_{U1})
P_{LMA} [TKey$_{AU}$, ExpiryDate$_{AU}$], SING$_U$ (P_{LMA} [TKey$_{AU}$, ExpiryDate$_{AU}$])
// Transaction key of agent A_U, denoted by TransactionKey(A_{U1})

Fig. 3. The protocol of the users' request for transaction certificates

The protocol of the users' request for transaction certificates. We use the following notation to represent messages and protocols in our paper. P_X , S_X denote the public and private keys of the entity X. CERT(X) denotes the digital certificate of entity X, K_X[M] denotes the encryption that uses the key K_X. SIGN$_X$ (N) denotes the signature of entity X on content N. H () denote a one-way collision-resistant hash function (e.g. SHA-1).

The protocol of the agent-to-agent transactions (one to one). The users can build one or more agents to negotiate with other agents. We assume that there exist two agents A_{U1} and A_{U2}, which are owned by the user U_1 and U_2 respectively. A_{U1} could be a customer agent and A_{U2} could be a broker or a supplier agent. The two agents exchange their transaction certificates, check the certificates and evaluate each other's transaction type and capability to confirm a safe transaction.

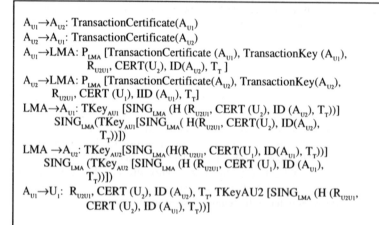

$A_{U1}\rightarrow A_{U2}$: TransactionCertificate(A_{U1})

$A_{U2}\rightarrow A_{U1}$: TransactionCertificate(A_{U2})

$A_{U1}\rightarrow$LMA: P_{LMA} [TransactionCertificate (A_{U1}), TransactionKey (A_{U1}), R_{U2U1}, CERT(U_2), ID(A_{U2}), T_T]

$A_{U2}\rightarrow$LMA: P_{LMA} [TransactionCertificate(A_{U2}), TransactionKey(A_{U2}), R_{U2U1}, CERT (U_1), IID (A_{U1}), T_T]

LMA$\rightarrow A_{U1}$: $TKey_{AU1}$ [$SING_{LMA}$ (H (R_{U2U1}, CERT (U_2), ID (A_{U2}), T_T))] $SING_{LMA}$($TKey_{AU1}$[$SING_{LMA}$(H(R_{U2U1}, CERT(U_2), ID(A_{U2}), T_T))])

LMA $\rightarrow A_{U2}$: $TKey_{AU2}$[$SING_{LMA}$(H(R_{U2U1}, CERT(U_1), ID(A_{U1}), T_T))] $SING_{LMA}$ ($TKey_{AU2}$ [$SING_{LMA}$ (H (R_{U2U1}, CERT (U_1), ID (A_{U1}), T_T))])

$A_{U1}\rightarrow U_1$: R_{U2U1}, CERT (U_2), ID (A_{U2}), T_T, TKeyAU2 [$SING_{LMA}$ (H (R_{U2U1}, CERT (U_2), ID (A_{U1}), T_T))]

Fig. 4. The Protocol of the Agent-to-Agent Transactions (one to one)

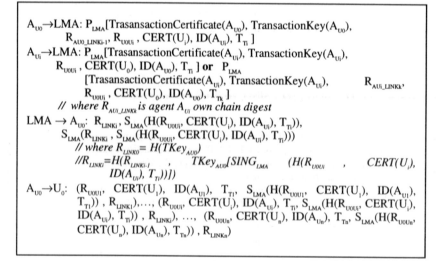

$A_{U0}\rightarrow$LMA: P_{LMA}[TrasansactionCertificate(A_{U0}), TransactionKey(A_{U0}), $R_{AU0\_LINKi-1}$, R_{U0Ui} , CERT(U_i), ID(A_{Ui}), T_{Ti}]

$A_{Ui}\rightarrow$LMA: P_{LMA}[TrasansactionCertificate(A_{Ui}), TransactionKey(A_{Ui}), R_{U0Ui} , CERT(U_0), ID(A_{U0}), T_{Ti}] **or** P_{LMA} [TrasansactionCertificate(A_{Ui}), TransactionKey(A_{Ui}), R_{AUi_LINKk}, R_{U0Ui} , CERT(U_0), ID(A_{U0}), T_{Tk}]

// where R_{AUi_LINKk} is agent A_{Ui} own chain digest

LMA $\rightarrow A_{U0}$: R_{LINKi} , S_{LMA}(H(R_{U0Ui}, CERT(U_i), ID(A_{Ui}), T_{Ti})), S_{LMA}(R_{LINKi} , S_{LMA}(H(R_{U0Ui}, CERT(U_i), ID(A_{Ui}), T_{Ti})))

// where R_{LINK0}= H($TKey_{AU0}$)

//R_{LINKi}=H($R_{LINKi-1}$, $TKey_{AU0}$[$SING_{LMA}$ (H(R_{U0Ui} , CERT(U_i), ID(A_{Ui}), T_{Ti}))])

$A_{U0}\rightarrow U_0$: (R_{U0U1}, CERT(U_1), ID(A_{U1}), T_{T1}, S_{LMA}(H(R_{U0U1}, CERT(U_1), ID(A_{U1}), T_{T1})) , R_{LINK1}),…, (R_{U0Ui}, CERT(U_i), ID(A_{Ui}), T_{Ti}, S_{LMA}(H(R_{U0Ui}, CERT(U_i), ID(A_{Ui}), T_{Ti})) , R_{LINKi}), …, (R_{U0Un}, CERT(U_n), ID(A_{Un}), T_{Tn}, S_{LMA}(H(R_{U0Un}, CERT(U_n), ID(A_{Un}), T_{Tn})) , R_{LINKn})

Fig. 5. The Protocol of Agent-to-Agent Transaction (one to many)

If the verification process succeeds, the two agents will start formal transaction negotiation. The effective results of the transaction will be confirmed by LMA in order that it ensures non-repudiation and integrity. The two agents A_{U1} and A_{U2} send their transaction certificates, keys and the transaction result (R_{U2U1}) to the LMA separately.

Firstly LMA checks the validity and expiry date of the two agents' transaction key. If anyone's key has been expired or invalid (based on owner's signature and certificate), error code will be returned and the transaction be declared illegal. If the contents of the transaction results are identical and the two agents have rights to deal with the transactions, the LMA will sign the transaction results and encrypt them using agent's transaction keys separately, and then send them back to the two agents.

The protocol of the agent-to-agent transactions (one to one). For common users, there are two ways to deal with transactions. Firstly the user can set up many agents and dispatch them to different site to meet with specified agents. Each agent will come back to its owner's host after its transaction done. Secondly the user can only set up one agent for multi-transactions with different agents. The agent roams in the E-Market and meets with other agents. We use the hash function, agent's transaction key and LAM signature to generate hash chain to link the intermediate results. We assume that the agent A_{U0} meets with the agents A_{U1}, A_{U2}, …, A_{Un} orderly. Of course we can predetermine the itineraries where the agents meet. On its itinerary, the agent carries a list of intermediate results and digest of intermediate result chain pair.

$A_{U\text{-}LMA1}$→LMA_1:TransactionCertificate($A_{U\text{-}LMA1}$), TransactionKey($A_{U\text{-}LMA1}$), LMA_2 // *Destination e-market*
LMA_1→LMA_2: P_{LMA2}[TransactionCertificate($A_{U\text{-}LMA1}$), CERT(LMA_1),
P_{LMA2}[$TKey_{AU\text{-}LMA1}$, $ExpiryDate_{AU\text{-}LMA1}$]
$SING_{LMA1}$(P_{LMA2}[$TKey_{AU\text{-}LMA1}$, $ExpiryDate_{AU\text{-}LMA1}$])]
LMA_2→LMA_1: P_{LMA1}[$SING_{LMA2}$(TransactionCertificate($A_{U\text{-}LMA1}$),
CERT(LMA_1)), $SING_{LMA2}$($P_{U\text{-}LMA1}$[$TKey_{AU\text{-}LMA1}$, $ExpiryDate_{AU\text{-}LMA1}$]),
$SING_{LMA2}$(P_{LMA2}[$TKey_{AU\text{-}LMA1}$, $ExpiryDate_{AU\text{-}LMA1}$])]
LMA_1→$A_{U\text{-}LMA1}$: TransactionCertificate($A_{U\text{-}LMA1}$), CERT(U_{LMA1}),
$SING_{LMA2}$(TransactionCertificate($A_{U\text{-}LMA1}$), CERT(LMA_1)),
// Cross e-market transaction certificate of agent $A_{U\text{-}LMA1}$,
// denoted by $TransactionCertificate_{LMA1\text{-}LMA2}(A_{U\text{-}LMA1})$
$SING_{LMA2}$($P_{U\text{-}LMA1}$[$TKey_{AU\text{-}LMA1}$, $ExpiryDate_{AU\text{-}LMA1}$]),
P_{LMA2}[$TKey_{AU\text{-}LMA1}$, $ExpiryDate_{AU\text{-}LMA1}$],
$SING_{LMA2}$ (P_{LMA2}[$TKey_{AU\text{-}LMA1}$, $ExpiryDate_{AU\text{-}LMA1}$])]
// Cross e-market transaction key of agent $A_{U\text{-}LMA1}$,

Fig. 6. The protocol of Agent Migration Request

When a result of intermediate transaction is generated, the agent A_{U0} sends back the latest result and the previous chain digests encrypted with the LMA's public key. The LMA compares received previous chain digests with its preserved previous one. If they are identical, the LMA calculates the new chain digest and sends the signed new digest to agent A_{U0}. To verify the integrity of collected results, the user U_0 only needs to recalculate the hash chain using his agent's secret transaction key. The trusted third party (TTP) solution for agent integrity in [15] is similar to ours, but they did not consider the case that agents could be hijacked and the intermediate results could be changed in its migration to TTP.

The protocol of agent migration request. Another question is how to prevent malicious agent from propagating to other E-Markets. The MA and LMAs play an important role on monitoring the agents' migration among multiple E-Markets. Fig 5 shows the protocol of agents' migration request from one E-Market to another. In order to be clear, only two markets (E-Market 1 and E-Market 2) are shown here. An agent has to apply to the LMA_1 if it wants to travel to another E-Market. The agent $A_{U\text{-}LMA1}$ sends its transaction certificate, key and destination to LMA_1. The LMA_1 sends its own certificate, $A_{U\text{-}LMA1}$'s transaction certificate, transaction key encrypted with LMA_1's public key and its certificate to LMA_2. LMA_2 checks validity of the received data and evaluates credit records of $A_{U\text{-}LMA1}$'s owner from MA, then decides whether or not to admit agent $A_{U\text{-}LMA1}$'s to enter according to local standards. If it does, LMA_2 signs $A_{U\text{-}LMA1}$'s transaction certificate, encrypts $A_{U\text{-}LMA1}$'s transaction key with its owner's public key and signs it (so later, agent $A_{U\text{-}LMA1}$'s owner will know LMA_2 has got right key), and then LMA_2 sends them back to LMA_1. LMA_1 assigns $A_{U\text{-}LMA1}$ the cross E-Market transaction certificates and keys.

When an agent leaves its original E-Market and migrates to another E-Market, it is under the supervision of the new E-Market's LMA. All the intermediate transaction results in the new E-Market are signed with the local LMA's private key and agent transaction key. The transaction protocol is same as what was described in previous section. All the actions that an agent performs in the E-Market are recorded in a form shown in table 2. Action place denotes the E-Market where the agent resides and deals. The content of the actions is described in the Action description section, in which different approaches are feasible. It could be expressed by natural language as well as by formal language. The LMA send these records to the MA who stores them as credit record of the agent's owner.

Table 2. The activity record form of the agent

Agent ID	Owner User Certificate	Action Place	Action Duration	Action Description

4. Implementation Considerations

The security architecture we proposed in this paper does not assume any specific attributes of the E-Market infrastructure, so that it is suitable for most of the E-Markets. But the elementary implementation problems are the certificate format and data exchange that we will spend more spaces to describe.

X.509 is the most widely used data format for public key certificate today. An X.509 certificate has been used to bind a public key to a particular individual or entity, and it is digitally signed by the issuer of the certificate authority (CA) that has confirmed the binding between the public key and the holder of the certificate. An X.509 certificate consists of the following:

- Version of certificate format
- Certificate serial number
- Subject's X.500 name (assigned by a naming authority)
- Subject's public key and algorithm information
- Validity period (beginning and end date)
- Issuer's X.500 name (certificate authority)
- Optional fields to provide unique identifiers for subject and issuer (Version 2)
- Extensions (Version 3)
- Digital signature of the certificate authority

The optional fields are available from Version 2 to make the subject name or the issuing certificate authority name unambiguous in case the same name has been reassigned to different entities. Version 3 provides the extension field for the integration of any number of additional fields to the certificate. These extensions make X.509v3 a truly open standard to support diverse needs.

The dynamic transaction-oriented certificate is a type of short-lived certificate (transaction key is a temporary key)that can be based on the X.509v3 certificates. Its lifetime is correlated with the expected length of the agent's transaction function (expiry date of transaction key).

The content of transaction type and capability could be expressed by natural language as well as formal language. We think XML is a better choice because it is the standard format for data exchange between inter-enterprise applications on the Internet.

5. Related Works

Mobile agent and its security has obtain many attentions from researcher all over the world, and many security issues were proposed, such as Authentication, Reputation and Trust, Secure Languages, Preventing Floods, and The problem of Malicious Hosts [16]. But it is strange that not many efforts have been spent on investigating the malicious agents issues whether in mobile agent systems or in agent-mediated electronic markets.

Necula proposes Proof-Carry-Code (PCC) approach that enables a computer system to determine automatically that program code provided by another system is safe to install and execute without requiring inter-pretation or run-time checking. The key idea is to attach the code with an easily checking proof so that its execution does not violate the safety policy of the receiving system. [17]

Berkovits describes a security architecture, which can ensure that an agent has not become malicious as a consequence of alteration to its state. He gives an example of traveling agent, with which a state appraisal function is used to check that the record list has not been altered in transit. [18]

Some other related works concentrate on preventing agent from being attacked by malicious servers. As these issues have some brilliant ideas concerning our architecture in some measure, so we'd like to briefly introduce some of them here.

Sander produces evidences that code can at least partially be protected against a malicious host. He identifies a special class of functions-polynomials and rational functions-together with encryption schemes that lead to a first non-trivial example of cryptographically hiding a function such that it can nevertheless be executed with a non-interactive protocol [19].

Palmer demonstrates that secure hardware can provide islands of trust even within untrusted hosts, at some cost [20]. Wilhelm suggests using tamper-proof hardware: processors that execute agents in a physically sealed environment to guarantee agents against tempering because even the owners cannot access the system internals [21].

6. Conclusion

Agent mediated electronic market is a new kind of online shopping approach that appears recently. It explores a new field that the autonomous agent technology is being applied to. One security issue of this style of electronic market lies in its lack of protection against the malicious agents. We compare the malicious agents with the PC viruses and find that the malicious agents are more harmful than PC viruses.

We proposed the MA and LMA architecture to solve this problem. Some agent transaction protocols are also addressed in detail to show how the agents operate after the security components were added. In our opinion, delivering the identification and migration checking task to some dedicated security mechanism could improve the security level and keep the dealing efficiency in each electronic markets. The architecture we proposed is based on dynamic transaction-oriented authorization schemes so that it is suitable to most types of current electronic market

Acknowledgments. Many people contribute to this work. Some provide valuable comments and suggestions that are so helpful to our paper. Without them, we cannot complete this paper easily.

We'd like to give our special thanks to Joris Claessens and T. O. Lee for their valuable comments in the cross-review.

References

1. D. Chess, B. Grosof, C. Harrison, D. Levine, C. Parris and G. Tsudik, "Itinerant Agents for Mobile Computing", (M. N. Huhns and M. P. Singh Eds), *Readings in Agent*, pp. 267-282, Morgan Kaufmann Publishers, Inc, 1997.
2. M. Crowley-Milling et al. "The Nodal System for the SPS," *CERN*, pp. 78-87, 1978.
3. J. E. White, Telescript Technology: The Foundation for the Electronic Marketplace, (General Magic Inc. Mountain View, CA, 1994.
4. Sun Microsystems, The HotJava Browser: A white paper, (white paper 1995).
5. T. Finin *et al.* "KQML as an Agent Communication Language," *Proceedings of the Third International Conference on Information and Knowledge Management*, ACM Press, Nov. 1994
6. M. R. Genesereth and F. E. Fikes, "Knowledge Interchange Format Version 3.0 Reference Manual," Technical report, Stanford University, Technical Report Logic-92-1, vol.1, no.1
7. P. Maes, R. H. Guttman and A. G. Moukas. "Agents that buy and sell". *Communication of the ACM,* March 1999/Vol.42, No.3, 81-91.
8. S. Loureiro, R. Molva and A. Pannetrat, "Secure data collection with updates," *Proceedings of Workshop on Agents in Electronic Commerce*, pp.121-130, Hongkong, 1999.
9. A. Romao, "Proxy Certificates: A mechanism for delegateing digital signature power to mobile agent," *Proceedings of Workshop on Agents in Electronic Commerce*, pp.131-140, Hongkong, 1999
10. X. Yi, S.C.Siew, Y. Miao and Y. Liu, "Secure Electronic Transaction Based on Software Agent," *Proceedings of Workshop on Agents in Electronic Commerce*, pp. 176-191, Hongkong, 1999

11. E. Palmer, "An Introduction to Citadel- a secure crypto coprocessor for workstations, " *in IFIP SEC'94 Conference*, Curacao, May 1994
12. F. Cohen, "Computer Viruses: Theory and Experiment," *Computers and Security*, vol.6, pp. 22-35, 1987
13. S. Loureiro and R. Molva, "Function hiding based on error correcting codes," M. Blum and C. H. Lee (Eds.) *Proceedings of Cryptec'99 -International workshop on Cryptographic Techniques and Electronic Commerce*, pp. 92-98, Hongkong, 1999
14. T. Sander and C. Tschudin, "Towards mobile cryptography," *Proceedings of the 1998 IEEE symposium on Security and Privacy,* California, 1998
15. A. Caglayan and C. Harrison. Agent Sourcebook. Wiley Computer Publishing, John Wiley & Sons, Inc. 1997.
16. D. Chess, "Security Issues in Mobile Code Systems," Giovanni Vigna (Eds.) Mobile Agents and Security, Lecture Notes in Computer Science, 1419, pp. 1-14, Springer-Verlag, 1998.
17. G. C. Necula and P. Lee, "Safe, Untrusted Agents Using Proof-Carry Code," Giovanni. Vigna (Eds) *Mobile Agents and Security*, Lecture Notes in Computer Science, 1419, pp. 61-91, Springer-Verlag, 1998.
18. S. Berkovits, J. D. Guttman and V. Swarup, "Authentication for Mobile Agents," Giovanni Vigna (Eds.) Mobile Agents and Security, Lecture Notes in Computer Science, 1419, pp. 114-136, Springer-Verlag, 1998.
19. T. Sander and C. F. Tschudin, "Protecting Mobile Agent Against Malicious Hosts," Giovanni Vigna (Eds.) *Mobile Agents and Security*, Lecture Notes in Computer Science, 1419, pp. 44-60, Springer-Verlag, 1998.
20. E. Palmer, "An Introduction to Citadel: a secure crypto-coprocessor for workstations," *Proceedings of IFIP SEC'94 Conference*, Curacap. Dutch Antilles, May 1994
21. U. Wilhem and X. Defago, "Objects Proteges Cryptographiquement," *Proceedings of RenPar 97'*, Lausanne, Switzerland, 1997

Secure Mobile Agent Digital Signatures with Proxy Certificates

Artur Romão[1] and Miguel Mira da Silva[2]

[1] Departamento de Informática,
Universidade de Évora
Rua Romão Ramalho,
59 – 7000-671 Évora, Portugal
a.romao@computer.org

[2] Departamento de Engenharia Informática,
Instituto Superior Técnico
Av. Rovisco Pais – 1049-001 Lisboa, Portugal
mms@dei.ist.utl.pt

Abstract. Security issues related to the usage of mobile agents in performing operations to which their owners have to be bound, such as payments, are of utmost importance if this kind of agents are to be used in electronic commerce. If this binding is achieved by means of digital signature techniques, this means agents have to carry the owner's private key to the host where they sign documents. This exposes the key to attacks because it is copied outside a protected environment. In this paper, we present a mechanism, called *proxy certificates*, that avoids the need for the agent to have access to the user's private key for digitally signing documents, but still binds the owner to the contents of those documents. In order to support our claims, we apply the mechanism to SET/A, an agent-based payment system we proposed in previous work. We also analyze the emerging technology of *attribute certificates* and argue that it is appropriate to implement proxy certificates.

1 Introduction

Utilization of mobile agents to facilitate electronic commerce operations is an appealing concept, especially when those operations are tedious or very difficult to perform by human users under certain conditions. For example, we proposed a payment system, called SET/A [11,12], whose goal is to allow a user to purchase and pay for goods and services on the Internet (using the SET protocol), even when she is not connected, using mobile agents. This mechanism can be used when the only way to connect to the Internet is an expensive, slow, error-prone network, using a device with limited computing power. This is the typical scenario in many mobile computing environments, and mobile agents have been proposed as a potential solution.

One of the most important problems with mechanisms like SET/A is that the user needs to be held responsible for certain operations performed by the

J. Liu and Y. Ye (Eds.): E-Commerce Agents, LNAI 2033, pp. 206–220, 2001.

agent, in a non-repudiable way. This means that the agent will have to digitally sign documents that prove those operations have occurred, something that it will only be able to do using the user's private key. However, if we consider that the agent is executing inside a potentially malicious host, it is easy to conclude that the private key is exposed to attacks that may result in the disclosure of the key.

In this paper we analyze this problem by describing an example where it occurs, and propose a solution, based on a mechanism that we call *proxy certificates*. This mechanism lets the owner of an agent delegate some power by issuing a special kind of certificate to the agent, so that it can sign documents on behalf of the owner without needing the owner's private key. In this paper we will not discuss SET/A itself or, more generally, the appropriateness of mobile agents for electronic payments. Their appearance here is for illustration purposes only.

The rest of the paper is organized as follows. Section 2 provides an overview of SET/A and discusses the security threats to the user's private key. We present the proxy certificate mechanism in Section 3, and discuss the security guarantees it provides in Section 4. In Section 5 we analyze the impact of proxy certificates in the original SET/A protocol. Similar mechanisms, called attribute certificates and mini-certificates, are presented and compared to our proposal in Section 6, and Section 7 concludes the paper.

2 Overview of SET/A

The purchase request transaction is the phase of the SET protocol that involves a direct interaction between the *cardholder* (buyer) and the *merchant* (seller). Both the cardholder and the merchant have digital certificates, issued by certificate authorities associated with the SET public-key infrastructure, that allow them to perform encryption and digital signature operations on documents.

During this transaction the cardholder sends a request to the merchant, who in turn sends a digitally signed acknowledgement. The cardholder then sends the *order information* (control information, card brand, bank identification, and a digest of the description of the goods) and the *payment instructions* (amount of the transaction, card account number and expiration date, among other elements).

The payment instructions are encrypted in such a way that only the *payment gateway* (a device operated by a financial institution for processing payments with the card brand used by the cardholder) is able to decrypt them. The merchant asks the payment gateway to authorize the payment and sends a response to the cardholder. If the authorization is granted, the merchant delivers the goods, but this operation is outside the scope of the SET protocol.

However, SET is a very complex protocol, and may not be suitable under some technical conditions, namely those in which the mobility of the users is determinant. Generally, the devices used in these environments have limited computational capacity and use slow and expensive connections to the Internet. SET may be too demanding for this kind of equipment and connectivity, mak-

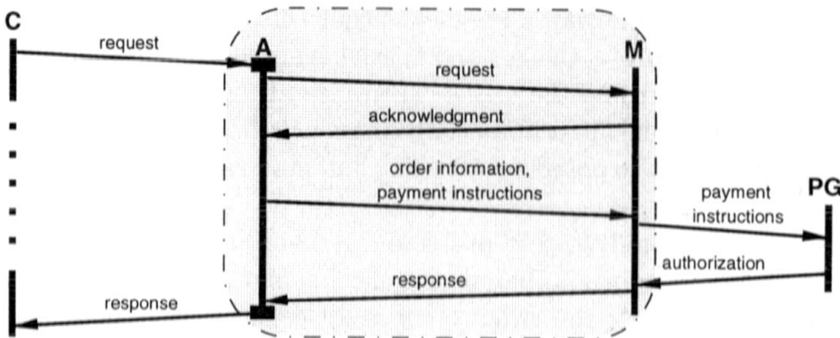

Fig. 1. SET/A purchase request transaction: Agent A shops with merchant M, on behalf of cardholder C.

ing SET transactions unsuitable for mobile users. In previous papers [11,12] we proposed a mechanism, called SET/A, guided by the SET rules and based on the *mobile agent paradigm*. With SET/A, the computational burden is taken away from the user's device, so it can be disconnected from the Internet while the transaction is running.

SET/A is based on an agent traveling from the cardholder's computer, carrying all the relevant information, to a remote (possibly the merchant's) server (see Figure 1). On arrival, the agent performs the cardholder's role and carries on a complete SET purchase request transaction with the merchant. From the merchant point of view, there will be no distinction between an agent and a real (i.e., human) buyer: a SET purchase request is being performed with another entity, which represents a cardholder with valid certificate and payment data.

2.1 Usage of SET/A

In a previous paper we outlined a scenario to illustrate a possible use of SET/A [12]. In that scenario, the agent migrates from the owner's environment (a mobile phone) to the server of a trusted third party (the cellular phone provider). The entire interaction with the merchant is conducted on this server. In order to buy a product, the agent carries two types of elements:

- *Secret data*, such as the credit card number and expiration date, and the cardholder's private signature key.
- *Specific code*, implementing whatever logic is necessary to carry on the transaction on behalf of its owner. For example, the agent uses this code, together with some additional data such as auxiliary variables and the cardholder's signature certificate, to negotiate the deal with the merchant (price, etc.).

The software for cryptographic and SET functionality is kept at the cellular phone provider's server, inside a secure processor. Before leaving the home environment, the secret data is encrypted with the public encryption key of the secure processor.

Upon arrival at the cellular provider's server, the agent installs itself inside the secure environment and uses the cryptographic and SET software. The agent then provides the secret data it carries for decryption by the secure processor.

From this point on, the agent is able to conduct a SET purchase request. The specific code enables the agent to implement its owner's policies when talking to the merchant (e.g., for negotiating the price, delivery conditions, etc).

This example shows that, if the agent is provided a reasonably secure and trusted environment, it is perfectly capable of performing an entire business transaction on a remote server on behalf of its owner. The server is operated by the cellular phone provider mostly for technical convenience, but it could also be operated by some other, more trusted third party, such as a notary or a government agency.

2.2 Problems with SET/A

Although the example above outlines an interesting use for agents, the solution is unacceptable under a strict security policy that forbids any highly secret data to leave the user's control. This happens, for example, when signing using the owner's private key, because the agent needs to have access to this key (which is part of the secret data described above) in order to be able to sign the payment.

Even though the execution environment is considered secure and trusted, the user obviously feels uncomfortable in letting her private key be copied to a remote host. In fact, this is a basic security assumption in the public-key cryptography context—the private key never leaves a trusted environment. Any security breach along the path or on the secure server compromises the key and lets an attacker sign documents on behalf of the user. In the case of SET/A, the attacker would be able to make payments since it is expected that the credit card data can also be discovered.

In order to increase security to an acceptable level, we need to devise a new method of letting the agent perform its role without needing the cardholder's signing (private) key.

3 Proxy Certificates

Our approach to solve the problem mentioned above is based on providing the cardholder with the capability to mandate the agent perform a set of operations on her behalf. These operations will be performed in such a way that the cardholder is held responsible for them (albeit indirectly via the agent).

In order to achieve this purpose, agents will have their own signature certificates, which we will call *proxy certificates*, issued and signed by their respective owners. In this section we will describe this mechanism, followed by an analysis of the guarantees it provides in the next section.

3.1 Notation

We use the following notation to specify the data elements and operations in the presentation:

CA	is the identity of a certification authority
$\mathtt{A}(X)$	is the identity of a mobile agent belonging to X
K_X	is the public key of X
K_X^{-1}	is the private key of X
$\{M\}$	is a message with contents M
$\{M\}_{K_X^{-1}}$	is a message with contents M signed by X
$\mathtt{C}\{X,K_X\}_{K_Y^{-1}}$	is the digital certificate of X issued by Y
$\mathtt{C}\{X,K_{\mathtt{A}(X)},[D]\}_{K_X^{-1}}$	is the proxy certificate of a mobile agent belonging to X, with additional data D

We also define two operations:

- Signature verification of $\{M\}_{K_X^{-1}}$:

  $$\mathtt{sig\_ver}(M,X) = M_1$$

  Verification is successful iff M equals M_1.
- Verification of $\mathtt{C}\{X,K_X\}_{K_Y^{-1}}$

  $$\mathtt{cert\_ver}(X,Y) = Z,K_Z$$

  Verification is successful iff $\mathtt{sig\_ver}(\mathtt{C}\{X,K_X\}_{K_Y^{-1}},Y)$ is successfull, in which case we have $Z = X$ and $K_Z = K_X$. The verification of a proxy certificate is similar, and we will not define a new operation for the sake of simplicity.

3.2 Issuing Proxy Certificates

As said above, a proxy certificate is issued and signed by the owner of an agent. Obviously, there is an associated key pair that is also generated by the agent's owner.

The certificate contains a validity period, the identity of the agent's owner, and a set of constraints indicating the valid operations that the agent is allowed to perform while using that certificate. In the context of SET/A, these constraints will typically specify the identity of the merchants that the agent may deal with, the products it may purchase and the (maximum) amount of money it may spend for each product and/or with each merchant.

The cardholder is bound to the actions performed (i.e., documents signed) by the agent through the owner's identity and signature in the proxy certificate. For this purpose, the identity in the proxy certificate must be the same as the identity in the cardholder's signature certificate (see Figure 2 for illustration).

Thus, a proxy certificate for an agent belonging to cardholder C is denoted as

$$\mathtt{C}\{C,K_{\mathtt{A}(C)},[constraints]\}_{K_C^{-1}}$$

(We ommit the validity period in the additional data section, since we assume that every certificate has a validity period.)

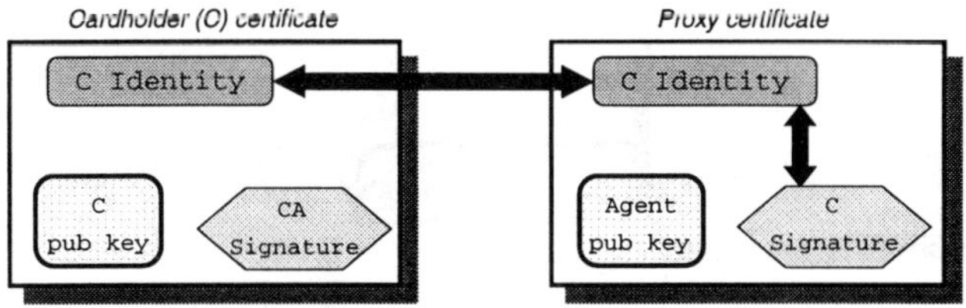

Fig. 2. Cardholder binding with a proxy certificate.

3.3 Using Proxy Certificates

When migrating to an external server the agent will carry its proxy certificate, which can be part of the data that composes the agent's specific code (see 2.1). The agent will also carry the cardholder's signature certificate, as before. The secret data includes the agent's private signature key, along with the usual secret data, but now excluding the cardholder's signature key.

I.e., the agent carries, among other elements:

$$\{\mathtt{C}\{C,K_{C}\}_{K^{-1}_{CA}},\mathtt{C}\{C,K_{A(C)},[constraints]\}_{K^{-1}_{C}},K^{-1}_{A(C)}\}$$

When the agent decides to purchase some good or service, it must check the details of the purchase (e.g., merchant, product, and price) against the constraints in its proxy certificate, and only proceeds if all of the constraints are satisfied.

In order to make a payment, the agent sends its proxy certificate and the cardholder's certificate (see below) to the merchant:

$$\{\mathtt{C}\{C,K_{C}\}_{K^{-1}_{CA}},\mathtt{C}\{C,K_{A(C)},[constraints]\}_{K^{-1}_{C}}\}$$

Besides the verification of signatures, discussed below, the merchant should check the constraints in the certificate in order to ensure that the agent is allowed to make the purchase. Even though the agent has already performed this check, the merchant should do it again to prevent possible malfunctions on the agent's behavior. It is assumed that in case of conflict, the merchant can only support his claims if he can provide a valid proxy certificate whose constraints allowed the agent to do the purchase being disputed. This protects the cardholder from attacks on the agent's behavior, for example, by forcing it to spend a large amount of money or to buy from a vendor that the cardholder would not want to do business with in the first place.

3.4 Signature Verification

The act of verifying a signature made by the agent on some message $\{M\}$ ($\{M\}_{K^{-1}_{A(C)}}$) represents more than simply binding the agent to the signed data. The cardholder has to be bound to the data, as well. Therefore, when verifying a signature, the merchant will first validate the cardholder's signature certificate (brought by the agent), i.e., performs

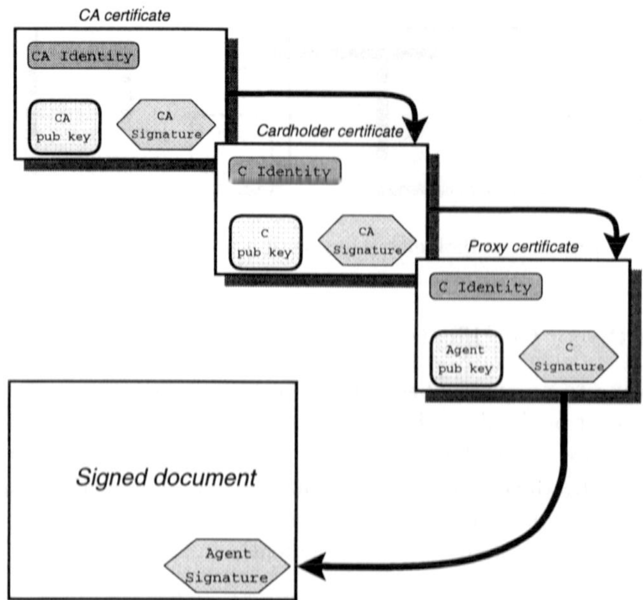

Fig. 3. Signature verification with proxy certificates.

$$\texttt{cert\_ver}(\texttt{C}\{C,K_{\text{C}}\}_{K^{-1}_{\text{CA}}},\text{CA})$$

and obtains C and K_{C}.

Next, the merchant validates the proxy certificate with

$$\texttt{cert\_ver}(\texttt{C}\{C,K_{\texttt{A}(C)},[constraints]\}_{K^{-1}_{\text{C}}},\text{C})$$

and obtains $\texttt{A}(C)$ and $K_{\texttt{A}(C)}$. This ensures that the cardholder has delegated powers (specified by the certificate constraints) to the agent.

Finally, the signature on the data is verified by doing

$$\texttt{sig\_ver}(\text{M},\texttt{A}(C))$$

Figure 3 illustrates the process.

The payment gateway will have to follow the same certification path in order to validate signatures made by the agent.

3.5 Certificate Expiration

A proxy certificate is issued for one agent, and the corresponding private key will only be used for signature operations as long as the agent needs that key. This means the certificate validity time may be shorter than usual (typically one year). In fact, we will present arguments below supporting that it *should* be shorter than usual. Depending on the time the cardholder expects that the agent will take to perform its tasks, the validity period of the certificate may be in the order of a few days or hours, or even minutes.

Nevertheless, proxy certificates should remain accessible in public repositories long enough to be used for signature verification, since they will be used in contexts where normal cardholder signature certificates are used. Therefore, proxy certificates should remain accessible for as long as normal certificates are (typically twenty years). The cardholder may use a public directory service to publish the proxy certificates.

3.6 Certificate Revocation

A certificate should be revoked when an abnormal condition invalidates one or more of the elements associated with the certificate, the most significant example being the compromise of the private key. Revocation is performed by the certificate issuer, usually upon request of the owner.

In the case of proxy certificates, the agent would have to request the cardholder to revoke the certificate. This introduces three kinds of problems: (1) communication mechanism to request the revocation; (2) distribution of the revocation information; and (3) fraudulent revocations.

The first two are technical problems. The agent may choose an asynchronous method to request the revocation (e.g., send an e-mail) and hope that the cardholder will eventually receive the request and act accordingly. If the agent wants to be sure that the certificate is revoked, it may choose to open some communication channel to the cardholder, send the request, and wait for a confirmation. The main difficulty with this scheme is that the cardholder has to be on-line at the moment the agent wants to ask for the revocation.

The second problem is potentially difficult to solve as well. The cardholder may choose an on-line method, such as OCSP [9], to provide information about the status of a certificate. This kind of methods generally have a very high cost in order to be effective (e.g., each response has to be digitally signed, and the on-line service has to be highly available), which makes them unsuitable to be used by the average cardholder.

An alternative to the methods above is the publication of certificate revocation lists (CRLs), a standard method for publishing this kind of information [7]. CRLs may be distributed via well-known Web addresses or directory entries (e.g., using LDAP [18]). While this may seem a better, less technically demanding alternative, it still requires the cardholder's intervention to digitally sign the CRL. The problem here is that the delay between the revocation request and the signing and publication of the CRL may be too long. A normal certification authority has a well-defined set of procedures to deal with this *time granularity problem*, but a user may take too long to be aware of the revocation request and to be able to sign and publish the CRL.

In any case, the establishment of some mechanism to revoke proxy certificates and provide information about them requires a significant increase in the resources required by mobile agent systems in order to support those certificates.

Finally, we have a security problem: fraudulent revocations. Information about a revoked certificate includes a timestamp and a trusted third party's digital signature. The timestamp, which is also generated by the trusted third party, specifies a moment in time after which the certificate is no longer valid and should not be trusted any more, and the signature attests the fact that the timestamp is valid. Therefore, a user may reject a digital signature made with a private key corresponding to a public key whose certificate has been revoked, as long as the signature has been generated *after* the time of revocation. If the owner of a revoked certificate had any chance of tamper with the revocation timestamp, she could pretend the revocation happened *before* the moment that she signed some document (e.g., a payment order) and thus repudiate the signature.

A malicious cardholder could instruct her agent to start a fraudulent revocation request after signing a payment order and thus being able to repudiate the transaction, possibly after receiving the goods. The fraud would consist in the cardholder putting an invalid (earlier) timestamp into the revocation information and then sign it. In other words, *the cardholder is not a trusted third party for revoking proxy certificates issued by her.* A possible solution would be to require the timestamp to be originated from some trusted source, for example using a digital notary service [5,15]. Again, the involvement of the cardholder and the technical requirements may be too demanding for this solution to make sense in practice.

We have analyzed the issue of proxy certificate revocation and identified important technical and security problems. While theoretically they seem to be manageable, the practical implications recommend some caution in dealing with these issues. Therefore, we feel that for the time being it is more appropriate to propose that proxy certificates cannot be revoked, especially since a short validity period solves most of the problem.

4 Discussion

In this section we discuss the implications of the proxy certificate introduced in the previous sections, in particular in the protection it offers to the cardholder's private key. The security issues related to the agent's private key are also discussed.

4.1 Cardholder's Private Key

We proposed proxy certificates in order to prevent the cardholder's private signature key to leave its (hopefully) protected environment, e.g., a smartcard or a password protected file in a cardholder's computer. We think that the binding between the agent's (signed) actions and the cardholder's identity provides enough evidence for the merchant and the payment gateway to accept this mechanism and let the agent be a surrogate for the cardholder.

As far as the cardholder's private key is concerned, proxy certificates provide complete protection, while at the same time not restricting the level of agent's functionality that the cardholder may require.

4.2 Agent's Private Key

The agent must carry its own private key in order to digitally sign documents. In this way, the agent's private key is vulnerable to the same kind of attacks we identified for the cardholder's private key: since the key is not under the direct control of its human owner,[1] it may not be conveniently protected. As such, the agent's key may be discovered by others and used to sign documents for which the cardholder will be responsible.

Proxy certificates do not solve the problem of private key compromise, but we have provided two mechanisms that will reduce significantly this possibility:

1. The limited lifetime of a proxy certificate makes it more difficult for an attacker to discover the private key before the certificate expires. Even attacks based on reverse engineering of the agent's object code may take too long to be effective. This is even more difficult if the agent runs inside a secure processor (see 2.1).
2. The constraint mechanism gives the cardholder the possibility to reduce possible damages, by allowing the agent to perform only a limited set of tasks. In other words, even if the private key is discovered, it may not be used to sign an arbitrary document. For example, it may not be used to spend a large amount of money, or to buy unwanted products from unwanted vendors (besides economical, this may have social implications, such as privacy, politics, and personal issues).

In any case, the agent's private key may still be discovered and used to attack the cardholder's safety before the proxy certificate expires. Under normal circumstances, if the agent (or the cardholder) were aware of this fact, the correct action would be to ask for certificate revocation. The fact that we prevent proxy certificates from being revoked (see 3.6) can be pointed as a serious limitation in our proposal.

However, it is important to note that the two other mechanisms (limited lifetime and power constraints) and the complete protection of the cardholder's private key (see previous Section) significantly reduce both the possibility of success of key discovery, and the damage that such an attack can inflict to the cardholder. On the other hand, future technological advances may solve the problems that we identified as preventing proxy certificates from being revoked.

5 Changes to SET/A

In order to use proxy certificates, we must introduce two important changes to the original SET/A protocol: (1) both the merchant and the payment gateway have to be aware of, and accept the fact that the certificate does not belong to

[1] For practical reasons, we consider that the cardholder is the "human owner" of the agent's private key. The issue here is that, in principle, a non-human (i.e., agent) owner is not as able to detect attempts to compromise the key as a human is.

the cardholder, and (2) the merchant (and maybe the payment gateway as well) needs to interpret the proxy certificate constraints.

The major disadvantage of these changes is that they neutralize one of the most important features of SET/A: it did not require any modifications to the SET software run by the merchant and the payment gateway.

5.1 Non-cardholder's Certificate

Since the agent was using the cardholder's key and certificate, neither the merchant nor the payment gateway needed to be aware of the fact that it was not the cardholder that was doing business with them. With proxy certificates, the merchant and the payment gateway need to accept that the cardholder delegates powers to the agent, which is incompatible with version 1.0 of the SET protocol [17] on which the original SET/A was based.

Note that proxy certificate validation does not introduce any addition to the SET protocol. Entities verify certificates by traversing the trust chain to the root key [17]. If we consider only the verification of the identities of certification authorities and the extraction of the entities' authenticated public keys, certification paths now have one more hop, but technically (and conceptually) there is no other difference.

5.2 Interpretation of Constraints

As stated in sub-section 3.3, the merchant should interpret the constraints in the proxy certificate to be sure that the purchase will not generate a conflict with the cardholder. While the SET protocol does not address this kind of verification, it can be regarded as an additional feature of the SET-compliant software used by the merchant, having no impact whatsoever on the execution of the protocol itself. A merchant may decide, for any reason, not to do business with a cardholder, and this decision may be made and implemented completely on top of the SET protocol.

The payment gateway may need to verify compliance with the proxy certificate constraints, for the same kind of reasons as the merchant does. If the verification fails, the payment gateway simply does not authorize the payment, according to the SET protocol. Nevertheless, this verification can only be made if the constraints apply to the amount of money that can be spent and the identity of the merchant, since SET does not allow the payment gateway to have knowledge of the product being purchased.

6 Related Work

In this section we compare our approach to that of other technologies, namely attribute certificates, and the WTLS mini-certificates. The former has the potential to be the basis for an implementation of proxy certificates. The later uses short-lived certificates in a context simlar to the one described in this paper: to overcome the problem of certificate revocation by clients with limited computing power and low bandwidth.

6.1 Protection from Malicious Hosts

The problem of protecting mobile agents from malicious hosts is one of the most challenging in this area, and several approaches have been proposed. For example, running the agent in secure hardware [20,21]: the agent migrates to a protected environment and all the confidential data is handled inside this environment. The example in Section 2.1 includes the utilization of secure hardware.

Another approach is to encode the agent in such a way that it is able to execute correctly in the host environment, but its secret data cannot be read or tampered with. Sander and Tschudin propose a solution based on so-called *encrypted functions* [13]. Hohl describes a conversion mechanism called *time limited blackbox protection* [6], that modifies the original structure of an agent in such a way that, within a certain time frame, it is hard for the host to reverse-engineer the executable code.

Our goal with proxy certificates is different from those of the above mechanisms: while secure hardware or agent enconding aim at protecting the agent itself and its data, we protect the owner's private key by eliminating the need for this key to be included in the agent's data. On the other hand, our mechanism is compatible with any of those cited above; in fact, it can benefit from them, since they provide an additional level of protection to the agent itself.

6.2 Attribute Certificates

The idea of an entity using digital certificates to delegate powers to others is not completely new. Standards committees (see below) recognized that certificates could be used to distribute *authorization information*, which led them to develop a specific class of certificates, called *attribute certificates*. These certificates bind one or more attributes to the certificates' owners. Attributes may specify, for example, that a person is authorized to sign contracts on behalf of a company, the maximum amount of money that those contracts may involve, roles, groups to which a user may belong to, and so on. They may also be associated to non-human users such as applications (or, in our context, mobile agents) that need access to resources.

Quoting Ford and Baum [4], "attribute certificates represent an important area of electronic commerce technology which is yet to be fully explored or developed." This concept has been incorporated into standards such as ANSI X9.57 [1], X.509 [7], and ECMA-219 [3]. New security infrastructure proposals, such as SDSI [10] and SPKI [2], also adopt this concept for delegating authorization and protecting resources. Nevertheless, only recently there is some interest from software vendors in this technology [8].

Attribute certificates are issued by so-called *attribute authorities*. These entities need not be specialized in certificate issuing activities, as are typical certification authorities. While certification authorities are trusted by the user community, attribute authorities need not enjoy this widespread trust. They may have only local jurisdiction over the users to which they may issue attribute certificates. For example, a company may issue attribute certificates to their employees, who in turn have their identity certificates issued by a central (e.g., governmental) certification authority.

Since attributes are likely to change more often than identities, lifetimes of attribute certificates are expected to be much shorter than those of identity certificates. Due to this fact, revocation of attribute certificates may be unnecessary since the duration of the exposure of certificates that should be revoked is likely to be very short.

It is obvious the similarity between the characteristics of attribute certificates and those we have proposed for proxy certificates in previous sections. More specifically, proxy certificates are issued "locally" (i.e., by the cardholder), they are used to authorize other entities to perform certain tasks as defined by a set of attributes (i.e., constraints) and, due to different reasons, they have short lifetimes and are never revoked. Therefore, if there will ever be an implementation of the proxy certificate mechanism, it is likely to be based on attribute certificates technology.

6.3 WAP Mini-Certificates

It is interesting to note that, in a different context, a technique using short-lived certificates is also used to deal with the certificate revocation problem. The WTLS protocol [16], which intends to provide security to the emerging WAP technology applications, uses certificates that have to be processed by mobile client devices. These lack the computational power and/or bandwidth to use the revocation methods discussed above (OCSP or CRLs). To solve this problem, VeriSign proposes a mechanism that uses short-lived (mini-) certificates, issued on a daily basis, that will certify the validity of other, longer-lived server certificates [19]. Mini-certificates are optimized in size, in order to be easier to parse and process by the client devices.

In this model, a client requests the mini-certificate that will confirm that the corresponding server certificate is still valid. (This also involves some kind of delegation, from the server certificate to the mini-certificate.) If the certificate is revoked, then mini-certificates for it are simply not issued any more.

This model is not appropriate for agent certificates, though. As explained before (see 4.2, the control over whether or not a private key is compromised is not possible for a mobile agent. Therefore, the agent is not capable (as a WAP server is) of determining when its certificate should be revoked, and stop issuing mini-certificates.

7 Conclusions

In this paper we proposed a mechanism, called proxy certificate, to overcome a security weakness we have found on the original SET/A proposal [11,12]. The problem consisted in having the cardholder's private key being carried by the agent to an external server, which violates a basic security precaution concerning the usage of public-key technology.

Proxy certificates allow the cardholder to delegate some powers to the agent, by issuing a certificate that restricts the agent's activities to a pre-defined set of operations. The agent carries its own private key, for signing payment orders, but the private key of the cardholder never leaves its secure environment. This mechanism does not provide complete security of the agent's key, but significantly reduces the risk of the key being compromised, mostly by shortening the lifetime of the proxy certificate to a period that would not be practical to impose on a normal (user identity) certificate.

In Section 5 we identified two modifications that have to be introduced in the original SET/A proposal. The most significant of these changes is that the certificate being used is not the cardholder's (see 5.1), something that is not dealt with by version 1.0 of the SET protocol. In our opinion, this represents the major drawback of the proxy certificate mechanism. At least in theory, this limitation could be eliminated by defining an extension to the protocol, which is something that has been done before [14].

However, the new protocol provides a safe and convenient way to delegate buying power on agents acting on behalf of users, something that was not taken into account in the original SET protocol. If agents do take off in the real world, we believe that a mechanism similar to the one proposed in this paper will be necessary to integrate those special requirements from agents into protocols like SET.

We have shown that our ideas make sense by analyzing an emerging technology, called attribute certificates, which can be used to implement proxy certificates. Attribute certificates are a relatively new concept, and their use is not yet as widespread as normal, public-key (or identity) certificates. One of the key contributions of this paper is the suggestion of a new area of application for this technology.

The discussion of proxy certificates in this paper was focused on the SET/A protocol, in order to solve a specific security problem. In the future we will work on the generalization of the proxy certificate concept, in order to apply it to other agent application scenarios.

References

1. American National Standards Institute. *ANSI X9.57: Public- Key Cryptography for the Financial Services Industry: Certificate Management*, 1997.
2. C. Ellison, B. Frantz, B. Lampson, R. Rivest, B. Thomas, and T. Ylonen. *SPKI Certificate Theory.* Internet Request for Comments 2693, September 1999.
3. European Computer Manufacturers Association. *Authentication and Privilege Attribute Security Application with Related Key Distribution Functions*, March 1996. Standard ECMA-219, 2nd Edition.
4. W. Ford and M. Baum. *Secure Electronic Commerce.* Prentice Hall, New Jersey, USA, 1997.
5. S. Haber and W. S. Stornetta. How to Time-Stamp a Digital Document. *Journal of Cryptology*, 3(2), 1991.
6. F. Hohl. Time Limited Blackbox Security: Protecting Mobile Agents from Malicious Hosts. In G. Vigna, editor, *Mobile Agents and Security.* Springer-Verlag, November 1997.
7. International Telecommunications Union. *ITU-T Recommendation X.509: Information Technology—Open Systems Interconnection—The Directory: Authentication Framework*, June 1997.

8. S. Laing. Attribute Certificates—A New Initiative in PKI Technology. White Paper, Baltimore Technologies, Inc., Dublin, Ireland, 1999.
9. M. Myers, R. Ankney, A. Malpani, S. Galperin, and C. Adams. *X.509 Internet Public Key Infrastructure Online Certificate Status Protocol–OCSP*. Internet Request for Comments 2560, June 1999.
10. R. Rivest and B. Lampson. *A Simple Distributed Security Infrastructure.* http://theory.lcs.mit.edu/ cis/sdsi.html.
11. A. Romão and M. Mira da Silva. An Agent-Based Secure Internet Payment System for Mobile Computing. In *Proceedings of the International Conference on "Trends in Distributed Systems for Electronic Commerce,"* Hamburg, Germany, June 1998. Springer LNCS 1402.
12. A. Romão, M. Mira da Silva, and A. Silva. *Secure Payments with Mobile Agents.* To appear in Journal of Distributed and Parallel Databases, 8(4), Kluwer Academic Publishers, October 2000.
13. T. Sander and C. Tschudin. Protecting Mobile Agents Against Malicious Hosts. In G. Vigna, editor, *Mobile Agents and Security.* Springer-Verlag, November 1997.
14. SET Secure Electronic Transactions, LLC. *Approved Extensions.* http://www.setco.org/extensions.html.
15. Surety Technologies, Inc. *Digital Notary Service.* http://www.surety.com/dns.html.
16. VeriSign, Inc. *Secure Wireless E-Commerce with PKI from VeriSign.* White Paper, January 2000. http://www.verisign.com/.
17. VISA International and MasterCard International. *Secure Electronic Transaction (SET) Specification*, May 1997. Version 1.0.
18. M. Wahl, T. Howes, and S. Kille. *Lightweight Directory Access Protocol (v3).* Internet Request for Comments 2251, December 1997.
19. The WAP Forum. *Wireless Transport Layer Security (WTLS) Specification.* November 1999. http://www.wapforum.org/what/technical.htm
20. U. Wilhelm and X. DeFago. Objets Protégés Cryptographiquement. In *Proceedings of RenPar'9*, Lausanne, Switzerland, May 1997.
21. B. Yee. A Sanctuary for Mobile Agents. In *Proceedings of the DARPA Workshop on Foundations for Secure Mobile Code*, Monterey, USA, March 1997.

Agent-Mediated Secure Electronic Transaction for Online Interdependent Purchases

Xun Yi, Chee Kheong Siew, and Yuan Miao

Information Communication Institute of Singapore
School of Electrical and Electronic Engineering
Nanyang Technological University, Singapore 639798
{exyi, ecksiew, eymiao}@ntu.edu.sg

Abstract. Because Internet trading provides customers with more convenient and more money-saving services than conventional trading, it has seen explosive growth in recent years and will have a major impact in shaping future markets. Certainly, it will be very advantageous for customers if on-line purchases, especially a series of on-line interdependent purchases, are capable of being more automated and secure than is currently the case, since the time and energy they spend will be dramatically reduced. This paper focuses on applying software agent technology together with cryptographic technology to automating and securing electronic transaction for a series of online interdependent purchases.

1 Introduction

Electronic commerce is emerging as one of the most important applications on the Internet, with the potential to revolutionize the whole structure of retail merchandising and shopping. By providing more complete information to purchasers and cutting transaction costs, it is reducing market friction and making markets more perfect.

The Internet is now considered to be the preferred environment for electronic commerce. Yet, there is still some resistance from the public to buying products and services on-line and paying for them over the Internet, for example, by browsing a company's Web server, ordering a product and paying for it by filling a form that includes credit card information. The main difficulty is that almost every Internet user has heard of credit card fraud performed by hackers eavesdropping connections used to send transaction data - despite the fact that very few of those attacks have actually succeeded. Even the deployment of secure servers based on protocols such as SSL or S-HTTP is not enough, since the credit card information is deposited in the server where it can easily be read by anyone with access to it (or even by unauthorized hackers).

The concern for protecting users' credit card information lead VISA and MasterCard, in association with major software and cryptography companies, to the devel

J. Liu and Y. Ye (Eds.): E-Commerce Agents, LNAI 2033, pp. 221-246, 2001.

opment of the SET protocol [18]. SET provides important properties like authentication of the participants, non-repudiation, data integrity and confidentiality. Each player knows only what is strictly necessary to play their role, for example, the selling company never knows the buyer's credit card information, and the financial institution authorizing the transaction is not aware of the details of the purchase, including the nature of the products, quantities, etc. Paying for something using a credit card under the SET protocol is clearly much more secure than doing it, say, in a restaurant, where the card is normally taken out of the customer's sight.

SET is expected to give buyers and sellers the necessary confidence to launch Internet commerce definitively (despite some technical and non-technical problems that still exists). From the buyer's point of view, SET should be very attractive, both to use (there will be many SET-compliant software tools to help the users with their credit cards on the Internet) and to trust (if we assume the financial institutions interested in its success are able to explain and convince users of its benefits).

SET is a very complex protocol, and may not be suitable under some technical conditions, such as mobile computing environments. Generally, the devices used in these environments have limited computational capacity and use slow and expensive connections to the Internet. SET may be too demanding for this kind of equipment and connectivity, preventing on-line transactions for mobile users.

Besides communication cost, SET is also very heavy for customer to order and pay for a series of interdependent goods or services on the Internet. For example, when you plan to go to an oversea city for business, you need to call some travel agencies firstly to book an airplane ticket to the city. Unless the ticket has been reserved, you can begin to consult some hotels in the city to book a room. Unless the airplane ticket and the room are reserved, you can indeed order and pay for the interdependent ticket and the room by running SET twice. You have to manually fill the order and payment forms twice. Without doubts, purchasing a series of interdependent goods or services on the Internet by using SET is quite boring for customers. It will consume a lot of time, energy and communication expense of customers.

Software agent technology offers a new paradigm for SET to overcome these difficulties mentioned above. A software agent is a software program that uses agent communication protocols to exchange information for automatic problem solving [5]. Unlike "traditional" software, software agents are personalized (incorporating cooperation, negotiation and conflict resolution), continuously running and semi-autonomous [8]. A software agent might have service capabilities, autonomous decision making and commitment features. These qualities are conducive to optimizing the whole buying experience and revolutionizing commerce as we know it today [10].

Guided by the SET rules and based on the mobile agent paradigm, SET/A is presented by Romao et al. [14]. With SET/A, the computational burden is taken away from the user's device, so it can be disconnected while the transaction is running. Notwithstanding the fact that software agents are able to simulate the entire person to person trading process, customers are wary about employing them to trade on their behalf, largely because of concerns about unknown risks they may face. The key to alleviating many of these concerns - to mitigating the risk - is the security of agents. In order to run, a mobile agent has to expose its code and data to the host environment that supplies the means for it to execute. Thus the agents are at risk of being tampered with, scanned or even terminated by malicious servers. SET/A depends on a secure execution environment installed at the merchant's server to protect an agent's confidential data (i.e., credit card information) against a malicious merchant. In our opinion, the solution is high cost for merchants and the required security is not easy to ensure.

After realizing this above problem, we try to apply software agent technology together with cryptographic technology to automating and securing electronic transaction for online interdependent purchases in this paper. We propose a new agent-mediated SET protocol, which avoids the security limit on the agent's execution environment in the merchant's terminal. In this proposal, in order to purchase a series of interdependent goods or services, a customer creates a mobile agent and launches it into the Internet. The mobile agent automatically roams among some specified online merchants and finds the most suitable sites where to purchase the series of interdependent goods or service. Then the mobile agent orders and pays for the series of interdependent goods or services by using SET protocol on behalf of customer. Finally, the mobile agent brings all purchase responses back to the customer.

The remainder of this paper is organized as follows: Section 2 introduces the fundamental cryptographic technology concepts necessary to explain secure electronic transaction. Section 3 outlines the Secure Electronic Transaction protocol (SET). Section 4 presents the agent-mediated secure electronic transaction for online interdependent purchases. The main security issues for mobile agents are discussed in Section 5. Conclusion is drawn in the last section.

2 Cryptographic Technology

Cryptographic technology is used to ensure the privacy and authentication of data on a network. To implement a mobile agent security policy, we need public key algorithms to provide data confidentiality, digital signature schemes for non-repudiation and to confirm data integrity, and authentication schemes to give assurance of an agent's identity (that is, the identity of the agent's owner). This section will briefly review these cryptographic principles.

2.1 Public-Key Cryptosystem

The concept of public-key cryptography was invented by Whitfield Diffie and Martin Hellman [4]. This contribution was the notion that keys could come in pairs - an encryption key and a decryption key. Since 1976, numerous public-key cryptography algorithms have been proposed. Only a few algorithms are both secure and practical. These algorithms are generally based on some computationally hard problem, such as the problem of factoring large numbers or the problem of calculating discrete logarithms.

Named after Ron Rivest, Adi Shamir and Leonard Adleman, the three inventors who first introduced the algorithm in 1978, RSA [13] has since withstood years of extensive cryptanalysis. RSA gets its security from the difficulty of factoring large numbers. The public and private keys are functions of a pair of large (100 to 200 digits or even larger) prime numbers. To generate the two keys, choose two large prime numbers p and q. Compute the product: $n=pq$. Then randomly choose the encryption key e such that e and $(p-1)(q-1)$ are relatively prime. Finally, use Euclid's algorithm to compute the decryption key d such that $ed=1 \pmod{(p-1)(q-1)}$. In other words, $d=e^{-1} \pmod{(p-1)(q-1)}$. Note that d and n are also relatively prime. The numbers e and n are the public key; the number d is the private key. The two primes, p and q, are no longer needed. They should be discarded, but never revealed.

To encrypt a message m, first divide it into numerical blocks such that each block has a unique representation modulo n (with binary data, choose the largest power of 2 less than n). That is, if p and q are 100-digit primes, then n will have just under 200 digits, and each message block m_i should be just under 200 digits long. The encrypted message c will be made up of similarly sized message blocks c_i of about the same length. The encryption formula is simply: $c_i=m_i^e \pmod n$. To decrypt a message, take each encrypted block c_i and compute: $m_i=c_i^d \pmod n$ because $c_i^d=(m_i^e)^d= m_i^{k(p-1)(q-1)+1} = m_i \cdot m_i^{k(p-1)(q-1)} = m_i \cdot 1 = m_i \pmod n$.

2.2 Digital Signature and Hash Function

Handwritten signatures on paper-based documents have long been used as proof of authorship of, or at least agreement on, the contents of such documents. We would like to do this sort of thing with electronic documents and information, but there are problems. Firstly, a bit stream is easy to copy. Even if a person's signature were difficult to forge (a graphic image of a written signature, for example), it is easy to move a valid signature from one document to another document. The mere presence of such a signature therefore means nothing. Secondly, documents are easy to modify after they are signed, without leaving any evidence of modification.

There are public-key algorithms that can be used for digital signatures. In some algorithms - RSA is an example - either the public key or the private key can be used for encryption. By encrypting a document using your private key you have a secure digital signature. The basic protocol is simple:

Alice can generate her signature on a document by encrypting it with her private key.

1) Alice sends the document with her signature to Bob.

2) Bob can use Alice's public key to verify the signature.

In practical implementations, public-key algorithms are often inefficient to encrypt long documents. To save time, digital signature protocols are often implemented using a one-way hash function. A one-way hash function, denoted as $H(M)$, operates on an arbitrary-length message M. It returns a fixed-length hash value h, where $h=H(M)$. There are many functions that take an arbitrary-length input and return an output of fixed length, but one-way hash functions have additional characteristics:

1) Given M, it is easy to compute h.

2) Given h, it is hard to compute M.

3) Given M, it is hard to find another message M' such that $H(M)=H(M')$.

Instead of signing a document, Alice signs the hash of the document. In this protocol, both the one-way function and the digital signature algorithm are agreed upon beforehand.

1) Alice produces a one-way hash of a document.

2) Alice signs the hash with her private key, thereby signing the document.

3) Alice sends the document and the signed hash to Bob.

4) Bob produces a one-way hash of the document that Alice sent. He then decrypts the signed hash with Alice's public key and compares it with the hash he generated. If they match, the signature is valid.

2.3 Authentication and Certificates

Authentication gives assurance of identity. It is the means of gaining confidence that people or things are who or what they claim to be. In other words, authentication relates to a scenario where some party has presented its identity and claims to be that party. Authentication enables some other party to gain confidence that the claim is legitimate.

The ISO authentication framework provides authentication across networks. The framework is certificate-based. Each user has a distinct name. A trusted certification authority assigns a unique name to each user and issues a certificate containing the name and the user's public key.

A X.509 certificate looks like:

```
Certificate :: = SIGNED SEQUENCE (
    signature AlgorithmIdentifier,
    Issuer Name,
    validity Validity :: = SEQUENCE (
        notBefore UTCTime,
```

```
                not After UTCTime)
          subject Name,
          subjectPublicKeyInfo SubjectPublicKeyInfo :: =
    SEQUENCE(
              algorithm AlgorithmIdentifier,
              subjectPublicKey, BIT STRING))
```

A Certification Authority (*CA*) signs all certificates. If Alice and Bob want to communicate, each of them has to verify the signature of the other person's certificate. If they use the same *CA*, this is easy. If they use different *CAs*, this is more complicated. Think of a tree structure, with different *CAs* certifying other *CAs* and users. On the top there is one master *CA*. Each *CA* stores the certificate obtained from its superior *CA*, as well as all the certificates issued by it. Alice and Bob have to traverse the certification tree, looking for a common trusted point.

Throughout the following discussion, each participant X in the framework has a pair of keys associated with it, one being publicly known (X_p , X's public key), the other one only known to X (private or secret key X_s). X 's public key is used to encrypt message M, meant to be read by X. The encryption is represented as $C=X_p(M)$. X can decrypt the result using its private key: $M=X_s(X_p(M))$. In this way, X can use Xs to create a digital signature, which can be verified by any party using X_p.

For simplicity, we assume only one certifying authority (*CA*) is involved in the framework. It provides each participant X with an X.509 certificate $Cert(X)$, while the public key of the certificate authority (CA_p) is known to all participants in the framework.

A simple example of authentication for access is given here. When Alice wants Bob to allow her to get access to Bob's computing resources, Alice can present Bob with her certificate obtained from the *CA* in advance with her signature on her access request. After receiving this information, Bob can verify the certificate with the *CA*'s public key and then Alice's signature with her public key retrieved from her certificate. Once she is validated, Alice is permitted by Bob to access his computing resources.

3 Overview of Secure Electronic Transaction (SET)

Visa and MasterCard have jointly developed the Secure Electronic Transaction protocol as a method to secure payment card transactions over open networks. SET is being published as an open specification for the industry. This specification is available to be applied to any payment service and may be used by software vendors to develop application.

3.1 Participants of the SET Protocol

The SET protocol is composed of several kinds of transactions, ranging from customer registration, merchant registration, to purchase requests, to payment authorization and payment capture. The participants of these phases are as follows:

1) Customer: In the electronic commerce environment, consumers and corporate purchases interact with merchants from personal computers. A customer uses a payment card that has been issued by a certificate authority. SET ensures that in the customer's interactions with the merchant, the payment card account information remains confidential.

2) Issuer: An Issuer is a financial institution that establishes an account for a customer and issues the payment card. The Issuer guarantees payment for authorized transactions using the payment card in accordance with the payment card brand regulations and local legislation.

3) Merchant: A merchant offers goods for sale or provides services in exchange for payment. With SET, the merchant can offer its customers secure electronic interactions. A merchant that accepts payment cards must have a relationship with an Acquirer.

4) Acquirer: An Acquirer is the financial institution that establishes an account with a merchant and processes payment card authorization and payments.

5) Payment Gateway: A payment gateway is a device operated by an Acquirer or a designated third party that processes merchant payment messages, including payment instruction from customers.

Each participant X in the SET protocol has two types of certificates: one is the signature certificate $\mathtt{Cert}_s(X)$ containing the signature public key of entity X, another is the key-exchange certificate $\mathtt{Cert}_k(X)$ containing the key-exchange public key used to distribute session keys for a symmetric cryptosystem.

3.2 Purchase Request of the SET Protocol

On the assumption that customers and the merchants have registered and obtained their certificates from the Issuer, the purchase request phase of SET can be outlined as follows (see Fig. 1):

Step 1. A customer (C), looks at a catalog (printed on paper, supplied on a CD-ROM, or available on-line on the Web) provided by a merchant (M) and, after deciding to purchase something, sends a request to the merchant's server. The request includes the description of the services or the quantities of the goods, the terms of the order and the brand of the credit card that will be used for payment.

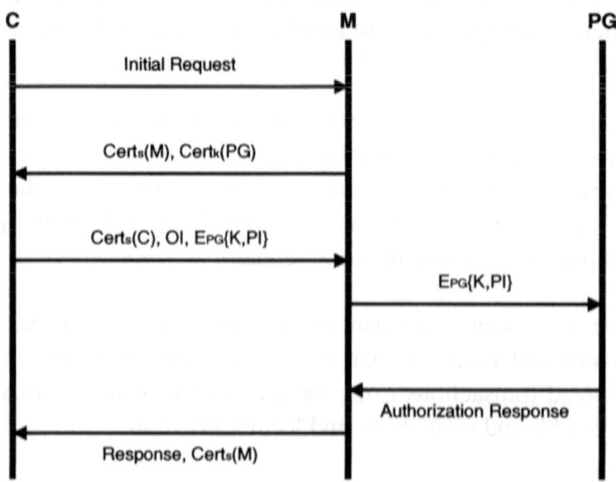

Fig. 1. SET Purchase Request Transaction

Step 2. The merchant receives the request and sends back its own signature certificate $Cert_s(M)$ and the key-exchange certificate $Cert_k(PG)$ of a payment gateway (PG). The merchant also sends a unique identifier, assigned to this transaction.

Step 3. The customer (i.e., his or her software) verifies the certificates by traversing the trust chain to the root key (the public signature key of a certificate authority (CA)) so as to assure itself of the authenticity and integrity of the data (the merchant had digitally signed it), and creates two pieces of information:

1) The Order Information (OI), containing control information verified by the merchant to validate the order, card brand and bank identification. The OI also includes a digest of the order description, which includes the amount of the transaction and other elements such as quantity, size and price of the items ordered, shipping and billing addresses, etc. This data, not included in the OI, will be processed outside the scope of the SET protocol.

2) The Payment Instructions (PI), containing the amount of the transaction, the card account number and expiration date, instructions for installment payments (if that's the case) and a couple of secret values to prevent guessing and dictionary attacks on the data, among other elements. The PI is encrypted with a randomly generated symmetric key K.

Both elements will contain the transaction identifier and are dually signed, so they can later be linked together by the payment gateway. Then, the encrypted PI (i.e.,

$E_k(PI)$) and the key (k) used to encrypt it are encrypted into a digital envelope (E_{PG}), using the payment gateway's public key. Finally, the OI and the digital envelope are sent to the merchant, along with the customer's signature certificate $Cert_s(C)$.

Step 4. The merchant verifies the customer certificate and the dual signature on the OI. The request is then processed, which includes forwarding the digital envelope to the payment gateway for authorization (the details of this operation are outside the scope of this description). After processing the order, the merchant generates and signs a purchase response, and sends it to the customer along with its signature certificate. If the payment was authorized, the merchant will fulfill the order by delivering the products bought by the customer.

Step 5. The customer verifies the merchant signature certificate, checks the digital signature of the response, and takes any appropriate actions based on its contents.

The software responsible for the customer's side of the protocol manages a data structure called a digital wallet, where sensitive data like certificates, private keys and payment card information are kept, usually in encrypted files. The merchant will have a more complex system composed of several parts, doing different jobs: managing the dialog with customers, signing messages and verifying signatures and certificates, asking payment gateways for payment authorizations, and so on.

4 Agent-Mediated Secure Electronic Transaction for Online Independent Purchase

On basis of the above SET protocol, we present an agent-mediated SET protocol for interdependent purchase.

4.1 Architecture of Agent-Mediated SET Protocol

Purchase conditions. Through the following discussion, we will consider such a scenario: Provided that a customer has already known which online merchant offers which goods or service, however he is not sure which merchant offer the lowest price to sell the goods or service. Now he wishes to order and pay for a series of goods or services C_1, C_2, ..., C_m from a series of online merchants. These goods or services and online merchants have the following constrained relationship:

I. It is known that $M(1,1)$, $M(1,2)$, ……, $M(1,n_1)$ offers C_1, and $M(2,1)$, $M(2,2)$, ……, $M(2,n_2)$ offers C_2, and so on. In other word, C_1 has to be purchased among $M(1,1)$, $M(1,2)$, ……, $M(1,n_1)$, and C_2 has to be purchased among $M(2,1)$, $M(2,2)$, ……, $M(2,n_2)$ and so on.

II. For C_i, the customer chooses the merchant who offers the lowest price and buys C_i in the value from the merchant.

III. Unless C_1, C_2, ……, C_i have been already reserved, C_{i+1} can be reserved.

IV. Unless all of C_1, C_2, ……, C_m have been reserved, the customer can indeed begin to order and pay for them and the on-line interdependent purchases can be finally completed.

The discussion about how the customer knows which merchant sells which goods or service is out of the range of this paper. The customer may firstly launch an agent to gather the trading information or look up it from some yellow page directories before the agent-mediated SET protocol starts.

Components of Agent-mediated SET Protocol. The architecture for agent-mediated SET protocol comprises the following three components:

1) Customer (*C*) - initializes purchase requests, generate and launch a secure payment agent (*A*) that orders and pays some goods or services on behalf of the *C*.

2) Agent Service Center (*ASC*) - keeps the encrypted payment information for the *C*, provides verification services to the *A* and re-encipher payment information according to requests from the *A*. The *ASC* is a trusted party and in charge of issuing certificates to customer and merchants.

3) Online Merchants (*M*) - each provides an Agent Meeting Place (*AMP*) for the *A* to run, accepts the order and payment of the *A* with SET protocol and finally delivers the ordered goods or services to the owner of the *A*, that is the *C*. These online merchants are denoted by $M(1,1)$, ……, $M(1,n_1)$, $M(2,1)$, ……, $M(2,n_2)$, ……, $M(m,1)$, ……, $M(m,n_m)$.

In addition, we suppose all customers and online merchants of the architecture have already obtained their certificates from the agent service center *ASC* in advance and know the public key of the *ASC*, i.e., ASC_p.

Structure of Secure Payment Agent. The Secure Payment Agent (A) defined here is a kind of mobile agent. Therefore, the A possesses the same structure as that of a general mobile agent. An A is designed for ordering and paying for some goods or services from a list of servers on the Internet. Each component of an A has a specific significance. When an A traverses a list of online merchants to order and pay for some goods, the A generally has the following kind of components:

1) Agent Passport - consists of the basic information required to permit the agent to flow from *AMP* to *AMP*. It includes the certificate of the agent's owner, error actions and addresses (i.e., the action that the *AMP* should take should an error occur while processing the agent), and goal and status information (i.e., a representation of the agent's goals and status). The route of the agent is specified in the goals.

2) Table of Contents (*TOC*) - provides a map of the structure of the agent. Each component has a size, type and importance. The size, as expected, is the size of the component. The type field contains a simple representation of what is required to process the component. The importance field describes whether the component is necessary for the agent to be instantiated at the *AMP*. This permits agents to carry obscure components through *AMP*s which do not support these components, and to avoid unpacking components which will not be used at any *AMP*.

3) Code and Data Component (*CDC*) - contains code and data executed on the list of merchants. There may be different code and data for different merchants, but here we simply assume that the same code and data is specific to all merchants.

4) Purchase Response Component (*PRC*) - contains the purchase response from a certain $M(i,j)$. The purchase response from the $M(i,j)$ should be signed with the secret key of the $M(i,j)$ to ensure its integrity, namely, $M(i,j)_S(PRC)$, where $M(i,j)_S$ the secret key of the M_i.

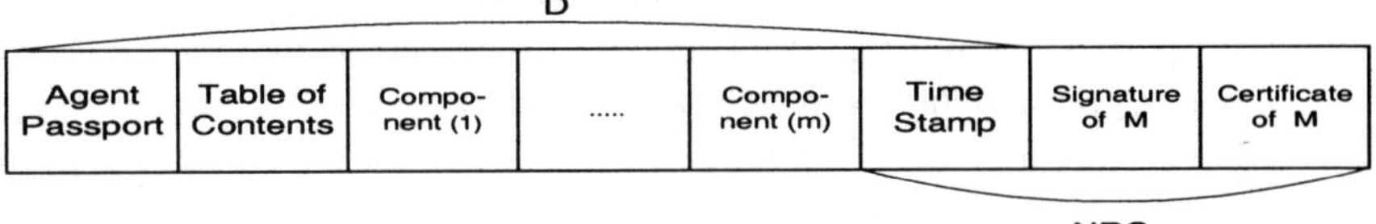

Fig. 2. Construction of a Secure Payment Agent (A)

5) Non-Repudiation Component (*NRC*) - contains the signature and certificate of some merchant *M* and the time stamp. It usually occupies the last component of the *A* and attaches right behind the corresponding *PRC*. For example, when the *A* is launched from M and roams into M', the *NRC* is the certificate of the M with the signature of the M on the part D and time stamp (as shown in Fig. 2).

In Fig. 2, the signature of M on D (denoted as $Sign_M$) is generated and verified in the following way:

1) M produces the hash value of D, that is $H(D)$.

2) M signs the hash value $H(D)$ with its signature secret key to generate its signature on the A, i.e.,

$$Sign_M = M_s(H(D)) \quad (1)$$

where M_s is the secret key of M.

3) The signature can be verified to be genuine if the following equation holds,

$$M_p(Sign_M) = H(D) \quad (2)$$

where the public key M_p of the M can be retrieved from the certificate $Cert_s(M)$ of the M.

4.2 Generation of the Secure Payment Agent

A purchase request transaction under the agent-mediated SET protocol has a few more steps than in SET, since a payment agent has to be generated by a customer.

Based on the purchase conditions I, II, III, and VI, the C creates a secure payment agent according to Fig. 2 as follows:

1) The customer's signature certificate ($Cert_s(C)$) is placed in the certificate portion of the secure payment agent.

2) The route of the secure payment agent is specified in the goal and status of its passport. As far as the goods or service C_1 is concerned, the order of the route is arranged from the best merchant to the worse one. In this case, we suppose the order is from $M(1,1)$ to $M(1,n_1)$. The same order rule is applied to the C_2, C_3, ..., C_m.

3) The code portion is occupied by a program. The description of this program is outside the scope of this paper.

   The order information (OI) (including the purchase conditions I, II, III and IV), the digest of the payment information PI (i.e., $H(PI)$), the dual signature of the customer C on OI and the payment information PI, are respectively placed in the data portion. Different from SET, the PI here does not contain the exact amount of transaction for each purchase. The exact amount of transaction for each purchase is actually determined by the agent service center ASC on basis of the purchase condition.

Both OI and PI contain a unique transaction identifier I_C assigned by C. There is only the same OI and PI for all merchants.

The dual signature of the customer on OI and PI is the signature of the customer on the message $H[H(OI)||H(PI)]$, where the symbol "||" denotes the concatenation of two messages. The dual signature is denoted as $Sign_C(H[H(OI)||H(PI)])$ which is generated in the following way:

$$Sign_C(H[H(OI)||H(PI)])=C_S(H[H(OI)||H(PI)) \quad (3)$$

where C_S is the signature secrete key of the C.

A random number R is generated and placed in the date portion of the payment agent.

4) The current time T is put into the time stamp portion.

5) The signature of the customer on the part D, which is computed as Formula (1) is placed in the signature portion as shown in Fig. 2.

Besides the payment agent, C needs to prepare for the protected payment information for the ASC.

The PI is firstly encrypted with a randomly generated symmetric key k, i.e., $E_k(PI)$ and then PI' is produced in the way:

$$PI'= ASC_p((k+I_C\bullet T+R), C_S(I_C||T||OI||H[H(OI)||H(PI)])) \quad (4)$$

where C_S is the secret (signature) key of the customer, ASC_p is the public key of the ASC, R is the random number generated by the payment agent and T is the current time.

The information sent the ASC comprises the Agent Passport, the Purchase Condition I, II, III, VI, $E_k(PI)$ and PI'. This information is sent to the ASC when the payment agent is launched from the C.

It should be pointed out that the ASC cannot retrieve k from PI' and then reveal the payment information PI because R is absent in the protected payment information provided to the ASC.

4.3 First Round of Secure Payment Agent Roaming

Once the secure payment agent is created, it is launched from the C into $M(1,1)$ initially, and then migrates from $M(1,1)$ into $M(1,2)$ and so on. The first round of the A roaming is illustrated in Fig. 3 (along the dashed line).

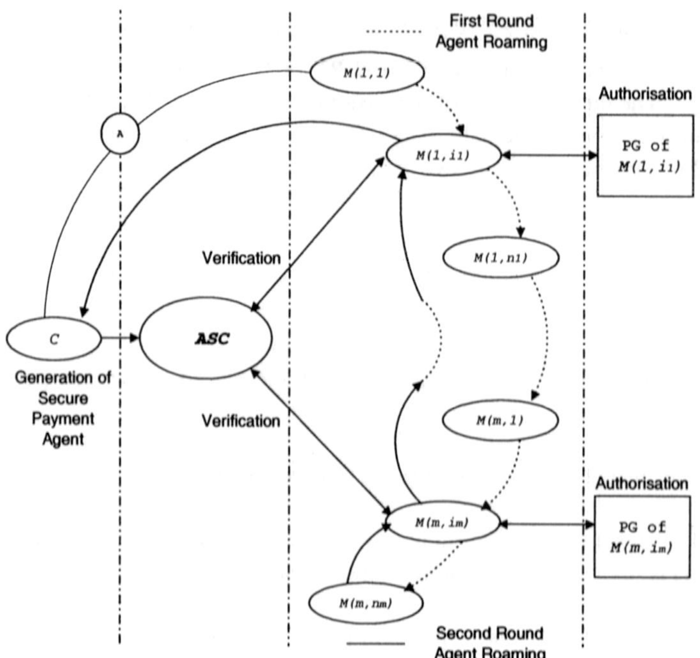

Fig. 3. Secure Payment Agent Roaming on Internet

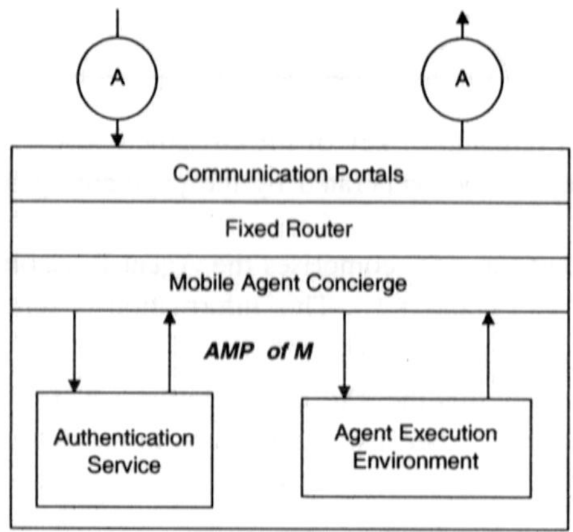

Fig. 4. Execution Process of the A at the AMP of M

We only deal with the general case in which the *A* is launched by the Agent Meeting Place of M^*, enters the Agent Meeting Place of *M* and later exits from it. The execution process of the *A* at the *AMP* of *M* is illustrated in Fig. 4.

The communication portals of *AMP* of *M* are responsible for managing the arrival and departure of mobile agents. For inbound services, they extract the arriving mobile agent A and pass it to the mobile agent concierge. The mobile agent concierge acts much as a concierge does in a full service hotel.

With the help of authentication services, the concierge can verify the following items:

1) Is $Cert_s(C)$ (from Agent Passport) issued by the ASC?

2) Is the signature C on the original A (from the NRC of the C) genuine?

3) Is the time stamp of the original A (from the NRC of the C) valid?

4) Is $Cert_s(M^*)$ (from the NRC of the M^*) issued by the ASC?

5) Is the signature M^* on the current A (from the NRC of the M^*) genuine?

6) Is the time stamp of the current A (from the NRC of the M^*) valid?

7) Have the previous purchase conditions (from the $PRCs$ of all the previous merchants) already satisfied?

Note that all signatures are verified based on Equation (2).

If each answer is yes, the concierge needs to give M^* a reply with $M_s(H(D))$ and $Cert_s(M)$ so as to announce that M^* has correctly received the A. M^* needs to keep this as non-repudiation evidence. Then the concierge extracts the Code and Data from the A according to the TOC and then sends it to an agent execution environment for it to run. Once the A resides and runs its code in the agent execution environment, it may ask M the following questions:

1) Do you sell some goods or service? If M is among the merchants from $M(i,1)$ to $M(i,n_i)$, the goods or service should be C_i.

2) If so, can you sell the goods or service in a price lower than the current lowest price? It should be pointed out that the decrease must be a multiple of a value specified in Code and Data Component (CDC).

3) If so, the A and the M cooperate to fill up an initial reservation form F. This form indicates the M can sell the goods or service in the price of $V(M)$ and will hold it for the C during some period.

After the A is supplied with the F, it may present the following requests:

1) Please encrypt the provided initial reservation form F with the signature secret key of the M and then attach the result $M_s(F)$ behind the A as an initial Purchase Response Component ($PRC(M)$).

2) Please sign the updated A as Formula (1) and then attach the current time, the signature and the certificate right behind the updated A as a Non-Repudiation Component (*NRC(M)*) of M.

Once the goal of the A in the M has been fulfilled, the A will ask the concierge to launch it to the next destination, i.e., M'. Until all merchants selling the goods or service C_i are visited, the mobile agent migrates to the first merchant offering the next goods or service, i.e, C_{i+1}.

If the M cannot offer the goods or service to the agent in the price lower than the current price, M is still required to do as above. In this case, the Initial Purchase Response Component simply takes the form of $M_s(N.A.)$.

If the A does not pass the verification check, the concierge handles the A in accordance with the information in the Error Actions and Addresses part from the Agent Passport.

In accordance with the route specified by the customer, the A traverses network from $M(1,1)$ to $M(m,n_m)$ in the above way. Until the agent traverses through all merchants on the list specified by the customer, the first round of the secure payment agent roaming ends. At the end, the A is filled with some initial reservation forms.

If one of the purchase conditions I, II, III and IV cannot be satisfied, the secure payment agent fails to accomplish its mission. It has to return the customer and asks the customer to reset the route and modify his purchase condition. For example, when the customer wants an agent to firstly roam a series of travel agencies to reserve an airplane ticket and then traverse a series of hotels to reserve a room, if the agent fails to reserve an airplane ticket for the customer, it does not need to traverse the series of hotels to avoid to waste time.

4.4 Second Round of Secure Payment Agent Roaming

In the first round of the secure payment agent roaming, we assume the agent has obtained the initial reservation forms relevant to C_1, C_2, ..., C_m from m merchants. $M(1,i_1)$ is the merchant who firstly offers the lowest price for C_1, $M(2,i_2)$ is the merchant who firstly offers the lowest price for C_2, ..., $M(m,i_m)$ is the merchant who firstly offers the lowest price for C_m. After the agent comes out of the last merchant $M(m,n_m)$, it migrates to the merchant $M(m,i_m)$. The second round of secure payment agent roaming begins.

Purchase Request Transaction between Secure Payment Agent and Merchant $M(m,i_m)$. As far as the merchant $M(m,i_m)$ is concerned, he does not know he has won the auction-like negotiation campaign for selling the goods or service C_m until the agent reenters the merchant server. After the agent resides in the merchant server, the agent-mediated SET protocol begins. The purchase request transaction between the A and the $M(m,i_m)$ can be illustrated in Fig. 5.

The purchase request transaction can be described as follows.

Initial Request. The agent *AMP(A)* resides in the environment and sends (now locally) an initiate request to the $M(m, i_m)$. The message indicates which payment card brand will be used for the transaction and which *ASC* will be used for certificate and signature verifications (i.e., $Cert_s(ASC)$), and requests a copy of the gateway's certificate. In addition, I_C , t and $H[H(OI)||H(PI)]$ are also sent to the $M(m, i_m)$.

Initial Response. When the $M(m, i_m)$ receives the request, it assigns a unique transaction identifier I_M to the message. It then provides the agent with an initial response, which ranges over the $M(m, i_m)$'s signature certificate ($Cert_s(M(m, i_m))$), payment gateway key-exchange certificate ($Cert_k(PG)$) that corresponds to the payment card brand indicated by the agent and $M(m, i_m)_s(I_C \ || \ I_M \ || \ T \ || \ H[H(OI)|| H(PI)])$, where $M(m, i_m)_s$ is the secret key of $M(m, i_m)$ and T is the time stamp of original agent.

Verification Request. The agent contacts the *ASC* by transmitting a verification request, which is composed of all Purchase Response Components (*PRC*s) which contain all initial reservation forms relevant to C_m and

$$\begin{array}{c} Agent\ Passport,\ Cert_s(M(m, i_m)), \\ Cert_k(PG),\ M(m, i_m)_s(I_C||I_M||T||H[H(OI)||H(PI)]) \end{array} \tag{5}$$

According to Agent Passport, the *ASC* can find the record corresponding to the customer *C*. On basis of the customer's Purchase Condition I, II, III, VI, *ASC* can know whether the agent has already obtained all Purchase Response Components relevant to C_m and judge whether $M(m, i_m)$ is the merchant who offers the lowest price to sell C_m by checking the verification request. If no problem, *ASC* verifies $Cert_s(C)$, $Cert_s(M(m, i_m))$, $Cert_k(PG)$, and decrypts PI' (see (4)) with its secret key-exchange key into

$$k + I_C \bullet T + R,\ C_S(I_C||T||OI||H[H(OI)||H(PI)]) \tag{6}$$

and decrypts $C_S(I_C||t||H[H(OI)||H(PI)])$ with the public key of the C into

$$I_C||T||H[H(OI)||H(PI)] \tag{7}$$

and decrypts $M(m, i_m)_s(I_C||I_M||T||H[H(OI)||H(PI)])$ with the public key of $M(m, i_m)$ into

$$I_C||I_M||T||H[H(OI)||H(PI)] \tag{8}$$

The *ASC* then compares the corresponding terms of (7) and (8). If there is no problem, it replies to the agent with a confirmation that includes:

$$PG_p((k+I_C \cdot T+R)+\ I_M \cdot T,\ ASC_s(V(M(m,i_m))),\ E_k(PI) \tag{9}$$

where PG_p is the payment gateway's public key obtained from the key-exchange certificate $Cert_k(PG)$ and $V(M(m,i_m))$ is the price offered by the merchant $M(m,i_m)$ to sell C_m.

It should be noted that *R* cannot be exposed to the *ASC* even though the *ASC* is a trusted center. The reason is that the *ASC* can retrieve the private key *k* if *R* is given.

Purchase Request. After receiving the above confirmation, the agent creates a digital envelope E_{PG} for the payment gateway, containing the following items:

$$E_{PG}=\{PG_p((k+I_C \cdot T+R)+I_M \cdot T+\ ASC_s(V(M(m,i_m))),\ I_C,\ I_M,\ T,\ R,\ E_k(PI)\} \tag{10}$$

The purchase request including

$$Cert_s(C),\ OI,\ H(PI),\ Sign_C(H[H(OI)||H(PI)]),\ E_{PG} \tag{11}$$

is then sent to the $M(m,i_m)$.

Authorization Request. After checking the certificate $Cert_s(C)$, in order to ensure that the order is signed using the customer's private signature key, $M(m,i_m)$ verifies the dual signature of the customer in the following way:

1) Because OI is known to the $M(m,i_m)$, it can compute the digest of OI, i.e., $H(OI)$.

2) Because $H(PI)$ is known to the $M(m,i_m)$, it can calculate the digest of $H(OI)||H(PI)$, i.e., $H[H(OI)||H(PI)]$.

3) The $M(m,i_m)$ can finally check the signature of the customer on $H[H(OI)||H(PI)]$ with Equation (2).

The purchase request is then processed, which includes forwarding the information

$$Cert_s(C),\ E_{PG},\ H(OI),\ Sign_C(H[H(OI)||H(PI)]),\ M(m,i_m)_s(V(M(m,i_m)) \tag{12}$$

to the payment gateway, for authorization.

Authorization Response. If I_C, I_M, R and T are compatible, the payment gateway should be able to obtain the correct k and then PI from $E_k(PI)$. If OI and PI agree, the dual signature can be verified with $H(OI), PI$ and $Sign_C(H[H(OI)||H(PI)])$ in a way similar to that outlined in the previous step. If there is no problem, this ensures that the PI has not been tampered with in transit and that it was signed using the customer's private signature key.

In addition, the payment gateway retrieves $V(M(m, i_m))$ from $ASC_s(V(M(m, i_m))$ and $M(m, i_m)_s(V(M(m, i_m))$ respectively with the public keys of ASC and $M(m, i_m)$ and checks if they are same.

If no problem, the *PG* formats and sends an authorization request to the Issuer via a payment system. Upon receiving an authorization response, the *PG* generates and digitally signs the authorization request message, which includes the Issuer's response and a copy of the *PG* signature certificate. Then the *PG* sends the authorization response to the $M(m, i_m)$.

Purchase Response. This step is the same as that of the SET protocol. After the OI has been processed, the $M(m, i_m)$ software generates and digitally signs a purchase response message, which indicates that the customer's order has been received by the $M(m, i_m)$. The response is then transmitted to the agent.

If the payment is authorized based on the amount of payment to the merchant $M(m, i_m)$ which is specified in the digital envelope E_{PG} by the agent service center *ASC*, the $M(m, i_m)$ will fulfill the order by shipping the goods or performing the services indicated in the order.

After obtaining the signed purchase response from $M(m, i_m)$, the agent attaches it behind the agent as $M(m, i_m)$'s Final Purchase Response Component and then asks the $M(m, i_m)$ to produce his Non-Repudiation Component and attaches the component behind the Final Purchase Response Component. The purchase request transaction between the secure payment agent and the $M(m, i_m)$ ends.

Purchase Request Transaction between Secure Payment Agent and Other Merchants. In the above stage, the A only finishes the mission of ordering and paying for the goods or service C_m, the A still needs to go back to reenter some merchants' server to order and pay for the other goods or services with SET protocol.

The route of the second round of the agent can be determined by those initial reservation forms which offer the lowest price to sell some goods or service to the agent. According to the above assumption, the second route is shown in Fig. 3 along the solid line, i.e.,

$$M(m, i_m) \rightarrow M(m-1, i_{m-1}) \rightarrow \ldots\ldots \rightarrow M(2, i_2) \rightarrow M(1, i_1)$$

During the second round of the secure payment agent roaming, the agent performs the same process in the merchants $M(m-1,i_{m-1}),\ldots\ldots, M(2,i_2), M(1,i_1)$ as in the merchant $M(m,i_m)$. In this way, the A can further order and pay for $C_{m-1}, C_{m-2}, \ldots\ldots, C_1$ with the agent-mediated SET protocol.

Secure Payment Agent Returning. After the secure payment agent comes out of the merchant $M(1, i_1)$, it returns to the customer's device and brings back all purchase responses. By these responses, the customer can represent the entire process of agent roaming on the Internet. He can check whether there is any conflict with his purchase conditions.

If no problem, the customer takes any appropriate actions based on their contents. After this, the agent-mediated SET protocol terminates.

5 Security Issues for Mobile Agent

Agent technology has received growing interest from the research community and has matured significantly in the last few years. However, the number of applications using this technology is still small. Electronic commerce is generally seen as one of the most promising application areas for mobile agents. For example, a buying agent leaves its host with the mission of querying several vendors about a certain product, determines which one offers the lowest price (or some other kind of preferred feature), buys the product from that one and pays for it. Clearly there is a perception that agents are suitable for this kind of activity and that the ability to pay is one of the desired properties they should have. A major concern is always how to do this in a secure way, in particular without revealing confidential information to the outside world.

Mobile agent security can be split into two broad areas [2]. The first involves the protection of host nodes from destructive mobile agents while the second involves the protection of mobile agents from destructive hosts.

5.1 Protection of Hosts from Malicious Agents

A mobile agent system is an open system [17]. Therefore, just like in any open system, the host nodes are subject to a variety of attacks, both old and new. Attacks on host security fall into four main categories:

1) Leakage: acquisition of data by an unauthorized party.

2) Tampering: alteration of data by an unauthorized party.

3) Resource stealing: use of facilities by an unauthorized party.

4) Vandalism: malicious interference with a host's data or facilities with no clear profit to the perpetrator.

The traditional methods of attack include eavesdropping, masquerading, message tampering, message replay and viruses. A mobile agent can employ any of these methods of attack, which in turn, can be guarded against using standard techniques such as cryptography, authentication, digital signatures and trust hierarchies.

However, a mobile agent is unique in that its code is executed by a host. Thus an executing mobile agent has automatic access to some of a host's resources. With this level of access a mobile agent can mount attacks by altering other local agents, propagating viruses, worms and Trojan horses, impersonating other users and mounting denial of service attacks [17]. The standard approach to this problem is to reject all unknown codes from entry into a host. This is not a viable solution in a mobile agent environment [8]. Telescript [19,20,21] provides three mechanisms that can be applied at various degrees of granularity.

Some research systems provide only partial protection for the hosts. Tacoma [7] provides hooks so that a developer can add their own encryption subsystem, but does not provide secure execution environments for all of its supported languages. Ara [11] enforces restrictions on the CPU time and memory usage, but does not yet protect resources such as the file system and network. Both Tube [6] and SodaBot [3] execute their agent inside secure interpreters that enforce some access restrictions. Since a high security level only can be achieved by the sacrifice of flexibility and increased expense, it is important to choose carefully the trade-offs among these factors.

5.2 Protection of Agents from Malicious Hosts

In comparison to the protection of host, protecting a mobile agent from attacks by malicious hosts is much more difficult. Since mobile agents are executed by hosts, they have to expose their data and code to the host environment. Thus the agents are at the risk of being tampered with, scanned or even terminated by malicious servers.

Some efforts have been made to solve the problem. However, current results are still far from satisfactory. The simplest method of protecting agents is to avoid supplying them with any important data. A non-critical agent will be free from the concern of being attacked. Obviously, such an agent will not be very useful in most cases. Limiting the confidential data that agents have usually limits the utility of these agents at the same time. S.Berkovits et al.[1] try to establish different degrees of trust among different parties and keep agents in secure routing zones to avoid them getting into malicious hosts. The problem is that this severely compromises the concept of an open agent system where new servers can join the system as new needs show up and the interests of the server owners may change dynamically. Tacoma [9] uses replication and voting schemes to handle malicious machines that either terminate an agent outright or provide the agent with incorrect information. Although this scheme prevents many kinds of attacks, it also has several drawbacks. T. Sander and et al. [15 ,16] came up with a very promising approach which exploits cryptographic functions. In this case, the mobile code performs an algorithm that, given some external inputs, computes a cryptographic value. The site has no clue about which function is actually computed and therefore cannot meaningfully tamper with algorithm execution and computation results.

In addition to the software approach, the use of tamper-proof hardware has been suggested [22]. Such devices are processors that execute agents in a physically sealed environment. The system internals are not accessible even by its owner without disrupting the system itself. While these systems can provide a high level of protection, they require dedicated (expensive) hardware. Therefore, they are not easily deployed on a large scale.

Protecting programs against attacks coming from the interpreter responsible for their execution is a challenging problem. Current consensus is that it is computationally impossible to protect mobile agents from malicious hosts. Instead of tackling the problem from a computational (difficult) point of view, current research [12] is looking at sociological means of enforcing good host behavior.

5.3 A Non-repudiation Approach to Achieve Security of Mobile Agents

In this section, we combine cryptographic technology and sociological means to propose a non-repudiation approach to securing mobile agents. We take the proposed agent-mediated SET protocol as the underlying object.

Login Data Bases (LDB). In the proposed agent-mediated SET protocol, each merchant (*M*) needs to set up a Login Data Base (*LDB*) reserving some information from passing mobile agents in order to provide non-repudiation evidence when any problem occurs.

Because there are probably a lot of mobile agents entering an *M* to order and pay goods or service every day, it is impossible for an *M* to keep full copies of passing agents in its records, since the *LDB* will then occupy a great deal of storage space. In view of this, the record structure of the *LDB* need to be optimized. Our solution to this problem is as follows in Fig. 6.

The record structure of a Login Data Base (*LDB*) is

Agent's Certificate	Time Stamp (0)	Previous Node	Time Stamp (1)	Signature (1)	Purchase response	Destination Node	Time Stamp (2)	Signature (2)

Fig. 6. The record structure of a Login Data Base (*LDB*)

In the above structure, the meanings of all symbols used are as follows:

1) Agent Certificate - the certificate of the agent, obtained from the original agent;

2) Time Stamp (0) - the time when the agent is generated, obtained from the original agent;

3) Previous Node - the certificate of the previous M^* from which the agent launches, obtained from the non-repudiation component of the previous M^*;

4) Time Stamp (1) - the time when the agent exists from the previous *M**, obtained from the non-repudiation component of the previous *M**;

5) Signature (1) - the signature of the previous *M** on the agent, obtained from the non-repudiation component of the previous *M**;

6) Purchase response - the initial reservation form or purchase response provided to the agent by the present *M*;

7) Destination Node - the certificate of the next *M'* to which the agent has gone, acquired from the reply of the next *M'*;

8) Time Stamp (2) - the time when the agent migrates to the next *M* from the present *M*;

9) Signature (2) - the signature of the next *M'* on the agent, acquired from the reply of the next *M'*.

Protection of Hosts against Malicious Agents. In the agent-mediated SET protocol, the Code and Data Component (*CDC*) is signed by the customer (*C*). No other parties can forge this signature on the basis of cryptography. Therefore, the *CDC* provides not only the code and data which will be executed by all merchants to achieve the order and payment mission, but also non-repudiation evidence, so that the *C* can not deny having generated the *CDC*. Once any problems such a virus altering other local agents, propagating viruses, worms and Trojan horses occur when a merchant runs the *CDC* on its agent execution environment, the *C* is probably malicious and will be accused.

Protection of Agents against Malicious Hosts. With the help of the *LDB*, the proposed agent-mediated SET protocol can provide protection for agents against a malicious merchant in the following respects:

On designing the architecture, each Purchase Response Component (*PRC*) is signed with the secret key of the responder. Except for the responder, others cannot do this because they do not know the secret key of the responder. In this way, we can prevent a malicious merchant from modifying a *PRC* belonging to others.

Although a merchant is permitted to put the *PRC* and Non-Repudiation Component (*NRC*) into an agent, any malicious manipulation (such as cutting or manipulating another merchant's *PRC*) will be detected by the *C* (because the *C* will be conscious of any malicious action if an agent has taken an error action, or if any *PRC* cannot produce significant purchase response or even completely disappears). In this case, the *C* will carry out the following check procedure and identify the malicious host.

1) The customer asks each merchant on the route list to commit their records (denoted as `Rec(M)`) about the agent with M_s`(PRC(M))`, where `PRC(M)` represents the initial reservation form or purchase response from the mer-

chant M. The motivation to prove themselves to be innocent drives all merchants except a malicious one to provide true records about the agent.

2) On basis of initial agent and all $Rec(M)$ and $M_s(PRC(M))$, the C can reconstruct the secure payment agent (A) in all stages in a recursive way.

3) Suppose all merchants before the merchant M have no problem and the merchant M' is right behind M, the customer C checks whether $(M')_p(Signature(2))$ is equal to $H(D)$, where *Signature (2)* is extracted from $Rec(M)$. If so, M has no problem. If not, M will be identified as malicious because it cannot provide the non-repudiation of receipt from M' which states M' has successfully received the correct agent A. In fact, M should repeatedly have transmitted the A to M' until $M'_p(Signature(2))=H(D)$ or delivered an error notification to the C.

If the agent is killed by a malicious merchant, the above check procedure can be also carried out to uncover the culprit. The first merchant who cannot provide a correct record about the agent will be identified as malicious.

6 Conclusion

SET is expected to gain wide acceptance as a secure Internet payment system since it combines the well-known credit card payment method with an elaborated security protocol. It is aimed at providing the necessary security through the authentication of the participants in a commercial transaction, as well as confidentiality of financial information. The fact that SET was developed by the major credit card companies is yet another factor contributing to its acceptance.

However, SET is a very complex and "heavy" protocol. Its complexity may prove it unsuitable for some on-line purchase cases. For example, when a customer wants to purchase a series of interdependent goods or services on the Internet, if he orders and pays for them by using SET, it will consume a lot of time, energy and communication expense of the customer.

Because software agents might have service capabilities, autonomous decision making and commitment, they can be applied to automate the on-line purchase with SET. In view of this, SET/A [14], based on the SET protocol and the mobile agent model, has recently been proposed. In order to protect an agent from a potentially malicious environment, SET/A depends on a secure execution environment in the merchant's server for an agent to run. However, the required security is not easy to ensure.

To remove the limitation on secure agent execution environment in SET/A and the difficulty for customers to order and pay a series of interdependent goods or service with SET, a new agent-mediated SET protocol has been proposed in this paper. By adding a trusted agent service center into the payment system, the secure payment agent is able to order and pay for a series of interdependent goods or services according to the purchase condition of customers after it is launched from the customer device. Under the assumption that the agent service center and the merchants never collude, our protocol can achieve the same security as the SET protocol, i.e., each player knows only what is strictly necessary to play their role, for example, the selling company and the agent service center never knows the buyer's credit card information, and the financial institution authorizing the transaction is not aware of the details of the purchase, including the nature of the products, quantities, etc.

As part of our future work, we intend to further optimize the agent-mediated secure electronic transaction protocol for interdependent purchases. In addition, we will try to use some agent languages to implement the agent-mediated SET protocol.

Acknowledgements. We would like to appreciate the valuable comments from Workshop on Agents in E-Commerce held in Hong Kong on December 14, 1999.

References

1. Berkovist, S., Guttman, J.D. and Swarup, V.: Authentication for mobile agents. Mobile Agent and Security. LNCS 1419 (1998).
2. Chess, D., Grosof, B., Harrison, C., Levine, D., Parris, C. and Tsudik, G.: Itinerant Agents for Mobile Computing. IEEE Personal Communications, 2(3) (1995) 34-49.
3. Coen, M. H.: SodaBot: A software agent environment and construction system. In Proceedings of the CIKM Workshop on Intelligent Information Agents, Third International Conference on Information and Knowledge Management (CIKM94), Gaithersburg, Maryland, Dec. (1994).
4. Diffie, W., Hellman, M.E.: New direction in cryptography. IEEE Trans. Information Theory, vol. IT-22, no.6, Nov. (1976) 644-654.
5. Green, S., Somers, F., Hurst, L., Evans, R., Nangle, B., Cunningham, P.: Software agent: A review. May (1997).
6. Halls, D., Bates, J. and Bacon, J.: Flexible distributed programming using mobile code. In Proceeding of the Seventh ACM SIGOPS European Workshop, Sept. (1996) 225-231.
7. Johansen, D., Renesse, R. V. and Scheidner, F. R.: Operating system support for mobile agents. In Proceeding of the Fifth IEEE Workshop on Hot Topics in Operating System (HTOS), May (1995) 42-45.
8. Maes, P.: Agents that reduce work and information overload. Communications of the ACM, 37(7) (1994) 31-40.
9. Minsky, Y., Renesse, R., Schneider, F.B. and Stoller S.D.: Cryptographic Support for Fault-Tolerant Distributed Computing. In Proceedings of the Seventh ACM SIGOPS European Workshop, Connemara, Ireland, September (1996) 109-114.
10. Moukas, A., Guttman, R., Maes, P.: Agent-mediated electronic commerce: an MIT media laboratory perspective. In Proceedings of the International Conference on Electronic Commerce (1999).
11. Peine, H. and Stolpmann, T.: The architecture of the Ara platform for mobile agents. In Proceeding of the First International Workshop on Mobile Agents (MA'97), LNCS 1219, Berlin, April (1997).

12. Rasmusson, L. and Janson, S.: Simulated social control for secure Internet commerce, In Proceedings of New Security Paradigms'96, ACM Press, September (1996).
13. Rivest, R.L., Shamir, A., Adleman, L.: A method for obtaining digital structures and public-key cryptosystem, Commun. ACM, vol.21, no.2, Feb. (1978) 120-127.
14. Romao, A. and Mira da Silva, M: An agent-based secure Internet payment system for mobile computing. In Proceeding of TrEC'98, LNCS 1402, Hamburg, Germany, June (1998).
15. Sander, T.: On cryptographic protection of mobile agents. In Proceedings of the 1997 Workshop on Mobile Agents and Security, University of Maryland, Oct. (1997).
16. Sander, T. and Tschudin, C.F.: Protecting mobile agents against malicious hosts. Mobile Agent and Security, LNCS 1419 (1998).
17. Tardo, J., and Valenta. L.: Mobile agent security and Telescript. In Proceeding of IEEE COMPCON'96, Feb. (1996).
18. Visa International and MasterCard International, Secure electronic transaction (SET) specification. Version 1.0, May (1997).
19. White, J. E.: Telescript technology: The foundation for the electronic marketplace. General Magic White Paper, General Magic, Inc. (1994).
20. White, J. E.: Telescript technology: An introduction to the language. General Magic White Paper, General Magic, Inc. (1995).
21. White, J. E.: Telescript technology: Scenes from the electronic marketplace. General Magic White Paper, General Magic, Inc. (1996).
22. Wilhelm, U. and Defago, X.: Objects Protégés Cryptographiquement. In Proceedings of RenPar'97, Lausanne, Switzerland, May (1997).

An Agent-Based Micropayment System for E-Commerce

T.O. Lee, Y.L. Yip, C.M. Tsang, and K.W. Ng

Department of Computer Science & Engineering, The Chinese University of Hong Kong, Shatin, N.T. Hong Kong, China
{tolee, ylyip, cmtsang, kwng}@cse.cuhk.edu.hk

Abstract. Recently, electronic commerce has become the focus of Information Technology development. Many electronic payment protocols and systems have been launched onto the Internet, but most of them induce complex cryptography and authentication mechanisms that incur relatively high processing costs and are therefore not feasible for micropayment transactions. For this reason, the mobile agent semantic is integrated to cope with the concerned difficulty. An agent-based transaction model is developed for processing micropayment transactions in a distributed environment and the corresponding system is built upon an OMG MASIF compliant agent platform. The novel agent-based transaction protocols are blends of the existing SET card payment and MilliCent micropayment protocols coupled with mobile agent characteristics respectively. As mobile agents can migrate to the desired communication peer and utilize the advantage of local interactions, goals like reduction of network traffic and simplification of communication protocol are readily attainable through such agent-based transaction protocols.

1 Introduction

Recently, electronic commerce has been a focus for research and development of Information Technology. For instance, a number of electronic payment protocols and systems have been made available on the Internet. However, only a minority of these systems is feasible for the micropayment scheme [3] that caters for transactions of small amount. Owing to the secure nature of electronic payment, most payment protocols involve complex data encryption and authentication that result in relatively high cost for a micropayment transaction. In this paper, the mobile agent technology is adopted to cope with such difficulty in a typical micropayment scheme.

Mobile agents can migrate to the desired communication peer and take advantage of local interactions. Through such a mechanism, advantages including a reduction of network traffic, a reduction of dependency on network availability as well as simplification of the communication protocol can be achieved. In this paper, an agent-based payment model is introduced for handling micropayment transactions efficiently and effectively in a distributed environment. In particular, the system prototype is built upon an OMG MASIF compliant agent platform. The agent-based protocol is a com

J. Liu and Y. Ye (Eds.): E-Commerce Agents, LNAI 2033, pp. 247-263, 2001.

bination of the existing SET [6] card payment and MilliCent micropayment protocols coupled with mobile agent characteristics. For the sake of convenience and readability, the enhanced protocols are named as SET/A [2] protocol and MilliCent/A protocol respectively in the rest of this paper.

The agent-based micropayment system is based on a customer-broker-merchant paradigm. Offline card payment transactions, which communicate using the SET/A protocol, are involved in the broker-merchant and broker-customer pairs. On the other hand, for simple online transactions, which occur more frequently between customers and merchants, the MilliCent/A protocol is chosen to be the candidate. Integrating both MilliCent/A and Set/A transaction protocols gives rise to our desired agent-based micropayment system which is described in the rest of this paper.

First, an overview of the current network standards and the architecture of our micropayment system are presented in sections 2 and 3 respectively followed with a description of the transaction protocols involved in section 4. Next we describe our system prototype in section 5 and justify the system performance in section 6 before we come to the conclusion in section 7.

2 Background

Business has been extended onto the Internet over this decade through which customer orders are registered online, but the payments are made on paper base like cheques to be collected through postal delivery with time lag. Recent technological developments on electronic payment mechanisms have made online payments possible over the Internet. Electronic payments are a paperless method of making payments that can be processed quicker and cheaper than traditional paper-based payment instructions. Therefore, electronic payments serve as the key for Internet shopping.

2.1 Payment Instruments

There are 3 common electronic payment instruments, namely the cash, the cheque and the card. Cash consists of a token that can be authenticated independently from the issuer through the use of self-authenticating tokens or tamper proof hardware whereas the authentication for cheque requires reference to the issuer. On the other hand, the card payment schemes provide a payment mechanism through the existing credit card payment infrastructure. The card payment scheme has many structural similarities to the cheque model except that solutions are constrained by the infrastructure.

These electronic payment instruments can be classified into 3 categories, namely the pre-paid system, the pay-now system and the pay-later system.

2.1.1 Pre-paid System

The pre-paid system is comparable to paying in cash. The participant may fetch an amount of money from his bank account and store it in an electronic purse, convert it to electronic money, or use a check certified by his bank. Examples are E-Cash from DigiCash and check from NetCheque.

2.1.2 Pay-Now System

The pay-now system differs from the pre-paid model by the fact that withdrawal of money from the bank account is only made at the time of paying.

2.1.3 Pay-Later System

The pay-later system is currently used with credit cards. The money is withdrawn at some time after the purchase is made. The system is equivalent to the pay-now system as the buyer sends some sort of form to the vendor in both systems. SET is a common example.

The comparison among the three payment models is summarized in Table 1.

Table 1. Evaluation on different payment methods

	Cash	**Check**	**Credit Card**
Transaction Cost	Low	Low	High
Atomic Exchange	Good	Fair	Poor
Consumer Base	Small	Medium	Large
Anonymity	High	Low	Low
Peer-to-peer Payment	Good	Good	Poor

The card payment instrument incurs the highest transaction cost whereas such cost associated with the cash payment instrument is the lowest among the three. This makes the cash payment instrument the best candidate for payment with amount on the cent base, otherwise the transaction cost would have accounted for a significant percentage over the total amount of payment.

2.2 Micropayment

Micropayments refer to low-value electronic financial transactions, ranging from a fraction of a cent to a few dollars [4]. It may sound that cents are useless for shopping in our daily lives. However, for a lot of services and goods we purchase in the bulk way, are actually composed of numerous units on the micro-base that add up to the dollar amount. If we break the price down to the per usage basis, most of these will fall in the cents regime.

Most existing and proposed protocols are appropriate for medium to large transactions, as the processing cost per transaction is typically several dollars plus a percentage. When these costs are applied to inexpensive transactions, say 50 cents or less, the transaction cost becomes a significant or even dominant component of the total purchase price, thereby effectively creating a minimum price for goods and services purchased.

Forcing online charges to be above some threshold reduces the options for service providers. Online services providing newspapers, magazines, reference works and stock prices all have individual items that could be inexpensive if sold separately. The ability to purchase inexpensive individual items would make these services more attractive to casual users on the Internet. In addition, secure low-priced transactions support grass-roots electronic publishing. A user who is not likely to open a ten-dollar account with an unknown publisher may be willing to spend a few cents to buy an interesting article. In view of the above arguments, micropayment has a great potential.

2.3 Protocols

Accompanies with the development of the Internet and electronic commerce in particular, people recognize a desire for reliability, privacy and security for their interaction over the open network. For these purposes, lots of protocols are launched onto the Internet for maintaining secure communication between the trading partners, among which MiliCent, SET and SSL has gained acceptance as the business standards.

2.3.1 MilliCent

MilliCent [9] is a lightweight and secure payment protocol for electronic commerce over the Internet. It is designed to support purchases costing less than a cent. It is based on decentralized validation of electronic tokens at the merchant's server without any additional communication, expensive encryption or offline processing.

The key innovation in the MilliCent protocol is the use of brokers and scrips. In the MilliCent protocol, a broker is responsible for account management, billing, connection maintenance and establishment of accounts with merchants. On the other hand, each scrip represents an electronic token that is only valid for a specific merchant. These scrips are to be validated locally by the merchants to prevent customer fraud such as double spending and invalid request. The interactions among the customer, the merchant and the broker in terms of the MilliCent protocol are illustrated in Figure 1.

Besides representing an account a customer has established with a merchant, a scrip keeps the balance of account as the value of itself. Whenever a purchase request is to be submitted, a customer retrieves the corresponding scrip and the merchant information from its databases. On the other side, the merchant carries out the verification and update of the scrip locally during payment processing. Only simple hash functions are performed for re-generating both the request signature and the scrip certificate that are to be compared with the received hashes for verification. Afterwards, the scrip is modified and returned to the customer.

The MilliCent protocol (Authentic but not private) is described as follows and summarized in Figure 2:

1. The customer sends both the purchase request and the merchant's scrip along with a request signature H(scrip, request, customer secret).
2. The merchant regenerate the customer secret from the customer ID embedded in the merchant's scrip together with the master customer secret in order to compare against the one embedded in the request signature for authentication.
3. The merchant's server checks for any double spending or expiration of the merchant's scrip.
4. The merchant performs the requested service and returns the change from the transaction by issuing a new scrip (i.e. scrip') together with the reply and the certificate of the old scrip (i.e. cert) embedded in the reply signature for the customer to validate the transaction.

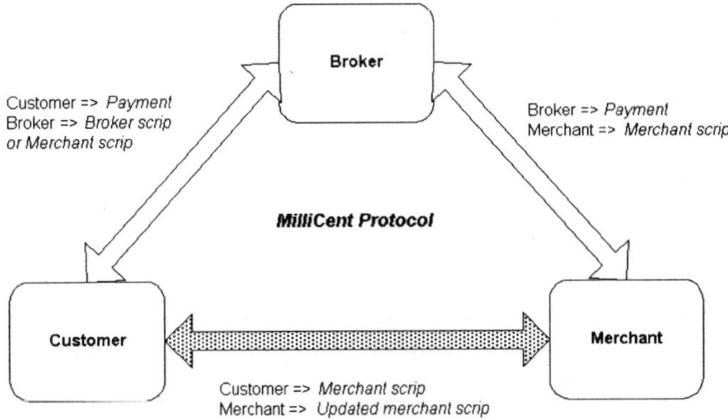

Fig 1. The MilliCent payment model

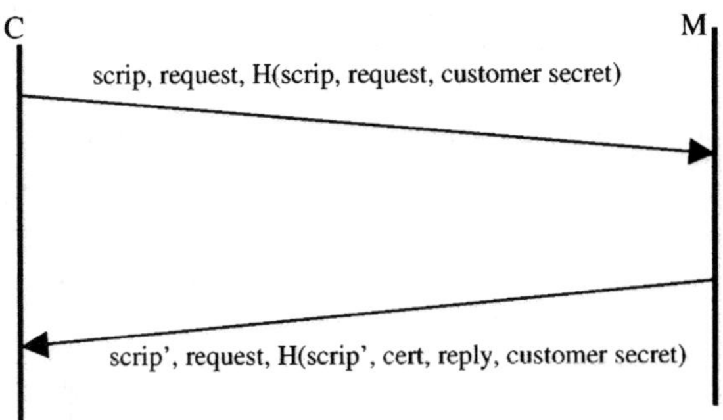

Fig. 2. The MilliCent payment protocol

2.3.2 SET

Although the Internet is now considered as the privileged environment for electronic commerce, major security threats like credit card frauds are likely performed by hackers that eavesdrop on the transaction channels. Therefore, a secure electronic transaction model, the Secure Electronic Transaction SET [6] protocol is introduced to facilitate safe and reliable business among merchants and cardholders over the Internet.

The conceptual interactions among the 4 parties in SET, the Cardholder, the Merchant, the Certificate Authority and the Payment Gateway are illustrated in Figure 3.

The SET protocol proceeds in four phases:

1. Certificate Issuance: the certificate authority (CA) issues signature and key exchange certificates to the trading parties.
2. Purchase Request: the cardholder purchases items or services from the merchant and supplies payment information to the payment gateway (PG).
3. Payment Authorization: the payment gateway authorizes payments from the cardholder to the merchant such that the latter could commit the transaction.
4. Payment Capture: the merchant captures funds that have been authorized by the payment gateway.

Certificate Issuance

1. The cardholder issues the issuance request to the CA
2. The CA receives the request and returns the appropriate digitally signed application form P along with its signature certificate.
3. The cardholder fills in and digitally signs the form. The filled-in form and the cardholder's public key (i.e. the public signature key and the public-key exchange key for the case of signature certificate and key exchange certificate issuance respectively) to be certified are encrypted with a symmetric key. Then the encrypted form and key are sent to the merchant along with the symmetric key embedded in a digital envelope.
4. The CA verifies the integrity and the information of P' and generates the corresponding certificate for the cardholder which is digitally signed and encrypted with a symmetric key to be sent back to the cardholder along with a digital envelope.
5. The cardholder then verifies the integrity of the certificate upon receipt and stores it securely.

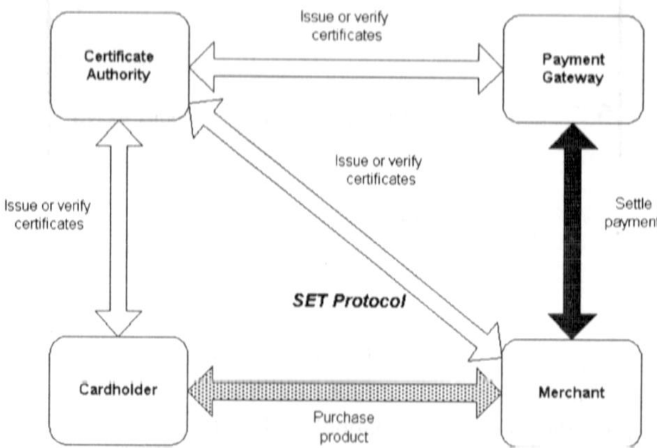

Fig 3. The SET payment model

Purchase Request

1. The cardholder issues the purchase request to the merchant
2. The merchant receives the request and returns a digitally signed reply with its signature certificate and the key-exchange certificate of the PG.
3. The cardholder verifies the certificates through CA and generates the order information OI and payment information PI pair. In particular, the PI is encrypted with a randomly generated symmetric key and a digital envelope is generated by encrypting both the encrypted PI and the symmetric key with PG's public key. The digital envelope is then sent to the merchant together with the OI and the cardholder's certificate.
4. The merchant verifies the cardholder's certificate and then forwards the digital envelope to PG for authorization.
5. Once the PG has authorized the payment, the merchant's server generates and returns a digitally signed purchase response to the cardholder.

2.3.3 SSL

The Secure Sockets Layer SSL [1] is a program layer created by Netscape for managing the security of network message transmissions in between the application and the Internet's TCP/IP layers. Under the SSL, messages are transmitted over the Internet securely with data fragmentation and reconstruction, data compression and decompression, data encryption and decryption as well as generation and verification of Message Authentication Codes MACs.

The SSL handshake protocol is first performed when the SSL client and server start communication. This handshake protocol is applied to authenticate the communicating partners, to negotiate the cryptographic algorithms (e.g. DES, RSA, etc) and the MAC algorithm (e.g. MD5, SHA, etc) for successive secure communications.

3 System Model

We integrate the mobile agent semantic into the standard MilliCent and SET protocols on top of SSL and come up with an electronic payment system that settles online micropayments between customers and merchants.

There are altogether five entities inherited from both the MilliCent and the SET models into our system, they are, the customer, the merchant, the broker, the certificate authority and the payment gateway. The merchants trade with their customers on scripts and the latter get services like online newspapers, magazines, reference work or stock prices in return.

The broker is introduced as a trustworthy entity to mediate between the customers and the merchants and to maintain the accounts for the customers C and merchants M. It maintains a long-term business relationship with both customers and merchants. In general, the broker serves as a scrip warehouse in which it buys multiple pieces of scrip from merchants, stores the scrip and sells the pieces one at a time to customers. The broker uses an agent-based card payment protocol, SET/A protocol [2] to buy merchants' scrips in large blocks and to sell significant amount of broker's scrips to the customers at a time. On the other hand, it sells individual scrip to customers based on an agent-based micropayment protocol, MilliCent/A protocol.

The payment gateway (PG) [6] is another trustworthy entity, mediating between the customer, the broker and the merchants, to settle transactions in between on top of the SET/A protocol. The broker, as a cardholder in terms of the SET protocol, uses a payment card to purchase blocks of scrip from merchants. The PG is responsible for processing the payment authorization and payment capture requests from merchants. The customer, in turn, purchases broker's scrip from broker in a similar manner through the PG.

The certificate authority (CA) [6] issues digital certificates to each system entity for a proof of identity. The CA is also responsible to provide the necessary information online for authentication between the trading parties throughout SET/A based transactions.

All system entities, particularly the customer, the broker, and the merchant communicate remotely over secure channels that provide external security like confidentiality, data integrity and mutual authentication. The SSL [1] as an industry-standard is one possible candidate, for it has been widely adopted in client-server products of leading vendors. On the other hand, all local runtime environments are assumed secure as both the merchant and the customer are authenticated at the SSL handshake protocol before the agent migrates to the merchant. In this sense, all local communications are subjected to no risk of being tampered.

Our payment system integrates both the MilliCent/A and the SET/A protocol to serve for electronic transaction between the customers and the merchants on the base of micropayment. The agent-based SET/A protocol is used for the transaction between broker and merchant as well as between customer and broker. On the other hand, customers and merchants trade on top of the MilliCent/A protocol. For instance, the scrip is implemented as a serializable object whose attributes are summarized in Table 2. The relations between the system entities are summarized in Figure 4.

Table 2. Attributes in scrip

Field Name	Format	Description
Merchant ID	16-bit integer	Identification of merchant
Value	16-bit integer	Value of scrip
ID	32-bit integer	Identification of scrip
Customer ID	16-bit integer	Identification of customer
Expiry Date	Date	CCYYMMDD
Certificate	Binary	128-bit MD5 hash

4 Agent-Based Protocols

A common card payment protocol and a micropayment protocol, SET and MilliCent respectively are used as a skeleton for the construction of the required agent-based protocols. Mobile agent technology is incorporated in both protocols in this micropayment system.

Mobile agents are software components that are able to move between different systems through the physical network. By moving to locations where the required information or logic is hosted, mobile agents can utilize the advantage of local communication to save system bandwidth and reduce the transaction cost.

The resulting agent-based protocols, namely MilliCent/A and SET/A are proposed on top of SSL. For instance, the authentication mode, server authentication with an unauthenticated client, is performed at the SSL handshake protocol such that the server is authenticated before the client issues a request. The MilliCent/A and the SET/A protocols are illustrated in the following sections.

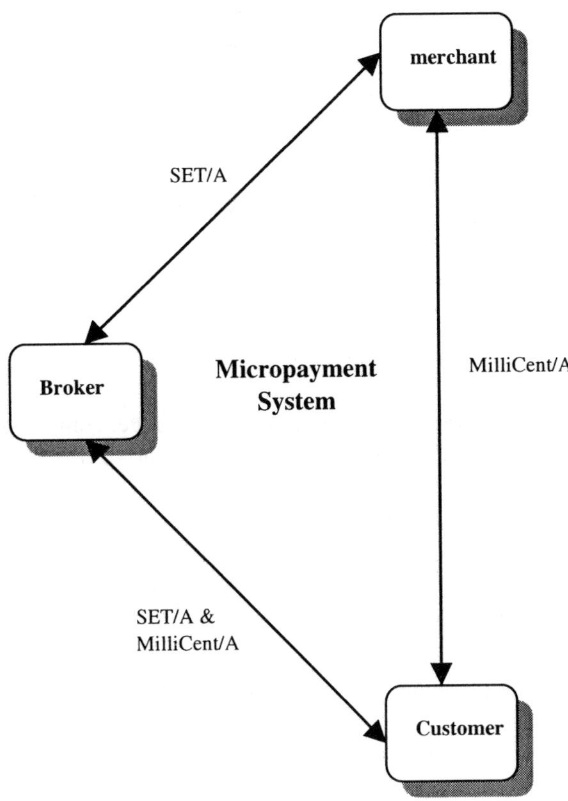

Fig 4. System architecture

4.1 MilliCent/A

We integrate the mobile agent technology in the MilliCent protocol [4, 5, 9] and come up with our MilliCent/A protocol. The mobile agent semantic is applied to move the key function from the client's to the server's host such that the customer software can be made thinner. From the customers' point of view, making a purchase request is equivalent to dispatching an agent. Whenever a purchase request is to be issued, the customer's server, which is a stationary agent, simply deploys the agent that carries the corresponding merchant's scrip with itself on its way to the merchant's server. The protocol is presented in Figure 5 and described as follows:

1. The agent A(C) migrates to the merchant's host along with the merchant's scrip and the customer secret specific to the merchant and issues purchase request locally to the merchant's server on behalf of the customer. (the dotted lines across C and M indicate a secure channel)

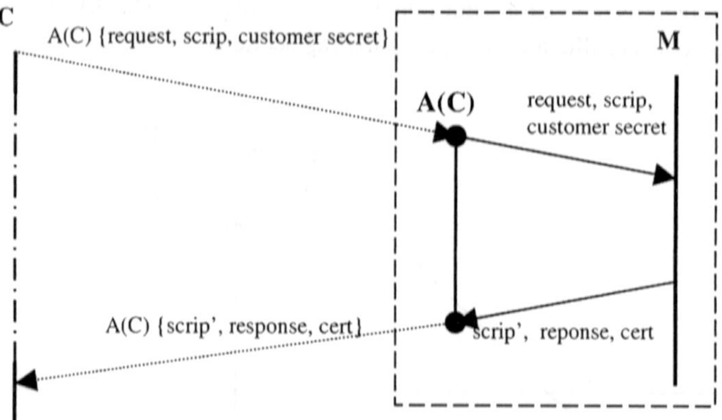

Fig 5. The MilliCent/A protocol

2. The merchant's server authenticates the customer by regenerating the customer secret from the customer ID embedded in the merchant's scrip and the master customer secret.
3. The merchant's server checks for any double spending or expiration of the scrip.
4. The merchant performs the requested service and returns the change from the transaction by issuing a new scrip (i.e. scrip') to the agent together with the response and the certificate of the old scrip (i.e. cert) for the agent to validate the transaction.

Afterwards the agent returns home with scrip' to and directly communicates with the customer for validation.

During the agent's life cycle, a large proportion of the transaction is performed off-line such that significant communication overhead between the customer and the merchant can be eliminated once the agent reaches the merchant's server. In general, the agent-based protocol contributes to the reduction of network traffic and the dependency on network availability. The customer trades broker's scrips for merchant's scrips from the broker in a similar manner.

4.2 SET/A

SET/A [2] is an implementation of the SET protocol [6] on top of the mobile agent semantic. It is designed to be as compatible with the original SET protocol as possible, with significant modification on the cardholder's role. On the contrary, the role of the merchant, whose interaction with the mobile agent remains more or less the same, as it would be with the cardholder in SET, is left intact.

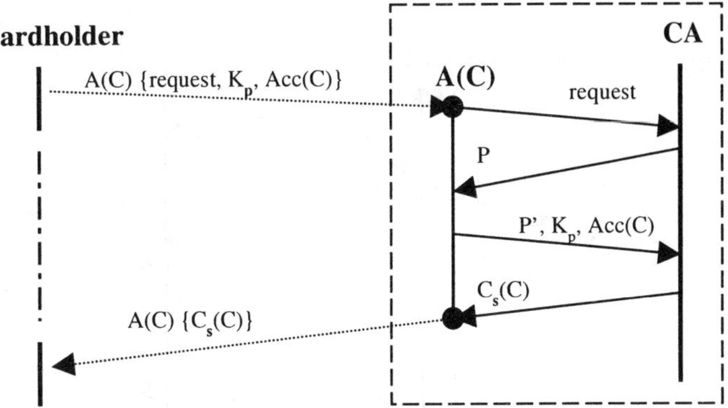

Fig 6. The SET protocol (Certificate Issuance phase)

4.2.1 Certificate Issuance

1. The cardholder's server dispatches a mobile agent A(C), which brings along the request, the cardholder's public key K_p to be certified (i.e. the public signature key and the public-key exchange key for the case of signature certificate and key exchange certificate issuance respectively) and the cardholder's account information Acc(C) to the CA peer.
2. The mobile agent issues a certificate issuance request to and interacts with the CA's server, locally on behalf of the cardholder.
3. The CA's server receives the request and returns the appropriate application form P.
4. The agent forwards the filled-in form P' to the CA's server along with K_p and Acc(C).
5. The CA's server verifies P' and generates the corresponding certificate $C_s(C)$ for the cardholder
6. Once the CA fulfilled the request, the mobile agent returns to the home server with the certificate.

The above protocol is summarized in Figure 6.

4.2.2 Purchase Request Phase

1. The cardholder's server dispatches a mobile agent A(C), which brings along with the request, the certificate $C_s(C)$ of the cardholder, the necessary information OI_PI_data for generating the order information OI and payment information PI, to the merchant peer.
2. The mobile agent issues the purchase request to and interacts with the merchant's server, locally on behalf of the Cardholder.

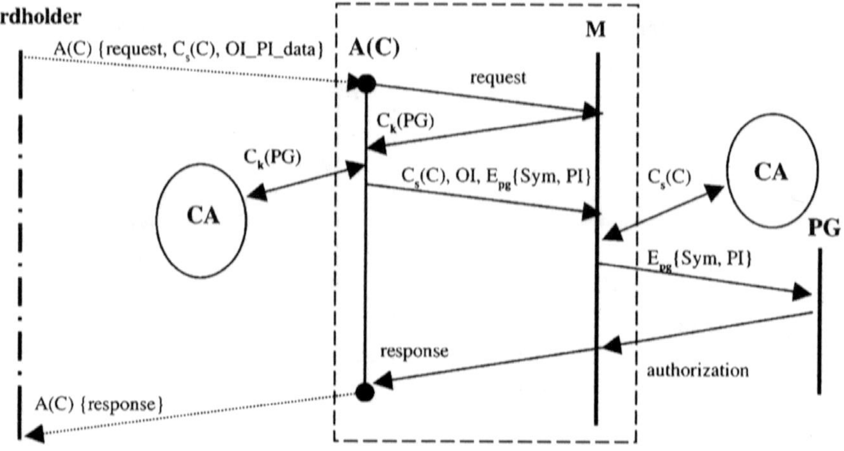

Fig 7. The SET/A protocol (purchase request phase)

3. The merchant's server receives the request and sends forward the key-exchange certificate $C_k(PG)$ of the payment gateway.
4. The agent verifies the certificate through CA and generates the OI and PI pair. In particular, the PI is encrypted with a randomly generated symmetric key K. Afterward, a digital envelope $E_{pg}\{Sym, PI\}$ is generated by encrypting both K and the encrypted PI with PG's public key. The digital envelope is then send to the merchant's server together with the OI and the cardholder's signature certificate.
5. The merchant's server verifies the cardholder's certificate and then forwards the digital envelope to PG for authorization.
6. Once the PG authorized the payment, the merchant's server generates and returns a purchase response to the mobile agent.
7. The mobile agent arrives at the home server with the purchase response and takes any appropriate action based on the content of the response.

The above protocol is summarized in Figure 7.

5 System Prototype

The IKV Grasshopper Development System 1.2 [7] has been chosen to be the development platform for the implementation of the above agent-based transaction protocols. The IKV Grasshopper 1.2 is a mobile agent platform that is built on top of a distributed processing environment. Under this architecture, the mobile agent technology and the traditional client/server paradigm can be integrated into an application. In addition, the IKV Grasshopper platform is the first mobile agent environment that is compliant to the Mobile Agent System Interoperability Facility (MASIF) standard of the Object Management Group (OMG) [8].

An experimental environment is built on top of the Grasshopper agent platform for demonstrating the micropayment system. This system prototype, basically composed of regions, places agencies and different types of agents, simulates transactions among the customer, the broker and the merchant. The system architecture is shown in Figure 8.

Remote communications are performed on top of SSL [1] with X.509 certificates compatible with the Grasshopper platform such that confidentiality, data integrity and mutual authentication are verified at the secure sockets layer.

Initially, all system entities including the customer, the broker, the merchant and the payment gateway raise certificate issuance requests, conforming to the initial phase of the SET/A protocol, to obtain certificates from the certificate authority. Afterwards, successive SET/A transaction phases are invoked between the broker and the merchant. The broker purchases blocks of scrip from the merchant through SET/A. Similarly, the customer purchases blocks of broker's scrips through SET/A from the broker. Afterwards, the customer trade individual broker's scrip for merchants' scrip and requests online documentation service from the merchants. The customer pays for the service with merchant's scrip through the MilliCent/A protocol. At the end, the merchant returns lines of text as receipt to the customer every time the transaction completes successfully.

6 System Performance

The system performance is evaluated based on the remote communications within the customer-merchant pair and the cardholder-merchant pair only in the MilliCent/A and the SET/A protocol respectively. The overhead in SSL (i.e. the SSL handshake protocol) is not included based on the assumption that as long as the service is delivered securely online from the merchant to the client through SSL after the payment is made, such a secure channel could be utilized for the Millicent/A protocol in the first place. On the other hand, since the remote communications between the cardholder-CA and merchant-CA pairs for verifying certificates in SET are out of the scope of evaluation, the SSL handshake protocol, serving for authentication purpose in particular, should reasonably be ignored in the SET/A as well. Further, the resources consumption in payment authorization within the merchant-PG pair in both SET and SET/A are ignored, for the underlying protocols are identically the same. The detailed evaluation is described as follows:

6.1 MilliCent/A Protocol

In the original MilliCent protocol, a merchant performs verifications on the correctness of a customer's request signature. The generation and verification of request signatures for authenticating the identity of scrip holders induce two hash functions. Further, the signing and verifying of merchant's response to guarantee message integrity induce another two hashes.

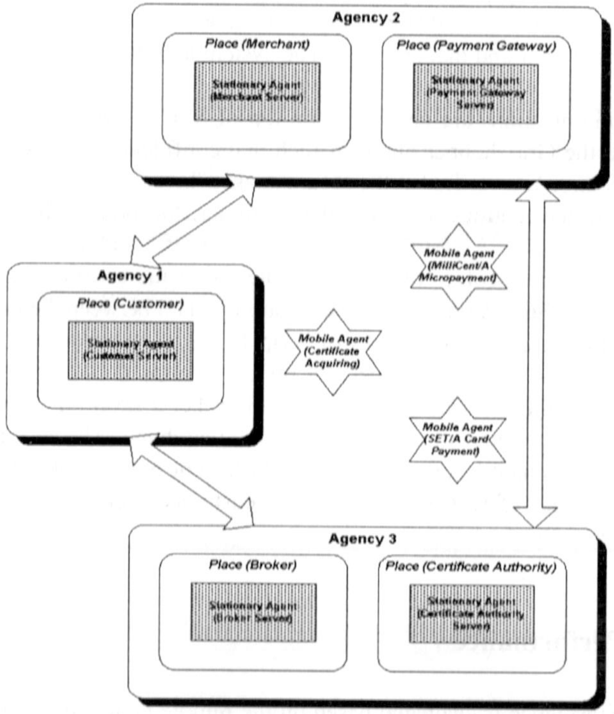

Fig 8. System prototype

In MilliCent/A, instead of generating a request signature, the mobile agent carries the customer secret to the merchant for direct verification such that two hashes are saved. Furthermore, since the agent is residing on the merchant's host, there is no need for proof of message integrity and hence no signing on the merchant's response and two more hash can be saved. However, these hash operations are saved at the expense of generation and verification of two Message Authentication Codes MACs in SSL, which induces two hash functions to be performed on each, and make up four additional hashes at the secure sockets layer.

In general, MilliCent/A completes in seven hashes, first for checking the old scrip, second for regenerating the customer secret, third for generating the new scrip plus additional four on authenticating the agent on its way to and form the merchant. Comparing to the MilliCent protocol, which induces seven hashes as well, both protocols are even in terms of local computation work.

On the other hand, the MilliCent protocol is likely to be implemented on a request reply paradigm such that the protocol may proceed in six or more remote messages and may induces additional hashes and cryptographic functions:

1. customer issues purchase initiation request
2. merchant responses with purchase initiation request reply
3. customer sends scrip
4. merchant returns validation results
5. customer confirms order
6. merchant commits the transaction and delivers the services

However, The MilliCent/A protocol induces exactly two network transmissions of mobile agent regardless of the underlying paradigm, for it has utilized the autonomy and the local processing ability of mobile agents. This comparison is summarized in Table 3.

Table 3. Resources consumption: MilliCent vs Millicent/A

Consumption	MiliCent	Milicent/A+SSL
Network Transmissions	6	2
Hash Functions Performed	7	7

6.2 SET/A Protocol

In both the certificate issuance and purchase request phase of SET/A, a significant number of cryptographic operations for purposes of certificate verification, message signing and encryption/decryption are reduced since the agent is supposed to be executing in a secure environment once it reached the server's host.

When the agent reaches the merchant's server, message signing can be saved for all request-and-respond communications. Since the agent knows well that it is communicating with the merchant by residing at its server, there is no need for proof of message integrity. However, the digital signatures are eliminated from the original protocol at the expense of supplementation with MACs in SSL for each agent migration. On top of that, the overhead for generating and verifying each MAC is relatively light compared to that for the digital signature in SET as the former does not require any asymmetric cryptographic operation.

For instance, the total number of MAC involved in SET/A is only two-third of the digital signatures in SET in the certificate issuance phase. In particular the SET/A protocol incurs two MACs and one digital signature in the purchase request phase and the underlying computation work is comparatively lighter than the three digital signatures in SET for the reason mentioned in the previous paragraph. As summarized in Table 4, we witness a reduction by about one-third in terms of message integrity verification for the certificate issuance and purchase request phases in SET/A.

In addition, symmetric encryption and decryption of messages can be avoided in the local communication between the agent and the merchant server in a secure environment. This is shown by the total reduction of digital envelopes for the certificate issuance in SET/A.

Table 4. Resources consumption: SET vs SET/A

Phase	Consumption	SET	SET/A+SSL
Certificate Issuance	Network Transmissions	4	2
	Digital Signaures / MACs	3	2
	Digital Envelopes	2	0
Purchase Request	Network Transmissions	4	2
	Digital Signaures / MACs	3	3
	Digital Envelopes	1	1

7 Conclusions

The mobile agent semantic brings an array of advantages that favor the development of electronic commerce over the Internet. Mobile agents are able to migrate actively from one physical network location to another. By moving to locations where the required information or logic is hosted, mobile agents are able to bring in the advantage of local communication over remote interaction via the network to distributed systems.

Seizing the opportunity to minimize processing cost for micropayment transaction, we have utilized such advantage of the mobile agent semantic and devised two agent-based transaction protocols. The agent-based protocols are blends of the existing SET card payment protocol and MilliCent micropayment protocol coupled with mobile agent characteristics. The corresponding micropayment system is built upon an OMG MASIF compliant agent platform. The system is based on a customer-broker-merchant paradigm. Offline interactions driven by the agent-based SET protocol are performed within the broker-merchant and broker-customer transaction pairs. On the other hand, simplified online interaction, conforming to the agent-based MilliCent protocol, takes place between the customer-broker and the customer-merchant transaction pairs.

The application prototype is built to demonstrate the performance of the proposed micropayment system. The performance evaluation of the micropayment system shows that the agent-based protocols outperform the original protocols in several areas.

Above all, security has been a major issue for agent-based environment. Security measures need to be introduced to protect the agents from both the hostile communication channels and malicious agencies. On the other hand, the servers need protection against attack form malicious agents as well. However, at the current development cycle, these security issues are left aside and supplemented with trust. Obviously, security is a critical issue in electronic commerce and, in turn, is the key problem we have to resolve in the future.

References

1. Alan O. Freier, Philip Karlton, and Paul C. Kocher, *Draft SSL 3.0 specification*, http://home.netscape.com/eng/ssl3/
2. Artur Romáo and Miguel Mira da Silva, *An Agent-Based Secure Internet Payment System for Mobile Computing*, Trends in distributed systems for electronic commerce: international IFIP/GI working conference, TREC'98, Hamburg, Germany, June 1999, pp. 76-93,
3. Carsten Schmidt and Rudolf Müller, *A Framework for Micropayment Evaluation*, http://macke.wiwi.hu-berlin.de/IMI/micropayments.html
4. Compaq, *An HTTP protocol for payment*, http://www.millicent.org/works/details/index.html
5. Compaq, *Millicent-specific elements for an HTTP payment protocol*, http://www.millicent.org/works/details/index.html
6. Grady N. Drew, Using SET for Secure Electronic Commerce, Prentice-Hall, Inc. 1999,
7. IKV++, *Grasshopper Technical Overview,* http://www.ikv.de/products/grasshopper/
8. OMG, http://www.omg.org/
9. Steve Glassman, Mark Manasse, Martín Abadi, Paul Gauthier, and Patrick Sobalvarro, *The MilliCent Protocol for Inexpensive Electronic Commerce*, proceedings of the 4th International World Wide Web Conference, December, 1995, http://www.millicent.org/works/details/index.html

Security Issues in M–Commerce: A Usage–Based Taxonomy

Suresh Chari[1], Parviz Kermani[1], Sean Smith[2], and Leandros Tassiulas[3]

[1] IBM T.J. Watson Research Center, Yorktown Heights NY 10598-0704
{schari,parviz}@us.ibm.com

[2] Department of Computer Science, Dartmouth College, Hanover NH 03755-3510
sws@cs.dartmouth.edu

[3] Electrical and Computing Engineering, Univ. of Maryland, College Park MD 20742
leandros@isr.umd.edu

Abstract. *M–commerce* is a new area arising from the marriage of electronic commerce with emerging mobile and pervasive computing technology. The newness of this area—and the rapidness with which it is emerging—makes it difficult to analyze the technological problems that m–commerce introduces—and, in particular, the security and privacy issues. This situation is not good, since history has shown that security is very difficult to retro–fit into deployed technology, and pervasive m–commerce promises (threatens?) to permeate and transform even more aspects of life than e–commerce and the Internet has. In this paper, we try to begin to rectify this situation: we offer a preliminary taxonomy that unifies many proposed m–commerce usage scenarios into a single framework, and then use this framework to analyze security issues.

1 Introduction

In the last few years, advances in and widespread deployment of information technology have triggered rapid progress in e–commerce. This includes automation of traditional commercial transactions (electronic retailing, etc.) as well as the creation of new transaction paradigms that were infeasible without the means of widely deployed information technology. New paradigms include electronic auctioning of purchase orders, as well as novel, money–less transaction models such as Napster [14]. E–commerce has heightened the focus on security both of systems and also for messaging and transactions [7,11].

In much the same way, recent advances in handheld *personal digital assistants (PDAs)*, wireless communication technology [17,19,26], and pervasive infrastructure [8,12,10,25,21] promise to extend this rich, comfortable environment to mobile users, and potentially to erase the distinction between the "off–line" and "on–line" worlds. As with e–commerce, we expect to see both the migration of current transaction models, as well as the emergence of new models made possible by this technology. Possible scenarios include:

J. Liu and Y. Ye (Eds.): E-Commerce Agents, LNAI 2033, pp. 264–282, 2001.

- "buying soda at a vending machine with a mobile phone"
- "trading stock from a wireless laptop, in an airport"
- "picking up a coupon while surfing the Web from a desktop, then squirting the coupon from a PDA into a kiosk at the grocery checkout."

This emerging area of *m–commerce* creates new security and privacy challenges because of new technology, novel applications, and increased pervasiveness.

Mobile applications will differ from standard e–commerce applications, because the underlying technology has fundamental differences:

- **Limitations of Client Devices.** Current (and looming) PDAs are limited in memory, computational power, cryptographic ability, and (for the time being) human I/O. As a consequence, the user cannot carry his entire state along with him, cannot carry out sophisticated cryptographic protocols, and cannot engage in rich GUI interaction.
- **Portability of Client Device.** PDAs have the potential to accompany users on all activity, even traditionally off–line actions away from the desktop. Besides creating the potential for broader permeation of e–transactions, this fact also makes theft, loss, and damage of client devices much more likely.
- **Hidden and Unconscious Computing.** Both to compensate for limited PDA storage, as well as to provide new ways to adapt a user's computing environment to her current physical environment, *pervasive computing (PvC)* often permits client devices to transparently interact with the infrastructure—without the user's direct interaction. This unconcsious interaction can include downloading executable content.
- **Location–Aware Devices.** When the user is mobile, the infrastructure can potentially be aware of the location of the user (e.g., in a particular telephone cell). This knowledge introduces a wide range of applications which have no analogue in the stationary user model.
- **Merchant Machines.** In the e–commerce world, the merchant (i.e., the party that is not the user) has powerful machines, with ample storage and computation, usually in a physically safe place. However, to fully exploit the potential interacting with mobile, PDA–equipped users, merchant machines may move out into the physical world. This move brings with its own challenges of increased physical exposure, limited computation and state, and limited interconnection.

Several of these applications scenarios have no analogues in stationary models. They give rise to new kinds of security issues—which need to be considered *before* designing protocols and deploying solutions. In this paper we aim to:

- to study the possible range of mobility scenarios,
- to propose a rudimentary taxonomy of possible application classes based on connectivity scenarios,
- to identify the security exposures and issues for each connectivity scenario
- to draw inferences from the discussion on exposures.

In Section 2, we introduce a set of entities which we are the main participants in the m–commerce world. In Section 3, we enumerate m–commerce usage scenarios based on these entities and their interaction. In Section 4, we consider the security and privacy implications of these scenarios. In Section 5, we try to generalize from this specific analysis to broader principles. In Section 6, we consider some directions for future research.

2 Entities

By definition, commerce involves commercial transactions between two or more entities. E–commerce moves at least some portion of this interaction to an electronic, computational setting. M–commerce goes further by moving some of this computation to a mobile platform. This characterization still leaves many variables open: Who are these entities? What are their computational platforms? How do these platforms interact during the course of an m–commerce transaction? We visit each question in turn.

2.1 Client Devices

Our basic model for a *client device* $\mathcal{C}$ is portable, moderately powerful computational device such as a PDA with a range of possible connectivity options which allows us to explore a wide range of mobility scenarios:

- $\mathcal{C}$ may have a physical connection to the client's desktop—but only when the client is at his desktop.
- $\mathcal{C}$ may itself be a wireless phone with a long–range wireless link.
- $\mathcal{C}$ may be equipped with a short–range link such as Bluetooth [17].

We make the simplifying assumption that the client device $\mathcal{C}$ is identified with the user of this device. At the application level, the authentication mechanisms for use in transactions will be different from those used at the link level to obtain services such as data transport. In some applications, this distinction will blur such as when the user uses the link–level authentication and authorization mechanisms to participate in transactions.

Physical security of the client device is a very useful property for the user to participate in protocols that can be proven, with high assurance, to be secure. While we do not assume that inexpensive devices such as current off–the–shelf cell–phones or PDAs (or, for that matter, desktop machines) offer sufficiently high resistance to physical attacks, we identify security exposures in protocols which could be avoided if $\mathcal{C}$ or $\mathcal{K}$ had these properties. With care, physical security can be imported into the client device via a secure hardware token such as a smart card or a smart button. Although the physical security of such devices is still in question [1,2,24], some smart buttons have had physical security independently evaluated at FIPS 140–1 Level 3 [15]. Physical security can be imported into desktops via a high-end, FIPS Level 4 secure coprocessor [23,27].

We note that, although many discussions of the physical security of client devices center on the resistance of the device to attack by a party other than the user, for many applications, it is important to consider resistance against attacks by the user himself. For example, an electronic wallet application may be subverted if a user can insert cash back into his wallet.

2.2 Kiosk Devices

A *kiosk device* $\mathcal{K}$ is our abstraction of the computational entity embodying the merchant with which the user participates in a transaction. In the normal e–commerce setting, the kiosk $\mathcal{K}$ is the server in the client–server model of interaction. However, in the broader world of m–commerce application scenarios, the kiosk $\mathcal{K}$ can have many form factors, such as:

- the normal web server/site which the client connects to either directly or through a proxy;
- an intelligent vending machine which the client can connect to using a local connectivity link;
- a passive identifying tag attached to painting in a museum.

From a security standpoint, there are different exposures depending on the entity that controls the physical location of the kiosk $\mathcal{K}$, and the points of attack against it. On one end, we have the kiosk as a backend server which can talk the WAP [26] protocol suite. In this setting, the client can directly establish a secure connection directly with this kiosk. This is similar to the traditional e–commerce model, where the kiosk $\mathcal{K}$ is a machine with large computational resources and broadband connections to other servers which it may contact to complete the transaction on behalf of the client such as a bank. The backend server can have strong security features such as being located behind a firewall, with access to a physically secure device. These features mitigate a number of security threats. However, a backend server with sophisticated connectivity might be subject the vulnerabilities that repeatedly surface in such complex boundaries.

At the other end, m–commerce introduces new scenarios where the kiosk $\mathcal{K}$ is a disconnected machine physically located in a remote setting. For instance, the kiosk $\mathcal{K}$ could be a vending machine and the client may connect to it using a local link. Here, the kiosk $\mathcal{K}$ does not have rich computational resources, and may also lack the ability to connect directly to a bank/payment center to verify the user's payment on–line. Since those with direct physical access to the device may not share the same interests as the owners of the kiosk $\mathcal{K}$, physical security issues [15] and physical protection of sensitive computation and data [23,27] become much more critical. Lack of high bandwidth connectivity also creates issues with maintaining and monitoring state at the device.

Early e–government initiatives gave serious consideration [9] to the security and usability issues of kiosks, since these were an avenue to bring information technology to broader populations than desktops could reach.

2.3 Infrastructure Servers

A fundamental difference between traditional e–commerce scenarios and their mobile counterparts is the role of the infrastructure. In mobile settings, the client device $\mathcal{C}$ and, very possibly, the kiosk $\mathcal{K}$ may suffer from fundamental restrictions such as a limited form–factor, very limited computational resources, small amounts of memory, lossy and high–latency connectivity., etc. Due to these limitations, the application frameworks are fundamentally different. For instance, a wireless–PDA wishing to access a web–site requires an intermediate machine to *transcode* the content so that it fits into its limited form–factor.

We abstract this external entity, which is part of the infrastructure potentially participating in mobile commerce transactions, as the *infrastructure server* $\mathcal{S}$. Examples of the infrastructure server include:

- **WAP Proxies.** In the WAP [26] architecture, the client device contacts a proxy using the WAP suite of protocols which then contacts a web server on the client's behalf. Besides bridging transport level differences in protocols on either side, the proxy also decrypts and re–encrypts data from the web server to the client. Other examples of such proxies are the Palm.Net proxy which manages user profiles besides transcoding content.
- **Wireless Gateway.** In another example, the user could potentially use the link level authentication mechanisms such as the *Subscriber Information Module (SIM)* of the wireless phone to pay for transactions. Here the infrastructure server is the wireless gateway which authorizes the use of the SIM for this transaction. This is the canonical "using a wireless phone to pay for soda at the vending machine" example.

By definition, the infrastructure machines is much more powerful than the other players in the m–commerce transaction. It can derive considerable physical security from its location but in a number of scenarios it can benefit from having physical security such as secure coprocessors.

Thus, we see that m–commerce introduces a critical distinction: the nature of client and kiosk technology introduces the need for this third element *which may be controlled by a party other than the user and merchant.*

Payment Gateways. Since commerce involves the exchange of services and merchandise for payment, implicit in all our discussions of m–commerce is the issue of electronic payment. (See [4] for an excellent overview of electronic payment systems.) We assume that financial institutions which facilitate payments are part of the infrastructure. In this section, we survey existing techniques for electronic payment systems.

We categorize electronic payment schemes based on what options are chosen for the following paramters:

- **Anonymity.** Can the spender can be tracked by the financial institution? (The scheme is *identifiable* if it can, *anonymous* otherwise)
- **On–line/Off–line Checks.** Is a connection with the bank required during the transaction?

Identifiable payment schemes contains sufficient information to reveal the identity of the person who originally withdrew the money from the financial institution, which can then further track the money as it moves in transactions. In contrast, anonymous payment schemes work more like paper cash; money can be spent without leaving a transaction trail. (Indeed, many researchers are particular about using "e-cash" or "e-money" *precisely* for those electronic payment schemes which are anonymous, atomic, and widely-accepted.)

As tempting as it may be to assert equivalence to paper, we note that real implementations of e-cash suffer from substantial differences [22]. For example, in the seminal DigiCash protocol [6]:

- Critical atomicity and anonymity properties will fail if the connection drops while Alice is receiving an e-dollar from Bob. [27]
- When Alice receives an e-dollar from Bob, she cannot turn around and spend it without first going to the bank.
- Alice cannot easily make change, without revealing her identity.

Once identified, many of these drawbacks can be overcome (e.g., [3].)

The main security exposure with anonymous e–cash is the problem of double spending. On–line schemes prevent double spending by requiring vendors to contact the financial institution during every sale, in order to determine whether a particular electronic dollar is still good. (In some schemes, the financial institution maintains a database of all the spent pieces of e-money; in others, it maintains a database of the unspent pieces.) This is very similar to the way vendors currently verify whether a particular credit card number corresponds to a valid account. Off–line schemes handle double spending in different ways:

- **Prevention.** Cash is stored on tamper–resistant smart cards which contain a small database of all transactions. Double spending can easily be detected since the hardware token (in theory) prevents tampering [13,27].
- **Detection.** Another approach is to *detect* double spending: a double spender is *identified* when the cash is redeemed at the bank. But rather than stopping double spending, this technique merely deters it. The main advantage of these schemes is that they do not require tamper–proof hardware.

3 Usage Models

In our abstraction of m–commerce, we thus have three entities: the client device $\mathcal{C}$, the merchant device $\mathcal{K}$, and the remote infrastructure $\mathcal{S}$. These entities interact during a transaction. For example:

- $\mathcal{C}$ may scan a barcode on $\mathcal{K}$
- $\mathcal{C}$ and $\mathcal{K}$ may establish a wireless Bluetooth link;
- $\mathcal{C}$ may establish a telephone link to $\mathcal{S}$
- $\mathcal{K}$ may establish a telephone link to $\mathcal{S}$
- $\mathcal{K}$ may be connected to $\mathcal{S}$ permanently via a LAN.

The interaction may not always involve the conscious action of the user: e.g., PvC's unconscious computing, where a PDA interacts on its own. The interaction may be unidirectional: e.g., client GPS. Furthermore, the user's perception of the interaction may differ substantially from the actual connection: e.g., the $\mathcal{C}$

may appear to connect to $\mathcal{K}$ directly, even though the connection is via a WAP gateway $\mathcal{S}$ that may in turn transparently redirect $\mathcal{C}$ to a different $\mathcal{S}$.

These three entities can interact with $2^3 = 8$ possible combinations of connectivity scenarios. For simplicity, we only consider connectivity at the time the transaction is being performed, and omit issues such as off–line connections. For example, in the soda–buying example, the kiosk $\mathcal{K}$ (vending machine) may be disconnected from the infrastructure when the transaction is actually performed, but may intermittently synchronize with a server to deposit the tokens to be redeemed for payment or these tokens may physically be removed from the kiosk through other means.

To formalize these scenarios consider a bit vector, where the most significant bit represents $\mathcal{K}-\mathcal{C}$ connectivity, the next $\mathcal{K}-\mathcal{S}$ connectivity, and the last $\mathcal{C}-\mathcal{S}$ connectivity. We case out the interesting connectivity scenarios. To be meaningful for m–commerce, both the client device $\mathcal{C}$ and the kiosk device $\mathcal{K}$ should be session–connected with at least one other entity. This gives a rudimentary taxonomy of five basic scenarios. In the following Section 3.1 through Section 3.5, we consider each in turn.

3.1 $\mathcal{K}-\mathcal{C}$ (100): Disconnected Interaction

In the *disconnected* case, illustrated by Figure 1, the client $\mathcal{C}$ and the kiosk $\mathcal{K}$ are disconnected from the infrastructure, and communicate with each other directly using a local link such as Bluetooth. Compelling examples include:

- **User at Vending Machine.** Here the client device $\mathcal{C}$ is a PDA, and the kiosk $\mathcal{K}$ is a vending machine. The user connects using a local connection, such as Bluetooth. A payment scheme for such a transaction needs to take into account that the kiosk $\mathcal{K}$ can perform no on–line checks (see Section 2.3).
- **Coupons.** Many payment–free examples are also possible: For example, schemes where a user retrieves *coupons* from one kiosk $\mathcal{K}$ and deposits them at others are arguably m–commerce.
- **Parking Validation.** Intermediate schemes are also possible. For example, a user's $\mathcal{C}$ might pick up a parking ticket in a parking garage, validate this ticket by interacting with a kiosk $\mathcal{K}$ in one of several nearby stores, and then inject his ticket (indicating he owes full value, or no value, if the ticket was validated) when he leaves the garage.
- **Local Services.** In many pervasive computing scenarios, traveling users access the devices they need—printers, video projectors—simply by pointing their PDA at them. When this access moves from "research lab conference room" to "cybercafe," then this money–less transaction can arguably become m–commerce.

3.2 $\mathcal{K}-\mathcal{S}-\mathcal{C}$ (011): Server-Centric Case

In the *server-centric* case (shown in Figure 2) the infrastructure server $\mathcal{S}$ is connected to both the client $\mathcal{C}$ and the kiosk $\mathcal{K}$. The $\mathcal{S}$ then acts as a proxy. Some examples are:

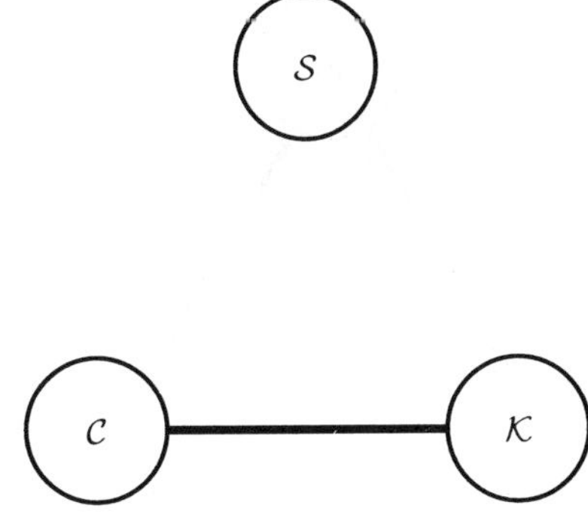

Fig. 1. The Disconnected Case: the client $\mathcal{C}$ and $\mathcal{K}$ interact directly, without on–line connection to the infrastructure $\mathcal{S}$.

- **WAP/Palm.Net.** Here the client device $\mathcal{C}$ is a wireless phone/PDA talking to a kiosk $\mathcal{K}$ which is a backend website. Since $\mathcal{K}$ and $\mathcal{C}$ do not talk the same protocol suite, the infrastructure server $\mathcal{S}$ performs the tasks of transcoding, splicing security protocols, etc. The three entities need not be in the same security domain, although this creates the obvious lack of end–to–end security since the proxy will decrypt and re–encrypt the content. This is the architecture of the emerging Wireless Applications Protocol suite [26]. The Palm.net [18] mode of interaction is similar, although in this case the server and the client device $\mathcal{C}$ talk the same set of protocols.
- **Vending Machines with On–line Checks.** The vending machine can make an on–line check when the user makes a payment for the transaction. In the example of buying soda using a cell–phone: the user calls a backend server, which transfers funds and calls the vending machine, to inform it to dispense the soda.
- **Location–Based Applications.** Other applications fitting this interaction model are location–dependent applications. If the user device is in contact with the infrastructure (for example, when the user's cellular PDA is turned on), the infrastructure can track the user's location, establish connection with a physically close kiosk, and assist in a potential transactional interaction. Examples of such transactions are the i–mode transactions deployed by NTTDoCoMo[16].

3.3 $\mathcal{K} - \mathcal{C} - \mathcal{S}$ (101): Client–Centric Case

In the *client–centric* case (shown in Figure 3), the client device $\mathcal{C}$ is connected to both the other entities, with a local link to the kiosk $\mathcal{K}$ and a wireless link to the infrastructure. Applications fitting this mode include: Imaginary Buffer Line

- **User State on Server.** The infrastructure alleviates the lack of memory on the client device $\mathcal{C}$ by keeping the user state. For instance, a user could

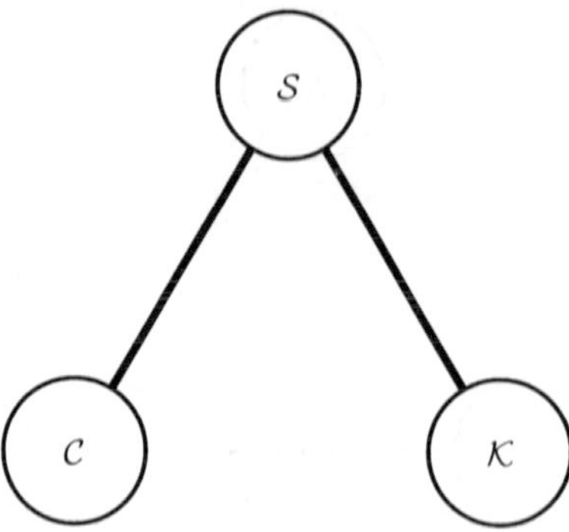

Fig. 2. The Server-Centric Case: the client and kiosk connect indirectly through the infrastructure server.

keep a repository of coupons on the server; when it is physically close to a kiosk $\mathcal{K}$ and wishes to participate in a transaction, the user device $\mathcal{C}$ can retrieve the appropriate coupon

- **Device State on Server.** The infrastructure could also store executables, so that the client device $\mathcal{C}$ only need store what its current context requires. (This model is often envisioned for speech-enabled PDAs: they pick up application-specific vocabulary from a kiosk in the user's physical environment.)
- **Cooltown.** The Cooltown scenarios ([8]) can fit into this case. The kiosks consist of very simple, passive tags. A client $\mathcal{C}$ interacts with a kiosk $\mathcal{K}$ by reading an identifier from the tag, then going into the infrastructure to retrieve the kiosk application.

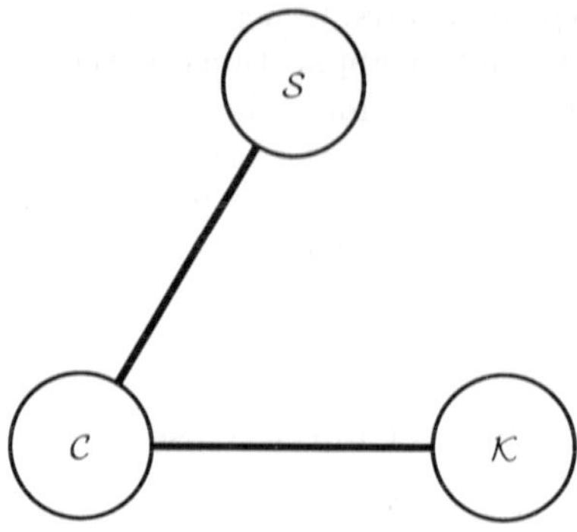

Fig. 3. The Client–Centric Case: the client device $\mathcal{C}$ connects both to the infrastructure and to the kiosk, but the kiosk is otherwise disconnected.

3.4 $\mathcal{C} - \mathcal{K} - \mathcal{S}$ (110): Kiosk–Centric Case

The *kiosk–centric* case (shown in Figure 4) is very representative of mobile application frameworks. The following are some examples:

- **ATM/Point–of–sale Terminal.** Here the user $\mathcal{C}$ communicates to the ATM or the Point–of–Sale terminal $\mathcal{K}$, which is connected to the infrastructure and can make on–line checks about the user during payment.
- **Traveling User.** Many proponents of pervasive computing predict scenarios where mobile users access remote infrastructure via local devices. For example, rather than carrying his file system—or a replica of a shared file system—with him, a user might simply point his $\mathcal{C}$ at a portal in a coffee shop or airport club, which in turn retrieves the data and potentially writes back changes. [20] Additionally, the backend server might use a large display on the kiosk to display non–secure information and display the sensitive information only on the user device.

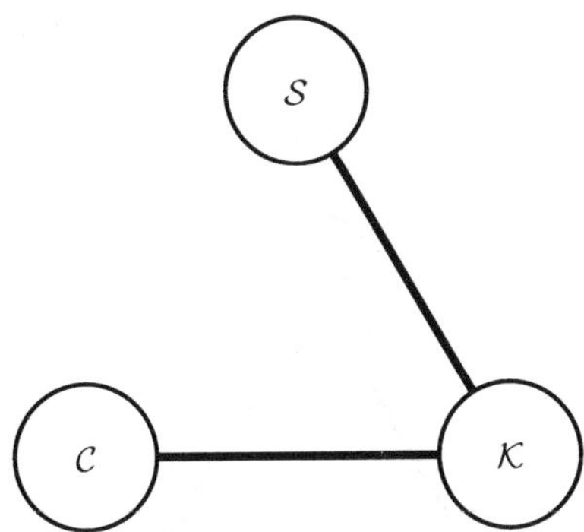

Fig. 4. The Kiosk–Centric Case: the client device $\mathcal{C}$ interacts directly with the kiosk, which in turn connects to the infrastructure.

3.5 Full Connectivity (111)

In the *fully connected case* (shown in Figure 5), all the entities are directly connected to one another. For example, suppose the client device $\mathcal{C}$ is a PDA with both Bluetooth and cell—phone capabilities, and the kiosk device $\mathcal{K}$ is network-connected.

The application scenarios here can include all the examples of the previous cases—if the technology supports it. Functionally, *any* transaction that can be performed in the fully connected case can be performed (with substantially more complicated protocols) in the biconnected models discussed above. However, full connectivity allows us to substantially simplify the protocols and obtain stronger security guarantees than similar applications in the other models. Full connectivity can also allow us to obtain other subtle security guarantees such as privacy and anonymity. For example, the user and kiosk might want to engage in some anonymous interaction, but both require backend resources to carry out this interaction. In this situation, using the infrastructure instead of a local connection to carry out the $\mathcal{K} - \mathcal{C}$ interaction would require some effective anonymous routing scheme, which can be expensive. The existence of all connectivity substantially reduces denial–of–service type attacks possible by implementing the same applications in other connectivity scenarios. (Section 4 will provide more discussion of these security issues.)

An application scenario possible with full connectivity, but not (easily) possible with weaker scenarios, is:

- **Proximity–Triggered Applications.** A kiosk and a client device both equipped with very short range connectivity like Bluetooth can detect when they are in close physical proximity. Additionally, if the client device $\mathcal{C}$ is connected to the backend through a wireless link and the kiosk $\mathcal{K}$ is connected to a LAN, one can think of several applications triggered by the kiosk $\mathcal{K}$ and client device $\mathcal{C}$ detecting physical proximity. (Detecting proximity can be possible without a direct $\mathcal{K} - \mathcal{C}$ interaction—e.g., both could use GPS—but this is much more complex.)

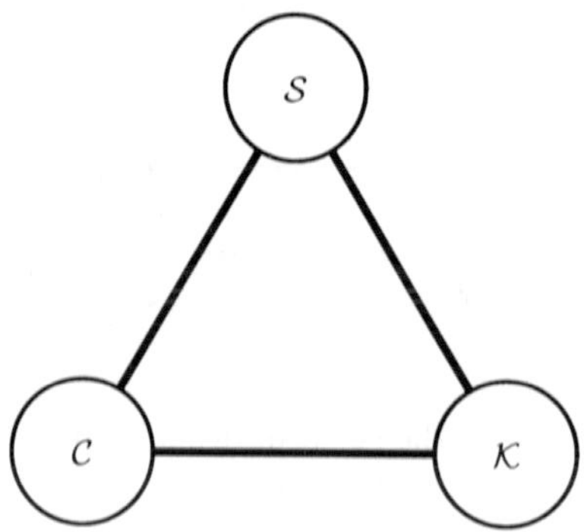

Fig. 5. The Fully Connected Case: all three entities are directly connected.

4 Security Exposures

In this section, we consider some of the security and trust issues raised by the cases and examples of Section 3. Besides the characteristics of the individual entities themselves, the security exposures and protocols are mainly decided by the connectivity between the entities. We consider each of the connectivity scenarios in turn. Essentially, the connectivity scenarios can be partitioned into three distinct classes:

- the disconnected case (Section 3.1);
- biconnected cases (Section 3.3, Section 3.2, Section 3.4)
- the fully connected case (Section 3.5).

We group the biconnected cases into one class since a number of exposures will be common. However, we will also point out individual differences in each of the cases.

4.1 Disconnected Interaction

At first glance, this case seems like the straightforward client–server interaction. However, the limitations of the PDA, and the fact that kiosks may be distributed in many physical locations, make this very challenging from a security perspective. We consider some problems.

Disconnection. In the disconnected case, by definition, both entities are disconnected from the infrastructure. Even if the kiosk $\mathcal{K}$ intermittently synchronizes with the infrastructure, neither it nor the client device $\mathcal{C}$ can have access to the latest state information. Conversely, neither the user nor the kiosk can update the information in the infrastructure. This immediately introduces a number of security exposures:

- **Double–Spending.** In the vending machine examples, the kiosk cannot check if the e-dollar or the coupon offered by $\mathcal{C}$ has already been spent somewhere else. Note that in some of the anonymous cash schemes, the protocol can detect *a posteriori*, if necessary, that double–spending had been done and identify the user [6].
- **Credential Freshness.** Most cryptographic protocols function by having one of more parties authenticate themselves during the transaction. With public keys, this is usually done by presenting a certificate which binds a public key with a name. Being disconnected, neither the client nor the kiosk can verify if the certificate is still valid and not been revoked.

Although these primary examples pertained to read-access (i.e., the client and kiosk were not able to read the current state in the infrastructure), write-access scenarios exist as well. For example:

- **Lack of Updates.** The kiosk cannot record that a particular e-dollar has been spent.

Many of the difficulties caused by disconnection can be characterized as a lack of *freshness*: the state at one $\mathcal{K}$ (or $\mathcal{C}$) lags behind or ahead the global merchant (or user) state. However, disconnection also eliminates economies of "information scale." For just example: the price a merchant charges for a commodity may directly depend on his cost, which can drop with quantities he buys. But if the merchant cannot know that each of 100 kiosks has each sold 10 units, his kiosks cannot reflect his wholesale price on 1000 units.

Integrity of State. The second related exposure is the possibility of *rollback.* Due to the limited physical security of off–the–shelf PDAs and the potentially exposed nature of kiosks, we must assume that, in the absence of extraordinary countermeasures, a dedicated adversary will be able to manipulate the internal state of both $\mathcal{C}$ and $\mathcal{K}$. This ability leads to a particularly acute security exposure. Interaction changes the state of the kiosk and the client in some well-defined way. However, because of the lack of connection, a delay exists between synchronizing this state with remote storage, and because of the lack of physical security, this uncommitted state may be subject to manipulation. Cryptographic techniques can prevent some types of manipulation. However, a device state can always potentially be rolled back to pre-interaction state. This creates a host of security and privacy challenges, typified by the following example:

– **Active Double Spending by Rollback.** Before spending e–cash at the vending machine, the client can record the complete internal state of the PDA, then restore this stored state afterwards and spend this cash again. Other variations exist—for example, a coupon marketing scheme might allow for unlimited distribution of a coupon, but require that a customer only use such a coupon on their first purchase.

Secure coprocessors and hardware tokens offers a potential solution to the problem of rollback, as discussed later.

Privacy of State. Another consequence of the lack of physical security is that the state at a device can be read and cloned. This exposure manifests itself in authentication. In the general case, if one entity cannot be trusted to keep its authentication secrets secret with high assurance, then the other entity can compensate by checking with some global state. But in the disconnected case, on–line checks are not possible.

Consider a user with a PDA interacting with a vending machine, with both entities disconnected from the infrastructure. How can the kiosk authenticate the client? Firstly, as pointed out, the kiosk can not check the freshness of the certificate presented. Secondly, even assuming that the certificate was not revoked, the certificate binds just binds a name to a public key which is confirmed by the possession of an equivalent private key. Without secure storage, this private key could easily have been obtained illegally.

4.2 The Biconnected Cases

The biconnected cases provide the potential to overcome some of the principal shortcomings of the disconnected case. Given our implicit assumption that both the user and the merchant have some portion of safe trusted storage in the infrastructure, then the entity that has a link to this infrastructure can also be a proxy extending this link to the other entity. The most natural example of this is in the server-centric case, where the server can route or forward $\mathcal{C} - \mathcal{K}$ communications to $\mathcal{K}$, and vice-versa. Note that the kiosk-centric and even the client-centric cases can carry out process of forwarding the messages to simulate full connectivity (if the device technology actually supports this.)

The main security issues which arise in this context are:

- **Active Translation.** The best example of the server-centric model is the Wireless Applications Protocol suite. Here the server (WAP proxy) needs to translate between the user's protocols and those of the kiosk since the client device $\mathcal{C}$ and kiosk do not speak the same protocols.
- **Privacy and Authenticity of Communications.** The intermediate entity can potentially try to attack the communications between the other two parties. Typically attacks involve altering the contents or the order of messages and replaying messages sent earlier.
- **Traffic Analysis.** Even if the intermediate entity does not actively modify the messages passing through, it will be aware of the frequency and length of the messages being exchanged. This can potentially lead to a substantial breach of privacy.
- **Denial of Service.** The intermediate entity can suppress messages meant for the other parties. This attack can especially crucial if one considers transactional protocols where the attacker may choose to stop sending "commit" messages.
- **More Points of Attack.** More complex message paths typically bring in more points of failure—and more points of attack. For example, if a portion of the link involves a LAN, then other devices on this network might carry out any of the attacks above.
- **Increased Failures.** The existence of more points of failure can increase the likelihood of failure of communications during a protocol. This can be a serious issue, since standard fault-tolerance techniques are not always orthogonal to security protocols—indeed, their naive application can actually subvert protocols (e.g., e–cash [27]).

Although we have grouped all the biconnected cases into one class, individual scenarios within this class bring their own concerns.

- **Client-Kiosk Identification.** Standard authentication techniques can address the problem of whether one party is in fact communicating with another party with a specific identity. But these techniques are effective only if one knows the identity in the first place.
  In many m–commerce interactions, the pairing of a $\mathcal{C}$ and $\mathcal{K}$ occurs because of physical co-location and user intention. For example, the user wants the system to know that he wants to buy from the vending machine in front of him—the user doesn't want to pre-load the serial number of a particular vending machine or to stand and punch in its serial number. Direct $\mathcal{C} - \mathcal{K}$ interaction techniques provide a painless way to address this problem—for example, the user communicates his intention by pointing his PDA at the vending machine, and a Bluetooth exchange establishes the rest. However, the server-centric case dispenses with this link. This situation can create some interesting risks. For example, a server trying to match a user to the closest vending machine may not necessarily be aware of the locked door separating the user from the physically closest machine.
- **Privacy Issues.** In applications based on cell–phones, by definition, the $\mathcal{S}$ will know the physical location of client device $\mathcal{C}$. This creates privacy

risks: for example, it might make it easier for a terrorist group to locate a particular targeted dignitary. With current technology, $\mathcal{C} - \mathcal{S}$ interactions appear to inevitably involve this technology, so we might reasonably conclude that complete user privacy cannot be possible in any server–centric or user–centric scenario.

4.3 Full Connectivity

In the fully connected case, the security exposures for all the above scenarios are substantially mitigated by the fact that there are direct connections between the different entities. For instance, several of the denial–of–service attacks possible in the biconnected cases are not possible in the fully connected case. In the biconnected case where the kiosk is forwarding user messages to the infrastructure, the kiosk can selectively drop messages. The protocol for the biconnected case has to be resistant to these attacks. However, with full connectivity, the protocols could be substantially simpler.

5 Discussion

In this section, we abstract from the discussion of security exposures in the previous section and discuss some approaches to mitigate these exposure. As before, we consider these topics based on connectivity.

5.1 Disconnected Case

As seen in the previous section, this case offers the most challenging scenario for security measures. At first glance, it would appear that the challenges in the disconnected case leave us with the following impossibilities:

- There is no effective way to do e-cash—or any other payment scheme—without risk of attacks such as double-spending.
- There is no effective way to prevent malicious rollback of a critical state transition.
- There is no effective way to authenticate the other party, against an adversary who may have extracted its secrets.

However, hardware which can guarantee physical security give us some mechanisms to address these problems:

- If both $\mathcal{C}$ and $\mathcal{S}$ were equipped with high–end secure coprocessors [23,27] that could be trusted to carry out their computation unmolested despite physical attack, then we could solve the cash problems. The technique could also extend to other state transitions—except, of course, where an adversary could benefit from simply destroying the device and losing all state.
- Suppose instead that the devices possessed "secure hardware" that takes the form of a non-reproducible label: for example, the random physical structure of the surface of the device contains some random number, that the other device can reliably read. In this scenario, the authentication problem could be solved.

Embedding secure coprocessors or secure hardware is essentially a way to deploy the infrastructure into the user device or the kiosk. Imaginary Buffer Line One might argue that a secure coprocessor at either entity in the disconnected case would transform the model into the equivalent of the biconnected case, because the coprocessor can become a trusted proxy for the missing party. (But on the other hand, one might argue that some problems of disconnection still could not be solved: two distinct coprocessors still cannot synchronize state.)

This reasoning suggests a potentially interesting avenue of theoretical work:

- What is a precise formulation of the transaction properties that cannot be achieved with the base disconnected case? Can we prove that this base case cannot achieve these properties?
- What minimal amounts of secure hardware (and of which type) do we need to add (and to how many entities) in order to achieve these properties?

In some sense, one can imagine a theory here similar to distributed and disconnected file systems: e.g., transactions that could be subverted if the other party has rolled back state require synchronization beforehand. It would be interesting to see if this reasoning could be formalized, and some general principles proven with this formalism.

Disconnected operation has one advantage over the other connectivity cases: transactions can be anonymous and privacy–preserving. Also, since no connections are made to the infrastructure, fault tolerance can be increased, since the trustworthiness or reliability of the infrastructure is irrelevant.

5.2 The Biconnected Cases

The connectivity models and examples described in the biconnected cases (Section 4.2) are in our opinion very representative of the security concerns in mobile applications.

Biconnected cases can simulate full connectivity by the entities establishing a three–party protocol: standard encryption and message authentication techniques can address the confidentiality and message ordering issues. However, the protocols must be carefully designed since the intermediate entity controls the entire data flow and can mount denial–of–service attacks. Care must be taken since not every protocol can be systematically hardened against selective denial-of-service. Techniques to hide the identity of parties in a networked connection are expensive and not always effective in practice. Techniques to hide the existence of communication are extremely expensive.

The case of the Wireless Applications Protocol [26] is an interesting example of the server–centric model. The setting here is the wireless client requesting a web page from the kiosk(the backend server) through the infrastructure server(the WAP proxy). Since the kiosk $\mathcal{K}$ and client device $\mathcal{C}$ do not speak the same protocol suite, the proxy has to translate and in the case of secure communication decrypt and re–encrypt the data. This is an obvious security hole unless the proxy and the kiosk are in the same security domain. One way to address this problem is for the server to contain a secure coprocessor which is controlled by the kiosk (backend server). The actual translation is done inside the secure coprocessor which essentially acts as an agent of the kiosk residing at the proxy [5].

Lastly, arguing that the biconnected cases are equivalent also overlooks the vastly different computational and I/O properties of the entities. It is impractical to assume that in the client–centric case that the kiosk could communicate to the infrastructure through the client: the client device C might not have the capability to support robust cryptography and, also, the user might not be willing to pay for the bandwidth required.

5.3 Full Connectivity

We only wish to note that privacy and the integrity of protocols can be substantially enhanced in the full connectivity model. Protocols can be proved to be correct without the existence of high assurance secure coprocessor.

6 Future Research Directions

As wireless and mobile computing continues to evolve, m–commerce application scenarios that go beyond the framework described above will emerge. Examples include:

- Ad-hoc networking of mobile devices will facilitate user-to-user connectivity without the intervention of more powerful entities. Hence there will be the opportunity for more casual interaction and new m-commerce models, directly between the users C, will emerge. For instance, when two users happen to be in the same environment may sell stock quotes one to the other or even sell access to the Internet (e.g., by sending email using the other user's laptop that is connected to the Internet). Again, an important issue here is the advertisement of services. The PDA of an individual may broadcast continuously the type of services that are available for use by other users and the "price" of those services. At the same time an individual may broadcast the type of services that he needs and they are not available to him from his own resources. Hence the PDA's will attempt to match services and requests when the users are in proximity, without the direct involvement of the individuals. Furthermore such a matching may occur even when the individuals are not in direct contact but they communicate through intermediate forwarding nodes.
- More sophisticated m–commerce models will enhance the flexibility of existing transaction paradigms. For instance the right m–commerce model might enable flexible subscription models for frequent travelers. When somebody registers and pays for a certain magazine, instead of having each issue of a magazine mailed to his house, he would like the flexibility to grab the magazine from the news stand in the airport if he wishes to do that instead or download it to his e–book from the info–kiosk.
- Finally the proliferation of micro–sensor technology in general and in particular the integration of sensors with communication transceivers will have

a significant impact on human I/O to the machine. Micro–sensor technology in combination with active badges will enable ubiquitous input to the computer without human intervention. Hence applications like automatic inventory and automatic ordering systems will become feasible. This will be useful for new distribution models for goods directly to the consumer.

7 Conclusion

Mobile application frameworks will likely be considerably different from the stationary user model, which creates a range of new security exposures. It is imperative to understand these exposures and design frameworks with security in mind *before* deploying applications and then retro-fitting security. In this paper we have identified some frameworks and their inherent exposures. We hope this spurs new research in secure protocols for mobile applications.

References

1. Anderson, R., Kuhn, M. Tamper Resistance—A Cautionary Note. 2nd USENIX Workshop on Electronic Commerce, 1996.
2. Anderson, R., Kuhn, M. Low-Cost Attacks on Tamper Resistant Devices. Preprint, 1997.
3. Camp, L.J. Reliability, Security, and Privacy in Electronic Commerce. Ph.D. thesis. Engineering and Public Policy, Carnegie Mellon University.
4. Camp, L.J., Sirbu, M., and Tygar, J.D. Token and Notational Money in Electronic Commerce. First USENIX Workshop on Electronic Commerce. July 1995.
5. Chari, S., Kaiserswerth, M., Rao, J.R. Network Security Issues in Pervasive Computing Devices. IBM Research Report RC 21592.
6. Chaum, D. Security without Identification: Transaction Systems to Make Big Brother Obsolete. Communications of the ACM, 28:1033-1044. October 1985.
7. Dierks, T., Allen, C. The Transport Layer Security Protocol. IETF Request For Comments 2246. Available online at `ftp://ftp.isi.edu/in-notes/rfc2246.txt`.
8. Hewllet Packard Laboratories Cooltown Appliance Computing. `cooltown.hp.com`
9. Hochberg, J., Smith, S., et. al. Kiosk Security Handbook. Los Alamos Unclassified Release LA-UR-95-1657, 1995. Los Alamos National Laboratory.
10. IBM Pervasive Computing, online at `http://www.ibm.com/pvc`
11. Kent, S., Atkinson, R. Security Architecture for the Internet Protocol. IETF Request for Comments 2401. Available online at `ftp://ftp.isi.edu/in-notes/rfc2401.txt`.
12. Kleinrock, L. Nomadic Computing & Smart Spaces. Keynote speak at Infocom 2000, Tel Aviv, Israel, March 2000. `http://www.cse.ucsc.edu/ rom/infocom2000/`.
13. The Mondex Electronic Cash Scheme. Documentation available online at `http://www.mondex.com`.
14. The Napster.com home page. `http://www.napster.com`.
15. National Institute of Standards and Technology. Security Requirements for Cryptographic Modules, Federal Information Processing Standards Publication 140-1. 1994.

16. The NTT DoCoMo i-mode applications. Documentation available online at `http://www.nttdocomo.com/imode`.
17. The Official Bluetooth SIG Website. Online at `http://www.bluetooth.com`.
18. The Palm VII handheld organizer. Documentation available online at `http://www.palm.com`.
19. Salonidis, T., Bhagwat, P., Tassiulas, L., LaMaire, R. Distributed Topology Construction of Bluetooth Personal Area Networks Preprint.
20. Satyanarayanan, M. Caching Trust Rather than Content. Carnegie Mellon University. Preprint, 2000.
21. Satyanarayanan, M. Fundamental Challenges in Mobile Computing. Fifteenth ACM Symposium on Principles of Distributed Computing May 1996, Philadelphia, PA Revised version appeared as: "Mobile Computing: Where's the Tofu?" Proceedings of the ACM Sigmobile April 1997, Vol. 1, No. 1.
22. Smith, S. Expressing and Enforcing Robust Behavior for Electronic Objects. The Federal Networking Council/MIT Internet Privacy and Security Workshop. May 1996. (Also: Los Alamos Unclassified Release LA-UR-96-1238.)
23. Smith, S., Weingart, S. Building a High-Performance, Programmable Secure Coprocessor. Computer Networks (Special Issue on Computer Network Security). 31: 831-860. April 1999.
24. Weingart, S. Physical Security Attacks and Defences. Cryptographic Hardware and Embedded Systems, August 2000.
25. Weiser, M. The World is not a Desktop. Interactions, Jan. 1994, pp. 7–8
26. The Wireless Applications Protocol Suite. Specifications available online at `http://www.wapforum.org`.
27. Yee, B.S.. Using Secure Coprocessors. Ph.D. thesis. Computer Science Technical Report CMU-CS-94-149, Carnegie Mellon University. May 1994.

Towards Distributed Workflow Enactment with Itineraries and Mobile Agent Management

Seng Wai Loke[1] and Arkady Zaslavsky[2]

[1] CRC for Enterprise Distributed Systems Technology
[2] School of Computer Science and Software Engineering
Monash University, Caulfield VIC 3145, Australia
swloke@dstc.monash.edu.au, A.Zaslavsky@csse.monash.edu.au

Abstract. Workflow technology is an important area of electronic commerce. The mobile agent paradigm offers a possible abstraction for flexible, adaptive, and dynamically extensible intra- and inter-organizational (even across the Internet) workflow systems. This paper describes two ideas we are exploring for mobile agent based distributed workflow enactment: an algebra of agent itineraries and its correspondence to workflow specifications, and a mobile agent control center for managing agents enacting workflows.

1 Mobile Agents for Distributed Workflow

There has been numerous workflow (also often called *business process*) management systems for automating and streamlining business process enactment.[1] Roughly, a *workflow* refers to a set of activities (or tasks) which need to be executed in some controlled order to realize a business purpose. Recent research aims to develop adaptive workflow technology with greater agility for coping with change [1]. In recent years, agent technology has been explored towards more flexible and robust workflow systems [2], and to facilitate workflow interoperability across organizations [3].

A recent strand of research explores the mobile agent paradigm for flexible intra-enterprise and inter-enterprise workflow enactment which includes workflow for virtual enterprises and supply-chain management and interaction with databases [4].

Mobile agents can be regarded as software components which on their own volition or invited can move from one host to another to perform computations. Mobile agents run within agent server programs which we call *places* that receive agents and execute them. A place typically has an address (e.g., `www.dstc.edu.au:888`). When at a place, an agent can utilise the resources at the place (e.g., if the place is interfaced with a database). Mobile agents may exhibit other agent attributes such as autonomy, social ability, adaptivity, and reactivity. Mobile agents encapsulating appropriate know-how can be used to

[1] See http://www.workflowsoftware.com.

J. Liu and Y. Ye (Eds.): E-Commerce Agents, LNAI 2033, pp. 283–294, 2001.

perform workflow activities by moving to and interacting with the appropriate resources (possibly over an Intranet or the Internet). In essence, a mobile agent could embody a workflow, encapsulating the business process logic (or part thereof) and execution state.

Potential benefits of the mobile agent paradigm for distributed workflow include the following:

Workflow extensibility and adaptability, and user customisability: these attributes refer to a workflow system which permits

1. *component-based extensibility*, where new places representing new business entities or interfaced to new databases (or software) can be added to the existing network of places, new workflows can be introduced by creating new agents (even at run-time to extend workflows on-the-fly [5]), agents can uptake or replace its components at run-time to cope with task changes (e.g., to interact with different databases), and an agent's *itinerary*, which describes the tasks of the agent and the locations where those tasks are to be performed, is viewed as an agent's component and can be altered before run-time or dynamically at run-time,
2. *reacting to events and adapting to changes*, where agents could utilise an event notification system and be interruptible at run-time and change their behaviour accordingly, and
3. *user involvement*, where users can not only define workflows, but also program their own workflow agents (e.g. to create ad-hoc workflows). In §2, we describe an agent itinerary language which has similar abstractions as workflow specifications. The user could also be involved with the agents at run-time. For example, the user might stop a running agent, modify it's itinerary, and then restart it.

(Dynamic) Workflow integration: two or more workflows which are simultaneously running can be integrated via communication between the agents enacting the workflows, or (for a tighter integration) by combining agent itineraries. We show a formal means of combining itineraries in §2.

Exception handling: agents consult a rule-base which tells them what to do with exceptions.

Workflow lifecycle monitoring: a workflow being enacted by an agent could be monitored by tracking the agent's activities. Also, other agents could be sent to interact with running agents to collect status information or to watch for deviations [6].

Workflow support for mobile devices: there has been much work on using mobile agents to support users of mobile wireless devices [7,8,9]. Such devices are limited in battery power, computational power, and may experience frequent disconnections. Mobile agents could be launched from mobile devices into a fixed network (or to other mobile devices) to perform tasks, without requiring the mobile device to be continuously connected. Mobile agents can also reduce network traffic over narrowband wireless networks by moving computation to databases instead of moving huge amounts of data to where computations are carried out.

Mobile agents offer an attractive solution for workflow involving such mobile workers. But mechanisms for adequate control of such agents are needed.

Remote installation of workflow components: in inter-organizational workflows where there is heterogeneous computational infrastructure across different organizations, lack of central management and high costs of integrating systems across organizations, mobile agents support ad-hoc workflows by being moved as software components to places as needed. Further benefits of mobile agents for inter-organizational workflow are detailed in [10].

These capabilities could be provided for both ad-hoc spontaneous workflows and repetitive production workflows. Mobile agents are also a natural abstraction for concurrent workflows - multiple agents enacting multiple workflows in parallel,and limited distributed local control - as delegated to the agents. Indeed, with the above potential benefits, there has been much work exploring mobile agent technology for workflow [11,6,12,5,10,13,14,15,16,17].

It is also our working hypothesis that the mobile agent is a convenient abstraction for distributed workflow systems. Our earlier work has developed an algebraic formalism for expressing mobile agent itineraries with an operational semantics defined by transition rules [18]. We show in this paper that our *itinerary algebra* can be used as compositional executable (at least in the sense of the transition rules) specifications of certain kinds of workflow. Hence, a contribution in this paper, different from the above cited work which implemented workflow applications with existing mobile agent toolkits or built new mobile agent based workflow systems, is a high-level language for programming (and reasoning with) mobile agent based workflows in a direct succinct manner. A second contribution is to argue that much work on mobile agent management can be applied to managing mobile agent based workflows, and so a *mobile agent control center* can control workflows by controlling the agents enacting the workflows. This control center could be a comprehensive tool with support for creating and deploying agents and hence workflows.

In §2, we present our algebra of itineraries, and in §3, we outline the components of a mobile agent control center which can be viewed as a workflow management system. We conclude with future work in §4.

2 Mobile Agent Itineraries as Executable Workflow Specifications

Our algebra aims to provide separation of concerns to simplify agent programming, where the mobility aspect of agents are separated from code details implementing the computations on hosts, and to encourage identification and reuse of patterns in mobility behaviour. We shall also see that our itineraries can function as workflow specifications.

For the algebra, we are currently using an object-oriented model of agents (e.g., with Java in mind), where an agent is an instance of a class given roughly by:
mobile agent = *state* + *action* + *mobility*

State refers to an agent's state (values of instance variables) possibly including a reflection of the agent's context. Action refers to operations the agent performs to change its state or that of its context. Mobility comprises all operations modifying an agent's location, including moving its state and code to other than the current location. While mobility assumes that an agent moves at the agent's own volition, the itineraries may be viewed as a specification or plan of agent movements.

We assume that agents have the capability of *cloning*, that is, creating copies of themselves with the same state and code. Also, agents can communicate to synchronize their movements, and the agent's code is runnable in each place it visits.

2.1 An Algebra of Itineraries

Let **A**, **O** and **P** be finite sets of agent, action and place symbols, respectively. Itineraries (denoted by $\mathcal{I}$) are now formed as follows representing the null activity, atomic activity, parallel, sequential, nondeterministic, conditional nondeterministic behaviour, and have the following syntax:

$$\mathcal{I} ::= \mathbf{0} \mid A_p^a \mid (\mathcal{I} \parallel \mathcal{I}) \mid (\mathcal{I} \cdot_{\oplus} \mathcal{I}) \mid (\mathcal{I} \mid \mathcal{I}) \mid (\mathcal{I} :_{\Pi} \mathcal{I})$$

where $A \in \mathbf{A}$, $a \in \mathbf{O}$, $p \in \mathbf{P}$, $\oplus$ is an operator which combines an agent with its clone to form a new agent, and Π is an operator which returns a boolean value to model conditional behaviour. We specify how $\oplus$ and Π are used but we assume that their definitions are application-specific.

We assume that all agents in an itinerary have a starting place (which we call the agent's *home*) denoted by $h \in \mathbf{P}$.

Below, we describe the meaning of the operators informally. In Loke *et al* [18] are more details of their operational semantics and algebraic properties. Given an itinerary I, we shall use $agents(I)$ to refer to the agents mentioned in I.

- *Agent Movement* (A_p^a). A_p^a means "move agent A to place p and perform action a". This expression is the smallest granularity mobility abstraction. It involves one agent, one move and one action at the destination. The underlying mobility mechanisms are hidden. So are the details of the action which may change the agent state or the context in which it is operating at the destination place:

$$a : states(A) \times states(p) \rightarrow states(A) \times states(p)$$

  In our agent model, each action is a method call of the class implementing A. The implementation must check that a is indeed implemented in A.
  $\mathbf{0}$ represents, for any agent A, the empty itinerary A_{here}^{id}, where the agent performs the identity operation $id \in \mathbf{O}$ on the state at its current place *here*.
- *Parallel Composition* ("$\parallel$"). Two expressions composed by "$\parallel$" are executed in parallel. For instance, $(A_p^a \parallel B_q^b)$ means that agents A and B are executed

concurrently. Parallelism may imply cloning of agents. For instance, to execute the expression $(A_p^a \parallel A_q^b)$, where $p \neq q$, cloning is needed since agent A has to perform actions at both p and q in parallel. In the case where $p = q$, the agents are cloned as if $p \neq q$. In general, given an itinerary $(I \parallel J)$ the agents in $agents(I) \cap agents(J)$ are cloned and although having the same name are different agents.

- *Sequential Composition ("·").* Two expressions composed by the operator "·" are executed sequentially. For example, $(A_p^a \cdot A_q^b)$ means move agent A to place p to perform action a and then to place q to perform action b. Sequential composition is used when order of execution matters. In the example, state changes to the agent from performing a at p must take place before the agent goes to q.
  Sequential composition imposes synchronization among agents. For example, in the expression $(A_p^a \parallel B_q^b) \cdot C_r^c$ the composite action $(A_p^a \parallel B_q^b)$ must complete before C_r^c starts. Implementation of such synchronization requires message-passing between agents at different places or shared memory.
  When cloning has occurred, sequential composition performs decloning, i.e. clones are combined using an associated application-specific operator (denoted by $\oplus$ as mentioned earlier). For example, given the expression $(A_s^d \parallel A_t^e) \cdot A_u^f$ and suppose that after the parallel operation, the configuration has clones. Then, decloning is carried out before continuing with A_u^f.
- *Independent Nondeterminism ("|").* An itinerary of the form $(I \mid J)$ is used to express nondeterministic choice: "I don't care which but perform one of I or J". If $agents(I) \cap agents(J) \neq \emptyset$, no clones are assumed, i.e. I and J are treated independently. It is an implementation decision whether to perform both actions concurrently terminating when either one succeeds (which might involve cloning but clones are destroyed once a result is obtained), or trying one at a time (in which case order may matter).
- *Conditional Nondeterminism (":").* Independent nondeterminism does not specify any dependencies between its alternatives. We introduce conditional nondeterminism which is similar to short-circuit evaluation of boolean expressions in programming languages such as C.
  We first introduce *status flag* and *global state function.* A status flag is part of the agent's (say, A's) state, written as $A.status$. Being part of the state, $A.status$ is affected by an agent's actions. $A.status$ might be changed by the agent as it performs actions at different places. A global state function Π need not be defined in terms of status flags but it is useful to do so. For example, we can define Π as the conjunction of the status flags of agents in a set Σ: $\Pi(\Sigma) = \bigwedge_{A \in \Sigma} A.status$. We can view Π as producing a global status flag. From the implementation viewpoint, agents in Σ must communicate to compute Π.
  An itinerary of the form $I :_\Pi J$ means first perform I, and then evaluate Π on the state of the agents. If Π evaluates to true, then the itinerary is completed. If Π evaluates to false, the itinerary J is performed (i.e., in effect, we perform $I \cdot J$).

The semantics of conditional nondeterminism depends on some given Π, expressed by writing "$:_\Pi$".

We next provide three example itineraries, the first two of which we view as ad-hoc workflows and the third, a workflow which crosses organizational boundaries.

2.2 Three Examples

Voting. An agent v, starting from home, carries a list of candidates from host to host visiting each voting party. Once each party has voted, the agent goes home to tabulate results (assuming that home provides the resources and details about how to tabulate), and then announces the results to all voters in parallel (and cloning itself as it does so). Assuming four voters (at places p, q, r and s), *vote* is an action accepting a vote (e.g., by displaying a graphical user interface), *tabulate* is the action of tabulating results, and *announce* is the action of displaying results, the mobility behaviour is as follows:

$$v_p^{vote} \cdot v_q^{vote} \cdot v_r^{vote} \cdot v_s^{vote} \cdot v_h^{tabulate} \cdot (v_p^{announce} \parallel v_q^{announce} \parallel v_r^{announce} \parallel v_s^{announce})$$

Note that we leave out brackets due to the associativity of the binary operators.

It is possible to combine the itineraries of different agents (representing different workflows) to form an itinerary expression (an integrated workflow). For example, suppose a different agent w is used to announce the voting results. Then we combine their behaviour as follows:

$$v_p^{vote} \cdot v_q^{vote} \cdot v_r^{vote} \cdot v_s^{vote} \cdot v_h^{tabulate} \cdot (w_p^{announce} \parallel w_q^{announce} \parallel w_r^{announce} \parallel w_s^{announce})$$

Meeting Scheduling. We use a two phase process for demonstration purposes:

1. Starting from home, the meeting initiator sends an agent which goes from one participant to another with a list of nominated times. As each participant marks the times they are not available, the list of nominated times held by the agent shortens as the agent travels from place to place. After visiting all places in its itinerary, the agent returns home.
2. At home, the meeting initiator selects a meeting time from the remaining unmarked times and informs the rest.

With four participants (excluding the initiator), the mobility behaviour for the agent m is given by:

$$m_p^{ask} \cdot m_q^{ask} \cdot m_r^{ask} \cdot m_s^{ask} \cdot m_h^{finalize} \cdot (m_p^{inform} \parallel m_q^{inform} \parallel m_r^{inform} \parallel m_s^{inform})$$

ask is an action which displays unmarked nominated times to a participant and allows a participant to mark times he/she is unavailable. *finalize* allows the meeting initiator to select a meeting time from the remaining unmarked times, and *inform* presents the selected meeting time to a participant.

Note that the expression of mobility is separated from the coding of these three actions. Also, this itinerary is similar in structure to the voting itinerary except for the agent, actions and places. Our itinerary expressions could aid the identification and reuse of patterns in workflow behaviour.

Sales Order Processing. We consider a scenario adapted from Papaioannou and Edwards [19] for processing sales orders in a virtual enterprise. Each sales order is carried out by a mobile agent which moves through several entities to process the order. We first name the entities. Let *us_sc* be a place where the agent can interact with the US stock control, *asia_sc* be a place where the agent can interact with the Asian stock control, *mat* be a place where the agent can purchase raw materials for manufacturing the products requested in a sales order, *man* be the place where the agent can place an order for products to be manufactured (i.e., *man* represents the manufacturer), and *ext* be a place where the agent can interact with an external buyer. Also, let *query* be an action where the agent queries a stock control, *report* be an action where the agent reports the results of a completed sales order, *buy_raw* be the action of purchasing raw materials, *buy_prod* be the action of buying products for a sales order, and *order* be an action of placing an order to have some products manufactured.

The business logic for processing a sales order is as follows. The agent first receives an order while at home. Then, one of the following takes place.

1. The agent checks with the US stock control to see if the requested products are available. If so, the agent returns home reporting this. We can represent this behaviour as $A_{us\_sc}^{query} \cdot A_h^{report}$.
2. Otherwise, the agent checks with the Asian stock control, and if the requested products are available, reports this at home. This behaviour is captured by $A_{asia\_sc}^{query} \cdot A_h^{report}$.
3. If the Asian stock control does not have the products available, the agent purchases raw materials for manufacturing the product and places an order for the product with the manufacturer. Thereafter, the agent reports what it has done at home. We write this behaviour as $A_{mat}^{buy\_raw} \cdot A_{man}^{order} \cdot A_h^{report}$.
4. Alternatively, if the agent cannot fulfill (3), for example, the raw materials are too expensive. The agent buys the products from an external buyer and reports this: $A_{ext}^{buy\_prod} \cdot A_h^{report}$.

In essence, there are four ways to process a sales order and we just want to perform one of them (each in the sense described above). We can capture the essence of the business logic as follows:

$$
\begin{aligned}
&(A_{us\_sc}^{query} \cdot A_h^{report}) \mid (A_{asia\_sc}^{query} \cdot A_h^{report}) \mid (A_{mat}^{buy\_raw} \cdot A_{man}^{order} \cdot A_h^{report}) \mid \\
&(A_{ext}^{buy\_prod} \cdot A_h^{report}) \\
= &(A_{us\_sc}^{query} \mid A_{asia\_sc}^{query} \mid (A_{mat}^{buy\_raw} \cdot A_{man}^{order}) \mid A_{ext}^{buy\_prod}) \cdot A_h^{report} \\
&\text{(by distribution of } \cdot \text{ over } \mid)
\end{aligned}
$$

However, the above itinerary does not model the fact that the four ways of processing a sales order are tried sequentially and the next way is used only when one way has "failed" (e.g., if the product is not in stock, then get it manufactured).

Using conditional nondeterminism, we can define the sales order agent's behaviour (and the business logic) more precisely as follows:

$$(A^{query}_{us\_sc} :_{\Pi} A^{query}_{asia\_sc} :_{\Pi} (A^{buy\_raw}_{mat} \cdot A^{order}_{man}) :_{\Pi} A^{buy\_prod}_{ext}) \cdot A^{report}_{h}$$

The operator is non-deterministic in the sense that the resulting configuration depends on the evaluation of Π. For example, assuming we use the definition of Π given earlier which is in terms of status flags, if no stock is available at us_sc, then, $A.status$ would be set to false. Note that it is left to actions of A to properly set $A.status$ to reflect the intended purpose of the application.

2.3 Discussion

Expressiveness. Formalisms for specifying workflows include workflow graphs [20], and Concurrent Transaction Logic with rule-based constraints. The concepts of sequence, alternative, concurrency, and synchronization in Sadiq and Orlowska [20] are present in our algebra. But our algebra also utilises concepts such as places (or locations) and cloning to model agent behaviour. We also have conditional workflows in the form of the conditional nondeterminism operator. The concept of iteration is present in an extension of our algebra in Loke *et al* [18] but it only allows a limited form of iteration: an agent performing the same action over an enumerated set of places. We do not have sub-itineraries (or sub-workflows) but our algebra is already inherently compositional. Modelling of compensation actions (in case of failure), and constraints as present in workflow specifications need to be included in our itineraries in order that our itineraries be used to not only program the behaviour of agents enacting workflows but also as (enriched) specifications of the workflows themselves. For example, let I and J be two itineraries. Then, a compensation action can be represented by:

J `compensates for` I on condition C

Suppose that $I = a^{update}_{db1} \cdot a^{update}_{db2}$, and I has completed (i.e. two databases have been updated). However, if on evaluation of C, it was found that I should not have been executed, then a (compensatory) itinerary $J = a^{report}_{dba1} \cdot a^{report}_{dba2}$ is executed (in this case to report to the database administrators what had happened). It is difficult to define C formally - C might be the output of a computer program which is executed after I has completed or based entirely on human considerations.

Our formal approach enables verification of properties and conformance to constraints, and well-defined combination of workflows.

Note that our notion of itineraries might appear static and inflexible, and does not allow expression of dynamic changes. However, the itinerary serves as an agent's mobility (sub-) plan and the agent need not be tied to an itinerary. For example, an agent could utilise a library of itineraries or change its itinerary.

An agent unable to execute its itinerary could suspend itself, uptake a different itinerary from the control center, and then resume. Itineraries could be interleaved with "check points" where the agent reports to the control center. Also, a small meta-itinerary language can be defined to express how one itinerary relates to another, of which the above compensation statement is one example. Another example is: on event E, perform I, where an agent performs different itineraries in responding to events. But this involves a more complex internal agent model and will not be discussed further in this paper.

Usage of Itineraries. One can directly program mobile agent based workflows in a high-level of abstraction as itineraries as we illustrated above. These itineraries augmented with details of tasks and places can then be translated into code of an underlying agent system and executed. Execution is then managed by the agent control center. Further work is needed to define such a translation.

In [21], we have also shown that itineraries can be mapped onto particular Workflow Petri Nets. This is particularly useful when the agents are used in inter-organizational workflows to synchronize the execution of a number of workflows in several organizations. Each organization's internal workflow is represented as a Workflow Net. This collection of Workflow Nets and the agent's itinerary expressed as a Workflow Net can be combined into one inter-organizational Workflow Net and analyzed together.

3 Mobile Agent Control for Workflow Management

The FIPA specification for agent management [22] describes an agent lifecycle and primitive commands on agents including create, invoke, destroy, suspend, resume, move and execute. We can create an agent control center for workflow management based on agent management ideas. To support the user throughout the agent lifecycle (or workflow lifecycle), the control center has eight components:

Agent creator/editor: this component lets users specify workflows and program the agents (and their itineraries) implementing the workflows. Programming of itineraries would be aided by a directory of places and the resources available at each place.

Agent store: this component permits storage of created agents and of partially executed agents (with state). The latter is useful for supporting long term workflows (e.g., book orders where an order is made but the workflow - and its associated agent - is suspended until the book arrives), and for agents waiting to be uploaded to mobile devices.

Component server: agent components are stored here (including itineraries) and could be dynamically uploaded by agents during run-time. We introduce the idea of *kernel agents* which encapsulates minimal functionality but uptake components when needed and drop unneeded components. We anticipate the size of agents to be important when a myriad of workflow agents are injected into the network.

Helper agents: Static helper agents run within the control center with which mobile agents could consult regarding decision-making (e.g., cost-efficiency computations to evaluate which site to go to perform a task) and exception handling.

Knowledge base of exception handling rules: these rules could be consulted by helper agents for advising the mobile agents or be loaded into the mobile agents at start-time. The rules might specify "set-plays" to capture agent behaviour for commonly occurring faults.

Agent scheduler: this component schedules the execution of agents. In order to avoid network congestion and overload at places, only a limited number of agents (e.g., the agent pool present in the Autopilot system [11]) might be used at any one time. The scheduler might also collect two or more similar workflows (e.g., with the same itinerary) for execution by one agent.

Run-time controller: this provides an interface for users to send commands to running agents. The commands should include the primitive ones mentioned above and application-specific ones (e.g., to add certain components to agents).

Event notification system: a publish/subscribe event notification service [23] is used for inter-agent communication. We route all messages between agents via the control center, permitting overriding at the control center and monitoring (and logging) of agent messaging.

4 Conclusion

Towards mobile agent based workflow, we have presented an algebra of itineraries which we view as executable workflow specifications. We have also presented a FIPA approach to a mobile agent control center to manage agents enacting workflows, and mentioned several avenues for further investigation (in §2.3).

Other work on mobile agent research can be integrated for building flexible and robust mobile agent based workflow systems. For example, the use of mobile agents for computation with mobile workers as mentioned in the introduction, system robustness based on mobile agent fault-tolerance [24], and transactional workflows with agents [25,16].

Having stated the potential benefits of mobility of agents for distributed workflow, a mix of static and mobile agents in a system might turn out to be the ideal in utility, performance and cost. Indeed, many existing workflow systems are client-server and might need to be "wrapped" by agents to interface with systems in other organizations or to interface with mobile agents synchronizing their workflow with the workflow in other organizations. Enterprise modelling [26] might also be useful to map out agent places.

Acknowledgements. The work reported in this paper has been funded in part by the Co-operative Research Centre Program through the Department of Industry, Science & Tourism of the Commonwealth Government of Australia.

References

1. *"Towards Adaptive Workflow Systems" Workshop at the Conference on Computer-Supported Cooperative Work* (1998) Online proceedings at <http://ccs.mit.edu/klein/cscw98/>.
2. Jennings, N.R., Faratin, P., Norman, T.J., O'Brien, P., Odgers, B.: Autonomous Agents for Business Process Management. Journal of Applied Artificial Intelligence (1999) Available at <ftp://ftp.elec.qmw.ac.uk/pub/isag/distributed-ai/publications/aaij991.ps.gz>.
3. Shepherdson, J.W., Thompson, S.G., Odgers, B.R.: Cross-Organizational Workflow Co-ordinated by Software Agents. In: Proceedings of the Workshop on Cross-Organisational Workflow Management and Co-ordination (1999) Available at <http://www.zurich.ibm.com/~hlu/WACCworkshop/papers/Shepherdson/waccWSPosition_1.html>.
4. Papastavrou, S., Samaras, G., Pitoura, E.: Mobile Agents for WWW Distributed Database Access. In: Proceedings of the 15th International Conference on Data Engineering, Sydney, Australia (1999) Available at <http://ada.cs.ucy.ac.cy/~cssamara/DBMS-Agents/Paper/papastavrous.ps>.
5. Chrysanthis, P.K., Znati, T.F., Banerjee, S., Chang, S.K.: Establishing Virtual Enterprises by Means of Mobile Agents. In: Proceedings of the Research Issues in Data Engineering Workshop, Sydney, Australia (1999) Available at <ftp://ftp.cs.pitt.edu/panos/MDBS/ride_99.ps.gz>.
6. Yan, Y., Kuphal, T., Bode, J.: Applications of Multiagent Systems in Project Management. In: Proceedings of the 2nd International Conference on Autonomous Agents (1998) Available at <ftp://fireflow.com/Agent98.zip>.
7. Gray, R.S., Kotz, D., Nog, S., Rus, D., Cybenko, G.: Mobile Agents for Mobile Computing. Technical Report TR96-285, Department of Computer Science, Dartmouth College (1996) Available at <ftp://ftp.cs.dartmouth.edu/TR/TR96-285.ps.Z>.
8. Kovacs, E., Rohrle, K., Reich, M.: Integrating Mobile Agents into the Mobile Middleware. In: Proceedings of the 2nd International Workshop on Mobile Agents (MA'98). Lecture Notes in Computer Science, Vol. 1477. Springer-Verlag, Berlin Heidelberg New York (1998) 124–135
9. Magedanz, T.: ACTS CLIMATE: An Overview. AgentLink News **2** (1999) 9–12 Available at <http://www.agentlink.org/newsletter/2/>.
10. Merz, M., Liberman, B., Lamersdorf, W.: Using Mobile Agents to Support Interorganizational Workflow Management. Applied Artificial Intelligence **11**(6) (1997) 551–572
11. Foster, S.S., Moore, D., Nebesh, B.A., Flester, M.J.: Control and Management in a Mobile Agent Workflow Architecture. In: Proceedings of the 3rd International Conference on Autonomous Agents, Seattle, U.S.A. (1999)
12. Cai, T., Gloor, P.A., Nog, S.: DartFlow: A Workflow Management System on the Web Using Transportable Agents. Technical Report PCS-TR96-283, Department of Computer Science, Dartmouth College (1996) Available at <ftp://ftp.cs.dartmouth.edu/TR/TR96-283.ps.Z>.
13. Dossick, S.E., Kaiser, G.E.: Worklets for Adaptive Workflow. In: Proceedings of the "Towards Adaptive Workflow Systems" Workshop at the Conference on Computer-Supported Cooperative Work (1998) Available at <http://ccs.mit.edu/klein/cscw98/paper13/>.

14. Cui G., White, G.M.: Experiments with Mobile Agents and Distributed Workflow Systems. In: Proceedings of the 1st International Workshop on Mobile Agents for Telecommunication Applications (MATA'99) (1999)
15. Brugali, D., Menga, G., Galarraga, S.: Inter-Company Supply Chain Integration via Mobile Agents. In: The Globalization of Manufacturing in the Digital Communications Era of the 21st Century: Innovation, Agility and the Virtual Enterprise. Kluwer Academic Pub. (1999) Available at <http://www.cim.polito.it/Articles/Art-Agents/98PROLAMAT.ps>.
16. Cichocki, A., Rusinkiewicz, M.: Providing Transactional Properties for Migrating Workflows. In: Proceedings of the Workshop on Cross-Organisational Workflow Management and Co-ordination at DEXA'99, Florence, Italy (1999) 90–94
17. Meng, J., Helal, S., Su, S.: An Ad-Hoc Workflow System Architecture Based on Mobile Agents and Rule-Based Processing. In: Proceedings of the International Conference on Artificial Intelligence, Las Vegas, Nevada, U.S.A. (2000) 245–251
18. Loke, S.W., Schmidt, H., Zaslavsky, A.: Programming the Mobility Behaviour of Agents by Composing Itineraries. In: Thiagarajan, P.S., Yap, R. (eds.): Proceedings of the 5th Asian Computing Science Conference (ASIAN'99). Lecture Notes in Computer Science, Vol. 1742. Springer-Verlag, Berlin Heidelberg New York (1999) 214–226
19. Papaioannou, T., Edwards, J.: Manufacturing System Performance and Agility: Can Mobile Agents Help? Special Issue of Integrated Computer-Aided Engineering (1999) Available at <http://luckyspc.lboro.ac.uk/Docs/Papers/Icae98.pdf>.
20. Sadiq, W., Orlowska, M.E.: Modeling and Verification of Workflow Graphs. Technical Report 386, Department of Computer Science, The University of Queensland, Brisbane, Australia (1996)
21. Loke, S.W., Ling, S.: Mobile Agent Itineraries and Workflow Nets for Analysis and Enactment of Distributed Business Processes. In: Proceedings of the International ICSC Symposium on Multi-Agents and Mobile Agents in Virtual Organizations and E-Commerce (2000) (to appear)
22. FIPA - Foundation for Intelligent Physical Agents. FIPA 98 Specification (Part 1) - Agent Management (1998)
23. Segall, B., Arnold, D.: Elvin has Left the Building: a Publish/subscribe Notification Service with Quenching. In: Proceedings of AUUG97, Brisbane, Australia (1997) Available at <http://www.dstc.edu.au/Elvin/doc/papers/auug97/AUUG97.html>.
24. Strasser, M., Rothermel, K.: Reliability Concepts for Mobile Agents. International Journal of Cooperative Information Systems **7**(4) (1998) 355–382 Available at <http://www.informatik.uni-stuttgart.de/ipvr/vs/Publications/ Publications. html#1998-strasser-02>.
25. Buchmann, A., Vogler, H.: Using Multiple Mobile Agents for Distributed Transactions. In: Proceedings of the 3rd IFCIS Conference on Cooperative Information Systems (CoopIS'98), New York, U.S.A. (1998) Available at <http://www.ito.tu-darmstadt.de/publs/papers/coopis98.ps.gz>.
26. Lupu, E., Milosevic, Z., Sloman, M.: Use of Roles and Policies for Specifying, Building and Managing Virtual Enterprises. In: RIDE'99 Workshop, Sydney, Australia (1999) Available at <http://www.dstc.edu.au/AU/staff/zoran/papers/DSTC-IC.ps>.

Enterprise Federation and Its Multi-agent Modelization

Huaglory Tianfield

School of Multimedia and Computing, Gloucestershire Business School
Cheltenham & Gloucester College of H. E., P O Box 220, The Park
Cheltenham, GL 50 2QF, England, UK
htianfield@chelt.ac.uk

Abstract. Federation is a self-organizing mechanism of socio-economic systems. Enterprise federation is an agile and self-organizing network of partner enterprises, which is capable of unifying two opposite ends in current societies and technologies, i.e. more and more complex product developments versus more and more specialized and miniaturized enterprises. This chapter makes thorough investigation into life-cycle organization of enterprise federation. First, a distinctive taxonomy of enterprise partnerships is presented. Then, concept and metrics of enterprise federation are put forward. Third, blueprints for creation, configuration, operation and dissolution of enterprise federation are specified. Fourth, multi-agent modelization is explored for enterprise federation. Fifth, case studies are presented based on global trends in trades and businesses to illustrate practices of enterprise federation. Finally, features of enterprise federation are summarized.

1 Introduction

In current societies and technologies, competitions in resources, competence, markets, etc. have become extremely severe. To win against competitions under such circumstances, specialized and miniaturized enterprises, limited in resources, competence, markets, etc., can survive and better operate, only if they come together to ally one another. At the same time, alliance among partner enterprises, i.e. enterprise partnership, is the most effective way of business doing in current information and globalized societies.

Enterprise partnerships raise new topics such as enterprise integration and enterprise federation. Recently many novel concepts have been put forward [1] [2] [3] [4], e.g.

- Virtual enterprises [5] [6] [7];
- Extended enterprises;
- Global enterprises;
- Agile enterprises [8];
- Network of (partner) enterprises;
- Project consortiums.

However, fundamentals of enterprise integration and enterprise federation have not well addressed. This chapter will investigate enterprise federation in both horizontal and vertical directions.

J. Liu and Y. Ye (Eds.): E-Commerce Agents, LNAI 2033, pp. 295-322, 2001.

2 Enterprise Partnerships

2.1 Product Development

Product life cycle refers to the whole life of a product from its birth to the end of its use, i.e. the whole progression along different stages experienced by a product from the raise of requirement to the end of use, or even to the reuse/recycling after use, as depicted in Fig. 1.

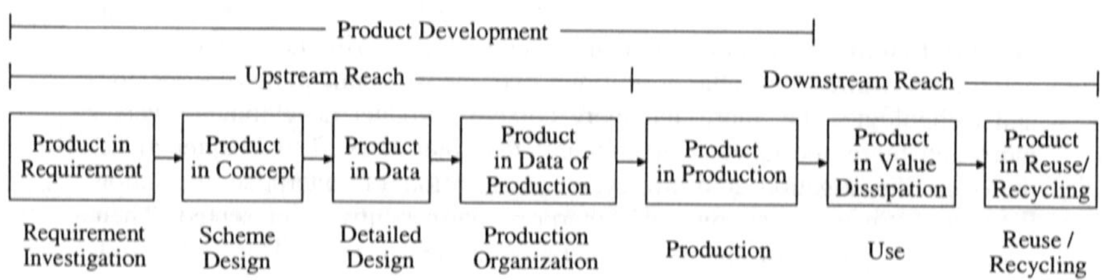

Fig. 1. Product life cycle

The range from requirement investigation to production organization is figuratively called the upstream reach of product life cycle, while from production to reuse/recycling the downstream reach. Shorter than the whole product life cycle, product development refers to the range of product life cycle from the raise of requirement to the completion of production, i.e. before the start of use.

Much beyond product life cycle, "processes related with product development" is a concept of broader sense. In fact, processes related with product development have three categories, as illustrated below: Upstream and downstream life-cycle stages, and the processes that are throughout all life-cycle stages and of great significance to product development, called life-cycle-through processes.

(1) Upstream life-cycle stages

- Requirement investigation
- R&D, scheme & detailed product design
- Production organization: production process planning (P^3) and production resource planning

(2) Downstream life-cycle stages

- Material acquisition, transport, inventory and supply
- Production preparation: tools, devices, machines and equipment
- Production: manufacturing, assembling and integration
- Test/examination, packaging, stock, delivery and installation
- Use and maintenance

Discard, reuse and recycling [9] [10] [11] [12]

(3) Life-cycle-through processes

- Quality and reliability
- Cost (consumption of resources) and value engineering
- Labors, human factors and safety
- Logistics

- Energy (electricity, gas, water, etc.)
- Funds (aggregation, input, deposit and circulation)
- Environmental protection
- etc.

For the convenience of statement, all processes related with product development are re-grouped into two general categories: Information-processing dominated processes and physical-resource-consumption dominated implementations. The former contain upstream life-cycle stages, planning for downstream life-cycle stages, and planning for life-cycle-through processes, while the latter contain downstream life-cycle stages, and implementations of life-cycle-through processes.

Criteria of product development are:

(1) Complete function and highest quality of product (maximum satisfaction to user requirements, utility, reliability, safety, etc.);
(2) Feasible schedule and shortest period of product development;
(3) High organizational and working efficiency, specifically

- consistency of team work, inter-stage information interchangeability, inter-stage transferability of the work done at early life-cycle stages to late life-cycle stages, particularly between upstream and downstream reaches of product life cycle,
- elimination of repeating at late stage the work that had been allocated to and actually done at early stage and thus making a detour of work from late stage to early stage. Here, "early" means information-processing dominated, and "late" means physical-resource-consumption dominated,
- success on (nearly) one time of physical-resource-consumption dominated implementations,
- adaptability to and resolvability of late and difficult-to-identify user requirement;

(4) Effective allocation and utilization of both physical and intangible resources;
(5) Robustness and agility over outside unpredictable uncertainties and changes;
(6) Creation of new jobs in organization.

2.2 Enterprise Engineering

An enterprise is an entity that is independent physically, organizationally, managerially, operationally, economically and culturally. The mission of an enterprise is to perform all or part of processes related with product development to meet market demands.

Enterprise resources refer to all of an enterprise, from physical resources: materials, parts, tools, machines, equipment, layouts of machines, technological processes, infrastructures, simple labors, funds, and energy (electricity, gas, water, etc.); to intangible resources: intellectual labors, organization of labors and routine businesses, information, management, operation, economy, legislation, and culture, and so forth.

Enterprise engineering is to realize product development by use of enterprise resources. It is about creation, configuration, operation and dissolution of enterprise.

Enterprise engineering has two strategic modes: non-partnership and partnership. While the former is concerned with single enterprise, the latter with multiple enterprises.

Schema of non-partnership enterprise engineering can be presented as follows.

- Creation and configuration of enterprise;
- Enterprise organization;
- Enterprise (e.g. finance, information, human resource, quality, energy, technology) management;
- Enterprise operation;
- Enterprise decision-making;
- Enterprise strategies, planning and targets;
- Enterprise legislation, culture;
- Entrepreneurship.

Schema of partnership enterprise engineering can be presented as follows.

- Enterprise integration [13];
- Information integration [14];
- Enterprise federation;
- Federated data interchange;
- Federated data management;
- Business doing;
- Business process cooperativity across enterprises;
- Cultural & legislative compatibility across enterprises.

2.3 Partnership Versus Non-partnership

Traditionally, processes related with product development are performed within one enterprise. Product development is realized by use of resources of one enterprise, as depicted in Fig. 2.

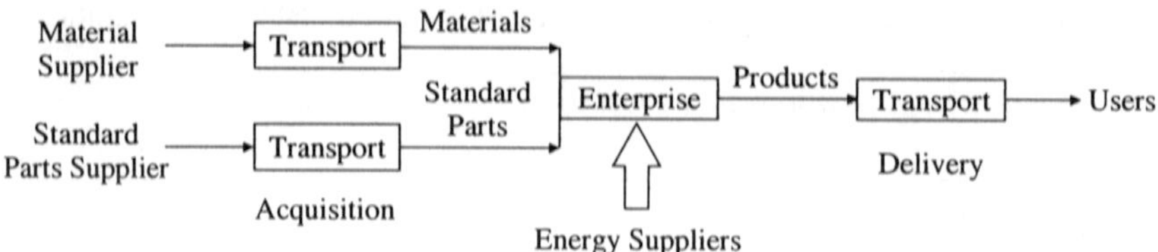

Fig. 2. Non-partnership enterprise engineering of product development

However, situation changes in current societies and technologies. Processes related with product development are or have to be performed across a group of partner enterprises. Product development is realized by use of resources of a group of partner enterprises, as depicted in Fig. 3.

Literally, there is no mode of enterprise engineering of product development that is strictly non-partnership. Even very traditionally, an enterprise always primarily needs involving outside, i.e. suppliers of materials, standard parts, tools, machines, energy and transports, as depicted in Fig. 4.

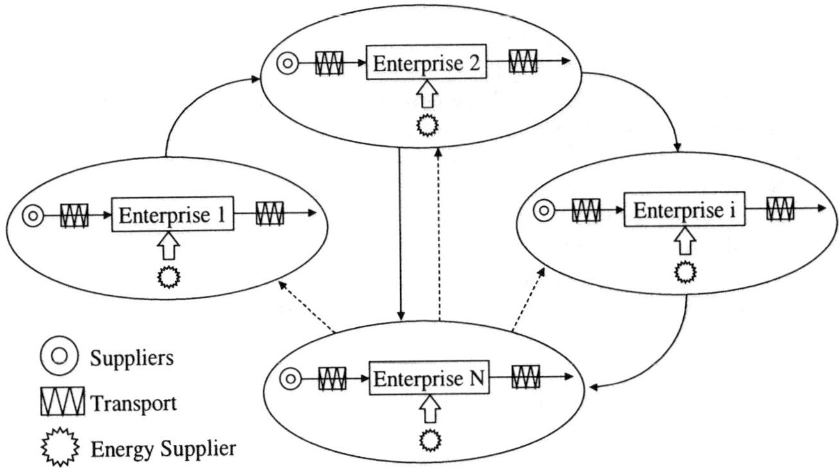

Fig. 3. Partnership enterprise engineering of product development

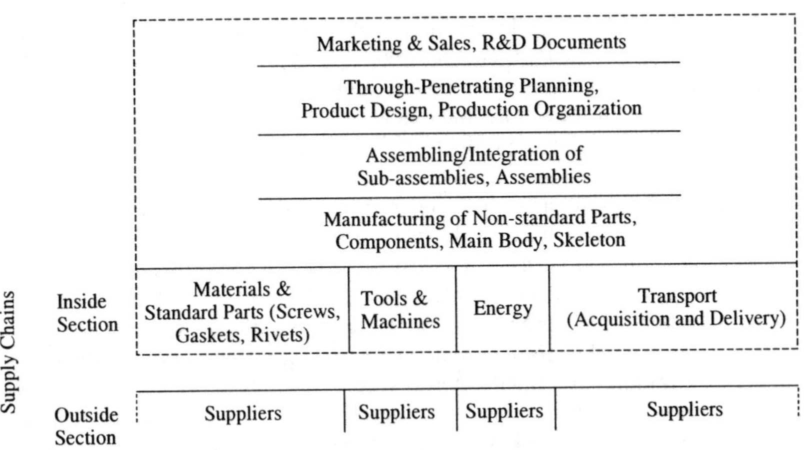

Fig. 4. An enterprise always primarily needs involving suppliers

However, an enterprise and its suppliers are not considered to form partnership enterprise engineering. What suppliers perform are only viewed as pseudo processes of product development.

Non-partnership enterprise engineering is relatively easier than partnership one, because the latter has to overcome difficulties brought forth by diverse variety of enterprise resources.

Facing instantaneously changing markets, non-partnership enterprise engineering may encounter problems. For instance, once bankrupt, non-partnership enterprise engineering has serious consequences, such as re-allocation of employees and re-orientation to new markets. Features of non-partnership enterprise engineering are:

- Relatively fixed;
- Huge and stiff organization;
- Big resistance to innovations;
- Ponderous reactivity to market changes;
- Big risk, centralized within one enterprise.

Comparatively, features of partnership enterprise engineering are:

- Network composed of a group of miniaturized enterprises;
- Agile organization;
- Rapid re-orientation to new markets;
- Timely reactivity to market changes;
- Reduced risk, decentralized among partner enterprises.

2.4 Motivations to Enterprise Partnerships

In current societies and technologies, below situations become increasingly prominent:

- entrepreneurial variety, specialization, miniaturization of enterprises;
- regional/global unbalances in resources, competence, markets, etc.;
- complex user requirements, hard delivery date, life-long after-sale supports (upgrading), and high degree of alliance required by large-scale products.

All of these make market competitions become extremely severe. Therefore, enterprise partnerships find following motivations:

- to exploit new potentials, new needs, essentially new markets, for both well-established products and explorative products. For example, well-established products are expanded into new regions, or existing products of partner enterprises are integrated into new products;
- to minimize risks, to decrease costs, and to shorten time to market. For example, it is faster and less risky to develop new large-scale products by allying existing enterprises than by establishing enterprises from scratches, or production is located in proximity of markets;
- to mutually complement in resources, competence, markets, etc. For example, dispersed enterprise resources are made to perform collective effects. Such complements in resources, competence, markets, etc. may not be outstanding locally or regionally, but is significant globally, since global unbalances exist badly.

Organization of enterprise partnership is to discover new market opportunities. However, it mostly can not win a bid if an enterprise partnership is not created and configured until a market opportunity already emerges to call for tenders. Any enterprise partnership has its life cycle, from creation to configuration and from operation to dissolution. Creation and configuration of an enterprise partnership take some time. While enterprise partnerships are not well created and configured, it is too late and hasty to catch newly emerging market opportunities. Market opportunities only await enterprise partnerships that are well-established, either fixed or evolving.

2.5 Enterprise Federation Versus Enterprise Integration

Enterprise partnerships can be classified as product-homogenous and product-heterogeneous ones. Enterprise partnership is product-homogenous if partner enterprises produce or are interested in homogenous kinds of products. Otherwise, enterprise partnership is product-heterogeneous if partner enterprises produce or are interested in heterogeneous kinds of products. Sometimes, product-homogenous and product-heterogeneous partnerships co-exist with one another.

Product-homogenous partnership is for quantity and variety of one kind of products, say to occupy markets overwhelmingly by monopolizing one kind of products. Common product-homogenous partnerships are investment-type, i.e. joint ventures, e.g.

- Capital/stock investment;
- Labor investment;
- R&D/design investment
- Technology (machine/equipment/production line/workshop) investment;
- Managerial investment (management modes inputted or managers immigrated);
- Logo/brand investment.

Product-heterogeneous partnership mainly aims at complex product developments, say to monopolize the latitude of markets by broad kinds of products. Product-heterogeneous partnerships further distinguish two different types: integration type partnerships and federation type partnership.

Integration type partnership is close and relatively fixed alliance among partner enterprises. It typically takes the form of trust, group corporate, etc. For instance, while its partner enterprises can remain independent to some extent, a group corporate is an enterprise, and there is a headquarters in the group corporate to issue commands to component enterprises.

On the contrary, federation type partnership is relatively loose alliance and temporary project consortium among partner enterprises, and is evolving, only existing over one or several projects, depending on market situations, never fixed.

The core of enterprise integration is information integration. Modern communication technologies and computer technologies have offered sufficient preparations and prerequisites for information integration in enterprises. Information integration becomes more difficult and important if processes related with product development, performed by the partner enterprises under integration, are regionally/globally dispersed. Literature [14] puts forward a hierarchy of information integration underpinning enterprise integration, as shown in Fig. 5.

Enterprise integration has below advantages:

- Better conventions, comprehensibility, and protocols among partner enterprises;
- Easier to set up through-penetration plans;
- Better segmentation and dispatch of tasks;
- In its marketing scope, enterprise integration is immediate to convince customers and more certain to win bids.

However, it can be seen that in order to obtain integrity of enterprise operation and management in a reactive and effective way, it is necessary in enterprise integration to build and maintain a large powerful integrated information system. This is costly, not to say the expensive re-engineering within component enterprises incurred by the creation and configuration of enterprise integration.

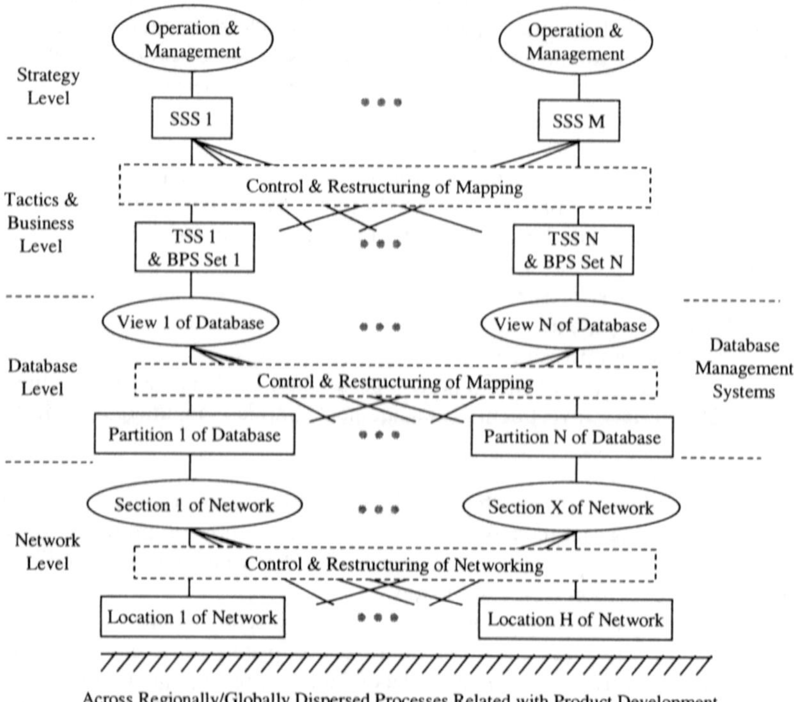

Fig. 5. Hierarchy of information integration underpinning enterprise integration. Legend: Ellipse: logic collection, Rectangle: physical entity, SSS/TSS: strategic/tactic support systems, BPS: business processing systems

In addition, while degree of integration goes up, enterprise integration may suffer form similar problems of non-partnership enterprise engineering.

3 Enterprise Federation

3.1 Concept of Enterprise Federation

Enterprise federation means an alliance where partner enterprises remain independent. Specifically, with the purpose of fulfilling specific projects emerging from markets, independent partner enterprises are federated to form an agile and self-organizing network, which is capable of unifying two opposite ends in current societies and technologies, i.e. more and more complex product developments versus more and more specialized and miniaturized enterprises. Strictly speaking, enterprise federation is not an enterprise already, but a way of business doing.

Prerequisites of enterprise federation are as follows:

- A project can not be fulfilled by any single enterprise;
- There are a group of enterprises, which are product heterogeneous and thus complementary to one another. They have to come together to ally one another, i.e. to form a project consortium, so as to secure and fulfill the project; and
- Partner enterprises remain independent within the project consortium.

None of regional/global geographical dispersal is prerequisite of enterprise federation. Essence of enterprise federation lies not in geographical dispersal, but in independence of partner enterprises.

Nevertheless, since enterprise federation is effective to solving global unbalances in resources, competence, markets, etc., while such partnership enterprise engineering is applied in a global circumstance, it is significant to global developments and prosperity. By taking use of mutual complements in resources, competence and markets, etc. on the globe, enterprise federation can achieve global optimization of partnership enterprise engineering. This can be illustrated by following scenario. It is supposed that there be five regions involved on the globe, as depicted in Fig. 6.

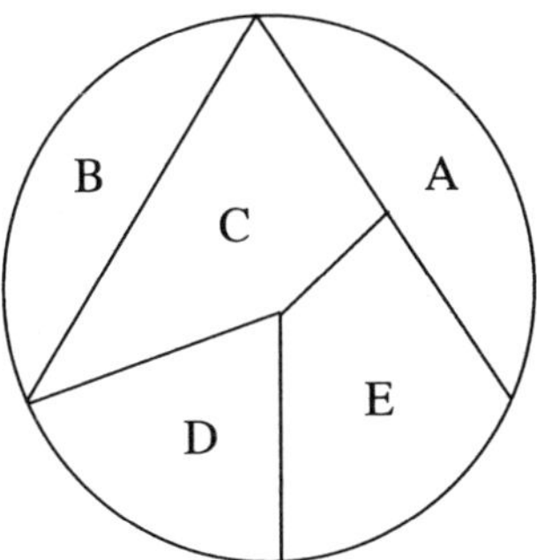

Fig. 6. Regions involved on the globe

An enterprise is good at one or several but not all processes related with product development. Any region has all enterprise resources necessary for a whole product development. However,

Region A: is most competent in through-penetration planning, product design, and production organization;

Region B: possesses cheap cost and labor, so suitable for labor extensive production;

Region C: is in superior proximity of markets;

Region D: is abundant in materials;

Region E: controls marketing and sales.

Therefore, most powerful partner enterprises from Regions A, B, C, D and E, respectively, should and also have to come to form enterprise federation for partnership enterprise engineering of product development. In such a global circumstance, federated data interchange and database management, and transport of components and sub-assemblies have to be considered properly.

3.2 Metrics of Enterprise Federation

Enterprise federation is an alliance in terms of segmentation. Thus, segmentation of processes related with product development can serve as metrics of enterprise federation.

There are two approaches to segmentation of processes related with product development. In the first place, segmentation of processes related with product development can be made along product life cycle dimension. Since product life cycle is a whole, such segmentation immediately reflects complements among partner enterprises.

Literature [15] [16] put forward a novel advanced life-cycle model, named stage-aligned information-substitutive concurrency and detour life-cycle model (SICODEL), for complex product development, as depicted in Fig. 7.

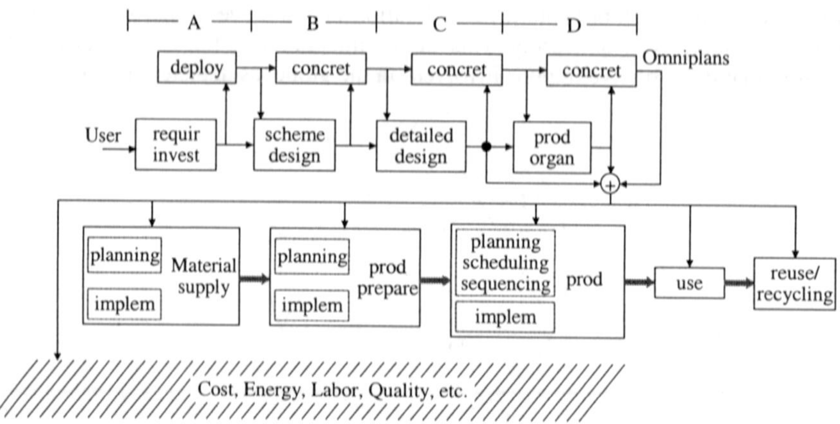

Fig. 7. Stage-aligned information-substitutive concurrency and detour life-cycle model (SICODEL) for complex product development [15] [16]. Abbreviations: concretize: concretization, deploy: deployment, implem: implementation, invest: investigation, organ: organization, prod: production, requir: requirement

The core idea of SICODEL is information-processing dominated design/planning first and physical-resource-consumption dominated implementations at the end. The underpinning means to realize the core idea of SICODEL is information-substitutive concurrency. That is, design/planning of downstream life-cycle stages and life-cycle-through processes proceeds and intertwines concurrently with upstream life-cycle stages. Thus, SICODEL is making an information-substitutive expansion of all processes related with product development, right before the start of physical-resource-consumption dominated implementations.

Specifically, SICODEL realizes the core idea through adding a line of through-penetration planning. So there become three lines:

- Line of through-penetration planning, represented by deployment and respective concretization from coarse granularity to fine granularity aligned with upstream life-cycle stages;
- Line of upstream life-cycle stages;
- Line of physical-resource-consumption dominated implementations.

Therefore, segmentation of processes related with product development can be made between the first two lines and the third line of SICODEL, or among the first two lines and the downstream life-cycle stages on the third line.

Federation can be formed among partner enterprises which perform segments of SICODEL. This can be expressed by below formula.

$$EF ::= (\oplus, \otimes)\ \{MS, PDO, SP, A/I, R/R\} \quad (1)$$

where ⊕, ⊗ are operators denoting "plus" and "federated with", respectively, and ⊕ has higher priority of operation over ⊗. EF: Enterprise Federation, MS: Marketing and Sales (requirement investigation), PDO: through-penetration Planning, product Design, and Production organization; SP: Supply, Production; A/I: product Assembling/Integration; R/R Reuse/Recycling.

Four instances of Equation (1) can be illustrated.

Instance (a), as depicted in Fig. 8(a),

First step (⊕):

None

Second step (⊗):

$$EF = \{MS \otimes PDO \otimes SP \otimes A/I \otimes R/R\} \quad (2)$$

This represents one of the widest ranges of federation. Most of individual processes related with product development, except PDO - through-penetration planning, product design, and production organization, are performed within individual partner enterprises, respectively, which are federated with one another.

Instance (b), as depicted in Fig. 8(b),

First step (⊕):

$(MS \oplus PDO); (SP \oplus A/I)$

Second step (⊗):

$$EF = \{(MS \oplus PDO) \otimes (SP \oplus A/I) \otimes R/R\} \quad (3)$$

Instance (c), as depicted in Fig. 8(c),

First step (⊕):

$(PDO \oplus SP \oplus A/I)$

Second step (⊗):

$$EF = \{MS \otimes (PDO \oplus SP \oplus A/I) \otimes R/R\} \quad (4)$$

Instance (d), as depicted in Fig. 8(d),

First step (⊕):

$(MS \oplus PDO \oplus SP \oplus A/I)$

Second step (⊗):

$$EF = \{(MS \oplus PDO \oplus SP \oplus A/I) \otimes R/R\} \quad (5)$$

This simply represents non-partnership enterprise engineering. All processes related with product development, except reuse/recycling, are performed within one single enterprise.

At a subordinate level, after the first two lines of SICODEL are completed, further segmentation of processes related with product development can be made along product geometry dimension. Specifically, at single downstream life-cycle stage, processes are segmented according to assembling of product. For instance, at production, there may be a number of enterprises which manufacture non-standard parts, components, sub-assemblies and skeleton of a large-scale product (e.g. aircraft, spacecraft, rocket, submarine, ship, galley, automobile, and computer……). Since product geometry is an integrity, i.e. all intermediate products should be able to be assembled into the final product under the overall product geometrical structure, these enterprises are mutually complementary.

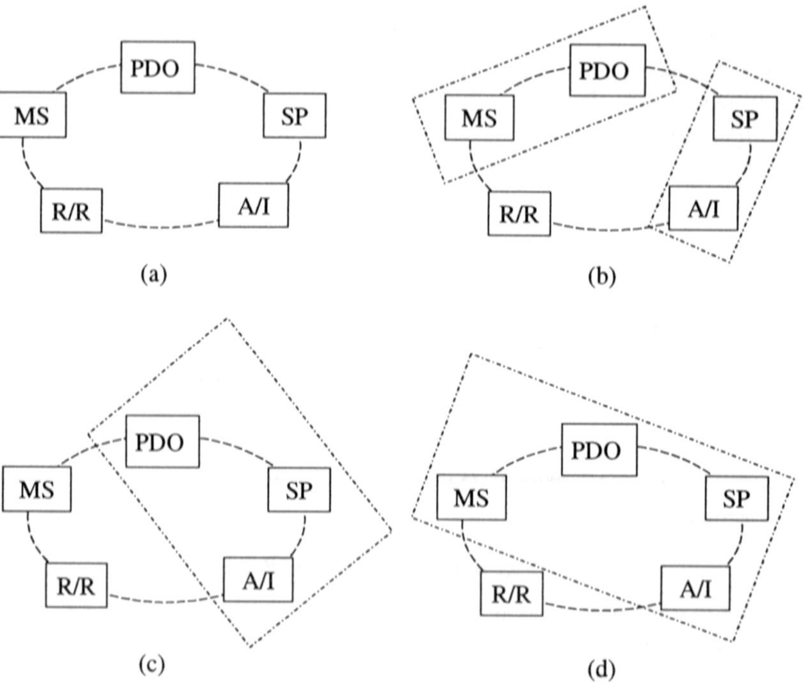

Fig. 8. Four instances of enterprise federation. Abbreviation: EF: Enterprise Federation, MS: Marketing and Sales (requirement investigation), PDO: through-penetration Planning, product Design, and Production organization; SP: Supply, Production; A/I: product Assembling/ Integration; R/R Reuse/Recycling

Therefore, Equation (1) can further become as follows.

$$EF ::= (\oplus, \otimes)\ \{MS, PDO, SP_1, SP_2, \ldots, SP_K, A/I, R/R\} \quad \textbf{(6)}$$

where SP_1, SP_2, …, SP_K represent geometry dimensional segments of a large-scale product into non-standard parts, components, sub-assemblies and skeleton.

Specifically, product assembling/integration has three ways:

- Skeleton-mode: Manufacturers of non-standard parts, components and sub-assemblies send products to manufacturer of skeleton to assemble/integrate;

- Equality-mode: Components and sub-assemblies to be assembled/integrated are almost equal in importance and/or workloads, and product assembling/integration is carried out by manufacturer of one of the components or sub-assemblies; and
- Third-party-mode: Product assembling/integration is carried out by a third party enterprise.

Correspondingly, there are three further types of enterprise federation across product geometry dimensional segments.

Equation (6) represents all combinations of ⊕ and ⊗ over product life cycle and/or geometry dimensional segments of processes related with product development, as illustrated in Fig. 9. Such combinations are market situated.

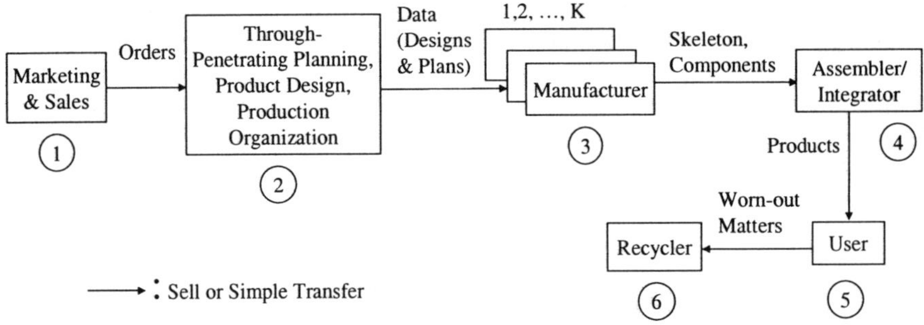

Fig. 9. Combinations of ⊕ and ⊗ over product life cycle and/or geometry dimensional segments of processes related with product development

Enterprise federation across different segments of SICODEL and further across different product geometry dimensional segments has different advantage and can address different emphases of product development. Advantages of enterprise federation result from its duality, i.e. decentralization and moderate alliance. For instance, resulting from decentralization of enterprise federation, federation between production enterprise and product assembler/integrator can take a mode in which product assembling/integration is located in proximity of markets. This alleviates delivery and saves transport cost. At the same time, resulting from moderate alliance of enterprise federation, federation between production enterprise and reuse/recycling enterprise can alleviate negative environmental effects and save materials.

4 Life-Cycle Organization of Enterprise Federation

Enterprise federation is a partnership that is unceasingly dissolved and formed again. It is evolving, never fixed. Therefore, an enterprise federation has a life. Four life-cycle phases can be identified for the organization of enterprise federation, as depicted in Fig. 10.

An initiator is necessary for enterprise federation, which can be acted by one of the below:

$$\text{or}\ \{\text{MS}, (\text{MA} \oplus \text{PDO}), (\text{MA} \oplus \text{skeleton manufacturer}), (\text{MA} \oplus \text{A/I}), \ldots\} \quad (7)$$

$$= MS \oplus (\text{or } \{\phi, \text{PDO, skeleton manufacturer, A/I}, \ldots\})$$

where "or" denotes logic OR and ϕ empty segment. Mostly an initiator is the exploiter and controller of trade and business.

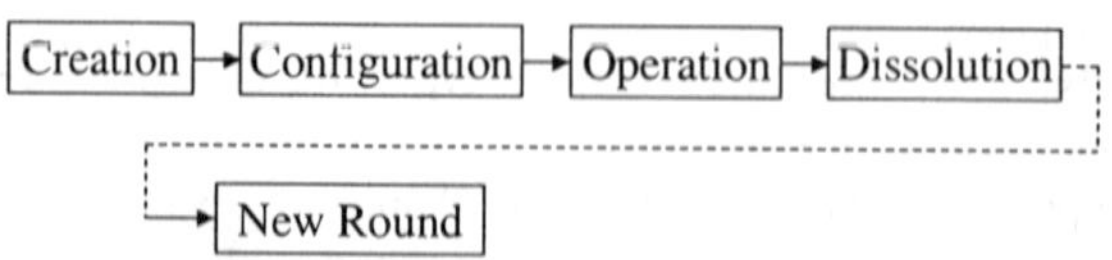

Fig. 10. Life cycle of enterprise federation

Enterprise federation is not only a technical problem, such as federated data interchange, federated database management and federated information systems, but more importantly, a problem of business process cooperativity across partner enterprises and cultural and legislative compatibility. Actually, in vertical direction, organization of enterprise federation involves a hierarchy of levels, as depicted in Fig. 11. That is, each life-cycle phase of enterprise federation further involves the levels of the hierarchy.

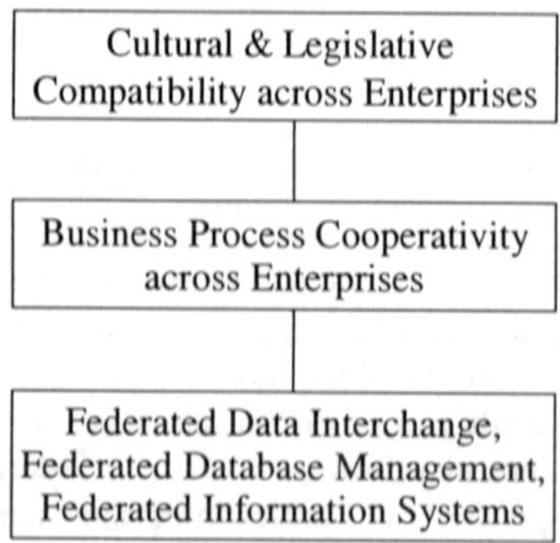

Fig. 11. Levels of enterprise federation

4.1 Creation of Enterprise Federation

Initiator of enterprise federation plays an important role at creation phase. Blueprints of creation phase are as follows:

- Recognition of new potential market opportunities, including range of markets, new products and services;
- Searching, clustering and aggregation of candidates to partner enterprises;
- Evaluation and selection of partner enterprises;
- Coalition, legislation, federation specification;
- Market-mechanism federation;
- Commitment formation, agreements;
- Responsibility segmentation and clarification, task dispatch, profit matching, and contracts;

- Which partner enterprises to perform what quantities of which components or business processes within what time frames;
- Assurance plans of standards, quality, supply, logistics, prices, delivery dates, etc.;
- Liability to risks, low profit or even loss from enterprise federation.

General qualifications of partner enterprises for enterprise federation may be:

- Federation sense, grown from analysis of market situations;
- Willingness to alliance and partnerships;
- Commitments, federation guarantee;
- Clear responsibility;
- Good price;
- Timely delivery dates;
- Competitiveness;
- Formal standards;
- Infrastructures: cultural, legislative, physical, and database and information systems;
- Federated data interchangeability, federated database management;
- Cultural and legislative compatibility, and business process cooperativity across enterprises;
- Uniform whole-appearance of end products to outside;
- Constant product qualities;
- Frequency of businesses.

Sometimes, specific situations may also be taken into account, such as:

- Proximity of materials;
- Proximity and pre-occupation of markets;
- Short and cost-saving transports of components and sub-assemblies;
- Cheap labors;
- Well-established supply chains, etc.

While geographical dispersal is not the prerequisite of enterprise federation, in a global circumstance, chances become much more to enterprise federation and freedoms of choice partners for federation become much wider.

Effective mechanism for creation of enterprise federation is market mechanism. Independent partner enterprises come together under biding, tendering and contracting. Initiator sends out calls for tenders and candidate partner enterprises submit tenders. Initiator evaluates tenders and determines partners. Successful partners draw up contracts with initiator and become contractors of initiator.

Procedure of creation of enterprise federation can be itemized as follows:

First, partner enterprises come together to form a project consortium;

Second, project consortium works out through-penetration plans, negotiates and revises them;

Third, project consortium jointly submits a tender. This also entails to assigning sub-tasks, contributions, delivery dates, and returns (payback) among partner enterprises;

Finally, when a bid is won, contracts and assurance plans upon quality, delivery dates, tasks, contributions, losses in case of failure, etc. are set up formally in writing.

4.2 Configuration of Enterprise Federation

Blueprints of configuration phase are as follows:

- Architectures of enterprise federation;
- Protocols of enterprise federation;
- Standard federation-ware, including federated data interchange, federated database management, federated information systems, data federation standards, protocols, interfaces;
- Logistic networking of partner enterprises.

Primary problem of configuration of enterprise federation is how partner enterprises can be facilitated for the data interchange and business process cooperation that enterprise federation requires. Usually a new operations management paradigm of product development requires a business process re-engineering to be implemented in the enterprise [17] [18]. However, re-engineering of underlying business processes within partner enterprises is expensive, and also unnecessary since enterprise federation is evolving, never fixed. For a universal implementation strategy for enterprise federation, a partner enterprise needs only to be facilitated for the data interchange and business process cooperation to the degree that enterprise federation requires.

Here, a conception of federation-ware is proposed. A federation-ware refers to a collection of hardware, software, databases, groupware, middleware, specifications and protocols to facilitate data interchange and database management among federated partner enterprises. Federation-ware enables partner enterprises to become nodes on the federation network of partner enterprises, and enables partner enterprises to be uniformly data interchangeable and business process cooperative, as depicted in Fig. 12.

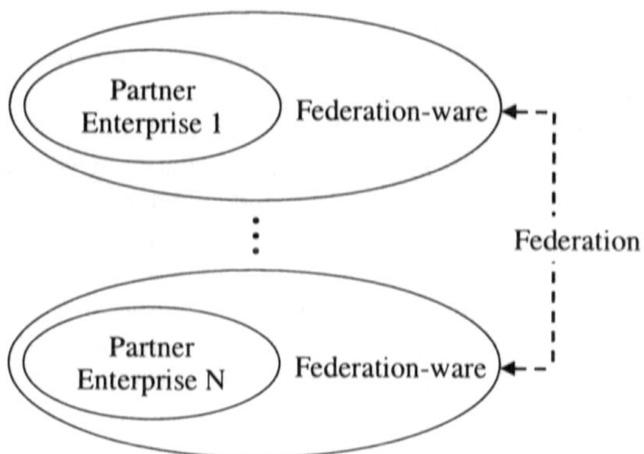

Fig. 12. Partner enterprises facilitated with federation-ware

Enterprise federation is already well prepared in today's information societies. Essential technical supports to enterprise federation, i.e. federated data interchange, federated database management and federated information systems, etc., are fully offered by modern information and communication technologies. Enterprises can be federated regardless of geographic dispersal and further globalization of trades and businesses. Information and communication technology overcomes geographic dispersal and lowers cost for organization among partner enterprises.

On the other hand, even geographically nearby, since they are independent, partner enterprises of enterprise federation need supports of federated data interchange, federated database management and federated information systems.

4.3 Operation of Enterprise Federation

Operation phase is the core of the organization of enterprise federation. Enterprise operation moves from non-partnership variants into federated ones. Blueprints of operation phase of enterprise federation are as follows:

- Coordination among partner enterprises;
- Federated marketing and sales management;
- Federated order management;
- Federated through-penetration planning, production planning and control;
- Federated cost control;
- Federated total quality management and control;
- Federated project management.

Operation phase of enterprise federation also performs:

- Operations evaluation of enterprise federation;
- Warning deficiencies of partner enterprises;
- Adequate adjustments of federation network of partner enterprises;
- Reconfiguration of federation network of partner enterprises.

Interactions among nodes on the federation network of partner enterprises can uniformly be modeled as multi-agent systems [19] [20] [21] [22]. Network and its self-organizing is a topic of operations research.

Two aspects of federation network of partner enterprises need to be considered. First is data flows among independent federation-ware facilitated partner enterprises, as depicted in Fig. 13. Data flows among partner enterprises are intensive in the case where initiator of enterprise federation takes over through-penetration planning, product design, and production organization.

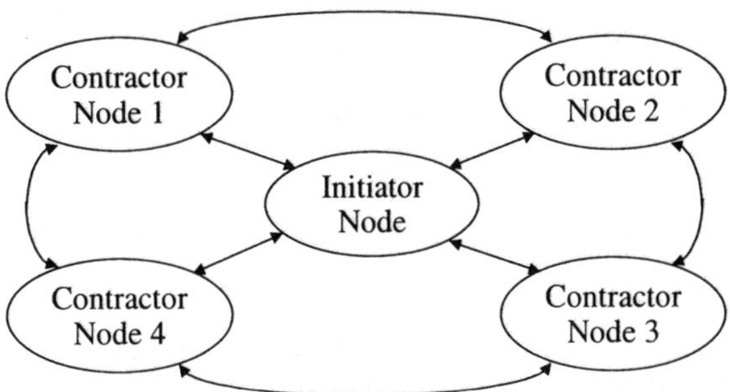

Fig. 13. Data flows among partner enterprises on federation network

Another is material flows among partner enterprises, as depicted in Fig. 14. For instance, while enterprise federation is formed across product geometry dimensional segments, transports of components and sub-assemblies need to be considered among partner enterprises.

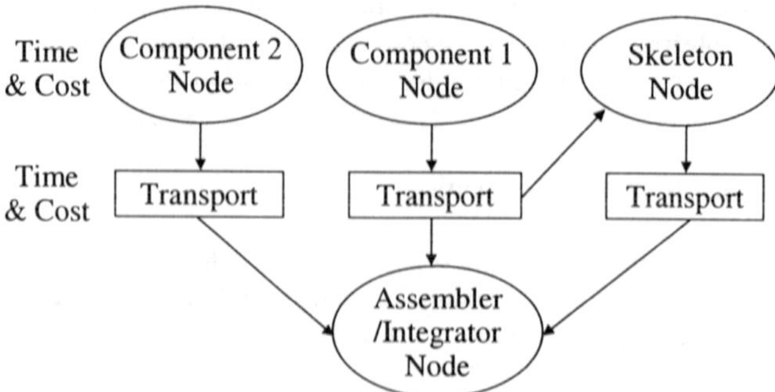

Fig. 14. Material flows in enterprise federation across product geometry dimensional segments

4.4 Dissolution of Enterprise Federation

Blueprints of dissolution phase are as follows:

- Clearance of economic relationships;
- Clearance of partnerships.

After an enterprise federation dissolves, former partner enterprises are released as non-partnership. When new projects emerging from markets, another new project consortium and enterprise federation may be formed.

5 Multi-agent Modelization of Enterprise Federation

5.1 Basic Concepts of Multi-agent Systems

Agent. Basically, an agent is assumed to have two abilities, autonomy and social ability.

Autonomy, ability of problem solving, to higher or lower degree, means that an agent makes decision about what to do based on its knowledge, without direct intervention of humans or others.

From this, optional attributes can further be derived, more or less. For instance,

Pro-activeness (antonym, passiveness), ability of goal-directing or planning, means that an agent is able to exhibit goal-directed behavior;

Reactivity (antonym, delibrativeness), ability of timely responding, means that an agent is able to perceive its environment and to respond in a timely manner to changes that occur in its environment; and/or

Other attributes, more or less, like learning, mobility, as appropriate in specific circumstances.

Social ability, ability of social communication, to higher or lower degree, means that an agent has its boundary distinguishing itself from its environment. An agent not only encapsulates some states (inaccessible by other agents), but more macroscopically packages some computational entities. An agent interacts with other agents via agent communication language.

An agent is a packaging of a set of capable computational entities, three of which, i.e. for scheduling, problem solving and social communication routing, respectively, are normative and others are informative, as depicted in Fig. 15. For example, for mobile agents, in addition to the three normative computational entities, entities for navigation and security are necessary.

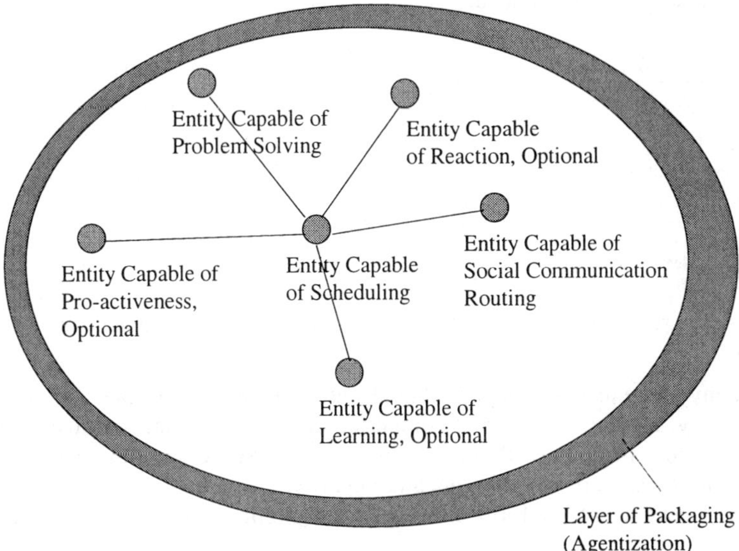

Fig. 15. Normative and informative computational entities of an agent

In research on agents, there has been a division, i.e. mental agency versus social agency.

Mental agency is concerned about an agent's mental state, typically described as belief, desire, intention, etc. Problems are specification, construction and programming of individual agents [23]. Example cases are such as agentization of humans, user interfaces, software (DBMS), etc. Some researchers boldly claimed that all efforts of traditional artificial intelligence had just been around specification, construction and programming of individual agents.

Social agency regards agents as social creatures that interact with one another. Basic problem is on social communication among agents [24].

Multi-agent Systems. In a multi-agent system, knowledge, skills, plans and activities of agents are coordinated to jointly take actions or to solve problems.

Coordination is required to determine organizational structure for a group of agents, to segment tasks, and to allocate resources. Coordination is a property of multi-agent systems. Cooperation is coordination among non-antagonistic agents, while negotiation is coordination among competitive or simply self-interested agents [25] [26]. Negotiation is required for detection and resolution of conflicts. Conflicts can result from simple limited resource computation to more complex issue-based computations where agents disagree because of discrepancies among their domains of expertise.

Agent Platform. Agent platform refers to a pragmatic computing environment which combines a variety of services into a unified and integrated execution model, as depicted in Fig. 16. In such a pragmatic computation point of view, an agent is an actor on an agent platform. It is through agent platform and life-cycle management that agent management is realized.

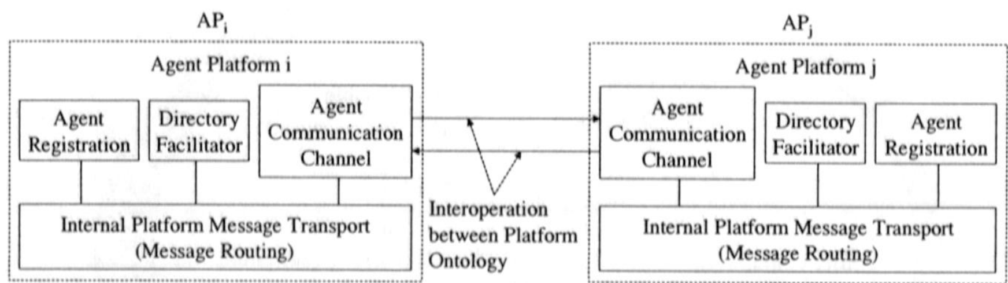

Fig. 16. Agent platform. AP_i and AP_j are supposed to be agent communication language compliant

Autonomy and equality of agents should not be understood in the same way as in human society. It is in the sense of computing environment platform that agents are said autonomous and equal with one another, never in the sense of human society and organization. Agents are autonomous and equal with one another, because they can uniformly access agent platform and enjoy the public services provided by agent platform.

Agent Social Communication. In order for a multi-agent system to solve problems coherently, agents must communicate amongst themselves. Agents communicate in order to achieve better the goals of themselves or of the society in which they co-exist.

Agent social communication is realized through agent communication language. Agent social communication remains as a problem, because of two sides. On the one hand, agents are open entities as they are capable of social communication. Social communication among agents is assumed at a higher level of discourse, i.e. contents of the social communication are meaningful statements about the agent's environment or knowledge. It is a kind of knowledge oriented communication. So, only message passing is not enough. Agents must be able to understand one another. This is one characteristic that differentiates agent social communication from, for example, other simple message-passing communication among strongly encapsulated computational entities such as method invocation in CORBA (common object request broker architecture).

For simplification of realization, on the other hand, common message passing mechanisms should be taken use of to realize knowledge oriented communication among agents. This requires that knowledge oriented communication should be properly encapsulated of itself.

Speech act theory involves a special class of actions, i.e. communicative acts. A communicative act is performed by one agent toward another. The mechanism of performing a communicative act is precisely that of sending a message encoding the act [27].

A message consists of message head referring to message type, and message body referring to contents of message. The message type defines the communicative act being performed, and the communicative act allows the recipient to determine the meaning of the contents of the message. Knowledge query and manipulation language (KQML) is a protocol for exchanging information and knowledge. The elegance of KQML is that all information for understanding the contents of a message is included in the communication itself.

5.2 Cooperation and Coordination in Enterprise Federation

Self-optimization of Partnership Enterprise Engineering. Enterprise federation is a self-optimization of partnership enterprise engineering. Creation, configuration, operation and dissolution of enterprise federation form a dynamic multi-agent model for product development [19] [20] [21] [22], where:

- A node on the federation network refers to performing product life cycle and/or geometry dimensional segments of processes related with product development;
- Performance of product development equals to the sum of performances of all nodes on the federation network;
- Each node has a number of candidate miniaturized enterprises which are motivated to qualify the nodeship to the federation network;
- The federation network is always evolving and self-organizing, to adapt itself to constant and unpredictable changes in markets.

Total cost of product development is equal to the sum of costs of product life cycle and/or geometry dimensional segments of processes related with product development. For each segment, there are a number of candidate partner enterprises, but only the best candidate is chosen for this segment. Best is judged in terms of:

- Low cost (cheap labor, low aging of machine)
- Timely completion of intermediate products
- Cheap raw materials (supply, transport, inventory)
- High efficiency and productivity
- Best commitment

Therefore, under such dynamic multi-agent organization, enterprise federation achieves self-optimization of partnership enterprise engineering through decentralized optimizations of candidate partner enterprises.

Inter-level Relation: Coordination. Inter-level coordination is the relation between a given level and several agents at adjacent lower level. Dialogue between the two levels ensures that decision frame of lower level can be constrained.

Hierarchical approach decomposes a whole problem into simpler problems. The upper-level agent defines decision frame to limit disagreements among lower-level agents and thus facilitates their decisions. To perform this, an upper-level agent assumes function of a coordinator. The coordinator's decision is made based on models of the organization under criteria assigned by the organization.

The decision frame worked out by the coordinator specifies the degree of liberty of lower-level agents and thus becomes a constraint upon lower levels. The decision frame is either accepted or if unsatisfactory, questioned by lower-level agents. In the latter case, a dialogue is established with the coordinator until all agents concerned are satisfied.

In such hierarchical decisional structures designated with only vertical dialogues, disagreement between two agents at the same level is only settled through the exchange of information between the coordinator and the lower-level agents in question.

Intra-level Relations: Cooperation. Horizontal dialogue designated between two agents at the same level assumes two functions:

- to settle local conflicts unforeseen by the coordinator, and
- to possibly increase potential optimality at the level.

Such horizontal dialogue will cause local revision of the decision frame without posing question about the coordinator's overall decision. However, if question rises about the coordinator's overall decision, disagreements that cannot be absorbed by cooperation at the level itself have to invoke a backtracking to upper level and thus a new coordination is started between the upper-level coordinator and the agents at this level.

Combining the above coordination and cooperation, agent social communication in compliance with organizational hierarchy can be proposed, as depicted in Fig. 17. In such a combined agent social communication process, deliberative (pro-active) provision and reactive provision are commutative. Reactive provision at higher level becomes deliberative one at lower level. In simple words, higher level is more deliberative than lower one.

6 Case Studies

Theory of enterprise federation is validated by practices of global trades and businesses in recent years.

6.1 Western European Economy

In Germany and France, especially during the re-allocation of former eastern German state-owned enterprises after the re-unification, former large state-owned corporations are privatized and miniaturized. In some trades and businesses, family-owned companies are encouraged. All efforts are to lower costs of product development, to increase agility of enterprises, and to enhance reactivity of enterprises to markets.

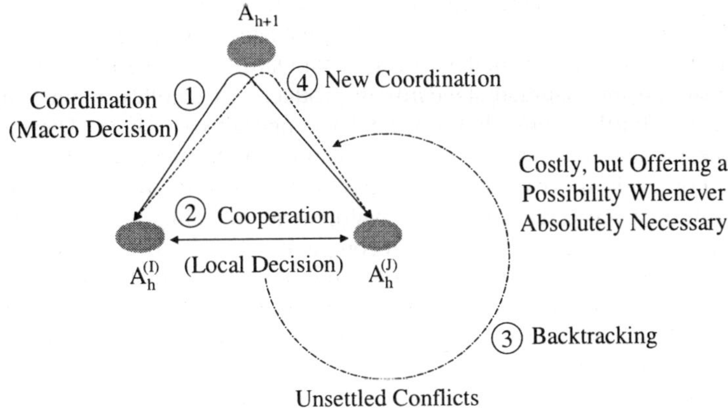

Fig. 17. Social communication process under organizational hierarchy. Working sequence: 1→2→3→4

6.2 Globalized Businesses of Aircraft Development

From late 80's, American aircraft corporations control marketing and sales, orders, R&D, product design, main production organization, total quality, and final product assembling and integration. At the same time, production of aircraft is dispersed all over the world and carried out using enterprise resources dispersed around the globe via a production network. Heads of aircraft are manufactured in China while tails of aircraft in Brazil.

6.3 Globalized Businesses of Laptops

In 90's, European traders of laptops control marketing and sales, orders, and final packaging and brand of laptops in Europe. Quality, R&D, through-penetration planning, product design, production organization, and production of mother boards and memory slices are carried out in Taiwan of China.

6.4 A State-Owned Enterprise in China and Its Externally-Associated Small Enterprises

A state-owned large-scale power station boiler works (PBW) of China is outlined below and its association with external small enterprises is analyzed to validate skeleton-mode product geometry segmented enterprise federation.

Power station boilers are energy products. Critical requirements are quality and safety. Demands of power station boilers are mainly in small batch, or even single product of its kind. Requirements in categories, structures and performances, materials and hard delivery dates vary with different loads, conditions and environments of boiler's operations. Detailed specifications upon geographical data, water quality data and fuel samples are usually attached in order contracts.

Large-scale power station boilers are non-standard, very often heavily deviating from national and international standards in products, assemblies, main components and even parts. Furthermore, they do not have unified categories. Therefore, it is difficult to establish universal designs of structures, performances and technological processes. For each specific boiler required by customers, it is necessary to do correspondingly specific research and development, including structure, thermal or hydraulic mechanics, energy conservation computation, and performance analysis and evaluation. These bring forth difficulties and complexities for product design, technological process design, material preparation, and even for workshop's production and on-site installation. Thus, a long period of product development is usually needed, one and half to two years or at least one year. All in all, development of power station boilers is order driven, user customized, and project management type.

On the other hand, in production of power station boilers, there is only a small amount of precision machining. Most technological processes are cold forging, riveting and welding. Welding is required very strictly for quality and safety. Products go out of workshops in the form of assemblies, and are to be assembled and installed on power station sites. Moreover, involving complex varieties, materials take a very heavy portion in product, and direct cost of materials usually occupies as high a percent as about 70% of total cost. Occupation ratio of circulating funds is very high and a great amount of funds is held up in material preparation stage, which heavily incurs indirect cost in a duplicated manner. All the above factors often make material cost stay at a very high horizon, and easily give rise to decreased profit in practice.

After orders are received, comprehensive plans are rapidly drawn up to properly organize and coordinate activities of departments of (structure and performance) design, technological process design, material supply, production, financial management, quality management, etc. Afterwards, execution of comprehensive plans is timely monitored to assure plans and schedules. Comprehensive plans involve all constraint specifications upon the activities of all departments in PBW. All final product documents, including safety manual, quality manual, operation manual, maintenance manual, environmental manual, recycling manual, etc., are formed from the initial comprehensive plans, and from their refinements in terms of subordinate plans at life-cycle stages and in life-cycle-through processes.

Functional blocks of product development of PBW can be depicted in Fig. 18. Drawing-up and monitoring of comprehensive plans are performed by the planning division of sales, operations and planning department.

Marketing and sales are controlled by PBW. Comprehensive planning, R&D, product design and technological deign are carried out in PBW. And skeletons and sub-assemblies of boilers are manufactured in PBW. Non-standard parts and components are contracted out to external small enterprises to manufacture. They receive design data and technological drawings, quality standard specifications, and strict delivery dates, all controlled by PBW, as depicted in Fig. 19.

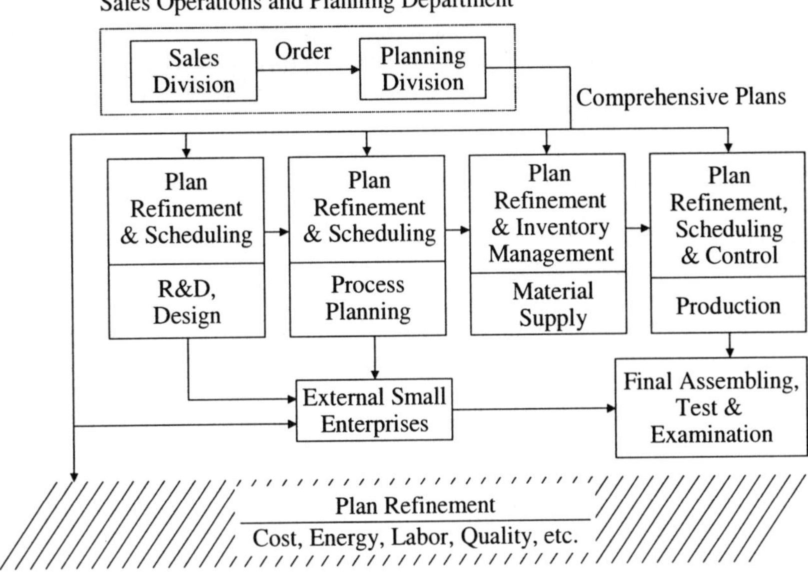

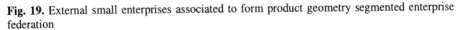

Fig. 18. Functional blocks of product development of PBW

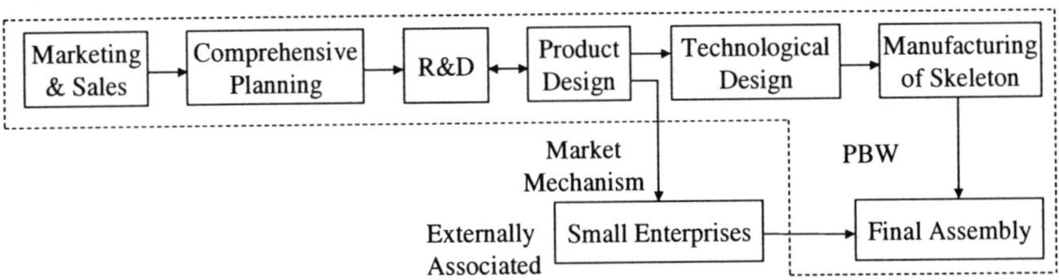

Fig. 19. External small enterprises associated to form product geometry segmented enterprise federation

7 Conclusions

In this chapter, a distinctive taxonomy has been presented for enterprise partnerships. Distinction between supply chains and enterprise federation has been made clear. Supply chains are pseudo components of product development, and management of supply chains is part of intra-integration of enterprise. However, enterprise federation is an agile and self-organizing network of independent partner enterprises which perform product life cycle and/or geometry dimensional segments of processes related with product development.

Furthermore, enterprise federation has been found to be distinctive from enterprise integration. Partner enterprises remain independent in enterprise federation, while partitions and barriers across partner enterprises need to be broken in enterprise integration.

Different from other operations management paradigms of complex product developments, which usually require business process re-engineering to be implemented in enterprises, re-engineering of underlying business processes within partner enterprises has been found to be unnecessary for enterprise federation. This shows enterprise federation is not only an agile and self-organizing, but, what is important, a cost-effective and easy-to-implement partnership enterprise engineering of product development.

This chapter has made thorough investigation into enterprise federation. Original contributions can further be summarized as follows.

(1) Concept and prerequisites of enterprise federation have been presented;
(2) Metrics of enterprise federation has been put forward in terms of product life cycle and/or geometry dimensional segments of processes related with product development. Market-situated combinations of $\oplus$ and $\otimes$ (operators denoting "plus" and "federated with", respectively) have been formalized;
(3) Life-cycle organization of enterprise federation, from creation to configuration and from operation to dissolution, has been presented and blueprints of every life-cycle phase have been specified;
(4) A conception of federation-ware has been proposed to facilitate implementation of enterprise federation across partner enterprises. Federation-ware enables partner enterprises to become nodes on the federation network of partner enterprises, and to be uniformly data interchangeable and business process cooperative;
(5) Multi-agent modelization has been explored for enterprise federation. Multi-agent social communication process under organizational hierarchy has been proposed.

Features of enterprise federation can be itemized as follows:

(1) Primary characteristic of enterprise federation is its duality, i.e. both decentralization and moderate alliance;
(2) Different from enterprise integration, organization of enterprise federation is evolving, formed according to situations of markets;
(3) Only those enterprises that best perform the product life cycle and/or geometry dimensional segments of processes related with product development are federated into the network of partner enterprises. So, self-optimization of partnership enterprise engineering becomes possible against outside uncertainties and changes;
(4) There is no stiffness and resistance brought forth by excessive centralization. Instead, partnership enterprise engineering of product development is decentralized and agile, and reactivity to instantaneously changing markets is greatly raised;
(5) Risks are totally decentralized among partner enterprises;
(6) Since no business process re-engineering is required, enterprise federation is a cost-effective and easy-to-implement approach to partnership enterprise engineering of product development;

(7) Current societies and technologies have simultaneously promoted and appreciated two opposite ends, i.e. more and more complex product developments versus more and more specialized and miniaturized enterprises. They have to be unified. Enterprise federation is an agile and self-organizing network of partner enterprises, which is capable of unifying the two opposite ends;
(8) Large-scale industrialization inevitably suffers from periodic economic crises. Enterprise federation in terms of specialized division and miniaturization may decentralize the dynamics of economic crises. Federation is a self-organizing mechanism of socio-economic systems.

References

1. Camarinha-Matos, L. M., Afsarmanesh, H., Marik, V. (eds.): Intelligent Systems for Manufacturing: Multi-agent Systems and Virtual Organizations. Kluwer Academic Publishers, (1998)
2. Morel, G., Vernadat, F. B. (eds.): Preprints of the 9th Symposium of IFAC on Information Control in Manufacturing (INCOM'98), Advances in industrial Engineering, volume I, Plenary Sessions. June 24-26, 1998, Nancy-Metz, France (1998)
3. Mårtensson, N., Mackay, R., Björgvinsson, S. (eds.): Changing the Ways We Work. Vol. 8 of Series "Advances in Design and Manufacturing". IOS Press, Amsterdam, Netherlands (1998)
4. Warnecke, H.-J.: The fractal company: A revolution in corporate culture. Springer-Verlag, Berlin, New York (1993)
5. Molina, A., Flores, M., Caballero, D.: Virtual enterprises: A Mexican case study. In: Camarinha-Matos, L. M., Afsarmanesh, H., Marik, V. (eds.): Intelligent Systems for Manufacturing: Multi-agent Systems and Virtual Organizations. Kluwer Academic Publishers (1998) 159-170
6. Goldman, S. L., Nagel, R. N., Preiss, K.: Agile competitors and virtual organizations. 1st edition, Van Nostrand Reinhold (Trade), New York (1995) 414 pages
7. Virtual Organization Net http://www.virtual-organization.net/
8. Kidd, P. T.: Agile manufacturing: Forging new frontiers. Addison-Wesley Pub Co. (1994) 388 pages
9. Tian, H., Binder, Z., David, B., Descotes-Genon, B., Dubois, M.: Toward exploitation of worn-out products. Proceedings of the Second World Manufacturing Congress (WMC'99), International Symposium on Manufacturing Technology (ISMT'99), September 27-30, 1999, Durham, UK (1999) 714-720
10. Tian, H., Binder, Z., David, B., Descotes-Genon, B., Dubois, M.: Functional model for exploitation of worn-out products. Proceedings of the Second World Manufacturing Congress (WMC'99), International Symposium on Manufacturing Systems (ISMS'99), September 27-30, 1999, Durham, UK (1999) 707-713
11. Tian, H., Binder, Z., David, B., Descotes-Genon, B., Dubois, M.: Novel information-substitutive process model for exploitation of worn-out products. Proceedings of the 1999 IEEE International Conference on Systems, Man, and Cybernetics (SMC'99), Vol. VI, October 12-15, 1999, Tokyo, Japan (1999) 416-421
12. Tian, H., Binder, Z., David, B., Descotes-Genon, B., Dubois, M.: Intelligent system for exploitation of worn-out products. Proceedings of the 1999 IEEE International Conference on Systems, Man, and Cybernetics (SMC'99), Vol. III, October 12-15, 1999, Tokyo, Japan (1999) 1101-1106

13. Kosanke, K., Nell, J. G., Vernadat, F., Zelm, M.: Enterprise integration-International consensus (EI-IC) EP 21859. In: Mårtensson, N., Mackay, R., Björgvinsson, S. (eds.): Changing the Ways We Work. Vol. 8 of Series "Advances in Design and Manufacturing". IOS Press, Amsterdam, Netherlands (1998): 745-756
14. Tian, H., Binder, Z.: Paradigm for information integration in enterprises. In: Mårtensson, N., Mackay, R., Björgvinsson, S. (eds.): Changing the Ways We Work. Vol. 8 of Series "Advances in Design and Manufacturing". IOS Press, Amsterdam, Netherlands (1998): 745-756
15. Tian, H.: Universal informatic process model for product materialization. Proceedings of the Second World Manufacturing Congress (WMC'99), International Symposium on Manufacturing Management (ISMM'99), September 27-30, 1999, Durham, UK (1999) 831-837
16. Tianfield. H.: Advanced life-cycle model for complex product development via stage-aligned information-substitutive concurrency and detour. International Journal of Computer Integrated Manufacturing, 13 (2000)
17. Qiao, F., Tian, H., Wu, Q., Shen, R.: Study of implementation strategies of enterprise business reengineering. Proceedings of International Conference on Management Science and the Economic Development of China, July 16-19, 1996, Hong Kong, China (1996) 493-500
18. Qiao, F., Wu, Q., Tian, H., Xu, W., Shen, R.: A Petri net based model for business reengineering. Proceedings of IEEE International Conference on Industrial Technology, December 2-6, 1996, Shanghai, China (1996) 141-146
19. Tianfield, H., Binder, Z., Unland, R.: Multi-agent interactions under organizational hierarchy. Preprints of the 2nd IFAC/IFIP/IEEE Conference on Management and Control of Production and Logistics (MCPL'2000), July 5-8, 2000, Session # S0 'Multi-agent Systems', Paper # P369, Grenoble, France (2000) 6 pages
20. Tianfield, H., Binder, Z., David, B.: Toward multi-gradation nested multi-agent systems. 7th International Symposium on Manufacturing with Applications (ISOMA'00), World Automation Congress (WAC'2000), June 11-16, 2000, Session # WeM5, Paper # ISOMA-9915, Maui, Hawaii, USA (2000) 6 pages
21. Tian, H., Unland, R.: On the hierarchical structure of multi-agent systems. Preprints of the 1st International IFAC/IFIP/IFORS Workshop on Multi-agent Systems in Production (MAS'99), December 2-4, 1999, Vienna, Austria, (1999) 271-276
22. Tian, H., Unland, R.: Formulating enterprise federation into multi-agent systems. Preprints of the 1st International IFAC/IFIP/IFORS Workshop on Multi-agent Systems in Production (MAS'99), December 2-4, 1999, Vienna, Austria, (1999) 229-234
23. Wooldridge, M.: Agent-based software engineering. IEE Proceedings on Software Engineering, 144 (1997) 26-37
24. Singh, M. P.: Agent communication languages: rethinking the principles. IEEE computer, 31 (1998) 40-47
25. Weiss, G. (ed.): Multiagent systems. The MIT Press (1999)
26. Green, S., *et al.*: Software Agents: A Review. www.cs.tcd.ie. May 27th 1997 (1997)
27. Foundation for Intelligent Physical Agents http://www.fipa.org/

User-Centered Agents for Structured Information Location

Xindong Wu[1], Daniel Ngu[2], and Sameer S. Pradhan[1]

[1] Department of Mathematical and Computer Sciences
Colorado School of Mines
1500 Illinois Street, Golden, CO 80401, USA
[2] School of Computer Science and Software Engineering
Monash University
900 Dandenong Road, Melbourne, VIC 3145, Australia

Abstract. This paper designs an electronic commerce system that integrates conventional electronic commerce services with contemporary WWW advantages, such as comprehensive coverage and agents for information search and selection. We use a user-centered approach and apply data mining techniques in the design of agents for information search and selection. There are various agents in this electronic commerce system to perform different functions. Among them, SiteHelper is a unique agent in our system compared to existing electronic commerce systems. It acts as a housekeeper for the system and as a helper for the users to find relevant information. In order to assist the users in finding relevant information at the centralized location (with Web links to the global Web), SiteHelper interactively and incrementally learns about each user's areas of interest and aids them accordingly, by deploying data mining techniques with incremental learning facilities as its learning and inference engines.

1 Introduction

Conventional commerce systems have traditionally stressed service, organization, and centralization. Electronic commerce systems have positioned themselves to absorb and take advantage of every new development including the World Wide Web (the Web or WWW for short). The bright colors, hypertext format, graphical user interfaces of the WWW have been widely used in the electronic commerce community to provide the access to multiple remote services. The World Wide Web has embodied flexibility, rapid evolution, and decentralization. Therefore, an electronic commerce system needs to bring together traditional notions of commerce systems with contemporary WWW capabilities.

In this paper, we use a user-centered approach and apply data mining techniques in the design of agents for information location. There are various agents in our electronic commerce system to perform different functions. Among them, the following three agents are important.

J. Liu and Y. Ye (Eds.): E-Commerce Agents, LNAI 2033, pp. 323–331, 2001.

- *Relevance Verification.* Our electronic commerce system has a dictionary to define the scope of documents[1] relevant to the system. The dictionary contains keywords in a hierarchy that describe areas of interests and related detailed topics. When the electronic commerce system is deployed at a different place with a different scope, only the dictionary will need to be changed. The Relevance Agent (RA) in the electronic commerce system verifies the relevance of recommended documents from sellers and Web users, using the dictionary.
- *SiteHelper.* This is a unique agent in our electronic commerce system compared to existing electronic commerce systems. In addition to conventional search engines, the SiteHelper agent acts as a housekeeper for the system and as a helper for the user to find relevant information. In order to assist the users to find relevant information at the centralized system (with Web links to the global Web), SiteHelper interactively and incrementally learns about each user's areas of interest and aids them accordingly. To provide such intelligent capabilities, SiteHelper deploys data mining techniques with incremental learning facilities as its learning and inference engines for incremental exploration of the electronic commerce system.
- *Document Updates.* Given the rapid evolution nature of Web documents, we design a document agent, DA, to check updates of the Web documents linked in the electronic commerce and report new entries from authorized users and the RA. The updates include revisions, insertions and removals.

Our electronic commerce system is centralized with WWW links to documents physically located on the Web, and provides intelligent agents that act as a housekeeper for the system and as a helper for the users to find relevant information. This approach begins from the centralized view of a conventional commerce system, seeks to provide access to the electronic commerce through digital means including the WWW, and maintains the advantages of decentralization, rapid evolution, and flexibility of the WWW.

2 Agent Structure with SiteHelper

The World Wide Web is rapidly becoming an "information flood" as it continues to grow exponentially [3,13]. This causes difficulty for users to find relevant pieces of information on the Web. According to the Internet Domain Survey by [17], the Internet has grown from only 617000 hosts in October 1991 to over 43 million hosts in January 1999 and in excess of 4 million Web servers in April 1999. It has been predicted that the number of connections on the Internet will exceed the number of people of the world by the turn of the millennium [6]. The amount of information on the Web is immense, and with such a speed of growth, the Internet and the Web have become a place of anarchy and chaos [8]. For Web users to use the Web and electronic commerce systems productively, they require

[1] A document in our electronic commerce system is a Web page with information for a product or a set of similar products.

better and smarter software like intelligent agents with AI capabilities to assist them. In the past 40 years, AI has found applications in many different domains, however, the systems built are mostly either very narrow or very brittle. The Web is an ideal environment for AI [9] to provide problem solving techniques, and support for users with methodologies like knowledge representation and data mining.

Commercial sites like Lycos, AltaVista, and many others are search engines that help Web users find information on the Web. These commercial sites use indexing software agents to index as much of the Web as possible. However, the enormous growth of the Web makes these search engines less favourable to the user because of the large number of pages they return for a single search. Thus it is very time consuming for the user to go through the list of pages just to find the information. To remedy this problem, many researchers are currently investigating the use of robots (or "spiders", "Web wanderers" or "Web worms") that are more efficient than search engines. These robots are software programs that are also known as agents, like WebWatcher, Letizia, CIFI, BargainFinder, Web Learner, Syskill & Webert, MOMspider and many others. Some of theses agents are called intelligent software agents [12] because they have integrated machine learning techniques. The Web page titled "Database of Web Robots Overview" at `http://info.webcrawler.com/mak/projects/robots/active/html/` lists 230 of these robots or agents as of July 20, 2000.

The advantages of the robots are that they can perform useful tasks like statistical analysis, maintenance, mirroring and most important of all; resource discovery. However, there are a number of drawbacks. Robots normally require considerable bandwidth to operate, thus resulting in network overload, bandwidth shortages and increase in maintenance costs. Due to the high demand of robots, network facilities are required to be upgraded - consequently resulting in budget increases. Robots generally operate by accessing external servers or networks to retrieve information, raising ethical issues as to whether people should improve their system just because too many robots are accessing their sites. Koster mentioned in his paper "Robots in the Web: threat or treat?" that a robot visited his site using rapid fire requests and after 170 retrievals from the server, the server crashed [5].

With these drawbacks of Web robots in mind, this paper designs an alternative way to assist the user in finding information in our centralized electronic commerce system (with Web links to the global Web) using incremental machine learning techniques. A software agent named SiteHelper is designed to act as a housekeeper for our electronic commerce system and a helper for the user to find relevant information on the system server. In order to assist the Web user to find relevant information at the centralized system site, SiteHelper interactively and incrementally learns about the user's areas of interest and aids them accordingly. To provide such intelligent capabilities, SiteHelper deploys data mining techniques with incremental learning facilities as its learning and inference engines.

2.1 Agent Architecture

SiteHelper in our electronic commerce system aids the users by learning about the users' interest and preferences through the generation of rules about the users. The rules are refined and improved through two learning processes: interactive incremental learning and silent incremental learning. SiteHelper first learns about a user's areas of interest by analyzing the user's visit records, and then assists the user in retrieving information by providing the user with update information about the electronic commerce.

Interactive incremental learning functions in cycles that interact with the user. SiteHelper prompts the user with a set of keywords in logical expressions and related documents which are likely of the user's interest, and asks for feedback. Considering the feedback SiteHelper makes changes to its search and selection heuristics and improves its performance.

Many Web servers implement a log file system that records user access information to their sites. The log files normally consist of the computer name and location on the Internet, the time of access and accessed Web pages. We implement such a log file system in our electronic commerce system. Silent incremental learning uses the log information as its starting point. SiteHelper extracts a log file for each user. From the log file, SiteHelper learns about the user's interest areas. It extracts a set of keywords in logical expressions about the user's interest areas according to the documents the user has visited in the past.

SiteHelper works differently from search engines and other kinds of agents like WebWatcher and World Wide Web Worm that help the user on the global Web. However, other Web sites can deploy SiteHelper to assist users in finding information in the same way as in our electronic commerce system. This design of SiteHelper avoids the drawbacks of existing robots. In addition, there are other advantages of having SiteHelper at a local Web site (like an electronic commerce). First, through incremental learning of the user's characteristics or interest areas, SiteHelper becomes an assistant to the user in retrieving relevant information. Second, SiteHelper has the potential to reduce user accessing and retrieval time, by displaying a list of changes that have been made since the user's last visit. Finally, SiteHelper can be easily adopted for other Web sites or electronic commerce systems.

Figure 1 shows the design of our electronic commerce system structure with the SiteHelper. The relevance verification agent (RA) and document updates agent (DA) have been mentioned in Section 1, and therefore we will concentrate below on how SiteHelper is designed.

- **Access Log.** Most Web sites allow global user access and have logging facilities in place [11] to record users' access details. The access log of a Web site records all Web transaction/request services by the Web server. The three main elements for each record are: the machine name with its Internet address from which the access is performed, the date/time of access and the Web page being accessed. We implement these facilities in our electronic commerce system.

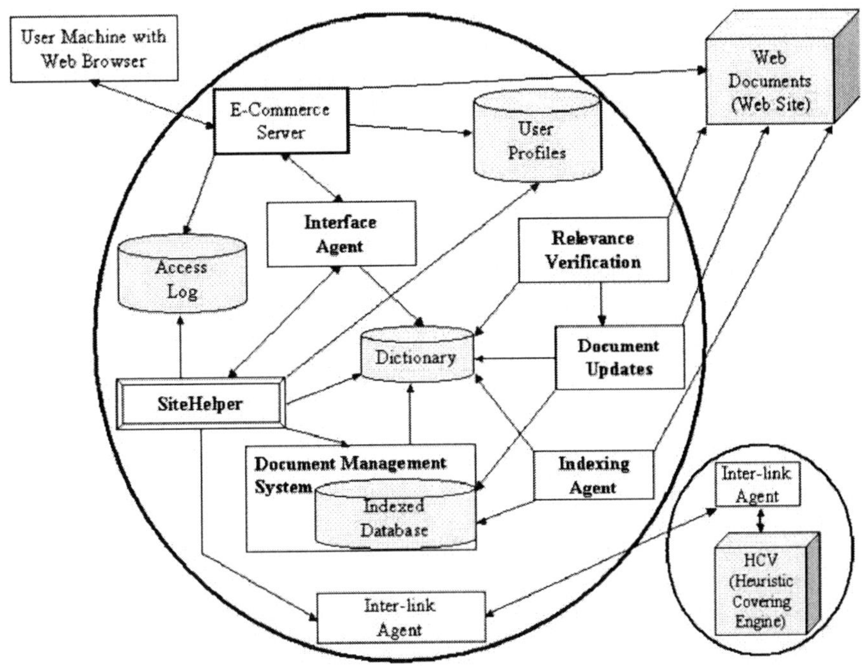

Fig. 1. Agent Structure with SiteHelper

- **Dictionary.** The dictionary is a list of keywords organized in a hierarchy that define the scope of the electronic commerce. It is used by various agents including the relevance verification agent (RA) mentioned in Section 1.
- **SiteHelper,** also referred to as the discovery agent. SiteHelper manages major communications and tasks of the electronic commerce system. In addition to conventional keyword-based search mechanisms, it reads the access log to collect records of documents that a user has accessed, and through the interface agent and the document management system, retrieves all the documents in the indexed database that the user has not visited. It also matches the records with the user profile to compile a set of references to document objects and passes them to the inter-link agent.

Of course, a user might access an electronic commerce for different purposes at different visits. If this is the case, the user can set up the user preferences (see the interface agent below) to stop SiteHelper from providing new and updated documents at some visits.

- **Inter-link Agent.** The inter-link agent forwards the system indexes from the discovery agent to the HCV engine for rule generation. Our electronic commerce system is designed across two different platforms, Windows NT and Unix. To establish the communication between the two, the inter-link agent is designed to run on both platforms.

- **HCV** [14,15]. The HCV induction engine is the "brain" of the discovery agent. It takes two input sets of documents; one set the user has seen, and the other the user hasn't visited. It generates rules in the form of conjunctions of keywords in the dictionary to identify the user's areas of interest, and forwards the rules to the user profiles.
- **Electronic Commerce Server.** This is the Web server for the electronic commerce system. It transmits information using the Hypertext Transfer Protocol (HTTP), and serves requests from external browsers for documents in the electronic commerce. It is the entry point for a user to use our electronic commerce system, with the user name and password to identify the user. Access details of the user are stored in the user profile.
- **Document Management System and Indexed Database.** The indexed database has an entry/index for each document in the electronic commerce system, and is managed by the document management system. A document here can possibly be a compound document that consists of many other simpler documents. Each entry in the database has a pointer to the corresponding document, with (a) a set of keywords from the dictionary to index the document, (b) a date and time to show when the document was last modified, and (c) a format indicator. The document entries can be nested to allow for compound documents to be searched.
- **Indexing Agent.** This agent traverses the electronic commerce weisite, indexes all relevant documents according to the dictionary and stores the results in the indexed database. It incrementally refreshes the indexes and automatically updates indexing when document updates are forwarded by the document updates agent mentioned in Section 1.
- **Interface Agent.** The interface is what the user sees. It presents a friendly interface that allows the user to interact with the system. The agent provides the user with the following functions: the bookmarking of interesting documents in the electronic commerce, navigation in the system, evaluation of retrieved documents, the setting up of user preferences, and a help system with hyperlinks using the semantic links between the keywords in the dictionary. We also have a facility on the electronic commerce interface for authorized sellers to submit relevant materials directly in electronic format.
- **User Profiles.** A user profile consists of the user's account details, areas of interest, access history, and the rules generated by the discovery agent.
- **User Machine with Web Browser.** A Web user can access our electronic commerce through a Web browser that supports the ActiveX technology, for example, the Microsoft Internet Explorer and Netscape Navigator with the ActiveX plugs-in.

3 Related Work

Assisting Web users by identifying their areas of interest has attracted the attention of quite a few recent research efforts. Two recent research projects reported in [2] and [16] are along this line. Three other projects, WebWatcher [1], Letizia [7] and Web Learner [10] also share similar ideas.

[2] develop a system that helps a Web user discover new sites that are of the user's interest. The system presents the user every day with a selection of Web pages that it thinks the user would find interesting. The user evaluates these Web pages and provides feedback for the system. The user's areas of interest are represented in the form of (keyword, weight) pairs, and each Web page is represented as a vector of weights for the keywords in a vector space[2]. From the user's feedback, the system knows more about the user's areas of interest in order to better serve the users on the following day. If the user's feedback on a particular Web page is positive, the weights for relevant keywords of the Web page are increased, otherwise decreased. Balabonovic & Shoham's system adds learning facilities to existing search engines, and as a global Web search agent does not avoid the general problems associated with search engines and Web robots. In addition, compared to SiteHelper, the (keyword, weight) pairs used in this system cannot represent logical relations between different keywords. This type of logical expressions is the starting point for knowledge representation and data mining with SiteHelper.

[16] investigate a way to record and learn user access patterns in the area of designing on-line catalogues for electronic commerce. This approach identifies and categorizes user access patterns using unsupervised clustering techniques. User access logs are used to discover clusters of users that access similar pages. When a user comes, the system first identifies the user's pattern, and then dynamically reorganizes itself to suit the user by putting similar pages together. An (item, weight) vector, similar to the (keyword, weight) vector used to represent each Web page in [2], is used in [16] to represent a user's access pattern. The system views each Web page as an item, and the weight of a user on the item is the number of times the user has accessed the Web page. This system does not use semantic information (such as areas of interest) to model user interests, but just actual visits. Also, it does not aim to provide users with newly created or updated Web pages when they visit the same Web site again. This is a significant difference in design between this system and our SiteHelper.

WebWatcher [1] is an agent that helps the user in an interactive mode by suggesting pages relevant to the current page the user is browsing. It learns by observing the user's feedback to the suggested pages, and it can guide the user to find a particular target page. A user can specify their areas by providing a set of keywords when they enter WebWatcher, mark a page as interesting after reading it, and leave the system at any time by telling whether the search process was successful or not. WebWatcher creates and keeps a log file for each user and from the user's areas of interest and the "interesting" pages they have visited, it highlights hyperlinks on the current page and adds new hyperlinks to the current page. WebWatcher is basically a search engine, and therefore does not avoid the general problems associated with search engines and Web robots. Although it has been extended to act as a tour guide [4], it does not support incremental exploration of all relevant, newly created and updated pages at a local site.

[2] The vector space approach is one of the most promising paradigms and the best-known technique in information retrieval.

Letizia [7] learns the areas that are of interest to a user, by recording the user's browsing behaviour. It performs some tasks at idle times (when the user is reading a document and is not browsing). These tasks include looking for more documents that are related to the user's interest or might be relevant to future requests. Different from WebWatcher, Letizia is a user interface that has no predefined search goals, but it assumes persistence of interest, i.e., when the user indicates interest by following a hyperlink or performing a search with a keyword, their interest in the keyword topic rarely ends with the returning of the search results. There are no specific learning facilities in Letizia, (but just a set of heuristics like the persistence of interest plus a best-first search), and therefore it does not perform incremental learning as SiteHelper does.

Web Learner [10] is similar to SiteHelper in that it learns about what a user is interested in and decides what new Web pages might interest the user. However, Web Learner generates keywords (called a feature vector) automatically from pages on the global Web, and does not provide facilities for incremental learning.

Our localized Web agent SiteHelper starts with the same idea of assisting Web users by learning and identifying their areas of interest. However, SiteHelper works with a centralized electronic commerce server which contains indexes to Web pages on the Web by using a keyword dictionary local to the electronic commerce. Further, based on the indexing of the Web pages on and linked to the electronic commerce server, SiteHelper supports interactive and incremental learning. The rules with logical conditions in SiteHelper are more powerful than the (keyword, weight) pairs used in some existing systems in representing users' areas of interest.

SiteHelper is different from existing search engines and robots on the World Wide Web in that it does not traverse the global Web, but acts as a housekeeper for a centralized electronic commerce server and as a helper for the user who visits the electronic commerce to find relevant information, with particular attention to the newly developed and modified documents in the electronic commerce.

4 Conclusions

As the Internet and World Wide Web continue to grow, more and more Web sites and electronic commerce systems are being set up. There have been many national efforts on electronic commerce systems in various countries. Our agent structure with SiteHelper is unique compared to existing electronic commerce efforts, and provides new capacities for electronic commerce systems to serve existing and new user communities.

The electronic commerce structure in Section 2 can be plugged in other electronic commerce systems by revising its keyword dictionary. In addition, the idea of having a localized agent to help the user find relevant information can be applied to many other domains. When a particular user visits an electronic commerce site (whether a specialized or a general system), the site allows the user to search for particular documents (or products). It can then log the user's searches as well as their browsing behaviour. From the log information, Site-

Helper can be used to learn about the user's areas of interest, and at the user's following visit, SiteHelper may prompt the user to look at those new/updated materials that match their areas of interest.

References

1. Armstrong, R., Freitag, D., Joachims, T. and Mitchell, T.: WebWatcher: A Learning Apprentice for the World Wide Web. In: *AAAI Spring Symposium on Information Gathering from Heterogeneous, Distributed Environments.* March 1995.
2. Balabanovic, M. and Shoham, Y.: Learning Information Retrieval Agents: Experiments with Automated Web Browsing. In: *On-line Working Notes of the AAAI Spring Symposium Series on Information Gathering from Distributed, Heterogeneous Environments.* 1995.
3. Berners-Lee, T., Gailliau, R., Luotonen, A., Nielsen, H. F., and Secret, A.: The World-Wide Web. *Communication of the ACM* **37**(August 1994).
4. Joachims, T., Freitag, D. and Mitchell, T.: WebWatcher: A Tour Guide for the World Wide Web. In: *Proceedings of the 15th International Conference on Artificial Intelligence.* Nagoya, Japan, August 23-29, 1997. 770-775.
5. Koster, M.: Robots in the Web: Threat or Treat? *ConneXions*, **9**(April 1995).
6. Lawrence, A.: Agents of the Net. *New Scientist*, 15 July 1995, 34-37.
7. Lieberman, H.: Letizia: An Agent That Assists Web Browsing. In: *Proceedings of the 1995 International Joint Conference on Artificial Intelligence.* Montreal, Canada, August 1995.
8. Murray, J.: Anarchy and Chaos on the Net. *IEEE Computer.* May 1995.
9. O'Leary, D.E.: The Internet, Intranets, and the Al Renaissance. *IEEE Computer*, January 1997, 71-78.
10. Pazzani, M., Nguyen, L. and Mantik, S.: Learning from Hotlists and Coldists: Towards a WWW Information Filtering and Seeking Agent. In: *Proceedings of IEEE 1995 Intl. Conference on Tools with Al.* 1995.
11. Pitkow, J. E. and Bharat, K.A.: WebViz: A Tool for WWW Access Log Analysis. In: *Proceedings of the First International World-Wide Web Conference.* Geneva, Switzerland, May 1994.
12. Riecken, D.: Intelligent Agents. *Communication of the ACM* **37**(July 1994).
13. Wiggins, R.W.: Webolution: The Evolution of the Revolutionary World-Wide Web. *Internet World.* April 1995, 35-38.
14. Wu, X.: *Knowledge Acquisition from Databases.* Ablex Publishing Corp., USA, 1995.
15. Wu, X.: Rule Induction with Extension Matrices. *Journal of the American Society for Information Science* **49**(1998), 5: 435-454.
16. Yan, T.W., Jacobsen, M., Garcia-Molina, H. and Dayal, U.: From User Access Patterns to Dynamic Hypertext Linking. In: *Proceeding of the Fifth International World Wide Web Conference.* Paris, France, May 1996.
17. Zakon, R.H.: Internet Timeline v4.1. `http://info.isoc.org/guest/zakon/Internet/History/HIT.html`

Using a Speech Technology Agent as an Interface for E-Commerce

Marie Devlin and Terri Scott

University of Ulster
Magee College
Northland Road
Derry
BT48 7JL, Northern Ireland
{m.devlin,tm.scott}@ulst.ac.uk

Abstract. This paper outlines an experiment set out to determine the usefulness of a Speech Technology Interface Agent for E-Commerce transaction tasks. There are a limited number of speech technology agents in use on the Web at present and there are none used in the E-Commerce scenario that combine both speech synthesis and speech recognition. The results of this experiment indicate that users would find such speech technology agents acceptable and useful for non-trivial tasks but that there is a need for technical improvements with regard to implementation and also a greater assessment of optimal task division between speech and traditional hyperlink navigation modalities. The latter has implications for all agent interaction on the Web as user acceptance and the usability of interface agent interaction is given little priority in the current research literature.

1 Introduction

New paradigms for interaction are required to support business procurement on the WWW. Animated agents can enhance human-computer interaction ensuring natural, meaningful and interesting dialogue. The traditional Web interaction style of navigation via hyperlinks is no longer singularly useful to the sophisticated user who requires quick solutions to the unsatisfactory response times, incomplete information and ambiguous search and retrieval methods that are symptomatic of increasing web traffic and poor design standards. In effect, an animated agent can convey more information than a *flat* HTML page by combining visual and auditory sources. Ideally, combining a Speech Technology interface agent with traditional Web interaction methods would result in a multimodal environment where users can act upon the world using the appropriate mode of interaction for certain classes of action in order to achieve information goals. Market research conducted by the International Data Corporation estimated that the amount of commerce conducted over the WWW will top 1 trillion dollars by 2003 and that in the same year the number of users who make purchases online will jump from 31 million in 1998 to more than 183 million.[6] The growth of average transaction size and the adoption of the Web as a vehicle

J. Liu and Y. Ye (Eds.): E-Commerce Agents, LNAI 2033, pp. 332–346, 2001.

for business procurement makes agent technology an attractive marketing solution. Agent technology introduces a new edge to Web utility. Animated agents decrease search times by expressing both emotional and intellectual content. This combination allows for an increase in the amount of information conveyed due to the human ability to combine many sources of information to perceive and understand. [10] This paper outlines an experiment that tested the significance of an interface agent that uses speech technology (both speech synthesis & speech recognition) to interact with the user in E-commerce situations. The experiment was unique in a number of respects in that there are few speech technology systems in use on the Web that utilise both speech synthesis and speech recognition. Those that do are not used in E-Commerce situations and also the interface agent, part of the CSLU Toolkit has never been tested for usability. The demonstration application (The CD Store) was tested using two methods, a variation of the predictive methods used in the Technology Acceptance Model [13], and the summative MUMMS method. [8]

2 The Use of Agent Metaphors for E-Commerce

Today's world of commerce involves prompt decision making, co-operation and communication between physically separated individuals. The imminent growth and increased diversity of WWW transactions and their importance in every day activities provides a growing need to communicate and exchange information and services in a more significant manner. Too often users are faced with unsatisfactory response times, incomplete information and ambiguous search and retrieval methods.

Eric Haseltine, Chief Scientist, Disney Interactive, highlights the importance of emotional content in human-computer interaction. Disney designed a language for composing scenes and has achieved results using emotional archetypes based on forms, colours, movements and expressions. Haseltine argues that animated agents can express both emotional and intellectual content and thereby increase the amount of information conveyed. In effect, an animated agent can convey more information than a *flat* HTML page and this is because information in a face is particularly efficient and effective form of communication.

We communicate best in face- to-face situations because we are able to combine many sources of information to perceive and understand, even when some of the information is ambiguous. When engaged in face-to-face conversations, our gestures, head movements and facial expressions indicate that we agree, disagree, are puzzled etc. Understanding these behaviours and incorporating them into Speech Technology Agents could provide a more graceful and effective interface than already exists. Therefore the animated conversational agent approach is, according to Haseltine,"a novel and important solution to problems of massive information overload and limited bandwidth on the Internet."[3]

Given the theory that using visual and auditory information may be able to convey more information to a user that a single modality interface, the utility of conversational agent interaction needs to be measured.

3 Single Mode Vs. Multi-modal Interaction

Ben Schneiderman observed that claims about intelligent software agents are *vague, dreamy and unrealised.* [15] However, there are those that would argue that other interaction methods such as Direct Manipulation have outlived their usefulness and are a frustrating way for users to interact with machines that are capable of showing more intelligence. In the everyday world, we act through language. Speaking is a *natural* way of communicating our goals to others and effecting changes in the world. In traditional Web interfaces, interaction is carried out by physical actions that are rapid and reversible. Users can navigate in the world by using cursor keys and the mouse, by selecting objects and clicking on them or by choosing operations from a menu. Combining a speech interface with this type of interaction mode results in a multi-modal interface where users can act upon the world by initiating physical or verbal commands and conversely the system can respond by speaking and/or by making changes in the virtual world. Speech offers three obvious benefits when compared to a typical Web page interface:

- Speech offers a way of issuing commands while allowing hands and eyes to remain free. Multiple actions can be simultaneously carried out using the different modalities of interaction.
- Users can refer to objects which are not present in their current view of the world. In a typical Web page interface, actions can only be applied to objects which are visually present. Users can use speech to select and manipulate objects which were in visual focus, will be in visual focus, are simply known objects, abstract objects etc.
- Naturalness - users are familiar with using language to act in the real world. The natural benefit needs to be tempered by using a restricted language set which the system can recognise and understand. Users may find it more natural to use spoken commands for certain classes of action, but these have yet to be determined.[12]

According to Oviatt, *"A multi-modal interface combining speech and Direct Manipulation (DM), (or other forms of interaction), can provide more efficient interaction than a single modality interface and allow us access to the benefits of both modalities"*[14].
It can also allow one modality to compensate for the limitations of the other e.g. a DM interface can compensate for the limitations of speech recognition by indicating throughout the display which objects are currently prominent for the system and a speech interface can make transactions more personal. Oviatt also maintains that the user is free to decide which modality to use depending on the naturalness of the action in comparison to using the other modality. A Speech Technology Agent has the advantages of being more eye-catching and interesting to the user and of providing a more personalised experience during the transaction.

4 The Importance of Creating a Visual Presence

Part of the important personalisation effect of conversational interfaces is the visual nature of conversational interaction. Communicating with a lifelike character that reacts to speech, just as a human being would, makes the conversation or transaction more like our everyday communications. A speaker's face and accompanying gestures influence speech perception, therefore rapidly conveying more information. Visual information presented by a talking face is also robust in that people are fairly good at using visual clues to aid speech recognition even when they are not looking at the speaker's lips.
Harry McGurk highlighted a quirk in human perception and provided a striking demonstration of the combined (bimodal) nature of speech understanding.[10] His research proposes that the brain simply combines sound and sight. Humans tend to combine both facial movements and sounds to understand spoken language. Visual speech and auditory speech information are both analysed in the brain to come up with an interpretation about what is being said. This is known as the *McGurk Effect* and occurs like so: Although viewers hear parts of speech that are completely different, they try to come up with meaningful words from the mix of visible and auditory speech (like when someone is speaking a foreign language, we try to translate it into ours or find similarities). According to Dominic Massaro, people believe speech is auditory and therefore visible speech shouldn't be very influential, but it is. [10] In the same vein as McGurk, he maintains that one of the key properties of bimodal speech is that of *complementarity* i.e. features of speech that are the hardest to distinguish acoustically are the easiest to distinguish visually and vice versa. The sensory integration of auditory and visual information in speech perception and the complementarity between these modalities shows clearly in Massaro's experiments that independently vary visual and auditory information. By testing both uni-modal and bimodal conditions, Massaro found that in unimodal presentations, acoustic recognition is more accurate than visual among hearing subjects who have not been trained in lip reading. He also found that, with regards to complementarity, not only do audible and visible speech provide two independent sources of information, but each also provides *strong* information where the other is weak.
Given these results and conclusions, a Speech Technology Agent that maintains a visual presence on a web page should provide a more comprehensive source of information for users, conveying knowledge more quickly and accurately. We prefer our messages embodied with a view. The image of a *person's* face provides a window into their motivations and emotions.
According to Oviatt,

> "Recent empirical studies have suggested that users prefer to interact multi-modally and that this can reduce errors and task completion time compared with a single modality interface."[14]

Therefore, both the bimodal, (visual and auditory), Speech Technology Agent and the use of mixed-modal interaction methods, (hyperlinks and the Speech Technology Agent), on E-Commerce sites hold the promise of being more *useful* to the user. Traditional evaluation methods do not cater for the *usefulness* factor.

5 Evaluation Methods

By using two methods of evaluation for our Speech Technology Agent, as opposed to one it was deemed possible to gain insight into both the usefulness and the usability of a conversational agent as a method of interaction and also to determine which mode of interaction is best for E-Commerce tasks. The MUMMS [8] method of evaluation is often used to measure the general usability characteristics of multi-media applications whereas the TAM [13] method introduces the concept of *usefulness* to evaluation and is capable of specific adaptation to deal with the issues of conversational agent technology.

6 The Technology Acceptance Model

The Technology Acceptance Model[13] is a theoretically grounded approach to the study of software acceptability that can be added to usability evaluations. It is a predictive rather than descriptive model and therefore cannot be used to diagnose specific design flaws. It can however help to predict system acceptability. Some models of technology acceptance have their roots in Innovation Diffusion Theory which seeks to identify perceived characteristics of technology that may be expected to influence user acceptance of that technology. However, in social psychology research, theorists seek to identify determinants of behaviour within the user rather than the technology. The Theory of Reasoned Action (TRA) has been used to more fully investigate how user beliefs and attitudes are related to *individual intentions to perform.*[13] According to TRA, attitude towards a type of behaviour is determined by the subject's belief about the consequences of that behaviour (based in the information available or presented to the individual) and the effective evaluation of those consequences.[13] Therefore the Theory of Reasoned Action can be used to provide insight into the usage behaviour of systems by showing the domino effect of external stimuli on user perceptions, henceforth to attitudes about the technology and finally to actual usage behaviour.
Davis's Technology Acceptance Model (TAM) is derived from TRA. [13] It helps us to predict user acceptance based on the influence of two factors : Perceived Usefulness and Perceived Ease of Use. TAM maintains that user perceptions of usefulness and ease of use determine attitudes towards using a system. *Behavioural Intentions to Use* are subsequently determined by these attitudes and these in turn can be used to predict actual system use. Within TAM Perceived Usefulness (U) is defined as *the degree to which a user believes that using a system will enhance their performance* and Perceived Ease of Use (EOU) is defined as *the degree to which a user believes that using a system will be free from effort.* TAM models Behavioural Intentions to Use (BI) as a function of the users attitude toward using the system (A) as shown in figure 1.

According to Davis,

> "Research has consistently shown that BI is the strongest predictor of actual use."[13] Therefore given this theory, if two systems offer identical functionality, but the user finds one easier to use, then that system is considered more *useful.* Consequently, TAM can be used to help predict

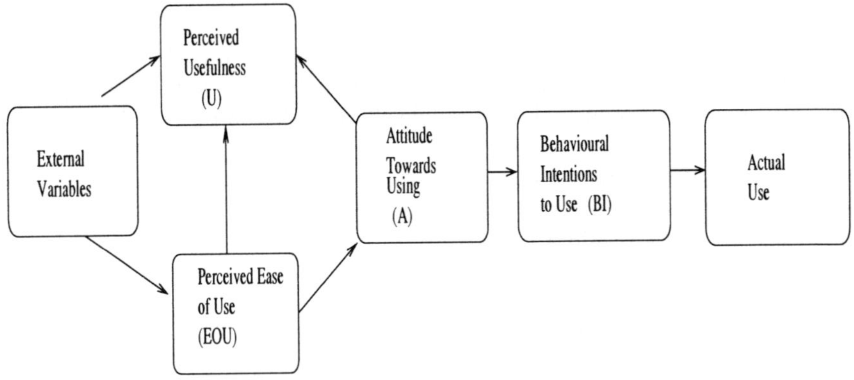

Fig. 1. Davis's Technology Acceptance Model, derived from TRA

problems before users have any significant experience with a system. Our adapted form of the TAM questionnaire consists of 15 questions (some of which elicit general demographic data). It uses scales of each variable used in TAM (i.e. Perceived Usefulness, Perceived Ease of Use, Attitude towards using and Behavioural Intentions to Use) which are defined below:[13]

- **Perceived Usefulness.** The degree to which a user believes that using a system will enhance performance
- **Attitude Towards Using.** Feelings of favourableness or unfavourableness towards using the technology
- **Perceived Ease of Use.** The degree to which a user believes using the technology will be free from effort
- **Behavioural Intentions to Use.** Indication of one's intentions to use the technology in the future.

Each variable is coupled to a set of specifically designed questions. Below are some examples of the adapted question scales designed to measure each of the variables:

Perceived Ease of Use:
I found it easy to get the application to do what I wanted
It would be easy for me to become skillful at using this application
I found the application easy to use
I am able to use the application

Attitude Towards Using:
I like the idea of shopping with an agent to assist me
I feel in control when using the application
Using the application is (pleasant /unpleasant)
I found the agent easy to converse with

Perceived Usefulness:
Using this application would improve my online shopping experience.
A conversational agent to help shop on the Internet is a (good/bad) idea
I would find a conversation agent useful for other Internet sites
An agent assistant would make my online shopping more pleasurable

Behavioural intentions to Use:
I would use an Internet shopping assistant
I will shop regularly on the Internet in future

7 The MUMMS Questionnaire

The MUMMS questionnaire (Measuring the Usability of Multi-Media Software) [8] was developed in response to the rapidly changing patterns of computing technology. The questionnaire is a way in which Multi-Media computer products can be assessed for quality of use by end users. The MUMMS method has been used extensively in research projects in Europe and it measures several quality scales

- *Affect:* how much the product captures the user's emotional responses;
- *Control:* the degree to which the user feels they, and not the product, are setting the pace;
- *Efficiency:* the degree to which the user can achieve their goals of interaction efficiently with the product;
- *Helpfulness:* the extent to which the product assists the user;
- *Learnability:* how easy it is for a user to get started and learn new features of the product.

The current version of the questionnaire has another sub-scale that relates to a concept the designers began calling *Excitement.*[8] This is the extent to which end users feel that they are *drawn into* the world of a multi-media application, and it seems to capture some of the strong emotive appeal which multi-media applications exercise over their users.
The questionnaire consists of a setof 48 statements that the user has to rate along a 5 point Likert Scale ranging from Strongly Agree to Strongly Disagree.

8 The CSLU Toolkit

We implemented our Speech Technology Agent using the CSLU Toolkit. The CSLU Toolkit is an easy to use set of tools and technologies for It includes interfaces for standard telephony and audio devices and software interfaces for speech recognition, natural language understanding, text-to-speech synthesis, speech reading and animation components.[2] The Toolkit's authoring environment integrates the core technologies of facial animation, speech recognition and understanding with other features such as word-spotting, dialogue repair and open microphone capability. The system comes complete with speaker independent and vocabulary independent speech recognition. In addition, several

vocabulary recognisers are included,(e.g. alpha digits) and a graphical authoring environment called RAD, (Rapid Application Developer).[5] It caters for Natural Language understanding via PROFER,(Predictive Robust Finite ParSER) which is modeled after Carnegie Mellon University's Phoenix System which can be used to extract semantic patterns from the output of the Toolkit's recognisers. The parser allows for spontaneous speech, tolerating such things as ungrammatical constructions etc.
The Festival text-to-speech synthesis system, developed at the University of Edinburgh, is integrated into the Toolkit and includes modules for normalising text, transforming text into a sequence of phonetic segments,assigning pitch and amplitude etc. The Toolkit comes with complete programming environments for both C and Tcl, which incorporate a collection of libraries and APIs. The libraries are portable across platforms. It also includes Natural Language Processing modules, developed in Prolog, which interface with the toolkit through sockets.[7]

9 Baldi - the Animated Conversational Agent

The conversational agent (Baldi) used for our evaluation of a Speech Technology Agent is incorporated into the CSLU Toolkit and is fairly primitive. It consists of a 3D talking face and a speech synthesis program that controls a wireframe model with a control strategy for co-articulation, controls for paralinguistic information and affect in the face, text-to-speech synthesis and synchronization of auditory and visual speech[4].
According to Ron Cole, Director of CSLU,

> *"Baldi's speech recognition is quite fallible and his conversatioal skills are quite limited. Unlike conversations among individuals, Baldi cannot engage in mixed-initiative dialogues using natural continuous speech. Baldi cannot understand the meaning of an utterance and generate an appropriate response based on this interpretation, as humans often do"* [4]

Therefore, our conversational agent is not strictly intelligent. It asks specific questions and then recognises or rejects specific words or phrases in response to these prompts. The speech recognition algorithm is designed to recognise a limited set of words or phrases produced by any speaker and to reject extraneous speech that is not in the recognition vocabulary. This may be a disadvantage in an application on the WWW that endeavors to make a conversational agent as realistically human as possible. Although Baldi's synthetic speech is highly intelligible, it sounds artificial and stilted compared to a human. When Baldi talks, the speech is synchronised with the movements in the face. He can change facial expressions to display an array of emotions such as anger, puzzlement etc. whilst listening to the user or producing speech. Baldi is a realistic rendering of a human to encourage the realness of the conversational experience. Facial movements are used to indicate his attention state.
Baldi is perhaps unique in one respect in comparison to other interface agents (MS Paperclip etc.) in that clear indication is given if a response is recognised

or not either by visual feedback or spoken dialogue that indicates he has not understood and whereas this is not true intelligence either,it is effective human-like behaviour with which the user can identify. Another factor for consideration is that there is a natural tendency for users to constrain themselves when *talking to a machine*. This perhaps should not concern us as according to McGlashan and Axling,

> *"Restricted language is not only a natural consequence of talking to machines but it is also a natural part of many everyday activities which are focused on a particular task."[9]*

Users may not be satisfied with this explanation and expect rather more from a system that proports to speak to them in natural language. The human-like facial features of Baldi could have both positive and negative connotations for the user's mental model. On a positive note, he appears very human. The user is presented with a 3D visual of Baldi's face which moves his mouth in sync with the words programmed to give the user instructions, information and guidance. Contrary to this, it may well be that the very fact that Baldi appears human could lead users to expect a larger degree of human intelligence and a more *normal* type of conversation. Human beings do not converse in a linear manner and are inclined to digress, become distracted or think ahead rapidly, whereas Baldi is incapable of responding spontaneously to anything outside the structured dialogue.

10 The CD Store

The application that was developed in order to evaluate the viability of conversational agent interaction is the CD Store. An online store should offer a number of services to its customers, just like a physical store. Customers should also be able to ask for information, sample the merchandise, order a product and purchase a product via a number of payment methods. In order to be competitive an online store should also have conventional business methods such as discounts, special offers and even competitions to attract custom. It should also ideally seek to emulate the personal shopping experience that a valued customer receives in the real world, with the sales assistant endeavouring to find the product that is right for a particular customer and even creating special accounts and tailoring services for them. In order to implement the CD store a conventional Web page was created. The page consisted of inactive images (jpeg, gif etc.) and hyperlinks. It also contains an online order form written in Java Script through which customers can request an e-mail bill or forward their credit card details.[1] Each of the purchasing tasks were created in the RAD environment of the Toolkit using generic and media objects. In addition, a login state was created so that frequent users would only have to enter their details once. The responses required from the user consist of keyword that are the catalyst for subsequent actions in the system. Customers could listen to clips from the CDs on offer via .wav files. The programming of the system was kept fairly simple. Images were added to make the interaction more interesting and to simulate the action of browsing through

CD covers in a conventional store. The user interacts with the CD Store via a series of menus presented by the agent (Baldi) in voice format.
The user then works through the system by responding to questions using a set of keywords that have been programmed into the recognition vocabulary. Once a request has been fulfilled, the agent will then move onto another set of options to present to the user.
The user can also opt to deactivate the agent and choose the more conventional method of interaction i.e. the selection of hyperlinks to more pages of mainly text-based menus. The agent controls the flow of the dialogue and therefore the user's progression throughout the conversational element of the CD store is restricted to the sequence if the options available. Questions within the system can be randomised to provide variety but some tasks need to be structured e.g. the agent needs to elicit information in a sequence in order to perform the purchasing task. It was also noted that the designers of the system had to anticipate a

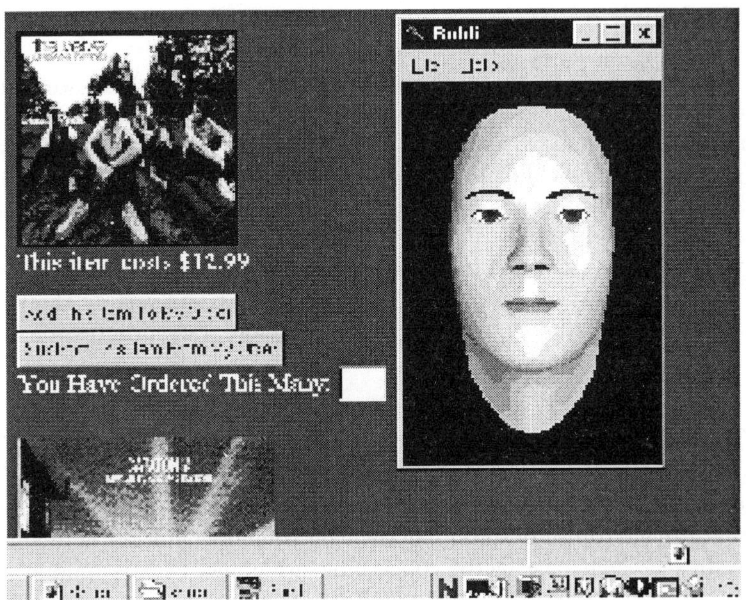

Fig. 2. A snapshot of the conversational agent Baldi and the online CD Store

finite set of user interaction patterns which left no room for user spontaneity. Conventional hyperlink interaction allows the user to browse casually through a web site and the system retains a memory of the path they have traversed. This was very difficult to emulate using the Speech Technology Agent. The underlying structure of the application became quite untidy but some of the difficulty was resolved by the use of sub-dialogues to separate distinct actions such as the Purchase option.

11 Technical Constraints

Dialogue systems should communicate with external information sources. Work has been ongoing at the University of Ulster[11] and an interface between the CSLU Toolkit and MS Access has been created toward this end. This enables designers to develop dialogues that retrieve information from a database. As regards implementation on the Web, there are functions to access live Web pages from the Toolkit, to read them and to parse them. There are no functions provided, however, to input data to Web pages to obtain further information, although this could be done with Perl scripts. Therefore for the purposes of our experiment we had to simulate the presence of Baldi in the live CD Store page. This involved running the CD Store application and Netscape Navigator in tandem to simulate a conversational agent on a Web page and proved quite effective as a prototype for evaluation.

12 Evaluation

There were 20 people in the user group tested. Of these 20, 10 were male, 10 were female. Eleven of the group were computing students at various levels of computing study (5 male, 6 female). The group also included 1 teaching assistant, 1 civil servant, 1 schoolchild, 1 researcher, 3 IT professionals (unspecified areas), 1 housewife and 1 lecturer in Computing Science. Of these, 7 were experienced MM users and 13 were inexperienced. Users were given a brief demonstration and description of the system and then were given free reign to *talk* to it themselves. There were no time factors involved or specific task analysis as the system is somewhat linear and dialogue is structured, therefore, task progression is similar for all users.

13 TAM Results

In general, the TAM results showed that the user group liked the application and found it easy to use despite experiencing some recognition and control difficulties. In particular the factor concerning usefulness that is unique to TAM provided value in the usability testing. A brief summary of the results for each measurement is given below.

Perceived Usefulness. Opinion among the user group was somewhat divided as to whether a Speech Technology agent would improve online shopping experiences but the majority of users did feel that the application was viewed as beneficial rather than a hindrance. The mixed feelings with regard to improvement capability may be due to the nature of the CD Store rather than significant to the usefulness of agent assistants but this merits further investigation.85% of users thought that the agent assistant made online shopping pleasurable and that the conversational dimension was an extremely good idea.

Perceived Ease of Use. Only 5% of users deemed it difficult to operate the CD Store agent and 90% felt that they could become skillful at using it quite easily. One slight disadvantage was that 30% of users found it hard to get the

application to do what they wanted all the time. The speech technology (synthesis & recognition) allows hands-free operation and this was thought beneficial to users who commonly multi-task.
Attitude towards Using. The majority of users found the application pleasant to use but 30% found the agent difficult to converse with at times and 40% did not feel in control when they were using the application. These results may be due to the fact that the agent controls the flow of dialogue and also to recognition problems that were observed.
Behavioural Intentions to Use. 80% of users agreed that they would use an Internet shopping assistant and 85% stated that they would shop regularly on the Internet in future. This question set was difficult to design as they could be viewed as closed questions. The measurement of this variable would merit further design consideration.
In general the TAM method proved a useful exercise for indicating reaction to and acceptance of Speech Technology Agents in E-Commerce. Even though the user group was small, the results indicate that the CD Store simulation agent was easy to use. The Usefulness factor was also clearly defined as 95% thought that having such an agent was a good idea. However, it was also clear from these results that users experienced some difficulties with the application. 30% of users found it difficult to control the application and therefore the structured dialogue in the application and the recognition difficulties need further and more rigorous investigation.

14 MUMMS Results

The six factors measured in the MUMMS questionnaire provided a clear indication of the usability level of the CD Store. The CSLU Toolkit Agent has never been subjected to usability testing and therefore the MUMMS questionnaire results are of general value. An overview of the results follows.
Affect
The CD Store scored a favourable 80% with regards to user enjoyment of the shopping session, however users were generally unhappy with the amount of control they had over the system and this was due to the linear nature of the tasks and the fact that Baldi initiates and controls the flow of interaction. The majority of users thought that the process of getting results from the application was not boring and repetitive. However some observations made it clear that users became frustrated when there was a recognition problem and the system repeated a complete dialogue sequence. This may have implications for dialogue length and again the structure of the CD Store. It also indicates that some of the dialogue in the application may be unnecessary and that hyperlink navigation may be more efficient and better suited to some of the tasks that users wished to perform e.g. menu selection.
Control
In general, the CD Store application was rated poorly in terms of user control. The majority of users became frustrated at using only the speech recognition as their main means of interaction. Many observed that using hyperlinks would be

quicker for some tasks e.g. searching. Again, this has implications for the classification of tasks that a Speech Technology Agent is most optimal for. Users observed that the application, while being easy to operate, was difficult to control. These may seem contradictory observations but users perceived the imperfections of the system yet still found it easy to understand without a help file. The majority of users did observe that the system had, in their view, been designed to suit its users.

Efficiency

The majority of users observed that the application was slow to operate and that sometimes it did not work the way that it should e.g. some users chose the Jazz category of music, and were taken to the Rock albums page. This was definitely a recognition problem. 45% of users thought that the application sometimes created problems for them and they found this quite frustrating. This is an important observation as it indicates that although the usability of the Speech Technology Agent is high, the technology has problems that can be compensated for with Hyperlink navigation and other methods of interaction.

Helpfulness

The system does not provide a Help file but the majority of users found that Baldi's corrections were quite helpful. The 20 user in the evaluation group received a brief overview of the application before they used and hence coped well, however, the addition of a Help file would be a bonus. One problem that was noted was that it was difficult to backtrack . Users could easily get lost in a larger application and the structured dialogue in the CD Store did not allow for this. Web sites have been criticised in the past for the same reason although he majority of site designers do provide site maps and navigation buttons.

Learnability

The Learnability results for the CD Store are the most favourable. The majority of users found that the application was easy to learn and remember (90%), and that it encourages the user to learn it (75%).

Excitement

The results for the Excitement factor were very positive as 95% of users thought that the application was presented in an attractive way and that it was original and exciting. It is also important to note that users did not view the agent as a gimmick i.e. 70% of users deemed that the tasks performed by the application were non-trivial.

15 Conclusion

The evaluation methods used to assess the usability and usefulness of the Speech Technology Agent were subjective in nature and whereas the results were favourable, they indicate that further more formal tests are needed.

Further work could include a more rigorous form of testing including traditional benchmark tests such as measuring transaction completion time and also a comparative analysis of performance between a *conventional* onlinestore and the CD Store with the Speech Technology Agent. E-Commerce Web sites need to maximise interest and minimise user effort given the dynamic nature of the Web and the increasing volume of information and traffic it supports.

The growth of commercial transactions on the Web make it imperative for Web designers to create more interesting, useful and efficient modes of interaction for the Web environment in order to capture customer imagination and fulfill business aspirations and user requests more optimally than is happening at present.

Speech Technology Agents provide an added dimension to the agent paradigm and to user experience but task definition and optimality need to be determined. Speech Technology Agents can also convey more information but this needs more exploration and comparison . The use of the Technology Acceptance Model (TAM) and the MUMMS questionnaire methods have provided insight into user opinion of such agents. The user evaluation results show that single mode interaction presents its own particular set of technical and usability difficulties, however, users are willing to embrace the technology because it is more exciting and easy to use. In this experiment, the agent metaphor has been shown as conducive to user goals and potentially capable of wide user acceptance. The general reaction to the CD Store example has been favourable among the small user group. However, it remains to be determined if Speech Technology Agents are the best solution to Web problems and E-Commerce requirements.

Acknowledgements. The authors would like to thank Professor Mike McTear, Valentina Tamma and Dr Simon Parsons for their assistance and kind comments.

References

[1] J. Burns and G. Smith. Html goodies. *http://www.htmlgoodies.com*, 1998.

[2] T. Carmell, J. Hosom, and R. Cole. A computer-based course in spectrogram reading. In *Proceedings of the ESCA/SOCRATES Tutorial and Research Workshop on Methods and Tool Innovations for Speech Science Education (MATISSE)*, UCL, April 1999.

[3] R.A. Cole. Tools for research and education in speech science. In *Proceedings of the International Conference of Phonetic Science*, San Francisco, 1999.

[4] R.A. Cole, D.W. Massaro, J. DeVilliers, B. Rundle, K. Shobaki, J. Wouters, M. Cohen, J. Beskow, P. Stone, P. Connors, A. Tarachow, and D. Solcher. New tools for interactive speech and language training: Using animated conversational agents in the classrooms of profoundly deaf children. In *Proceedings of the ESCA/SOCRATES Tutorial and Research Workshop on Methods and Tool Innovations for Speech Science Education (MATISSE)*, pages 45–54, UCL, 1999.

[5] S. Suttonand R. Cole, J. DeVilliers, J. Schalkwyk, P. Vermerlen, M. Macon, Y. Yan, E. Kaiser, B. Rundle, K. Shobaki, P. Hosom, J. Wouters, D. Massaro, and M. Cohen. Universal speech tools, the cslu toolkit. In *Proceedings of the International Conference on Spoken Language Processing*, pages 3221–3224, 1998.

[6] Information Society Commission. Information society commission update. *http://www.infosocomm.ie*, 1999.

[7] P. Connors, A. Davies, G. Fortier, K. Gilley, B. Rundle, C. Soland, and A. Tarachow. Participatory design: Classroom applications and experiences. In *Proceedings of the ESCA/SOCRATES Tutorial and Research Workshop on Methods and Tool Innovations for Speech Science Education (MATISSE)*, 1999.

[8] J. Kirakowski. Background notes on the sumi questionnaire: The use of questionnaire methods for usability assessment. *www.ucc.ie/hfrg/questionnaires.html*, 1996.

[9] S. MacGlashen and T. Axling. Talking to agents in virtual worlds. *UKVRSIG'96, (United Kingdom Virtual Reality Special Interest Group, www.sics/se/ Scott/papers/ukvrsig96/ukvrsig96.html)*, 1996.

[10] D.V. Massaro and D.G. Stork. Speech recognition and sensory integration. *American Scientist Magazine*, May-June 1998.

[11] McTear M.F. Using the cslu toolkit for practicals in spoken dialogue technology. In *Proceedings of the ESCA/SOCRATES Tutorial and Research Workshop on Methods and Tool Innovations for Speech Science Education (MATISSE)*, 1999.

[12] M.F.McTear. Modelling spoken dialogues with state transition diagrams: experiences with the cslu toolkit. In *International Conference on Spoken Language Processing*, 1998.

[13] M.G. Morris and A. Dillon. How user perceptions influence software use. *IEEE Software Magazine*, pages 21–26, July-August 1997.

[14] S. Oviatt. Multimodal interfaces for dynamic interactive maps. In *Proceedings of CHI'96*, pages 95–102, 1996.

[15] B. Schneiderman. Direct manipulation versus agents: Paths to predictable, controllable and comprehensible interfaces. In J.M. Bradshaw, editor, *Software Agents*, chapter 6, pages 97–106. AAAI Press/M.I.T, 1997.

Author Index

Lecture Notes in Artificial Intelligence (LNAI)

Vol. 1847: R. Dyckhoff (Ed.), Automated Reasoning with Analytic Tableaux and Related Methods. Proceedings, 2000. X, 441 pages. 2000.

Vol. 1849: C. Freksa, W. Brauer, C. Habel, K.F. Wender (Eds.), Spatial Cognition II. XI, 420 pages. 2000.

Vol. 1856: M. Veloso, E. Pagello, H. Kitano (Eds.), RoboCup-99: Robot Soccer World Cup III. XIV, 802 pages. 2000.

Vol. 1860: M. Klusch, L. Kerschberg (Eds.), Cooperative Information Agents IV. Proceedings, 2000. XI, 285 pages. 2000.

Vol. 1861: J. Lloyd, V. Dahl, U. Furbach, M. Kerber, K.-K. Lau, C. Palamidessi, L. Moniz Pereira, Y. Sagiv, P.J. Stuckey (Eds.), Computational Logic – CL 2000. Proceedings, 2000. XIX, 1379 pages.

Vol. 1864: B. Y. Choueiry, T. Walsh (Eds.), Abstraction, Reformulation, and Approximation. Proceedings, 2000. XI, 333 pages. 2000.

Vol. 1865: K.R. Apt, A.C. Kakas, E. Monfroy, F. Rossi (Eds.), New Trends Constraints. Proceedings, 1999. X, 339 pages. 2000.

Vol. 1866: J. Cussens, A. Frisch (Eds.), Inductive Logic Programming. Proceedings, 2000. X, 265 pages. 2000.

Vol. 1867: B. Ganter, G.W. Mineau (Eds.), Conceptual Structures: Logical, Linguistic, and Computational Issues. Proceedings, 2000. XI, 569 pages. 2000.

Vol. 1881: C. Zhang, V.-W. Soo (Eds.), Design and Applications of Intelligent Agents. Proceedings, 2000. X, 183 pages. 2000.

Vol. 1886: R. Mizoguchi, J. Slaney (Eds.), PRICAI 2000: Topics in Artificial Intelligence. Proceedings, 2000. XX, 835 pages. 2000.

Vol. 1898: E. Blanzieri, L. Portinale (Eds.), Advances in Case-Based Reasoning. Proceedings, 2000. XII, 530 pages. 2000.

Vol. 1889: M. Anderson, P. Cheng, V. Haarslev (Eds.), Theory and Application of Diagrams. Proceedings, 2000. XII, 504 pages. 2000.

Vol. 1891: A.L. Oliveira (Ed.), Grammatical Inference: Algorithms and Applications. Proceedings, 2000. VIII, 313 pages. 2000.

Vol. 1902: P. Sojka, I. Kopeček, K. Pala (Eds.), Text, Speech and Dialogue. Proceedings, 2000. XIII, 463 pages. 2000.

Vol. 1904: S.A. Cerri, D. Dochev (Eds.), Artificial Intelligence: Methodology, Systems, and Applications. Proceedings, 2000. XII, 366 pages. 2000.

Vol. 1910: D.A. Zighed, J. Komorowski, J. Żytkow (Eds.), Principles of Data Mining and Knowledge Discovery. Proceedings, 2000. XV, 701 pages. 2000.

Vol. 1916: F. Dignum, M. Greaves (Eds.), Issues in Agent Communication. X, 351 pages. 2000.

Vol. 1919: M. Ojeda-Aciego, I.P. de Guzman, G. Brewka, L. Moniz Pereira (Eds.), Logics in Artificial Intelligence. Proceedings, 2000. XI, 407 pages. 2000.

Vol. 1925: J. Cussens, S. Džeroski (Eds.), Learning Language in Logic. X, 301 pages 2000.

Vol. 1930: J.A. Campbell, E. Roanes-Lozano (Eds.), Artificial Intelligence and Symbolic Computation. Proceedings, 2000. X, 253 pages. 2001.

Vol. 1932: Z.W. Raś, S. Ohsuga (Eds.), Foundations of Intelligent Systems. Proceedings, 2000. XII, 646 pages.

Vol. 1934: J.S. White (Ed.), Envisioning Machuine Translation in the Information Future. Proceedings, 2000. XV, 254 pages. 2000.

Vol. 1937: R. Dieng, O. Corby (Eds.), Knowledge Engineering and Knowledge Management. Proceedings, 2000. XIII, 457 pages. 2000.

Vol. 1952: M.C. Monard, J. Simão Sichman (Eds.), Advances in Artificial Intelligence. Proceedings, 2000. XV, 498 pages. 2000.

Vol. 1955: M. Parigot, A. Voronkov (Eds.), Logic for Programming and Automated Reasoning. Proceedings, 2000. XIII, 487 pages. 2000.

Vol. 1967: S. Arikawa, S. Morishita (Eds.), Discovery Science. Proceedings, 2000. XII, 332 pages. 2000.

Vol. 1968: H. Arimura, S. Jain, A. Sharma (Eds.), Algorithmic Learning Theory. Proceedings, 2000. XI, 335 pages. 2000.

Vol. 1972: A. Omicini, R. Tolksdorf, F. Zambonelli (Eds.), Engineering Societies in the Agents World. Proceedings, 2000. IX, 143 pages. 2000.

Vol. 1979: S. Moss, P. Davidsson (Eds.), Multi-Agent-Based Simulation. Proceedings, 2000. VIII, 267 pages. 2001.

Vol. 1991: F. Dignum, C. Sierra (Eds.), Agent Mediated Electronic Commerce. VIII, 241 pages. 2001.

Vol. 2003: F. Dignum, U. Cortés (Eds.), Agent-Mediated Electronic Commerce III. XII, 193 pages. 2001.

Vol. 2007: J.F. Roddick, K. Hornsby (Eds.), Temporal, Spatial, and Spatio-Temporal Data Mining. Proceedings, 2000. VII, 165 pages. 2001.

Vol. 2033: J. Liu, Y. Ye (Eds.), E-Commerce Agents. VI, 347 pages. 2001.

Vol. 2035: D. Cheung, G.J. Williams, Q. Li (Eds.), Advances in Knowledge Discovery and Data Mining – PAKDD 2001. Proceedings, 2001. XVIII, 596 pages. 2001.

Vol. 2039: M. Schumacher, Objective Coordination in Multi-Agent System Engineering. XIV, 149 pages. 2001.

Lecture Notes in Computer Science

Vol. 1998: R. Klette, S. Peleg, G. Sommer (Eds.), Robot Vision. Proceedings, 2001. IX, 285 pages. 2001.

Vol. 1999: W. Emmerich, S. Tai (Eds.), Engineering Distributed Objects. Proceedings, 2000. VIII, 271 pages. 2001.

Vol. 2000: R. Wilhelm (Ed.), Informatics: 10 Years Back, 10 Years Ahead. IX, 369 pages. 2001.

Vol. 2001: G.A. Agha, F. De Cindio, G. Rozenberg (Eds.), Concurrent Object-Oriented Programming and Petri Nets. VIII, 539 pages. 2001.

Vol. 2002: H. Comon, C. Marché, R. Treinen (Eds.), Constraints in Computational Logics. Proceedings, 1999. XII, 309 pages. 2001.

Vol. 2003: F. Dignum, U. Cortés (Eds.), Agent Mediated Electronic Commerce III. XII, 193 pages. 2001. (Subseries LNAI).

Vol. 2004: A. Gelbukh (Ed.), Computational Linguistics and Intelligent Text Processing. Proceedings, 2001. XII, 528 pages. 2001.

Vol. 2006: R. Dunke, A. Abran (Eds.), New Approaches in Software Measurement. Proceedings, 2000. VIII, 245 pages. 2001.

Vol. 2007: J.F. Roddick, K. Hornsby (Eds.), Temporal, Spatial, and Spatio-Temporal Data Mining. Proceedings, 2000. VII, 165 pages. 2001. (Subseries LNAI).

Vol. 2009: H. Federrath (Ed.), Designing Privacy Enhancing Technologies. Proceedings, 2000. X, 231 pages. 2001.

Vol. 2010: A. Ferreira, H. Reichel (Eds.), STACS 2001. Proceedings, 2001. XV, 576 pages. 2001.

Vol. 2011: M. Mohnen, P. Koopman (Eds.), Implementation of Functional Languages. Proceedings, 2000. VIII, 267 pages. 2001.

Vol. 2012: D.R. Stinson, S. Tavares (Eds.), Selected Areas in Cryptography. Peoceedings, 2000. IX, 339 pages. 2001.

Vol. 2013: S. Singh, N. Murshed, W. Kropatsch (Eds.), Advances in Pattern Recognition – ICAPR 2001. Proceedings, 2001. XIV, 476 pages. 2001.

Vol. 2015: D. Won (Ed.), Information Security and Cryptology – ICISC 2000. Proceedings, 2000. X, 261 pages. 2001.

Vol. 2018: M. Pollefeys, L. Van Gool, A. Zisserman, A. Fitzgibbon (Eds.), 3D Structure from Images – SMILE 2000. Proceedings, 2000. X, 243 pages. 2001.

Vol. 2020: D. Naccache (Ed.), Topics in Cryptology – CT-RSA 2001. Proceedings, 2001. XII, 473 pages. 2001

Vol. 2021: J. N. Oliveira, P. Zave (Eds.), FME 2001: Formal Methods for Increasing Software Productivity. Proceedings, 2001. XIII, 629 pages. 2001.

Vol. 2022: A. Romanovsky, C. Dony, J. Lindskov Knudsen, A. Tripathi (Eds.), Advances in Exception Handling Techniques. XII, 289 pages. 2001

Vol. 2024: H. Kuchen, K. Ueda (Eds.), Functional and Logic Programming. Proceedings, 2001. X, 391 pages. 2001.

Vol. 2025: M. Kaufmann, D. Wagner (Eds.), Drawing Graphs. XIV, 312 pages. 2001.

Vol. 2026: F. Müller (Ed.), High-Level Parallel Programming Models and Supportive Environments. Proceedings, 2001. IX, 137 pages. 2001.

Vol. 2027: R. Wilhelm (Ed.), Compiler Construction. Proceedings, 2001. XI, 371 pages. 2001.

Vol. 2028: D. Sands (Ed.), Programming Languages and Systems. Proceedings, 2001. XIII, 433 pages. 2001.

Vol. 2029: H. Hussmann (Ed.), Fundamental Approaches to Software Engineering. Proceedings, 2001. XIII, 349 pages. 2001.

Vol. 2030: F. Honsell, M. Miculan (Eds.), Foundations of Software Science and Computation Structures. Proceedings, 2001. XII, 413 pages. 2001.

Vol. 2031: T. Margaria, W. Yi (Eds.), Tools and Algorithms for the Construction and Analysis of Systems. Proceedings, 2001. XIV, 588 pages. 2001.

Vol. 2033: J. Liu, Y. Ye (Eds.), E-Commerce Agents. VI, 347 pages. 2001. (Subseries LNAI).

Vol. 2034: M.D. Di Benedetto, A. Sangiovanni-Vincentelli (Eds.), Hybrid Systems: Computation and Control. Proceedings, 2001. XIV, 516 pages. 2001.

Vol. 2035: D. Cheung, G.J. Williams, Q. Li (Eds.), Advances in Knowledge Discovery and Data Mining – PAKDD 2001. Proceedings, 2001. XVIII, 596 pages. 2001. (Subseries LNAI).

Vol. 2037: E.J.W. Boers et al. (Eds.), Applications of Evolutionary Computing. Proceedings, 2001. XIII, 516 pages. 2001.

Vol. 2038: J. Miller, M. Tomassini, P.L. Lanzi, C. Ryan, A.G.B. Tettamanzi, W.B. Langdon (Eds.), Genetic Programming. Proceedings, 2001. XI, 384 pages. 2001.

Vol. 2039: M. Schumacher, Objective Coordination in Multi-Agent System Engineering. XIV, 149 pages. 2001. (Subseries LNAI).

Vol. 2040: W. Kou, Y. Yesha, C.J. Tan (Eds.), Electronic Commerce Technologies. Proceedings, 2001. X, 187 pages. 2001.

Vol. 2045: B. Pfitzmann (Ed.), Advances in Cryptology – EUROCRYPT 2001. Proceedings, 2001. XII, 545 pages. 2001.

Vol. 2053: O. Danvy, A. Filinski (Eds.), Programs as Data Objects. Proceedings, 2001. VIII, 279 pages. 2001.